JN065623

# out APIR

sia Pacific Institute of Research (APIR) was founded in 2011, with the aim of
ting sustainable development in the Asia Pacific region and Kansai/Japan.[1] In
oidly globalizing economic environment, APIR has been conducting timely
economic forecasts, as well as research in various fields, such as economy,
e, business, etc. We have also been actively providing academic insights into
iomestic and global issues. APIR has extensive connections with the academia,
iment, and industry, especially in the Kansai area. Many leading companies,
izations and universities are supporting APIR's activities. We are constantly
ig to expand our global network through collaborative research, seminars and
erative activities.

Kansai is an area located in the center of Japan and has a huge market with a population of
approximately 20.35 million and a GRP of approximately JPY 87,587 billion.

# Kansai and the Asia

## Economic Outlook
## 2023-24

APIR ASIA PACIFIC INSTITUTE OF RESEARC

**Ab**

The A
supp
the r
macr
finan
both
gove
orga
striv
coo

**Mission:**

As a problem-solving think tank, we develop solutions for problems faced by the Asia-Pacific region and contribute to the creation of new vitality and the advancement of sustainable development in both Japan and the Asia-Pacific region.

1. Research that provides logical and factual evidence for developing policies and business strategies.
2. Research, that is accumulating for future forecasts and is being used as a frame for identifying issues and making policy suggestions.
3. Research, the results and data of which are used as a public property and foundational research.

Based on research results, we make practical suggestions and provide information for the economic, academic, and governmental communities at the appropriate time. We also develop excellent human resources for the future.

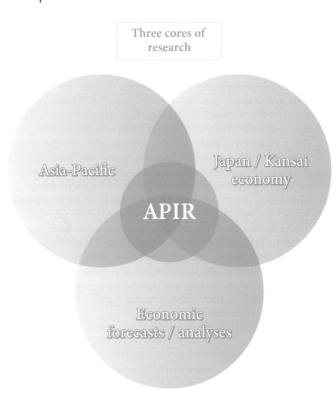

Three cores of research

Asia-Pacific

Japan / Kansai economy

APIR

Economic forecasts / analyses

# MESSAGE FROM THE RESEARCH DIRECTOR

Asia Pacific Institute of Research
Research Director  *MIYAHARA, Hideo*

In 2022, the Japanese economy continued to be affected by COVID-19, as it was in 2021, in terms of the movement of people and goods. On the other hand, the world has already lifted behavioral restrictions, and economic activities have resumed. In 2023, supply shortages caused by globally disrupted supply chains have been overcome, and economic activities have recovered. However, the situation concerning Russia and Ukraine is still very complicated so that energy and food supplies continue to be affected, and countries around the world are suffering from steep inflation. This inflation has caused Western countries to shift from easing monetary policy to tightening it, and there are concerns about the possibility of recession affecting the world economy if the tight monetary policy continues for a long period.

In China, the GDP growth rate for the full year of 2022 was 3.0% (National Bureau of Statistics), much lower than the 5.5% target of the Chinese government, due to the lockdown in each city caused by its comprehensive zero corona policy. In 2023, however, China revised that policy and moved into a new phase, lifting the previous restrictions. This is expected to lead to full-fledged economic activities in the country.

In Japan, although behavioral restrictions were gradually lifted in 2022, infection spread during the seventh wave in August and the eighth wave in December, and tourism and service industries were severely affected, as in the previous year. In addition, soaring natural resource prices and price hikes for food and other commodities have continued to impact household budgets. On May 8, 2023, however, the classification of COVID-19 under the Infectious Disease Control Law was lowered from category 2 to category 5, making it equivalent to seasonal influenza, and various restrictions were lifted, leading to a recovery in the tourism and service industries that were so greatly affected by the corona disaster. On the other hand, regarding economic security issues, the U.S.-China conflict is intensifying. Depending on Japan's economic security policy, there is a possibility that trade with China may be affected, negatively impacting the Japanese and Kansai economies.

The new trend in 2023 is that the rate of wage increase was 3.89% (Nikkei's Survey on Wage Trends), the highest figure in 31 years. According to the Ministry of Health, Labour and Welfare (2022: Analysis of Labor Economy), Japan's nominal and real wages in 2020 were 111.4 and 103.1, respectively, compared with the indicator of 100 in 1991. Since the respective averages for the G7 countries excluding Japan were 227.0

and 131.4, Japan is clearly behind the other six countries. In order for Japan to shift to a virtuous cycle that leads to continuous productivity growth and further consumption in the future, continuous wage increases, not just transitory ones, are essential.

The theme of the Osaka-Kansai Expo, which will be held in April 2025, is "Design Future Society for Our Lives," and its concepts are (1) co-creation of our future society, (2) online platform for sharing challenges and solutions from around the world, and (3) place to create and share new ideas. People, things, and wisdom will gather from around the world to find solutions to various issues. Preparations are currently underway to host the event, but the recent sharp rise in building material costs and labor shortages are making it difficult to arrange the event as planned. I hope that the public and private sectors will work together to overcome these difficulties and convene this event.

The Osaka IR (Integrated Resort) zone development plan was finally approved by the national government on April 14, 2023, and, together with the 2025 Expo, it will be a catalyst for the Osaka and Kansai economies in the future. By codeveloping entertainment facilities, casinos, hotels, MICE (Meeting, Incentive travel, Convention, Exhibition/Event) facilities, restaurants, and many other visitor attractions, Osaka is expected to allure a great deal of domestic and foreign investment, and attract many more visitors, making them of growing industries in this area in the future. The project will further lead to the promotion of tourism in the wider Kansai region, hopefully leading to a ripple effect on the economy of the entire region.

In light of these circumstances, this year's "Asia Pacific and Kansai: The Kansai Economic White Paper 2023" has two themes: "The Dawn of the Post-Corona Era: Changes and Challenges" for the Asia-Pacific region in Part I; and "A Crossroads for its Economic Turnaround" for the Kansai economy in Part II.

The first part focuses on the challenges and prospects of the Asia-Pacific region from an international political and economic perspective, as a main issue surrounding the region in 2023.

The second part of the report, dealing with a crossroads for Kansai's economic turnaround, discusses the current state and future prospects for the Kansai economy, as well as issues such as its labor market, DX (Digital Transformation), and human resource support and cultivation in the Kansai region, while also considering the tourism industry in this region. It also discusses the industrial structure that is expected to turn the Kansai economy around into the future.

In this way, this book includes hints for considering the future from a variety of perspectives. In addition, as in the previous year, Part III summarizes the status of the Osaka-Kansai Expo as Expo 2025 Chronology and, from this year, tourism in Kansai is described as Tourism Chronology.

The Asia Pacific Institute of Research (APIR) will continue to develop the results of its research into practical applications, aiming to be a frontrunner in contributing to the development of the Asia Pacific and Kansai economies, including that of Japan.

Finally, I would like to express my sincere gratitude to all those who have contributed to the publication of this book.

February 2024

# Table of Contents

# Editors & Contributors

| | |
|---|---|
| **Editor in Chief** | HONDA, Yuzo |
| **Associate Editors** | INOKI, Takenori; INADA, Yoshihisa; |
| | MATSUBAYASHI, Yoichi; GOTO, Kenta |
| **Production Editors** | NOMURA, Ryosuke; MIYAMOTO, Ei; |
| | NITTA, Yosuke |

## Contributors

### HONDA, Yuzo

Director of Research, APIR
Professor Emeritus, Osaka University
Professor Emeritus, Kansai University
Ph.D. in Economics (Princeton University, 1980)
Preface; Chapter 1, Section 2

### INOKI, Takenori

Research Advisor, APIR
Professor Emeritus, Osaka University;
Professor Emeritus, International Research Center for Japanese Studies
Ph.D. in Economics (Massachusetts Institute of Technology, 1974)
Chapter 1, Section 1

### INADA, Yoshihisa

Director of Research & Director of Center for Quantitative Economic
Analysis (CQEA), APIR
Professor Emeritus, Konan University
Ph.D. in Economics (Kobe University, 1992)
Part II Summary, Introduction; Chapter 2, Section 1~4, Column C;
Chapter 3, Section 1, 2; Chapter 4, Section 1, 2; Chapter 5, Section 1

### MATSUBAYASHI, Yoichi

Senior Research Fellow, APIR
Professor, Graduate School of Economics and Faculty of Economics, Kobe
University
Ph.D. in Economics (Kobe University, 1991)
Chapter 2, Section 1

## GOTO, Kenta

Senior Research Fellow, APIR

Professor, Faculty of Economics, Kansai University

Ph.D. in Area Studies (Kyoto University, 2005)

Chapter 1, Column A

## KAJITANI, Kai

Senior Research Fellow, APIR

Professor, Graduate School of Economics, Kobe University

Ph.D. in Economics (Kobe University, 2001)

Chapter 1, Section 3

## KIMURA, Fukunari

Senior Research Fellow, APIR;

Chief Economist, Economic Research Institute for ASEAN and East Asia
(ERIA)

Professor, Faculty of Economics, Keio University

Ph.D. in Economics (University of Wisconsin-Madison, 1991)

Chapter 1, Section 4

## SHIMODA, Mitsuru

Director & Chief Researcher, Applied Research Institute, Inc.

Master of Economics (Tezukayama University, 1999)

Chapter 2, Section 2, Column C; Chapter 5, Section 1

## IRIE, Hiroaki

Professor, Junior College Division, Kindai University

Ph.D. in Economics (Kwansei Gakuin University, 2012)

Chapter 2, Section 3, Column C; Chapter 5, Section 1

## SHIMOJO, Shinji

Senior Research Fellow, APIR

Professor, Faculty of Software and Information Technology,
Aomori University

Professor Emeritus, Osaka University

Ph.D. Engineering Science (Osaka University, 1986)

Chapter 5, Section 2

### SHIMOYAMA, Akira
Professor, Faculty of Economics, Osaka University of Economics
Ph.D. in Economics (Kwansei Gakuin University, 2010)
Chapter 2, Column C; Chapter 5, Section 1

### TAKABAYASHI, Kikuo
Senior Research Fellow, APIR
Professor, Osaka University of Economics and Law
Professor Emeritus, Kwansei Gakuin University
Ph.D. in Economics (Kyoto University, 1989)
Chapter 5, Section 1

### KARAVASILEV, Yani
Research Fellow, APIR
Lecturer, Kyoto Bunkyo University
Ph.D. in International Public Policy (Osaka University, 2017)
Chapter 1, Section 5

### YOSHIDA, Shigekazu
Staff, APIR
M.A. in Economics (Kobe University, 2009)
Chapter 1, Column B

### LU, Zhaoying
Research Fellow, APIR
Ph.D. in Economics (Osaka University, 2021)
Chapter 2, Section 4

### KUO, Chiu-Wei
Research Fellow, APIR
Ph.D. in Economics (Kyoto University, 2016)
Chapter 3, Section 3

### TERADA, Kenji
General Manager, Outreach Department, APIR
Seconded from Osaka Gas Co., Ltd.
Chapter 3, Section 2; EXPO 2025 Chronology

## IMAI, Ko

Former Chief Program Officer and Research Fellow, APIR
Seconded from Resona Bank, Limited.
Chapter 1, Section 1

## ASHIKAGA, Tomoyoshi

Chief Program Officer and Research Fellow, APIR
Seconded from DAIKIN INDUSTRIES, LTD.
Chapter 5, Section 2; Tourism Chronology

## INOUE, Kenji

Chief Program Officer and Research Fellow, APIR
Seconded from OBAYASHI CORPORATION
Chapter 4, Section 1; Tourism Chronology

## TOKOYAMA, Kuriko

Senior Advisor, APIR
EXPO 2025 Chronology

## URABE, Saki

Staff, APIR
EXPO 2025 Chronology; Tourism Chronology

## NOMURA, Ryosuke

Deputy Chief Research Fellow, APIR
M.A. in Economics (Konan University, 2014)
Chapter 1, Column B; Part II Summary; Chapter 2, Column C;
Chapter 3, Section 1, 3; Chapter 4, Section 1, 2; Chapter 5, Section 1;
EXPO 2025 Chronology; Tourism Chronology

## MIYAMOTO, Ei

Program Officer and Research Fellow, APIR
Seconded from MUFG Bank, Ltd.
Part I Summary

**NITTA, Yosuke**
Program Officer and Research Fellow, APIR
Seconded from TAKENAKA CORPORATION
Part I Summary; EXPO 2025 Chronology; Tourism Chronology;
Statistical Annex

(As of March 31, 2024)

# PREFACE:
# WILL JAPAN BE BACK?

*HONDA, Yuzo*

The stubbornly high inflation seems to have started cooling off in the US, standing at 3.1% in November 2023. Industrial production has virtually levelled off throughout 2022 and 2023. Both prices and production suggest that the US economy is decelerating, although the third-quarter GDP growth remains at the respectable 3.0%, and the unemployment rate at a low 3.7% in November.

To cope with the outbreak of the Covid-19 pandemic in 2020, the US government and the Federal Reserve Board (FRB) took bold expansionary fiscal and monetary policies, respectively. This, together with the global surge in energy and food prices, has induced the current high inflation in the US. The switch to contractionary monetary policy by the FRB since the beginning of 2022 has pushed up the short-term interest rate (the 3-month Treasury Yield) roughly from 0.1% to 5.4%, and the long-term interest rate (the 10-year Treasury Yield) from 1.6% to 3.9%. The rise in interest rates and the reduction in the monetary base have led to the current slowdown in real spending in the US.

Now, the question is whether or not the slowdown of the US economy will turn into a recession in the beginning of 2024. I believe even if that should happen to be the case, the recession would be mild, with the appropriate management by the FRB. Overall, the US economy seems to be on a right track.

The rise in interest rates in the US has not only curbed spending, but it has also had a huge economic impact all over the world, including Japan. More specifically, the widening interest rate differential between Japan and the US has led to the depreciation of the yen against the US dollar from 115 yen per dollar at the beginning of 2022 to 143 yen on December 21, 2023, a depreciation of approximately 24%. The yen depreciation, together with the global surge in energy and food prices, has reduced the purchasing power of people in Japan through the rising prices of imported goods. As a result, domestic consumption has decreased, which has had a negative impact on the Japanese economy.

With some time lag (called "J curve effect in macroeconomics"), however, the yen depreciation has produced a favorable environment for Japanese business firms, exporting manufacturers in particular, generating handsome profits in 2023. The improved performance of those businesses has enabled them to make new investments and raise wages. According to the Nihon Keizai Shinbun Survey from December 16, 2023, the 874 leading Japanese companies are going to make total fixed investments worth 32 trillion yen for the 2023 fiscal year, which is an impressive 17.3% increase from the previous year. Indeed, there is a possibility that the expansionary monetary policy, which has been implemented by the Bank of Japan (BOJ) for more than a decade, might have helped to lay the basic foundations needed to rebuild the Japanese economy, which has been stagnating since the bubble burst in 1990.

Whether or not Japan will be back is yet to be seen, but at least there seem to be some structural changes happening in recent exports and foreign direct investment. Japanese firms have been putting more weight on the US both as a trading partner and as a destination for direct investment. For example, Japanese direct investments in North America amounted to 9.0 trillion in 2021 and 8.1 trillion yen in 2022, significantly exceeding the 5.6 trillion yen in the pre-pandemic 2019. Also, Japan's exports to the US exceeded those to China in 2023, in contrast to the previous year.

In order for the Japanese economy to get back on a steady growth path, two factors seem to be indispensable. The first one is investment by private businesses: with the necessary funds at hand, firms need to make new investment, which embodies the technological innovation, so that their products and services may become more competitive on the global market.

Second, it is essential for the BOJ to take an appropriate monetary policy to support the real sector. There has been constant and strong upward pressure on the Japanese long term interest rate through arbitrage since the FRB began to take a contractionary monetary policy at the beginning of 2022. This upward pressure on the long term interest rate from the US has collided with the BOJ's monetary policy to keep the rate around the zero percent, leading the Nikkei 225 Index to exceed its highest peak of 38,915 yen recorded at the end of 1989 for the first time in 34 years, and also the yen-dollar exchange rate to hover around 150 yen per dollar in February 2024. In general, it takes some time for exogenous shocks on financial (asset price) variables (like stock prices and exchange rates) to have full impacts on income (flow) variables (like consumption and investment), and we have to wait and see how this will happen in the near future. In the meantime, however, the recent violent behavior of financial variables is now posing a difficult problem on whether the BOJ should keep or modify the current yield curve control (YCC) policy in the future.

Part I of this year's Economic Outlook discusses the economic status quo in the major countries along the Pacific Rim surrounding Japan. Part II outlines the performance of the Japanese economy in general, and that of the Kansai area in particular. Given that the Osaka-Kansai Expo will be held in 2025, and that international tourism in Japan is resurging, we have added two chronologies - an EXPO 2025 Chronology and a Tourism Chronology - in Part III for your convenience. Part IV contains a Statistical Annex. Although this Economic Outlook is an abridged English-language version of the original Economic Outlook 2023 published by APIR in Japanese, some of the authors have updated their manuscripts in order to provide readers with the latest information.

# Part I

## THE DAWN OF THE POST-CORONA ERA: CHANGES AND CHALLENGES

*MIYAMOTO, Ei; NITTA, Yosuke*

Part I summarizes the current situation and challenges in the world's major economies and the Asia-Pacific region in the dawn of the post-corona era. It discusses various challenges and prospects facing the world economy, including inflation, energy issues, and human rights issues.

Section 1 outlines the current state of the world economy and some major factors that could disrupt the structure of the Japanese economy, and provides an outlook for the future.

Section 2 analyzes the challenges facing the U.S. economy, namely high inflation and recession risk, and explains the impact of U.S. economic trends on the Japanese economy.

In Section 3, the first half describes the background and problems of the real estate market risks facing the Chinese economy. The second half of the paper discusses the fiscal problems faced by local governments.

Section 4 discusses the economic strategies of Japan and Japanese firms in the face of the deepening confrontation between the U.S. and China. The first half of the paper analyzes the decoupling policies of the U.S. and Japan. The second half describes Southeast and South Asia's continuing economic growth and the strategies that Japan and Japanese firms should adopt with ASEAN.

Column A discusses the issue of "business and human rights" in the development of global value chains (GVCs), and explains the need for companies overseeing GVCs to take responsibility for respecting human rights not only for their "direct business partners" with whom they have contractual relationships, but also for their "indirect business partners" they have no business contracts with, from the perspective of universal human rights. Finally, the column describes the challenges for Japanese companies to implement mechanisms to ensure their responsibility to respect human rights in GVCs, expanding mainly in Asia.

Section 5 examines the household debt problem in Asian countries. The impact of household debt on the economy is analyzed from various angles, including the rate of increase in outstanding household debt, its determinants, and its composition. The section then focuses on housing loans, which account for the majority of household debt, and discusses measures that Asian countries should take in the future, considering trends in housing prices and other factors.

Column B examines global demographic trends based on the World Population Prospects 2022 issued by the United Nations. The first half of the column presents the demographic trends of the world's major regions, and the second half presents the demographic characteristics of the world's major countries. Finally, the important points derived from this data and new issues that have been identified are discussed.

# Chapter 1

# MAJOR ISSUES IN THE ASIA-PACIFIC REGION IN 2023–2024

## Section 1
## TRANSFORMATION OF THE INTERNATIONAL ORDER AND THE WORLD ECONOMY

*INOKI, Takenori, IMAI, Ko*

Looking back on the world situation in 2022, although the coronavirus disease (hereafter, COVID-19) is showing signs of being under control, events continued to remind us that we have entered a new phase of global political and economic divide and conflict, as evidenced by the Russian invasion of Ukraine in February. Frequent extreme weather events and natural disasters around the world also indicate that climate change has become an issue of global significance that can no longer be taken lightly.

It is needless to point out once again that China has become a global player in international politics and the world economy since the beginning of this century. Like Japan, however, China's declining and aging population has been a major stumbling block to economic growth. China's total fertility rate (TFR) has dropped below 1.2, lower than that of Japan. Until the Cultural Revolution, China's TFR was around 6.0, and the "One-Child Policy" was introduced in 1979 as a solution to the food shortage problem. However, this radical policy was abandoned due to the labor shortage and wages improved with economic growth, and from 2021, "three children" were allowed, and various pronatalistic measures introduced.

Meanwhile, in Russia, the TFR temporarily dropped to around 1.2 at the end of the 20th century, and the government launched a policy of providing generous benefits to parents with two or more children. Although the birth rate has recovered somewhat since then, the Putin administration's concerns about a declining population appear to be quite strong. The Russian government seems to be facing a significant crisis due to the decline in the number of troops and the tendency of professional personnel to leave the country.

The future appears uncertain for the authoritarian states like China and Russia when considering indicators such as the working-age population and economic vitality. Expansion and growth are typically the results of virtuous cycles, but once the economy moves into a contractionary phase, numerous challenges arise. It is undeniable that the territorial expansionism of the Xi Jinping regime and the imperialism of contemporary Russia are in part uncontrolled actions driven by fears of future governance challenges stemming from a shrinking population and economic stagnation. However, government intervention in childbearing in a liberal democratic state is unlikely to have much effect unless each individual is able to envision a positive outlook towards marriage and family.

The spread of COVID-19 and Russia's invasion of Ukraine had the effect of changing energy prices and the flow of food imports and exports by severing supply chains and blocking trade ports. Furthermore, in response to the pandemic, all countries were forced to launch aggressive fiscal measures as part of their economic policies. Now that the virus is in the process of being contained, it is necessary to take a long-term perspective on fiscal discipline, as the pandemic has temporarily caused a marked increase in public debt worldwide. Although there has been a slight decline in public debt as concerns about the virus have eased in Europe and the United States, it remains considerably high. This high level of public debt and its increase will exert inflationary pressure.

It remains to be seen whether the global inflation, fluctuating with highs and lows, will be transitory or become chronic and persistent. What stance will be taken on the issue of fiscal discipline in the future, when a large amount of funds will be needed for defense spending and economic restructuring? The first step is to determine the nature of inflation, which will be a difficult task. Japan's monetary authorities, under the leadership of new Bank of Japan Governor Ueda, have made it clear that, unlike other major advanced economies, they will continue their large-scale easing measures, but will also begin a review of their monetary policy over the past quarter century and its side effects.

Section 1 provides an overview of the current global economic challenges and identifies major factors that could destabilize the Japanese economy, along with discussing potential future scenarios.

## 1. Current State of Inflation and Situation in Each Country

The supply- and demand-side factors of inflation are linked by a complex causal relationship that includes the inflation expectations of each economic agent, and are largely determined by domestic monetary and fiscal policies, as well as exchange rates (currency fluctuations). In 2022, the impact of Russia's invasion of Ukraine led to a dramatic increase in energy and food prices, which further intensified inflationary pressure on the global economy, especially in the euro zone. In the case of Japan, which had been in a chronic "deflationary state," inflation has so far remained low by world market standards. Nevertheless, rising food and energy prices has been a contributing factor preventing companies from increasing wages in 2022. The sharp rise in energy and raw material prices is believed to have been a "cost-push" force. Table 1-1-1 shows the movements of the consumer price index (CPI) in major countries.

In 2021, the U.S. experienced a significant increase in the annual average inflation rate. This was sometimes attributed to "temporary inflation" resulting from the release of "pent-up demand" that had initially been suppressed by the COVID-19 pandemic. However, the average annual inflation rate continued to rise to 8% in the subsequent year of 2022. In response, despite the looming risk of a recession beginning in March 2022, the Federal Reserve Board (FRB) took decisive action, aggressively raising interest rates to curb inflation. This level of inflation, reaching 8% YoY, marked the highest since the second oil crisis.

In the eurozone, inflationary trends have become more pronounced, similar to those in the United States. Consumer prices have surged in major countries such as France, Germany, and the United Kingdom. Fears of inflation due to fiscal expansion triggered by Russia's invasion of Ukraine prompted the European Central Bank (ECB) to sharply raise interest rates by 0.75% in September 2022, followed by another 0.75% increase at the October meeting of its Executive Board. When inflation expectations themselves increase, a mechanism may be set in motion that further exacerbates actual inflation. The policy of raising interest rates is considered to be a precautionary measure against such

**Table 1-1-1**     Consumer Price Indexes and Estimates: 2015-25

| Country | 2015 | 2016 | 2017 | 2018 | 2019 | 2020 | 2021 | 2022 | 2023 | 2024 | 2025 |
|---|---|---|---|---|---|---|---|---|---|---|---|
| France | 0.1 | 0.3 | 1.2 | 2.1 | 1.3 | 0.5 | 2.1 | 5.9 | 5.0 | 2.5 | 2.1 |
| Germany | 0.7 | 0.4 | 1.7 | 1.9 | 1.4 | 0.4 | 3.2 | 8.7 | 6.2 | 3.1 | 2.3 |
| Japan | 0.8 | -0.1 | 0.5 | 1.0 | 0.5 | 0.0 | -0.2 | 2.5 | 2.7 | 2.2 | 1.6 |
| UK | 0.0 | 0.7 | 2.7 | 2.5 | 1.8 | 0.9 | 2.6 | 9.1 | 6.8 | 3.0 | 1.8 |
| USA | 0.1 | 1.3 | 2.1 | 2.4 | 1.8 | 1.3 | 4.7 | 8.0 | 4.5 | 2.3 | 2.1 |
| China | 1.5 | 2.1 | 1.5 | 1.9 | 2.9 | 2.5 | 0.9 | 1.9 | 2.0 | 2.2 | 2.2 |
| Russia | 15.5 | 7.0 | 3.7 | 2.9 | 4.5 | 3.4 | 6.7 | 13.8 | 7.0 | 4.6 | 4.0 |

Note 1: Annual average inflation rate of consumer prices for the specific year
Note 2: Estimates for France and Russia in 2022 and all countries in 2023, 2024, and 2025
Source: Prepared by the author using data from International Monetary Fund, World Economic Outlook Database, April 2023

"forecast effects."

For Russia and China, both facing economic and political challenges, pinpointing a single reason for the changes in inflation rates is difficult. In Russia, the depreciation of the ruble prompted the Russian central bank to take the emergency step of raising its policy rate to 20% to avoid the risk of inflation caused by the depreciation of its currency. The IMF's Economic Outlook estimates Russia's average annual inflation rate at 14% in 2022.

In China, inflation has remained slightly below 2% for the past year. Even before the outbreak of the pandemic, prices in China had been relatively stable. Consumer demand has been suppressed (pent-up) by the "ZeroCOVID Policy" due to the spread of the coronavirus infection. A heightened sense of caution due to the real estate crisis might also have had a substantial impact.

The impact of the unilateral interest rate hike policy of the U.S. has been significant for the world as a whole. This policy not only led to the dollar's appreciation but also caused currencies of countries with substantial trade volumes with the U.S. to depreciate, leading to a sharp increase in import prices. These soaring import prices essentially exported inflation from the U.S. to the rest of the world, altering global trade flows.

## 2. Change and Recovery in Trade Volume

In 2021, as the impact of the new coronavirus somewhat weakened, there was a general recovery in global trade. However, the degree of recovery varied across different industry sectors and products. Industries such as telecommunications equipment, precision instruments, and transportation vehicles, which suffered from a shortage of semiconductors due to supply chain disruptions, showed a remarkable recovery, while trade in the energy sector, where price hikes were conspicuous through 2022, showed a high rate of increase in terms of value.

All countries and regions observed a noticeable decrease in trade. It's worth noting that the "trade in services" sector was hit harder by the coronavirus spread than the trade in goods, with severe restrictions on people's movements, especially across borders, severely impacting the travel and transportation industry. According to United Nations Conference on Trade and Development (UNCTAD) Trade Statistics, YoY, the value of exports of travel services fell by 81.8% in the second quarter of 2020. However, in the first quarter of 2022, the value of exports of travel services showed a sharp and rapid recovery, with an increase of 88.5%, demonstrating a quick rebound from the sudden downturn.

Since global trade was in a recovery phase, increases in both imports and exports were observed in almost all countries, including China, the United

States, Germany, Japan, and the Netherlands. However, it should be noted that changes in the value of trade varied by country, with some countries recording a widening trade deficit and others posting large surpluses. The largest trade deficits are observed in the U.S., Germany, Japan, and the Netherlands.

The main causes of the growing deficits appear to differ from country to country. In the Eurozone, energy prices have been rising since the beginning of the war of aggression against Ukraine in 2022, which has had a major impact on the area. In Japan, not only energy prices but also the rapid depreciation of the JPY contributed to the increase in imports. In the U.S., the trade deficit with China (China accounts for one-third of the total U.S. trade deficit) had been shrinking due to "Additional Tariff Measures" implemented during the tariff war against China under the previous Trump administration. However, over the past year, imports from China have begun to expand, resulting in a goods trade deficit in excess of $1 trillion.

It is undeniable that the "tariff surcharge" has increased inflationary pressure on U.S. retailers and consumers by adding tariffs on many daily necessities, including clothing made in China. There are reports of considerations to review this measure under the Biden administration, but there are also opposition opinions within the Democratic Party. However, some predict that eliminating tariffs on China, the U.S.'s largest trading partner, could suppress the domestic consumer price index by 1% or more. Under these circumstances, the Biden administration is faced with a difficult choice: protect manufacturing workers or contain inflation. Figure 1-1-1 illustrates the changes in China's imports and exports from January 2020 to April 2023.

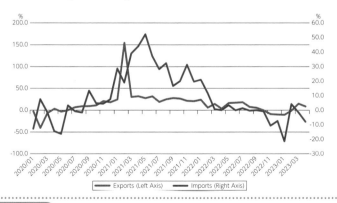

Exports (Left Axis)    Imports (Right Axis)

**Figure 1-1-1**    China's Imports and Exports YoY : January 2020 - April 2023

Source: Compiled by the author using data from the General Administration of Customs of the People's Republic of China

China is the world's largest exporter and second-largest importer, while the United States occupies the contrasting positions of being the world's largest importer and second-largest exporter. The United States lags far behind China in exports, and its second place and huge trade deficit clearly show the problems of U.S. trade with China.

## 3. Current Public Debt Outstandings

How did the ratio of national debt (total general government debt including national, regional, and social security funds) to GDP change as a result of Russia's invasion of Ukraine during the COVID-19 pandemic? As mentioned earlier, the U.S. Fed has been raising interest rates since March 2022, and it is necessary to consider the risk factors implied by these rate hikes. It is crucial to contemplate the implicit risk factors due to these hikes, such as the potential expansion of domestic private-sector debt, leading to financial crises in countries aligning with U.S. policies. The U.S. Fed's "inflation control" measures are not unrelated to its policy of raising interest rates, as bank failures that have been occurring in the U.S. since the spring of 2023 demonstrate.

The Bank for International Settlements (BIS) statistics, Credit to the non-financial sector, allows us to calculate the debt of the non-financial sector as a percentage of GDP in three categories: "general government debt,"

**Table 1-1-2**   Nonfinancial Sector Sectoral Debt of Major Countries as % of GDP

| Country | 3rd Quarter of 2022 | | |
|---|---|---|---|
| | General Government | Non-Financial Corporations | Household Accounting Departments |
| Canada | 90.1 | 113.8 | 103.2 |
| France | 109.6 | 164.1 | 66.5 |
| Germany | 64.0 | 73.4 | 55.7 |
| Italy | 142.2 | 69.6 | 42.6 |
| Japan | 231.3 | 116.8 | 67.9 |
| Korea | 44.2 | 119.2 | 105.3 |
| UK | 94.9 | 69.5 | 84.5 |
| USA | 103.5 | 78.8 | 75.2 |
| China | NA | 158.2 | 61.4 |
| Hong Kong | NA | 279.2 | 94.8 |
| India | NA | 52.2 | 35.5 |
| Russia | NA | 72.8 | 21.0 |

Note: Data for NA not yet published
Source: Prepared by the author using data from Bank for International Settlements (BIS)

"non-financial corporate debt," and "household debt."

As for the debt-to-GDP ratio of the non-financial sector, except for Hong Kong, where the debt situation of government finances and corporations is in a special position, Japan, as is well known, is the top country in terms of the severity of the debt situation of the non-financial sector (416.0%). Japan's debt situation is characterized by the fact that the debt-to-GDP ratio of the "general government debt sector" is by far the highest by sector. However, the debt-to-GDP ratio of the non-financial corporate debt sector is lower than those of France and Korea, and the debt-to-GDP ratio of the household debt sector is lower than those of Korea, Canada, the United Kingdom, and the United States.

At the end of 2021, the U.S. Congress passed a bill to raise the legal limit on federal government debt to $31.4 trillion to avoid a so-called "Government Shutdown," but by the end of January of the following year, it exceeded $30 trillion for the first time, marking a severe situation. Such government shutdowns are not uncommon in U.S. history, and in May 2023, the U.S. again faced the problem of a government shutdown and default if the debt ceiling was not raised. The crisis was averted in exchange for the Republicans cutting education and social programs in pursuance of a further increase in the debt ceiling from its current level of $31.4 trillion.

In addition to Greece and Italy, Portugal, Ireland, Spain, and other euro-zone countries with heavy government debt, as well as China and South Korea, which are facing significant risks due to an overheated real estate market, are confronted with significant challenges in navigating the issue of rising interest rates.

## 4. Changes in Military Expenditures of Major Countries

The impact of Russia's invasion of Ukraine on world trade has been discussed earlier. The nature of this impact varies depending on the nature of trade with Russia, and the impact of import restrictions from Russia on the economy of the country varies qualitatively. For example, the EU saw a significant change in the value of its imports and exports to Russia in March 2022, the month following the start of the war of aggression against Ukraine. Export restrictions on Russia reduced the supply of high-tech products such as semiconductors, and the value of exports dropped by almost half from 7.37 billion euros in February to 3.84 billion euros in March. On the other hand, primary commodities such as wheat and natural gas were highly dependent on imports from Russia, so imports could not be completely shut down immediately, and the value of imports has increased due to soaring energy prices.

At the same time, we will examine changes in the size and composition of each country's fiscal expenditures, particularly with respect to military spending. Russia's aggression against Ukraine, which has had a major impact on international relations, has also aggravated Russia's own finances through a significant increase in military expenditures. Comparing the "ratio of military expenditures to GDP" of major countries between 2019 and 2022 using data from the Stockholm International Peace Research Institute (SIPRI), no significant changes can be seen.

However, significant increases in absolute military expenditures can be observed in most major countries, including the United States (+9%), the United Kingdom (+20%), Germany (+14%), and France (+13%) among the major NATO countries. It is noteworthy that while the U.S. is the world's largest military spender, China, in second place with the reunification of Taiwan in mind, has recorded a 22% increase. Although Russia's military spending in 2022 increased around the time of the invasion of Ukraine, the total increase in military spending for the entire year of 2022 is negligible, partly due to previous financial strains. For a more accurate assessment, reviewing the 2023 data will be necessary.

**Table 1-1-3**    Military Expenditures of Major Countries as % of GDP (SIPRI)

| Country | Percentage of GDP | | Percentage of government spending | |
|---|---|---|---|---|
| | 2019 | 2022 | 2019 | 2022 |
| USA | 3.43% | 3.45% | NA | NA |
| Australia | 1.88% | 1.90% | 4.82% | 5.02% |
| India | 2.55% | 2.43% | 9.14% | 8.26% |
| China | 1.68% | 1.60% | 4.91% | 4.79% |
| Japan | 0.99% | 1.08% | 2.66% | 2.53% |
| Korea | 2.67% | 2.72% | 11.85% | 10.57% |
| Myanmar | 2.19% | 3.05% | 10.81% | 14.24% |
| USSR | NA | NA | NA | NA |
| Finland | 1.35% | 1.72% | 2.54% | 3.22% |
| France | 1.84% | 1.94% | 3.32% | 3.43% |
| Germany | 1.26% | 1.39% | 2.81% | 2.75% |
| UK | 1.98% | 2.23% | 5.14% | 5.29% |
| Iran | 2.01% | 2.59% | 13.92% | 17.32% |
| Saudi Arabia | 8.13% | 7.42% | 23.15% | 27.79% |

Note: Data for NA not yet published
Source: Organized by the author using data form Stockholm International Peace Research Institute (SIPRI)

## 5. Trade Policy Change and Anti-Globalization

Finally, I would like to add a comment on the outlook for the global economy from the perspective of changes in trade policy and the possibility of bloc formation.

The EU acted swiftly to impose sanctions against Russia, suspending imports of Russian coal in August 2022 and initiating a phased embargo on oil and natural gas. These measures must have been a difficult choice for the EU. In fact, the EU as a whole is not completely aligned. The pro-Russian Orban government in Hungary has allowed some oil imports from Russia, for example.

Another contributing factor to the food crisis was the destabilization of the world grain market due to the massive disruption in the supply of Ukrainian wheat. Despite mediation efforts by Turkey and the UN, resulting in the lifting of the blockade on the port of Odessa, turmoil persists in the grain market. Notable importers such as Indonesia, Turkey, and China continue to face challenges, keeping the market in a state of flux. Additionally, the market has been adversely affected by extreme weather conditions, adding another layer of instability.

This movement toward trade fragmentation and a bloc economy had already occurred with the severing of the supply chain by the coronavirus. The conflict in Ukraine also caused major cracks in the trade structure due to energy and food transportation problems, revealing a serious dilemma of "the separation of politics and economy." A prime example of this is that, from the perspective of national security, the U.S. further strengthened its efforts to hinder China's technological progress by limiting trade with non-friendly countries and restricting exports to China of products whose "technology and equipment are for both civilian and military use" (so-called dual use).

In 2022, the WTO's Dispute Settlement Subcommittee concluded that these U.S. tariff measures "do not constitute a war or a state of emergency in international relations" and that the U.S. "tariff increases" were not allowed. Since then, the U.S. has been steering its policy toward building a strong supply chain and preventing the military diversion of high-tech technology in China, including subsidy measures to attract semiconductor manufacturing companies to the country through the "CHIPS and Science Act" of August 2022 and focusing on concluding a framework trade agreement to exclude China. The global cooperative framework of U.S. politics and trade policy in recent years has been geared toward so-called "friend-sharing," a strategy that emphasizes trade and supply chains with U.S. allies and friends, while keeping China in mind.

Economics can lucidly explain the benefits from free trade and globalization. But how do we deal with situations in which citizens of countries that

Part I

Part II

Part III

Part IV

prosper from free trade face difficulties that offend public sentiment, such as widening income inequality within a country? Unless sufficient consideration is given to this point, the future of free and multilateral trade is not bright. The shift in national security policies by Germany and other EU countries, reducing dependence on the Chinese and Russian economies, is a political maneuver to navigate away from significant economic and political dilemmas. It is not uncommon to find situations where economic interests and the maintenance of peace are incompatible. Striking the right balance is a task left to domestic politics and diplomacy.

## References
BIS
  https://data.bis.org/topics/TOTAL_CREDIT
Cristina Constantinescu (2022)
  As global mobility restrictions have been lifted, travel services are making a comeback.
  https://blogs.worldbank.org/trade/trade-and-development-chart-travel-rebounding-covid-19-hit
General Administration of Customs of the People's Republic of China
  http://www.customs.gov.cn/
IMF World Economic Outlook Database
  https://www.imf.org/en/Publications/WEO/weo-database/2023/April/select-country-group
Stockholm International Peace Research Institute
  https://www.sipri.org/databases/milex/sources-and-methods.

# Section 2
# THE U.S. ECONOMY AIMING FOR A SOFT LANDING[1]

*HONDA, Yuzo*

## 1. Introduction

Since March 2020, there has been a rapid spread of the corona virus across the United States. As the disease spread, spending and production dropped sharply, and the U.S. unemployment rate hit a record 14.7% in April 2020. This was the highest unemployment rate in the U.S. after the Great Depression. To cope with the situation, the government and the Federal Reserve Board (FRB) immediately implemented bold expansionary fiscal and monetary policies.

Some economists, including professor Lawrence Summers, warned from the outset that the expansionary policies by the government and the FRB were too excessive in scale. In retrospect, they were right. As they correctly worried, the U.S. economy was experiencing high inflation. Unfortunately for the government and the FRB, Russia invaded Ukraine in February 2022. The Russo-Ukrainian war caused a sharp rise in global natural resource and food prices, which exacerbated inflation in the U.S. In September 2022, the U.S. CPI inflation rate reached 9.1% year on year.

Faced with high inflation, the FRB took a sharp turn toward tightening monetary policy in 2022. This time, the FRB tightened monetary policy sharply, feeling anxious that high inflation might come to stay. As a result, as shown in Figure 1-2-1, the inflation rate peaked in September 2022 and has since been steadily declining. Nevertheless, as of March 2023, the inflation rate was 5.0%, which is still much higher than the 2% target. Further monetary tightening is necessary. On the other hand, the growth rate of production has already declined due to the effects of monetary tightening, and the real economy has now virtually leveled off. If monetary tightening continues, the economy might fall into recession in the latter half of 2023 or 2024. In addition, in March and May 2023, three U.S. regional banks went bankrupt due in part to the rapid and drastic monetary tightening.

In this Section 2, we report the above recent trend of the U.S. economy aiming for a soft landing from such high inflation, from a macroeconomic

---

1) I would like to thank Koichi Hamada and Karavasilev Yani for their helpful comments in the preparation of this paper. However, any possible remaining errors are solely my own.

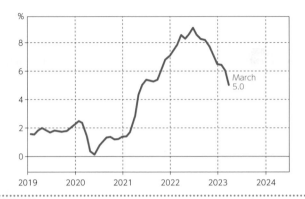

**Figure 1-2-1**　U.S. CPI Inflation rate

Source: Federal Reserve Bank of New York

perspective and consider its implications for the Japanese economy.

Section 2 is organized as follows. Subsection 2.2 describes the FRB's policy shift toward tighter monetary policy after 2022, and Subsection 2.3 examines the current situation of the U.S. real economy in the wake of the FRB's monetary tightening. Subsection 2.4 explains the relationship between high inflation and the risk of recession, one of the current challenges, and Subsection 2.5 considers another current challenge, the relationship between high inflation and the failure of three regional banks. Subsection 2.6 discusses the impact of the above U.S. economic movement on the Japanese economy.

## 2. FRB's Switch to Contractionary Monetary Policy

As shown in Figure 1-2-1, the U.S. economy was hit by rapid inflation from 2021. In order to cope with high inflation, the FRB changed its previous stance of monetary easing, and swiftly tightened monetary policy in 2022. This subsection presents data on this tightening and explains its contents.

### (1) Federal Funds Rate

Table 1-2-1 shows the timing at which the policy interest rate has been changed. The FRB has raised its policy interest rate, the federal funds rate, seven times in 2022 and three times already in 2023. As a result, the federal funds rate rose to 5.00-5.25% on May 5, 2023.

The characteristics of these policy interest rate changes are twofold: The first is the rapid increase in interest rates in a short period of time, and the second is the large size in the range of respective changes. In this short period,

**Table 1-2-1**    Federal funds rate change: timing and range

| Month of Change | Increase | Level |
|---|---|---|
| March 2022 | 0.25% | 0.25% to 0.50% |
| May | 0.50% | 0.75% to 1.00% |
| June | 0.75% | 1.50% to 1.75% |
| July | 0.75% | 2.25% to 2.50% |
| September | 0.75% | 3.00% to 3.25% |
| November | 0.75% | 3.75% to 4.00% |
| December | 0.50% | 4.25% to 4.50% |
| February 2023 | 0.25% | 4.50% to 4.75% |
| March | 0.25% | 4.75% to 5.00% |
| May | 0.25% | 5.00% to 5.25% |

Source: Federal Reserve System

the policy interest rate rose by approximately 5% from 0% at the beginning of 2022. The policy interest rate was raised by 0.75%, three times the normal level, in each of the four changes from June through November 2022, and by 0.50%, twice the normal level, in May and December 2022, as shown in Table 1-2-1. All of these indicate the FRB's rapid shift toward monetary tightening.

## (2) Interest rate on reserves

The FRB controls its policy interest rate, the federal funds rate, to its target through changes in interest rate on reserves (private banks' deposit accounts at the FRB). As shown in Figure 1-2-2, the FRB raised this interest rate on

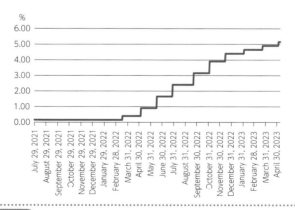

**Figure 1-2-2**    Interest on reserves (July 2021 to May 2023)

Source: Federal Reserve Bank of St. Louis

reserves from 0.15% to 0.4% in March 2022 and then rapidly increased it to 5.15% in May 2023. This also demonstrates how the FRB has quickly tightened its monetary policy.

## (3) Monetary base

Another measure of monetary policy stance is monetary base (the sum of cash and private bank deposits at a central bank). As shown in Figure 1-2-3, the monetary base peaked in December 2021 and then began to rapidly decline. Recognizing clearly the risk of high inflation, the FRB raised its short-term policy interest rate and stopped quantitative easing (QE) in March 2022, and began quantitative tightening (QT) in June 2022. We can also observe this quick shift to monetary tightening through the shrinkage in the size of the FRB's balance sheet.

Using Figure 1-2-3, we call your attention to the following four points. First, the FRB dramatically increased the monetary base after the Lehman Shock in 2008. Second, the FRB spent for more than six years from 2008 through 2014 expanding the monetary base to recover from the recession after the Lehman Shock, whereas it rapidly expanded the monetary base in a very short period of time from 2020 to 2021 under the current corona virus recession. The same is true for the case of monetary base contraction. The FRB took the longer period of time from 2014 through 2019 to gradually reduce the monetary base for the case of the global recession due to the Lehman Shock, whereas it shrank the

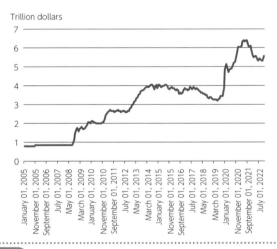

**Figure 1-2-3**     Monetary Base (January 2005 - March 2023)

Source: Federal Reserve Bank of St. Louis

monetary base rapidly in the shorter period from 2021 to 2022 for the case of the corona pandemic. Third, the magnitude of the monetary base change due to monetary expansion and contraction (vertical change in Figure 1-2-3) at this time is as large as that during the deep recession from the 2008 global financial crisis. Finally, the FRB's rapid expansion of the monetary base within a short period of time, followed by its rapid contraction immediately afterward, is one of the main causes of recent financial institution failures.

## 3. Current Status of the U.S. Economy

Subsection 2.3 describes the current state of the U.S. economy following the monetary tightening by the FRB explained in Subsection 2.2.

### (1) Production and Expenditures

Expansionary fiscal and monetary policies to cope with the corona pandemic led to a relatively smooth recovery of production and expenditures in the U.S. economy until the end of 2021. Durable consumption goods such as automobiles, computers, and electronics increased relatively steadily even in 2022, when monetary tightening began. On the other hand, housing investment fell sharply in both price and quantity due to rising interest rates. As a whole, as shown in Figure 1-2-4, the upward trend in production has weakened since 2022 and roughly remained flat. However, the level of production has already exceeded the pre-corona pandemic level in 2022.

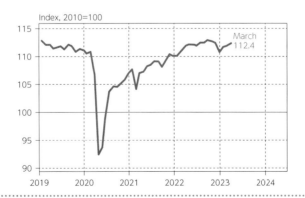

| Figure 1-2-4 | Production of the U.S. Economy |

Source: Federal Reserve Bank of New York

Part I

Part II

Part III

Part IV

## (2) Prices

Prices rose sharply from 2021 due to several factors, including bold expansionary fiscal and monetary policies. In addition to these factors, the global surge in natural resource prices, following Russia's invasion of Ukraine, further pushed up domestic prices, and the consumer price inflation rate in June 2022 recorded 9.1% year on year.

Thanks to the contractionary monetary policy by the FRB as well as the slowdown in global natural resource price surge, inflation has begun to improve and recovered to 5.0% as of March 2023. It is still, however, well above the 2% target.

When considering future inflation rates, people's inflation expectation rate is important. The one-year inflation rate forecast by the University of Michigan's consumer survey peaked at 5.4% in March and April 2022 but has been declining ever since, falling to 3.6% as of March 2023, as the actual inflation rate has been decelerating. The University of Michigan's inflation forecast rate is an inflation rate expected by consumers, while the breakeven inflation rate (BEI) is an inflation rate expected by investors. The BEI inflation rate forecast for the next five years is slowly declining from over 3.5% to under 2.5%, as the actual inflation rate has somewhat subsided.

Another factor affecting an inflation rate is the world natural resource and food prices. The price level of WTI crude oil, one of the leading indicators of energy prices, peaked in March 2022 at US$123.6 per barrel, and it has decreased since then. Prices have recently remained in the high range of $70-$80 per barrel. However, the rate of price increase has been slowing down.

## (3) Unemployment Rate

The unemployment rate was 14.7% in April 2020, when the new corona virus widely spread. Thanks to bold expansionary fiscal and monetary policies, however, the unemployment rate has recovered quite rapidly, and has been relatively low since 2022. The unemployment rate in April 2023 was 3.4%, and the adverse effect of monetary policy tightening has not yet appeared.

This is the current situation of the U.S. economy. In summary, although production is virtually leveling off, the economy as a whole has not as yet deteriorated and the labor market remains tight. Inflation has fallen significantly, but is still high at 5%.

## 4. The Primary Challenge Facing the U.S. Economy: High Inflation and Risk of Recession

The U.S. economy is currently facing at least two challenges: The risk of recession and the risk of bank failures. This Subsection 2.4 describes the first challenge: high inflation and the risk of recession.

The overall CPI inflation rate has fallen to 5.0% as of March 2023. However, the 5.0% level is still too high for people to live with in general and well above the target of 2.0%. Furthermore, the core CPI inflation rate excluding food and energy, shown in Figure 1-2-5, remained high at 5.6% as of March 2023. This indicates that the transient decline in food and energy prices contributed signifi-cantly to the fall in the overall CPI inflation rate from 9.1% to 5.0%. All of these factors suggest that there still remains a considerable risk that high inflation might remain into the future.

Both consumption and investment in the real economy were quite strong in 2022, with the exception of housing investment, and the unemployment rate was low at 3.4% in April 2023. The labor market was also tight, with the 2.6% increase of an employment rate year on year (Figure 1-2-6).

The high level of overall CPI inflation rate, the persistently higher level of core CPI inflation rate, active spending, and the tight labor market suggest the need for further monetary tightening.

One reason why tightening policy has not been fully effective is that the monetary base, which expanded rapidly and urgently during the outbreak of the new corona virus, has not been fully shrunk. In the market there still remains more than 1.5 times the base money in the pre-pandemic period. The glut of

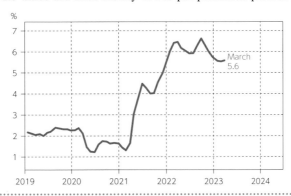

**Figure 1-2-5**    Core CPI inflation rate excluding food and energy (year on year)

Source: Federal Reserve Bank of New York

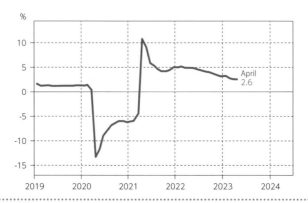

Figure 1-2-6    Employment Growth (year on year)

Source: Federal Reserve Bank of New York

base money in the market is one of the reasons why the core inflation rate has remained high, and thus, QT should continue.

However, as we move into 2023, the effects of monetary tightening to date are actually eroding the strength of expenditures in the economy. If monetary policy continues to be tightened further, production and expenditures might turn downward, and the economy might face the risk of entering recession. We are now in the difficult situation in which we must decide whether to continue tightening monetary policy or to return to a neutral monetary policy stance.

As for an outlook, although the inflation rate has fallen to 5%, that level is still too high, and the FRB is likely to continue tightening for the present. As a result, there is certainly some risk that the U.S. economy might fall into a recession in late 2023 or in 2024, but even if a recession should occur, it is unlikely to be major if other conditions remain the same.

## 5. Second Challenge: High Inflation and Financial System Stabilization

In Subsection 2.4, we discussed the relationship between high inflation and the risk of recession. In March 2023, a rapid shift to monetary tightening by the FRB resulted in another serious problem: The failure of some U.S. regional banks.

### (1) Liquidity and Bank Run

There are at least two possible reasons for a bank failure: First, as in a manufacturing business firm, the bank might go bankrupt if it is inefficient in its operation. Second, the bank also might fail if it runs short of liquidity. (Liquidity is a measure of each asset, i.e., how easily the asset can be converted into cash without loss. By definition, cash is the most liquid asset and real estate such as land is the least liquid asset.) Whatever the reason, even if it is merely a rumor or a lie, if it causes people to rush to a bank to withdraw their deposits, that alone can cause the bank to fail. In fact, this has happened many times in the past. In the United States, during the Great Depression in the early 1930s, people lined up in front of banks to withdraw their deposits. During the chaos, the U.S. financial authorities were forced to simultaneously close and terminate all banking businesses in the U.S. In Japan, the financial panics in 1927, when bank runs occurred frequently, are well known.

## (2) Failure of Three Regional Banks

In just over a year from the beginning of 2022 to the present, the FRB raised the policy interest rate by 5%, converted QE to QT, and rapidly reduced the monetary base. This shift to tighter monetary policy caused bond prices to fall sharply and brought about unexpectedly large capital losses for regional banks, comprising one of the reasons for the failures of the three regional banks at the time. As shown in Table 1-2-2, Silicon Valley Bank and Signature Bank failed in March 2023, and First Republic Bank failed in May.

One of the differences between the recent U.S. regional bank failures and the traditional bank runs described above is the speed of people to withdraw their deposits. In past bank runs, it took many days for depositors to wait in line and gradually withdraw their deposits, but in the case of the Silicon Valley Bank failure, for example, newspapers reported that about a quarter of the deposits were withdrawn in one day.

Information on whether a bank holds a large amount of bonds that incur capital losses is available on the Internet. This kind of information is spread via social networking sites (SNS) and the Internet, and instantly affects the stock price of the bank in question. A decline in a stock price increases the risk of failure, not only because of a lack of liquidity, but also because of unsound and inefficient management. As a result, the depositors of the bank in question will rush to withdraw their deposits through Internet banking and other means. The

**Table 1-2-2**    U.S. Regional Bank Failures

| bankruptcy date | Bank Name |
| --- | --- |
| March 10, 2023 | Silicon Valley Bank failed. |
| March 12, 2023 | Signature Bank failed. |
| May 1, 2023 | First Republic Bank failed. |

massive outflow of deposits further erodes the bank's credibility, and financial instability will increase dramatically. For these reasons, banks now are likely to fail in a much shorter period of time than in the past. One of the characteristics of this series of bank failures is that they occurred within a very short period of time once the banks' issues had surfaced.

## (3) Bank Term Funding Program (BTFP) and Federal Deposit Insurance Corporation (FDIC)

When the three regional banks failed, the two immediate actions taken by the U.S. financial authorities were (1) to create the Bank Term Funding Program (BTFP) and (2) to fully protect the deposits of the banks. These two measures induced depositors not to panic and minimized turbulence in the financial system. So how do these two measures work?

When deposit outflows occur, they may spread not only to the bank in question but also to other similar banks. If these deposit outflows are left uncontrolled, confidence in the financial system as a whole could be lost. Hence, the FRB must play the role of "lender of last resort" as a central bank and provide ample liquidity to the financial market. It is essential to prevent banks from failing by lending them the funds they need so that they do not run short of reserves (cash held by private banks and/or their deposits at the central bank) when deposit outflows occur. BTFP is the FRB's measure to secure the funds at the congress, which allows the FRB to make emergency loans as needed.

The second countermeasure was an immediate decision by the financial authorities to protect all deposits in the failed banks so that depositors would not suffer losses. In so doing, they prevented bank runs or a 'domino-toppling' expansion of bank failures.

The FDIC was established in the United States in 1933 as a countermeasure to the frequent bank failures that occurred from the 1920s through the Great Depression. Thanks to the FDIC, it was expected that deposits would be protected in the event of a bank failure. The existence of this system aimed to prevent people from running to banks to withdraw their funds.

However, there is a cap of $250,000 (approximately equals to JPY 33 million) on the amount of settlement deposits that can be protected under this system, and deposits exceeding this limit are not protected. The financial authorities, fearing a further spread of financial instability, have immediately decided to protect all of the bank's deposits, including those not covered by FDIC deposit insurance, to pacify the situation. As a result, the number of failed banks is currently limited to three as shown in Table 1-2-2.

## (4) FDIC System and Moral Hazard of Banks

Since the financial authorities have decided to protect deposits exceeding the amount protected by FDIC insurance, why do they not protect the entire amount of deposits without setting a ceiling on deposits from the outset?

If there were no ceiling on the amount of deposits to be protected, depositors would lose their incentive to choose a bank with which to deposit their money, since the full amount of their deposits would be protected anyway, regardless of which bank they chose. In other words, for depositors, all banks would be equal. If this were to happen, there would now be an incentive for banks to take risks (this behavior is called "moral hazard"). Since there is generally a trade-off between risk and return, banks will tend to take higher risks in search of higher returns. This is because depositors are generally indifferent to their choice of banks and will not leave their own banks, even if said banks take riskier behavior. It is not desirable for banks to take riskier behavior, since banks have the public mission of playing a key role in the settlement system. For these reasons, institutional protection of the full amount of deposits is considered difficult. Yet despite these difficulties, the FDIC system is expected to be improved in some way based on the experience currently being acquired.

## (5) Are High Inflation Control and Financial Stability Policies Compatible?

If bank failures were left uncontrolled, deposits would flow out of the banking sector, and the amount of bank loans would decline. The reduction in credit would lead to a reduction in spending in the private sector. To avoid this, the FRB should inject ample funds through the BTFP into the private sector to make up for the shortfall of needed funds.

The latest slight upturn in the monetary base balance in Figure 1-2-3 can be attributed to the FRB's emergency additional supply of liquidity to cope with the failure of two regional banks in March.

When people withdraw their bank deposits all at once, as was the case with the three regional bank failures, the monetary base flows out from the financial sector to the nonfinancial sector. If left uncontrolled, the money multiplier will decrease (i.e., the economy's overall loans and deposits will decline), resulting in a large reduction in the money supply (a part of which are deposits). If the monetary base flows out from the financial sector, and if the central bank does not modify the amount of the monetary base, it is equivalent to reducing the money supply to the economy as a whole, thus tightening monetary policy. The monetary policy stance becomes neutral only when the central bank supplies additional monetary base equal to the amount of funds flowing from financial sector to nonfinancial sector. It is important to understand that deposit outflows, if left uncontrolled, are equivalent to tightening monetary policy. Therefore, the latest increase in the monetary base in Figure 1-2-3 cannot be immediately interpreted as an easing of monetary policy. It is more likely that the necessary monetary base is injected simply to compensate for the shortfall of funds.

Here is one obvious question. The increase in the monetary base to stabilize the financial system, as shown in Figure 1-2-3, will work as monetary easing, which might conflict with the contractionary monetary policy currently employed to control high inflation. Will the FRB give priority to the financial system stabilization policy and ease the monetary tightening policy?

In fact, the FRB could manage to pursue both high inflation control and financial system stabilization policies simultaneously by adopting the following approach. Since the effects of monetary policy are broadly economy-wide, general monetary policy measures should be allocated to controlling high inflation. On the other hand, pinpoint policy measures, such as the BTFP, should be allocated to specific purposes to fully protect the deposits of failed banks and to stabilize the financial system. In this way, the two measures could be consistent with each other, and the FRB could deal with the two challenges simultaneously. If bank failures should continue to occur frequently in the future, this approach would not work, in which case another approach would be needed. But at least the above approach has successfully dealt with the current issues to date.

The U.S. economy is currently aiming for a soft landing from high inflation, and although it faces the two risks described here and in the previous subsection, overall the real economy is generally on a steady recovery path. However, the monetary base stock is still quite high, so it may take some time for inflation rate to reach the 2% target. The risk of future bank failures also needs due attention.

## 6. Impact on the Japanese Economy

Subsection 2.6 briefly describes the impact of the movement in the U.S. economy on the Japanese economy.

### (1) JPY depreciation due to the interest rate differentials

The BOJ has set its short-term policy rate at minus 0.1% since January 2016 and has supported its 10-year long-term interest rate at near 0% since September 2016. On the other hand, the FRB has raised the policy market interest rate by roughly 5% with its tightening monetary policy since early 2022. Long-term interest rates have risen accordingly. The interest rate differential between Japan and the U.S. has widened significantly, and the yen-dollar exchange rate has swung sharply toward a depreciation of the yen against the U.S. dollar. In 2022, the yen depreciated against the dollar to a 150-yen-per-dollar level at one point, but was subsequently bought back. The yen-dollar exchange rate at the end of 2021 was 115 yen per dollar, while it was 132 yen per dollar at the end of 2022, implying that the yen weakened against the dollar by about 15% during the year of 2022.

The global surge in natural resource and food prices, coupled with the depreciation of the JPY, caused the prices of imports into Japan to soar, and high inflation became a problem in Japan as well. High inflation is particularly problematic for people whose incomes are fixed at nominal values, as it directly affects their livelihoods and reduces their spending.

However, the depreciation of the JPY also alters the conditions of competition for domestic firms with foreign firms, with domestic products becoming cheaper than foreign products. When the JPY depreciates, Japan's trade balance and production are negatively affected at first by the depreciation. Within six months to two years, however, the effects will be reversed, and positive effects for the Japanese economy will expand and dominate. (In macroeconomics, this reversal effect is called the "J-curve effect." For details, see Honda (2022).)

The Japanese economy had been experiencing a gradual depreciation of the yen since 2021, but the sharp monetary tightening in the U.S. from the beginning of 2022 led to its rapid depreciation. As a result, the first adverse part of the J-curve effect appeared in 2022, and the trade deficit of the Japanese economy in 2022 was extremely large. However, the subsequent positive aspects of the J-curve effect are expected to appear and favorably impact Japan's current account balance and production in the future.

## (2) The Impact of the FRB's Monetary Tightening on Japan's Regional Bank Management

The tightening of U.S. monetary policy from 2022 has already begun adversely affecting the management of Japanese banks. Rising interest rates in the U.S. have caused a significant deterioration in the "net gains/losses on other securities" account through valuation losses on foreign and domestic bonds and equities held by Japanese banks. In particular, "gains on other securities" of regional banks, facing a severe business environment, have been rapidly declining since the end of March 2021, and many individual regional banks have already recorded net losses.

If the Japanese and/or U.S. monetary authorities raise interest rates in the future, the valuation losses will increase further and have a greater negative impact on bank management. We need to continue closely monitoring the figures in the "gains/losses on other securities" account.

## (3) U.S. economy

The impact of the U.S. economy on the Japanese economy would be quite different, depending on whether or not the U.S. economy succeeds in a soft landing. In terms of total trade values in exports and imports, China is Japan's No.1 trading partner with the U.S. No.2. In terms of export value alone, however, the U.S. was the No.1 export partner and China was No.2 in April 2023. Therefore, boom or recession in the U.S. economy has a significant impact on Japan's exports.

As discussed in Subsection 2.3, while the U.S. economy has generally performed well as a whole, the contractionary monetary policy after 2022 might cause the U.S. economy to fall into recession in the second half of 2023 or in 2024. Although the possibility is slight, if the U.S. economy were to fall into a serious recession, Japan's trade and current accounts would incur commensurate damage, leading to a major blow for the Japanese economy.

## (4) Risk of U.S. financial system instability

Another concern for the Japanese economy is the collapse of the three U.S. regional banks. If no other banks go bankrupt, there will no problems. However, the FRB is still in the process of tightening monetary policy. Raising interest rates by the FRB could worsen the banks' balance sheets through capital losses from bond possession. If more and more banks should fail, the U.S. financial industry could fall into turmoil and also seriously impact the Japanese economy.

In that case, the impact would be on both real and financial sectors in the Japanese economy. If the financial turmoil were transmitted to the real sector in the U.S. economy, Japanese firms' exports to the U.S. as well as local production in the U.S. would decline. This would have a direct effect on the real sector in the Japanese economy. If the U.S. real economy should fall into recession, the FRB would ease its monetary policy significantly, inducing JPY appreciation.

Looking back, the global recession of 2008 began with the bursting of the real estate bubble in the United States in mid-2006. The resulting turmoil remained within the financial industry for about two years. When the Lehman Brothers went bankrupt in September 2008, the turmoil quickly spread to the real economy. As soon as the U.S. economy fell into recession, the FRB dealt with it by boldly easing monetary policy, while the Bank of Japan was late and its intervention was minimal. This difference in monetary policy between the FRB and the Bank of Japan led to the extreme appreciation of the JPY, which in turn brought about a disastrous impact on the Japanese economy. Recalling this bitter experience, we cannot take our eyes off the developments in the U.S.

financial industry.

## References

Yuzo Honda (2022), "JPY depreciation and Japanese firms: Positive effects expand with time lag" (Japanese title: *Enyasu to Nihon Kigyo: Zikansa Tomonai Purasu Koka Kakudai*), Nihon Keizai Shimbun, Morning Edition, Keizai Kyoshitsu, September 13.

## Section 3
# RISKS IN THE CHINESE ECONOMY:
# REAL ESTATE AND LOCAL PUBLIC FINANCE

*KAJITANI, Kai*

## 1. The Real Estate Market Slump and Its Macroeconomic Background

In the aftermath of China's 'zero-Covid' policy, uncertainty about the future of the Chinese economy has never been higher. China's GDP (gross domestic product) showed a modest recovery in the first quarter of 2023, increasing by 4.5% year on year. On the other hand, the consumption of large durable consumer goods such as automobiles remains sluggish, and the real estate market remains a major source of economic uncertainty due to an imbalance between supply and demand for housing, especially in small and medium-sized cities. Although it seems to have recovered from its temporary slump, the real estate market remains a major source of concern for the economy.

In consideration of the above, the purpose of this paper is to analyze trends in the real estate market, which is the greatest risk factor for the Chinese economy over the medium to long term, and then to reassess the problem from the perspective of a "rational bubble" and its demise. The risks faced by local government finances, which are closely related to the slump in the real estate market, are discussed as well.

First, let us examine the aspects of the current real estate market slump. In February 2020, when lockdowns were implemented in Wuhan and other cities, the Chinese government swiftly embarked on a policy of monetary easing. This policy and the implementation of thorough zero-Covid measures to suppress the infection were initially successful, and the real estate market quickly recovered to pre-pandemic levels, even showing signs of overheating. In August 2020, the government, fearing growing public criticism of the soaring housing market, established "three red lines": (1) an asset-liability ratio of 70% or less, excluding advances; (2) a net debt-to-equity ratio of 100% or less; and (3) cash holdings that exceed short-term liabilities. A decision was made not to provide loans to real estate companies that did not meet these conditions. However, as a result of this policy, many real estate companies, which had been borrowing at low interest rates to service their growing debts, began to struggle for funds, and in July 2021, stock prices and corporate bonds of real estate companies plummeted, triggered by fears of default by real estate giant Evergrande Group. In September of the same year, the average price of new condominiums in 70 major cities in China dropped for the first time in six years and five months, and the real estate market rapidly cooled. The economic impact of the prolonged lockdowns, best exemplified by the lockdown that was implemented in Shanghai for about two months from the end of March 2022, further exacerbated the situation.

In the summer of 2022, the issue of homebuyers refusing to pay their loans due to the suspension of construction of properties they had already purchased became a social problem. As a result, the catchphrase for real estate policy became *bao jiao lou, bao min sheng* (ensuring delivery of housing and protecting people's wellbeing). In November of the same year, the "Notice on Financial Support for the Stable and Healthy Development of the Real Estate Market" ("Article 16: Finance") was announced, and the policy bank provided special loans to *bao jiao lou*, supported developers who had fallen into business risks, and guaranteed financial interests to homebuyers, among other measures to support housing construction and prevent further price declines. In January 2023, the government reasserted its stance on stabilizing the real estate market by relaxing the "three red lines" for only 30 major companies (China Research Office, Research & Advisory Department, 2022). As a result of these government measures, new condominium prices in 70 major cities rose an average of 0.3% MoM in February 2023, marking the first increase in 18 months, however the housing market recovery still lacks strength.

Apart from the microeconomic aspect of the management of individual real estate companies, the destabilization of the real estate market can be attributed to three macroeconomic trends: (1) fiscal and monetary policies following the Covid-19 pandemic; (2) the long-term development strategy for China's urbanization; and (3) the end of the intergenerational resource transfer scheme through a continuing rational bubble.

This paper focuses mainly on the third trend, which is closely related to the problems afflicting China's real estate market. In the following paragraphs, this topic is analyzed in detail from a macroeconomic perspective.

## 2. Dynamic inefficiencies and "rational bubbles"

Before analyzing China's real estate market from the perspective of "rational bubbles," we first briefly explain the concept of "rational bubbles" in recent macroeconomics.

Sakuragawa (2021) pointed out that as long as the economic (GDP) growth rate exceeds the lending interest rate, an asset bubble can persist for a long time even in a steady-state economy. Such a persistent bubble is referred to as

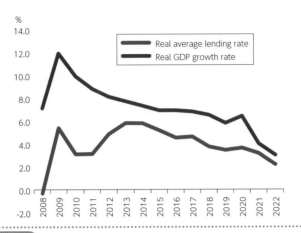

**Figure 1-3-1**    GDP Growth Rate and Average Lending Rate

Note: The real average lending rate is the weighted average of financial institution lending rates substantiated by the commodity retail price index.
Source: CEIC Data, National Bureau of Statistics.

a "rational bubble." Sakuragawa also argues that in a low-interest-rate economy, in which the GDP growth rate exceeds the interest rate, bubbles keep moving from one sector to another. For example, after the real estate and stock bubbles of the 1980s ended, a bubble emerged in Japanese government bonds, which is the cause of Japan's huge budget deficit.

In China, the GDP growth rate has consistently exceeded the average lending rate since the Great Recession (Figure 1-3-1). In macroeconomics, a situation in which economic growth exceeds the interest rate under steady-state conditions is called a dynamically inefficient state. When investment is saturated in a decentralized economy, the Pareto-optimal allocation of resources among different points in time cannot be achieved through market transactions, and there is room for the government and other economic actors to improve the total welfare by forcibly redistributing resources. In explaining the resource allocation problem in a state of dynamic inefficiency, the so-called overlapping generations model is often used, as in Tirol (1985) and others.

The model assumes that all people live for two periods: 'youth' and 'old age.' In their youth, people work and earn income, and they consume a portion of that income. In their old age, people live off the savings they accumulated in their youth. Now consider an economy where investment is saturated, and the rate of return on real investment is low, i.e. the real interest rate is lower than the rate of economic growth. To simplify the discussion, we assume that the ratio of people in each generation is constant. In such a case, young people are forced to save under low interest rates for their own consumption in old age (Figure 1-3-2).

Even without the government's semi-mandatory reallocation of resources, as described above, this sort of dynamic inefficiency can be eliminated through the successive purchase of assets whose value increases in tandem with economic growth, such as real estate assets. In this way, the welfare of all economic agents can be improved. Tirol proved that in order to achieve efficient intergenerational capital transfers, it is necessary for assets that have no fundamental value to be traded as having a certain value, and that value tends to expand over time. This is the situation in which the so-called "rational bubbles" occur.

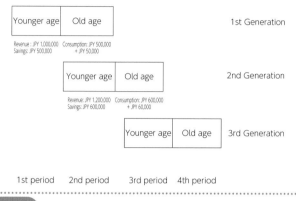

**Figure 1-3-2**    **Asset Formation with Market Interest Rates**

Source: Prepared by the author

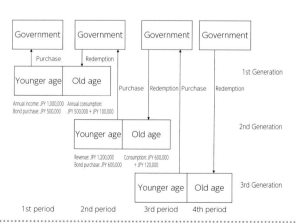

**Figure 1-3-3**    **Cases in which the government issues bonds with interest payments equal to the economic growth rate**

Source: Prepared by the author

## 3. The "Rational Bubble" and China's Real Estate Market

### (1) High growth due to excess accumulation of capital

One of the important issues in viewing China's real estate market as a "rational bubble" is that "capital overaccumulation" has become the norm as a result of the high growth of the Chinese economy led by vigorous domestic investment.

Under the Hu Jintao administration this state of excessive capital accumulation became exacerbated. This is attributable to three major factors: (1) a decline in the labor participation rate due to state-owned enterprise reforms and intensified competition among enterprises; (2) an increase in retained earnings (corporate savings) by non-state-owned enterprises that had difficulty borrowing from financial institutions; and (3) a high savings rate by the household sector due to the delayed development of social security systems (Kajitani, 2012). In particular, the stimulus packages implemented after the Great Recession increased the degree of government intervention in the market, leading to what some economists have criticized as "national progress and national regression." Such stimulus packages combined with excessive fixed capital investment led by local governments did not bring about a fundamental solution to the problem of excessive capital accumulation, but instead postponed the problem through state intervention in the market.

When the economy is in such a state of "excessive capital accumulation," the productivity of fixed capital investment declines, consumption is suppressed, and excessive fixed asset investment is sustained, even though economic welfare would clearly increase if current investment were reduced and consumption were increased. The reason why fixed capital investment keeps growing despite its low productivity is generally attributed to the fact that earnings = capital gains (losses) from the rise (fall) in asset prices fill the gap between the time preference rate and the productivity of investment. On the other hand, in an economy like China, where the government has strong authority over fixed asset investment, it is necessary to consider the possibility of excessive capital accumulation due to aggressive investment activities without regard to government profitability.

As already mentioned, the overlapping generations model theoretically suggests that such a state of excess capital accumulation occurs even though each economic agent tries to maximize consumption in a decentralized market economy. When such excessive accumulation of capital occurs, the economy is said to be in a dynamically inefficient state. Based on an empirical analysis of the dynamic efficiency of the Chinese economy, Kajitani (2012) points out that the real estate market is likely to have been in a state of "rational bubble" since the

Great Recession.

## (2) Inadequacies of the levy-based social security system

As mentioned above, another major determinant of the excessive capital accumulation in China is the inadequacy of the levy-based pension system. China's public pension system consists of the compulsory 'Basic Pension for Civil Servants and Urban Employees,' and the voluntary 'Basic Pension for Urban and Rural Residents.' The latter was established in 2014 by integrating the 'New Rural Social Pension' and the 'Basic Pension for Urban Residents' for urban non-regular workers, and it is voluntary. The pension benefit amount is only one-twentieth that of the Basic Pension for Civil Servants and Urban Employees, and its insufficient level is problematic (Katayama, 2017).

On the other hand, the 'Basic Pension for Civil Servants and Urban Employees' is a two-tiered pension insurance plan that combines a levy-type common fund as the source of the pension with an accumulation-type individual account. The individual account is a pension account in the employee's name, and the employee and employer accumulate premiums in proportion to wages.

As shown in Subsection 3.2, it is widely known that when the economy is dynamically inefficient, intergenerational resource transfers, such as levy-based pensions, can eliminate the excessive accumulation of capital and thereby raise economic welfare (Futagami, 2012).

In other words, in a dynamically inefficient state, if the government establishes a social insurance system, such as an old-age pension system, and enhances services such as social security, excessive capital accumulation can be suppressed and the economic welfare of all generations can be improved. In contrast, if the social security system is not sufficiently developed, excessive capital accumulation will continue and the economy will be stuck in a dynamically inefficient state.

As already mentioned, China's current public pension system does not provide sufficient pensions to the peasantry and urban informal workers, who make up the majority of the population. Even for urban formal workers, pensions that do not include intergenerational resource transfers are heavily weighted toward the accumulation system, which does not include intergenerational resource transfers. If dynamic inefficiency is the cause of the recent asset bubbles in China, it is clearly due in part to the government's failure to provide adequate intergenerational resource transfers, as exemplified by the public pension system.

In his recent book, Olivier Blanchard argues that in an economy where interest rates, the "safe rate of interest" (the yield on government bonds), remain at very low levels, sometimes below the effective lower boundary of the growth rate and even the real rate of interest (Blanchard, 2023). Blanchard argues that the government could improve economic welfare by increasing the issuance of public debt and conducting aggressive fiscal policy. Applying this argument to the current state of the Chinese economy, the policy implication would be that the government should aggressively spend money, especially to improve the inadequacies of the levy-based pension system and to improve intergenerational resource transfers.

### (3) Real estate ownership as a means of retirement security

Under these circumstances, where intergenerational resource transfers through levy-based pensions have been insufficient, people have purchased condominiums in order to secure rent-free accommodation for their retirement. In addition, relatively affluent urban families often purchase a second condominium for their sons to live in after they get married. This is because parents as well as grandparents are willing to provide financial support for the purchase of a condominium, since in present-day China finding a marriage partner is almost impossible unless the person who is seeking marriage (usually a man) owns a condominium whose price continues to rise (Saito, 2023). At the same time, parents expect their sons and daughters to support them in their old age. Against the backdrop of such social values, there is empirical evidence that the price increase of condominiums is greater in areas with a larger proportion of the male population (Wei et al., 2017).

The strong demand for condominiums in urban areas and the inadequacy of the levy-based pension system have driven the continuous rise in real estate prices in China since the beginning of this century, and has also been the cause of excessive capital accumulation via vigorous real estate construction.

## 4. The future of rational bubbles and the problems facing local finances

It is unclear whether a hard landing in the real estate market and widespread economic turmoil can be avoided as the overaccumulation of capital in the Chinese economy begins to dissipate.

From a macroeconomic viewpoint of economic theory, rational bubbles in the real estate market should theoretically become unsustainable once the overaccumulation of capital is eliminated and the GDP growth rate stops exceeding the lending interest rate. Even if this happens, it is possible to achieve a certain level of economic growth while temporarily suppressing people's dissatisfaction under low interest rates. This could happen either by encouraging intergenerational transfers by widely holding government bonds with low interest rates, or by expanding the levy-based public pension system, which currently only covers urban full-time employees, to all citizens, as was the case in Japan after the collapse of the bubble economy.

Another concern is the situation of local government finances. The finances of local governments have been largely supported by the sale of farmland and other land holdings. The tightening of the real estate market, as described in this paper, has caused a significant drop in this income, and the financial situation of many local governments has deteriorated significantly. Some local governments, such as Hegang City in Heilongjiang Province, are reported to have cancelled their staff recruitment plans and announced that they were implementing a financial restructuring plan, effectively "going bankrupt."

In response to this situation, an editorial in the April 24, 2023 issue of the influential economic journal "Caixin Weekly" warned once again that the severe economic impact of the Covid-19 pandemic, falling prices in the real estate industry, and various tax exemptions were worsening the debt problems of local governments. The May 22nd issue of the same journal's special feature article, "The Debt Issuance Boom of Local Government Financing Vehicles," points out that Local Government Financing Vehicles, which have been a breeding ground for local government "hidden debt," are increasing their debt through the issuance of bonds known as "municipal bonds," thereby increasing the risk to local government finances. According to a think tank's estimate, at the end of 2022, local government hidden debt amounted to RMB 52-58 trillion, which is 1.5-1.7 times the amount of official debt outstanding.

Financing through the issuance of "municipal bonds" by Local Government Financing Vehicles has been used by many local governments since the establishment of Local Government Financing Vehicles to implement economic stimulus measures after the Global Recession.

However, according to an article in Caixin Weekly, the issuance of more complex bonds, so-called "structured bonds," has been a major characteristic of recent municipal bond issues.

A typical example is the asset-backed securities (ABS) scheme, in which Local Government Financing Vehicles uses its own funds to purchase municipal bonds it has issued, posts them as assets, and uses them as collateral to raise new funds. This is strictly regulated as a way to reduce the participation of outside capital and issue bonds at interest rates lower than the market level, which distorts the market. For example, in 2023, the government issued a notice restricting new financing by firms whose own bonds account for more than 50%

of the net assets of Local Government Financing Vehicles, and tightened penalties for firms that do not comply with the new restrictions.

At the same time, however, some local governments, such as those in Guizhou Province, have been experiencing financial difficulties, and it is said that they are no longer able to resolve their debts on their own. In many cases, these local financing platforms have asked the local or central government to reschedule (review the repayment terms of) the municipal bonds they have issued.

In a well-known case, in December 2022, Zunyi Daoqiao Construction Group, headquartered in Zunyi City, Guizhou Province, defaulted and announced a debt restructuring that postponed the repayment date by 20 years and only required interest payments for the first 10 years. It is clear that the state of local government debt is posing risks to the Chinese economy as a whole, and this is a problem that cannot be left unaddressed.

Some economists in China have pointed out that the reason for this tightness in local government finances is that the central government does not spend enough money, thereby imposing an excessive burden on local governments, which is a very plausible explanation.

If the soft landing from the "rational bubble" situation in the real estate market is to be achieved, it is necessary to maintain the current rate of economic growth, to suppress the sharp decline in exchange rates while continuing the low-interest-rate policy. In the meantime, it is necessary to expand and improve the social security system while minimizing the level of social unrest that will accompany the decline in real estate prices. Additionally, since the declining birthrate and aging population are bound to become more serious and the government's fiscal burden is expected to increase, it will also be necessary to review the current fiscal system that places much of the burden, from the provision of social security to economic stimulus measures, onto local governments.

In this context, the decision by the Standing Committee of the National People's Congress in October 2023 to issue RMB one trillion in special government bonds and allow a budget deficit of 3.8% of GDP is a notable move. Will this catalyze the Chinese government to adopt a more proactive fiscal policy? In any case, we will continue to keep a close eye on China's real estate market and local government finances for some time to come.

## References
[Japanese]
China Research Office, Research & Advisory Department (2022), "China
     Launches Financial Real Estate Support Policies: Caution on Cooling Real

Estate Market" (Japanese title: *Chugoku wa Kinyumen no Fudosan Shien Seisaku o Uchidasu –Fudosan Shijo no Hiekomi ni Keikai–*), *MUFG Bank (China) Economic Weekly Report*, 574th Edition, November 22, 2022.

Futagami, K. (2012), *Dynamic Macroeconomics* (Japanese title: *Dogaku Makuro Keizaigaku*), Nippon Hyoronsha

Kajitani, Kai (2012), "An Empirical Analysis of Dynamic Inefficiency in the Chinese Economy: An Examination Using the AMSZ Criterion" (Japanese title: *Chugoku Keizai no Dogakuteki Hikoritsusei ni Kansuru Jissho Bunseki –MSZ Kijun wo Mochiita Kento–*), *Journal of the National Economy*, Vol. 206, No. 5.

Katayama, Yuki (2017), "On China's Pension System (2017)" (Japanese title: *Chugoku no Nenkin Seido Nitsuite [2017]*), *Nissay Research Institute for Basic Studies Bulletin*, Vol. 62

Saito, Junko (2023), *Sin Chinese - Radical Change in Society and Troubled Youth* (Japanese title: *Shin Chugokujin –Gekihen Suru Shakai to Nayameru Wakamono Tachi–*), Chikuma Shinsho

Sakuragawa, Masaya (2021), *An Economic Theory of Bubbles: Low Interest Rates, Long-Term Stagnation, and Financial Degradation* (Japanese title: *Baburu no Keizai Riron: Teikinri, Choki Teitai, Kinyu Rekka*), Nihon Keizai Shimbun Publishing Co.

[English]

Abel, Andrew B., Mankiw, N. Gregory, Summers, Lawrence H., and Zeckhauser, Richard J. (1989). "Assessing Dynamic Efficiency: Theory and Evidence." *Review of Economic Studies*, 56, 1-20.

Blanchard, Olivier (2023), *Fiscal Policy under Low Interest Rates*, MIT Press.

Tirol, Jean (1985), "Asset Bubbles and Overlapping generations" *Econometrica*, 53, 1499-1528.

Wei, Shangjin, Zhang, Xiaobo, and Yin Liue (2017), "Home ownership as status competition: some theory and evidence," *Journal of Development Economics*, 127, 169-186.

[Chinese]

Yi, Gang (2021), "The People's Bank of China, China's Interest Rate System and Interest Rate Marketization Reforms," *Journal of Financial Research*, 9th period, 2021.

Part I

Part II

Part III

Part IV

## Section 4
## ECONOMIC STRATEGIES OF JAPAN AND JAPANESE COMPANIES TOWARD EAST ASIA

*KIMURA, Fukunari*

# 1. U.S.-China Conflict and Production Networks

## (1) Countermeasure to changing circumstances

The U.S.-China confrontation, which began in 2018 under the Trump adminis-tration as a tariff war, has gradually expanded its scope to include competition over technological hegemony among the superpowers and issues of human rights and political regimes, and the degree of confrontation has deepened fur-ther under the Biden administration. Japan, an ally of the United States, has been forced to undertake a major review of its security policy. However, there are signs that the tide is turning in the area of economic security, particularly with regard to export controls in the high-tech sector.

Certainly, the deterioration of sentiment toward China in Washington, D.C., is extremely strong, and it is unlikely that the U.S. and China will move toward reconciliation anytime soon, as the US enters presidential election mode over the next year. Meanwhile, a speech given by Jake Sullivan, Assistant to the President for National Security Affairs, at the Brookings Institution on April 27, 2023, suggested that the White House is trying to settle the current issue. He said that export controls over China are "with a small yard and a high fence," and that the goal is de-risking and diversifying, not decoupling, as European Union President Von der Leyen has suggested. In the context of export control, the US is introducing strict controls to decouple some high-tech sectors, but creating an environment in which other economic activities can develop freely, i.e., decoupling is only partial. This statement is considered to be an indication of the intention to reflect the voices of the economic community that values business with China, which is not readily apparent, although there are probably many competing opinions in Washington, DC.

European countries are visiting China one after another, starting with German Chancellor Scholz in November 2022, accompanied by businessmen, separating politics and economics, in an attempt to expand their business pres-ence in China. In fact, the U.S. also continues its close economic relationship with China, and in 2022, despite the slowdown of the Chinese economy in the second half of the year, both imports and exports reached all-time highs for the entire year. While the impact of export controls in the high-tech sector, especially as it determines the direction of cutting-edge innovation, cannot be ignored, there is little concern of the world as a whole being split in half. A pragmatic approach is becoming clear: continuing the confrontation with China, but taking immediate economic gains while taking risks into account.

Japan and Japanese companies have seemed to be so caught up in the security debate to prepare for the worst-case scenario that they have stopped thinking. In export control, too much reliance is placed on the anticipation of the other party's moves between the government and the private sector, and excessive careful attention is limiting free economic activities. Certainly, in relations with China, it may be difficult for Japanese companies to start moving aggressively because of the detention of Japanese VIP in March 2023. However, it should be well understood that that is exactly China's strategy to divide the West. And just because the strategy toward China is difficult, can it be said that Japanese companies are embarking on expanding their activities to the Association of Southeast Asian Nations (ASEAN) and other parts of the world? We must not forget the economy. The government needs to create the economic environment and companies need to develop their corporate strategies, while assessing where their competitors are drawing the line and trying to increase their economic activity.

## (2) Japan's decoupling policy

The set of policies called economic security-related policies are a mixture of various objectives and measures, but here we will review Japan's decoupling-related policies, especially from the perspective of supply chain decoupling.

First, for a middle power like Japan, which is sandwiched between two superpowers, a distinction should be made between defensive and offensive decoupling policies in light of their immediate objectives. Defensive decoupling policy here refers to the policy of increasing domestic supplies or supplies from a third country in order to reduce dependence on a specific country when there is a risk of sudden supply disruptions of critical commodities in the case of geopolitical tensions. On the other hand, offensive decoupling policy is a policy of restricting the supply of critical commodities to another country with the intention of damaging it.

In the case of Japan, most of the policies adopted so far are defensive decoupling policies. A certain degree of risk management has first been promoted by the private-sector. In particular, the "China+1 strategy" (i.e., separating Chinese operations from the rest of the world) was adopted early toward that country, and was carefully reexamined especially after the Senkaku Islands issue and China's rare earth export restrictions in 2010.

Part I

Part II

Part III

Part IV

After 2020, against the backdrop of geopolitical tensions that rose with the new Corona pandemic, two types of METI subsidies were established for Japanese companies: the "Subsidy for Domestic Investment Promotion Projects for Supply Chain Measures" and the "Support Program to Strengthen Overseas Supply Chains for Demonstration Projects and Project Feasibility Studies". Although not officially specified, the former was intended to encourage production bases located in China to return to Japan, while the latter was intended to diversify production bases from China to ASEAN and other regions. While these policies have produced some results, they have not caused a major leave of Japanese companies located in China.

Furthermore, the Law for the Promotion of Economic Security, enacted and promulgated in May 2022, states that the first of its four pillars is to ensure a stable supply of critical commodities. In December of the same year, the law designated 11 critical commodities (antimicrobial agents, fertilizers, permanent magnets, machine tools and industrial robots, aircraft parts, semiconductors, storage batteries, cloud computing programs, natural gas, critical minerals, and ship parts) and announced a policy of providing financial assistance. Some of the critical commodities are intended as a kind of industrial policy, but most of them are defensive decoupling policies.

Most of the offensive decoupling policies related to Japan have taken as countermeasures to the extraterritorial application of U.S. export controls. Japan itself expanded export control items in 2018 and 2021, but this has not had a significant impact.[1] The introduction of export controls on 23 items of semiconductor manufacturing equipment (scheduled to take effect in July) announced at the end of March 2023, in line with the US, is a new step forward.

A defensive decoupling policy considers how much risk to take in relation to costs, and therefore is considered to be a restraint that limits the scope of decoupling rather than an orientation of total decoupling. On the other hand, an offensive decoupling policy is one in which a middle power such as Japan is likely to keep pace with its ally, the U.S., rather than deciding how far to go based on its own strategy. As long as any decoupling policy is implemented against the market mechanism, it will incur certain costs and leads to the problem of who will bear those costs. In the case of offensive decoupling policies, in particular, it is highly likely that the costs will be borne by industries and companies in which Japan is internationally competitive.

---

1) Hayakawa, Ito, Fukao, and Deseatnicov (2023) used econometrics to analyze whether exports declined for items that Japan placed under new export controls in 2018 and 2021, but found no statistically significant decline.

## (3) Impact of U.S. Export Controls on Japan

The U.S. export control policy in the high-tech sector, which is an offensive decoupling policy for the U.S., could affect not only China, but also Japan and other countries that cooperate with the U.S. How large are the effects?

First, at the industry and sector level (general machinery, electrical machinery, transportation equipment, and precision machinery), no clear offensive decoupling effects are detected based on international trade data, at least until the end of 2022 (Ando, Hayakawa, and Kimura 2023, forthcoming). East Asian machinery exports recovered quickly from COVID-19 and are back on a growth path. This differs significantly from North America and Europe. There was a slight slowdown from the second half of 2022. The reasons for this include the lull in special demand due to the nest egg demand associated with the new corona, the slowdown in the smartphone market, the end of the semiconductor boom, China's zero corona policy, and rising transportation costs due to the war between Russia and Ukraine. In addition to these factors, geopolitical tensions may also be a factor, but it is not clear at the industry or sector level. In particular, China remains an important trading partner for Japan. There are signs of a certain degree of reorganization of production networks to deal with the tariff war between the U.S. and China. For example, in Vietnam and Mexico, which are used as detour points, we observe an increase in exports to the U.S. and foreign direct investment, including Chinese firms. However, the impact of export controls is not clearly seen.

The effects of export control are detected in more detailed product level or for specific companies. Ando, Hayakawa, and Kimura (2023) focus in particular on the tightening of U.S. export controls on Huawei in August 2020 and attempt to quantify the effects using detailed product data on Japanese exports to China. They found that the reduction in Huawei's production of telecommunications equipment reduced Japan's exports by reducing demand for various components used in telecommunications equipment, rather than by the extraterritorial application of U.S. technology exports. The magnitude of the reduction in Japan's exports was about 3% of Japan's annual exports to China. Ando, Hayakawa, and Kimura (forthcoming) analyzed the effect of export controls on U.S. semiconductor manufacturing equipment from November 2022 using data on U.S. exports to China and found that U.S. exports of it to China decreased by about 16-36%. If the export controls on Japanese semiconductor manufacturing equipment scheduled to be introduced in July 2023 were to result in a similar reduction in Japanese exports to China, it would result in a 5-11% reduction in exports of it.

Thus, statistically significant effects were observed at detailed product level and for companies. However, the magnitude is not so large at the macro level. Offensive decoupling and other restrictions on economic activities in the name of security may increase in the future. However, it is highly likely that complete decoupling of supply chains will not be achieved. If we believe that the final result will be only partial decoupling, governments and companies will have to take appropriate measures to deal with the situation.

## 2. Asian Economies Remain Vibrant

### (1) Growing Southeast and South Asia

In 2023, developed countries are experiencing a marked economic slowdown, if not a recession, and according to the IMF (2023), economic growth in developed countries is projected to slow down from 2.7% in 2022 to 1.3% in 2023 and 1.4% in 2024. Japan's growth rate remains as low as ever, and many media reports take the tone that the entire world is in a recession. However, Asian economies continue to grow robustly.

China has been in a slump since the second half of 2022 and is having a difficult time recovering from the new corona pandemic while also dealing with its own structural economic problems. Although many believe that China will not be able to return to its previous growth trajectory, the ADB (2023) still its forecasts economic growth of 5.0% in 2023 and 4.5% in 2024 (Table 1-4-1). Since a large economy can grow at such a high rate, it still has the potential to create many business opportunities.

Southeast and South Asia have already returned to their previous growth trajectory and are growing further. In 2022, Southeast Asia as a whole recorded growth of 5.6%, with Malaysia, Vietnam, and the Philippines performing particularly well at 8.7%, 8.0%, and 7.6%, respectively, and Indonesia and Cambodia at 5.3% and 5.2%. In 2023, it is expected to see a slight slowdown due to the economic downturn in developed countries, but the region is becoming increasingly attractive as a production base and a market. South Asia as a whole is growing at 6.4% in 2022, enjoying a large potential for growth, and is expected to continue to grow after 2023.

It is inevitable that Japan and Japanese companies will seek a deeper relationship with the Asian economy.

| Table 1-4-1 | Economic growth rates of Asian developing economies (fact and forecast) (%) | | | |
|---|---|---|---|---|
| | 2021 | 2022 | 2023(f) | 2024(f) |
| **East Asia total** | **7.9** | **2.8** | **4.6** | **4.2** |
| China | 8.4 | 3.0 | 5.0 | 4.5 |
| South Korea | 4.1 | 2.6 | 1.5 | 2.2 |
| Taiwan | 6.5 | 2.5 | 2.0 | 2.6 |
| **Southeast Asia total** | **3.5** | **5.6** | **4.7** | **5.0** |
| Brunei | -1.6 | -0.5 | 2.5 | 2.8 |
| Cambodia | 3.0 | 5.2 | 5.5 | 6.0 |
| Indonesia | 3.7 | 5.3 | 4.8 | 5.0 |
| Laos | 2.3 | 2.5 | 4.0 | 4.0 |
| Malaysia | 3.1 | 8.7 | 4.7 | 4.9 |
| Myanmar | -5.9 | 2.0 | 2.8 | 3.2 |
| Philippines | 5.7 | 7.6 | 6.0 | 6.2 |
| Singapore | 8.9 | 3.6 | 2.0 | 3.0 |
| Thailand | 1.5 | 2.6 | 3.3 | 3.7 |
| Vietnam | 2.6 | 8.0 | 6.5 | 6.8 |
| **South Asia total** | **8.4** | **6.4** | **5.5** | **6.1** |
| Bangladesh | 6.9 | 7.1 | 5.3 | 6.5 |
| India | 9.1 | 6.8 | 6.4 | 6.7 |

Note: This table includes data of countries other than those listed ones.
Source: ADB (2023)

## (2) Japan's relative position

At the same time, it is necessary to be well aware of the position of Japan and Japanese companies in the eyes of Asian countries.

Figure 1-4-1 shows the value of imports and exports by country and region for the 10 ASEAN countries. Even in 2020, when the impact of the corona pandemic was most severe, the decline in ASEAN's trade, especially exports, was very small. This is largely because ASEAN countries succeeded in mitigating the spread of the virus to a considerable extent, and ASEAN countries were able to enjoy the positive demand shocks created by the work-at-home and stay-at-home effects of the corona pandemic. In 2021, both imports and exports grew strongly.

What is even more remarkable is China's share of imports and exports in this region. While ASEAN countries' internal trade is just over 20%, China accounts for 16% of ASEAN's exports and 24% of its imports (in 2020 and 2021). In particular, imports from China have come to exceed the sum of imports from Japan, the U.S., and Europe. Although the depth of economic engagement cannot be measured by trade volume alone, and direct investment in ASEAN and technology flows must also be taken into account, there is no doubt that

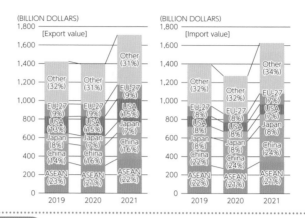

**Figure 1 - 4 - 1**    Exports and Imports of ASEAN Countries by Country or Region

Source: ASEAN Secretariat Website

ASEAN countries are becoming increasingly involved with China. On the other hand, Japan accounts for only about 8% of both imports and exports, while the U.S. accounts for only 15% of exports and 7-8% of imports. It is clear that Japan is not in a situation where it can force ASEAN to select the U.S. or China as a sole partner.

Kumagai et al. (2023) use the IDE-GSM model of the Institute of Developing Economies to simulate the impact on countries around the world if the Western and Eastern camps start decoupling their supply chains by imposing a 25% tariff mutually. The results show that both camps would naturally be negatively affected, but third countries that do not belong to either camp, such as ASEAN countries, would be positively affected because they could continue to trade with both camps. There is certainly an economic incentive for third countries, especially those deeply involved in the East Asian production network, to remain neutral.

## (3) Strategies of Japan and Japanese Companies toward ASEAN

If offensive decoupling ultimately remains part of the supply chain, Japan's economic diplomacy with ASEAN will be extremely important. ASEAN, along with China, is the region where the core international production network for the machinery industry in East Asia is deployed, and it has less policy risk in the sense that China bears. Japan is not the only friendly country to ASEAN, but Japanese companies have built up a solid track record, and Japan has earned a great deal of trust. Taking into consideration that geopolitical tensions are difficult to resolve in the short term, ASEAN is a valuable counterpart in maintaining the economic vitality of "other economies" outside of export controls.

Japan and Japanese companies should adopt the following three strategies to deal with ASEAN. First, it is important to explain well to ASEAN countries the supply chain decoupling policies adopted by developed countries, and to have them understand that there is room for ASEAN to be involved in decentralization of supply sources, especially in industries and products that are subject to defensive decoupling policies. Also, Japan and Japanese companies should firmly explain that there are few cases in which ASEAN needs to immediately deal with the extraterritorial application of U.S. export controls in the high-tech sector, but rather that they open up the possibility for ASEAN to accept high-tech-related investment in the future.

Second, although the era of Japan as a prominent player in ASEAN was over, Japan must continue its efforts to further deepen economic ties with ASEAN countries. Japan has contributed greatly to the development of economic infrastructure and the creation of international production networks, particularly in the manufacturing sector, in ASEAN. While the importance of these contributions will not diminish in the future, the emphasis of ASEAN's economic development strategy is shifting toward services and urban amenities. The ASEAN is particularly interested in digital and sustainability.

Third, Japan, together with ASEAN, must preserve the rules-based trading regime as much as possible and emphasize its importance to the world. Since the 1990s, East Asia has led the world in the development of an international division of labor based on tasks, especially in the machinery industry, and the preconditions for this were a rules-based trading regime and a long-lasting peace. In the future, technological progress will make possible a more sophisticated international division of labor, but these two preconditions must continue to be met in order to make effective use of the division of labor.

One of the major problems with the current policy measures to geopolitical tensions is that developed countries are openly violating existing trade rules for reasons of security. A prominent example of this is the domestic priority for subsidies in high-tech sectors such as advanced semiconductors. It may be difficult to push back the logic of security or the structure of confrontation between the superpowers head-on, but this does not mean that the trading regime based on rules should be seriously damaged. It is essential to keep other economic activities under trade rules as broadly as possible, while ensuring the consistency with trade rules of security policies as much as possible. China may not agree with the content of trade rules, but it feels a strong desire to be respected as a respectable country that abides by the rules in the international arena[2]. There are still many meanings of international rules.

ASEAN can be a valuable partner in advocating the importance of a rules-based trading regime. ASEAN has utilized globalization in economic development most effectively in the past 40 years under international rules. ASEAN should not free-ride on global policy governance, as it has done in the past, but should take responsibility for its own development.

There are many ways in which Japan and ASEAN can cooperate to preserve the rules-based trading regime. First, in relation to the World Trade Organization (WTO), the second tier of dispute settlement, the Appellate Body, has ceased to function with zero members due to the U.S. blockade. As a result, cases of so-called "appeals into void" have been piled up, in which appeals are filed to the Appellate Body, which does not function after the panel of first instance reached a conclusion.[3] In March 2023, Japan announced its participation in the Multi-Party Interim Appeal Arbitration Arrangement (MPIA), which is intended to temporarily replace the functions of the Appellate Body. However, Singapore is the only ASEAN country that has already joined the MPIA, and it is important to encourage other ASEAN countries to do so. In addition, Japan is co-chairing a joint statement initiative for e-commerce, and Japan could cooperate with ASEAN, which is also taking steps to establish its own rules.

We would also like to promote the use of the mega-FTAs (Free Trade Agreements) that Japan has concluded with ASEAN countries. In particular, the Regional Comprehensive Economic Partnership (RCEP) agreement covers the whole East Asia, including China, and is expected to reduce policy risks within the region by actively using such opportunities as regular meetings[4]. In the Indo-Pacific Economic Framework (IPEF) currently under negotiation, a substantial agreement was reached in May 2023 on supply chains, the second of four areas: trade, supply chains, clean economy, and fair economy[5]. The agreement is to cooperate in preparation for sudden supply disruptions of critical commodities such as semiconductors and critical minerals. It is not clear to what extent this will be effective, but it is not a matter of course to force the stakeholders to

---

2) See Watanabe, Kamo, Kawashima, and Kawase (2021).
3)  For example, the EU sued Indonesia for a nickel ore export ban and domestic processing requirements (DS592), and Japan sued India for higher tariffs on ICT products (DS584), both of which have been appealed out of court after the panel decision. See Trade Policy Bureau, Ministry of Economy, Trade and Industry (2023) and WTO website.
4)  See Kimura (2022) for a discussion of the role that RCEP could play.
5)  Japan External Trade Organization (JETRO), "Business Brief: U.S. Department of Commerce Announces Substantial Conclusion of IPEF Supply Chain Agreement, Offers Measures to Realize Business Benefits," Accessed on May 29, 2023.

declare which side they will be on.

Geopolitical tensions are a major headwind for free economic activity, but they have not run the entire world. We must pursue a balanced economic diplomacy and corporate strategy to ensure sound rules and vigorous economic activities as broadly as possible.

## References

Ando, M., Hayakawa, K., and Kimura, F. (2023) "Supply Chain Decoupling: Geopolitical Debates and Economic Dynamism in East Asia", submitted to Asian Economic Policy Review. Forthcoming in the JCER Discussion Paper Series.

Ando, M., Hayakawa, K., and Kimura, F. (forthcoming) "The Threat of Economic Deglobalization from Cold War 2.0: A Japanese Perspective", Asian Economic Papers.

Asian Development Bank (ADB) (2023) Asian Development Outlook, April 2023, Manila: ADB.

Hayakawa, K., Ito, K., Fukao, K., and Deseatnicov, I. (2023), " The Impact of the Strengthening of Export Controls on Japanese Exports of Dual-use Goods", International Economics, 174, pp. 160-179.

International Monetary Fund (IMF) (2023) World Economic Outlook April 2023: A Rocky Recovery, Washington, DC: IMF.

Kimura, F. (2022), "Significance and Role of RCEP" (Japanese title: *RCEP no igi to yakuwari*). In Kimura, F., and Nishiwaki, O. (eds.), "Structural Transformation of International Trading Regime: The US-China Confrontation WTO, Regional Economic Integration, and Japan" (Japanese title: *Kokusai Tsusho Chitsujo no Chikaku Hendo: Beichutairitsu·WTO·Chiikitogo to nihon*), Keiso Shobo: 207-228.

Kumagai, S., Hayakawa, K., Gokan, T., Isono, I., Sukhniran, K., Tsubota, T., and Kubo, Y. (2023), "The Impact of Global 'Decoupling' on the World Economy: IDE-GSM Analysis (Summary Version)" (Japanese title: *Gurobaru na 'Dekappuringu' ga Sekai Keizai ni Ataeru Eikyo -IDE-GSM- Niyoru Bunseki [Gaiyoban]*), IDE Policy Brief, No. 1 (February 6).

Trade Policy Bureau, Ministry of Economy, Trade and Industry (2023), "The 2023 Report on Compliance by Major Trading Partners with Trade Agreements (WTO, FTA/EPA and IIA)" (Japanese title: *2023nemban Fukosei Boeki Hokokusho: WTO Kyotei oyobi Keizai Renkei Kyotei·Toshi Kyotei kara Mita Shuyokoku no Boeki Seisaku*), METI.

Watanabe, M., Kamo, T., Kawashima, F., and Kawase, T. (2021), "A Study on the Background of China's Declaration of Intention to Join the CPTPP (Revised

Version)" (Japanese title: *Chugoku no CPTPP Sanka Ishi Hyomei no Haikei ni Kansuru Kosatsu [Kaiteiban]*), RIETI Policy Discussion Paper Series 21-P-016 (September 11).

| Column A | Considering Business and Human Rights: What are Universal Human Rights? |
|---|---|

*GOTO, Kenta*

## 1. Introduction.

In September 2022, the Japanese government released "Guidelines on Respecting Human Rights in Responsible Supply Chains" to promote corporate efforts to respect human rights. One month earlier, "Guidelines for Responsible Business Conduct for the Textile and Clothing Industry of Japan" was formulated by the Japan Textile Federation under the auspices of the Ministry of Economy, Trade and Industry. While the latter is specific to the textile sector, the industry still encompasses many subsectors from upstream to downstream, and the size of the actors varies from small to large companies. The position of each company in the textile industry value chain is different, and the management issues they face involve a variety of stakeholders. The fact that the guidelines were developed through constructive dialogue between workers and employers was groundbreaking.[1]

These guidelines are all based on key international standards related to business and human rights (BHR), such as the Organization for Economic Co-operation and Development's (OECD) "Guidelines for Multinational Enterprises on Responsible Business Conduct (MNE Guidelines)," the International Labour Organization's (ILO) "Tripartite Declaration of Principles concerning Multinational Enterprises and Social Policy (MNE Declaration)," and the United Nations' "Guiding Principles on Business and Human Rights (Guiding Principles)"[2]. The development of those guidelines in Japan has been based on the growing attention within the government on issues related to BHR since the inauguration of the Kishida administration.

Shortly before these movements in Japan, the Biden administration, which also emphasized human rights, took office in the United States.

---

1) Workers were represented by the Japanese Federation of Textile, Chemical, Commerce, Food and General Services Workers' Unions (UA Zensen). The International Labour Organization (ILO) office in Japan provided technical assistance in the development of the guidelines. The author had the opportunity to participate in the development process as one of the ILO's advisors.
2) Guiding Principles on Business and Human Rights: Implementing the United Nations' "Protect, Respect and Remedy" Framework.

All businesses should recognize the intrinsic value and importance of human rights and respect it in their daily operations, not because it is "required." However, it may still be important to understand the broader international political and economic context in which human rights issues have evolved to become central to business activities. One example in which this has manifested itself is the Indo-Pacific Economic Framework (IPEF). The IPEF is one of the main policies of the Biden administration related to the Asian region, which, unlike previous regional trade agreements, is now being discussed with an emphasis on "values," such as human rights. We will discuss IPEF in the final part of this column. These broader international political-economic dynamisms will most likely affect the institutional context in which businesses must operate in the near future. [3]

While the need for a technical response on BHR has been recognized, the discussion and understanding of the significance and universality of the issue of human rights, however, do not seem to have matured, at least not in the Japanese business world. As such, this column will take a step back and think of what "human rights" would mean for contemporary businesses, particularly in a globalizing context where it should be considered an issue that must be extended beyond the boundaries of individual companies and countries connected in global value chains (GVCs). Why should companies located in Japan be concerned not only with human rights issues within the boundaries of their country or companies, but also with those of workers of foreign business partners and even the local communities in which these partners operate? Given the context of GVCs, what is the underlying philosophy that mandates companies to bear responsibility for the human rights of workers of suppliers with which they have no direct contacts or contractual relationships? In order to address these questions, the next part briefly reviews how BHR became a prominent issue in GVCs, and then reviews its core principles, by focusing on the concept of universal human rights. This column will also discuss the challenges that this poses to businesses in the era of

---

3) In "Kansai and the Asia Pacific Economic Outlook 2002," the author reviewed the current situation of "Business and Human Rights" in Japan from both institutional and business perspectives, and discussed management issues related to the issue. Please refer to Goto (2023) for details.

globalization, and attempts to draw implications on the potential opportunities for Japan and Asia.

## 2. GVC Development and Human Rights

BHR is an old but contemporary issue. Its origins date back more than half a century to the 1960s, when the influence of corporations began to extend beyond national boundaries. The progression towards the free trade regime at a global scale in the postwar era led to the internationalization of business activities by multinational enterprises (MNEs) in developed countries, which has been recognized as a major contributor to the environmental and social problems in developing countries. It was an era in which, for example, human rights violations under policies such as the apartheid in South Africa were increasingly recognized as being problematic, and companies doing business with such countries were criticized. The MNE Guidelines and MNE Declaration were the international community's response requiring businesses to respect human rights (Yoshimura, 2021).

Economic globalization peaked during the rise of neoliberalism in the 1980s and the post-Cold War period that followed in the 1990s.The key characteristic of GVCs, which have evolved since, is that it intricately connects firms from various countries with different factor endowments through complex intra- and inter-firm relationships. Firms in developing countries with a comparative advantage in labor-intensive processes participate in GVCs by undertaking such processes. Lead firms in developed countries that organize and manage GVCs have a strong influence on the firms in other countries connected to them and on the local economies in which they operate. Therefore, when a human rights issue arises in a company in a developing country connected to a GVC, the lead firm in the developed country that coordinates the GVC is held primarily responsible. Such GVCs have developed most extensively in Asia, which has also been the main driver of the region's economic growth (Goto, 2019).

BHR became a critical issue for businesses particularly when the United Nations Human Rights Council unanimously endorsed the UN Guiding Principles (UNGP) in 2011. This was largely driven by the

Part I

Part II

Part III

Part IV

widespread view that corporations in developed countries, including Japan, have encouraged or been complicit in human rights abuses in the process of improving their competitiveness through the formulation of GVCs. The UNGP include three requirements: (1) the obligation of states to respect, protect and fulfill human rights and fundamental freedoms; (2) the responsibility of businesses to comply with all applicable laws and to respect human rights; and (3) to have in place appropriate and effective remedy mechanisms and to guarantee access to them in the event of human rights violations or non-compliance. It is important to note that, while the protection or extension of human rights has traditionally been considered the role of the state, now the responsibility of corporations has also been clearly stated (Goto, 2023).

The UNGP requires businesses to respect the human rights particularly of the workers not only in their own companies in their home countries, but also in their overseas operations. These include workers of their suppliers with whom they have no capital (ownership) relationships. The UNGP further stipulates the responsibility to respect the human rights not only of those workers of "direct suppliers," but also of "indirect suppliers" with which they may have no direct contractual relationships. In many cases, Japanese companies are in a position to configure and manage GVCs in Asia, and given their stronger position in those chains, it is understandable that they are expected to lead responsible business practices by example. The UNGP, however, is asking for more. Why should Japanese businesses be concerned and take action when there are potential human rights violations of those workers of business partners in foreign countries, even when there are no direct contracts? To address this question, it would be useful to revisit the concept of universal human rights.

## 3. The Concept of Universal Human Rights

The Universal Declaration of Human Rights of 1948 states that "All human beings are born free and equal in dignity and rights." (Article 1) and that "Everyone is entitled to all the rights and freedoms set forth in this Declaration, without distinction of any kind, such as race, color, sex, language, religion, political or other opinion, national or social origin, property, birth or other status" (Article 2). As can be understood from the Declaration, human rights are inherently "international" (Yokota, 2021) and universal in nature. It would be useful to take a look at this concept, according to the views presented by Tsutsui (2022).

Humanitarianism is a concept similar to human rights, and includes dimensions such as relief of the weak, equality, justice, freedom, and dignity. Institutions based on this concept have existed since ancient times. For example, the Mesopotamian civilization's Code of Hammurabi, which was written in the B.C. era, reflects these values. Tsutsui, however, sees the current human rights ideals as transcending these humanitarian concepts by virtue of their universality. The first key concept to understanding the nature of this difference is the distinction between in-groups and out-groups.

The idea of natural rights, that people are born with inherent rights, has existed since ancient Greece, and later took root in Western Europe with the spread of Enlightenment thought. However, these natural rights were applied to "members of society" as defined by social, political, and cultural factors, and were often understood in a limited manner. In other words, although people were considered to be born with rights, the scope of "people" was limited to in-groups such as "residents of a country" and "adult males within that country," excluding people with specific attributes such as women and foreigners. The arbitrary treatment of people who did not belong to such groups is evident in the history of the world, including that of Japan. In fact, the distinction between in-groups and out-groups is a characteristic that is widely seen in human society. It has been considered the role of the state to give priority to the in-group and to protect the lives and rights of its members. However, the concept of universal human rights is revolutionary in the sense that it holds that certain human rights must be guaranteed to everyone, regardless of the distinction between in-groups and out-groups.

It was not until after World War II that the concept of human rights as universal rights was established, which states that people must be guaranteed basic human rights simply because they are human beings. The Universal Declaration of Human Rights, whose definition is cited earlier, was the first to specifically define human rights as universal rights in an international context. Tsutsui evaluates the universal human rights

Part I

Part II

Part III

Part IV

that emerged at this time as revolutionary and a landmark in the history of mankind. Tsutsui also points out the 1970s, when interest in universal human rights grew rapidly in the international community, and the 1990s, when institutions related to human rights began to take effect after the Cold War, as important milestones in the promotion of universal human rights. Understanding human rights as a universal concept in this way makes it clear that distinctions between in-groups and out-groups, defined by boundaries such as corporations and nations, cannot be reasons to neglect the respect for human rights.

Tsutsui further states that the second key concept that distinguishes modern universal human rights from the humanitarianism of the past is the exception to the principle of non-intervention in internal affairs of states. This means that if there is a violation of human rights in another country against some of its citizens, it should not be ignored as an internal affair of another country. The principle of non-intervention granting exclusive sovereignty over its territory started since the Peace of Westphalia in 1648, and domestic affairs has since often been regarded as sacred for states. Therefore, given the reality of international politics, the affirmation of intervention in internal affairs may only be a theoretical possibility. Nevertheless, under the universal human rights concept, domestic human rights violations in the name of state sovereignty are not allowed, at least in theory, and this concept itself has been groundbreaking. If this exclusion of non-intervention underlies the concept of universal human rights in BHR, then companies overseeing GVCs will need to take action toward human rights issues of those connected in their value chains in distant countries, even when their connections remain indirect. In other words, from the perspective of universal human rights, it is essential that Japanese companies, as the lead-firms of GVCs in Asia, take some action to improve the situation when there are human rights violations in, for example, the labor conditions of suppliers with which they do not have direct contracts.

## 4. Challenges for Japanese Companies

On May 27, 2023, a ministerial-level meeting of the IPEF was held in Detroit, MI, in the U.S. Unlike the Comprehensive and Progressive

Agreement for Trans-Pacific Partnership (CPTPP) or the Regional Comprehensive Economic Partnership (RCEP), this U.S.-led initiative, which includes 14 countries including Japan, does not address issues related to market access such as tariff reductions. Instead, discussions are underway in the four areas of "fair and resilient trade (Pillar I)," "supply chains (Pillar II)," "clean economy (Pillar III)," and "fair economy (Pillar IV). Discussions in relation to IPEF are different because of a strong emphasis on "values."

At the Detroit meeting, it was announced that there had been an agreement on Pillar II related to resilience of supply chains. However, there has been one issue in this agreement that has not received much attention from the Japanese media, that being the establishment of an "IPEF Labor Rights Advisory Board" as a mechanism to ensure respect and promotion of labor rights, based on a tripartite structure of government, workers, and employers. Labor rights are at the heart of the BHR agenda, and the ILO's core labor standards (10 conventions and 1 protocol in 5 areas, including "Recognition of the right to freedom of association and collective bargaining," "Prohibition of forced labor," "Prohibition of child labor," "Elimination of discrimination," and "Safe and healthy working environment") are generally referred to as minimum rights to be respected. In Asia, however, BHR is not yet frontloaded in policy discussions. As there may be diverse reactions to human rights issues, various challenges may rise when it comes to mainstreaming BHR into practice.

In Japan, respect for human rights by businesses has so far remained a voluntary requirement. However, in Europe and other areas, it is becoming mandatory (Goto, 2023). Even if the IPEF negotiations proceed and a framework is agreed upon, it will not be enforceable unless member countries ratify the framework and enact it into domestic law. Nevertheless, it is possible that such legal measures for businesses to respect human rights might be taken in Japan in the future.

If a legal framework would be established to respect human rights and to conduct due diligence along their entire value chains, businesses would most likely respond with strong incentives. However, we must remember that it should be a natural obligation for those companies to operate in a manner that fully respects human rights, considering the

Part I

Part II

Part III

Part IV

magnitude of their influence. In addition, in light of the universality of human rights, demands for respect for human rights and criticism of human rights violations cannot be used arbitrarily in relation to specific countries or companies, as discussed earlier. One of the main challenges to mainstream human rights in business practice is to design and implement a mechanism for dialogue that is inclusive of a diverse set of stakeholders in accordance with the principles of universal human rights throughout the entire value chain.

Given these challenges, what can Japanese businesses offer, especially to their partners in Asia? In addition to formal regulations and rules, business practices aligned with respect for human rights can also emerge in the pursuit of competitiveness without regulatory enforcement. In economic terms, they can be considered as institutions in forms of informal equilibria. For example, Japanese management practices often emphasize long-term, stable inter-firm and employment relationships, which may entail practices consistent with the ideas behind BHR (Goto and Arai, 2018; Goto, 2022). Whether these "good practices" can be applied in other contexts, or the external validity of such specific cases, is of course a question that should be addressed. However, such good "*de facto*" practices are often embedded as tacit knowledge in the daily operations of Japanese companies, and sharing them with Asian partners and adapting them to local contexts may provide new insights to mainstream human rights concerns into business strategies. Identifying such good practices and reevaluating them from the BHR perspective may have important implications.

## References

Goto, K. 2023. "Business and Human Rights in the Era of Globalization" in *Kansai and the Asia Pacific: Economic Outlook 2022-2023*, Osaka: Asia Pacific Institute of Research, pp. 56-66.

Goto, K. 2022. *Responsible Supply Chains in Asia: The Case of Japan's Electronics Industry*. Tokyo: ILO.

Goto, K. 2019. *What is the Asian Economy? Its Growth Dynamism and Japan's Future* (Japanese title: *Ajia Keizai toha Nanika? Yakushin no Dainamizumu to Nihon no Katsuro*). Tokyo: Chuo-Koron Shinsha Publishers (in Japanese).

Goto, K. and Yukiko A. 2018. *More and Better Jobs through Socially Responsible Labour and Business Practices in the Electronics Sector of Viet Nam*. Geneva: ILO.

Tsutsui, S. 2022. *Human Rights and the State: The Power of Ideas and the Reality of International Politics* (Japanese title: *Jinken to Kokka Rinen no Chikara to Kokusai Seiji no Genjitsu*). Iwanami Shoten (in Japanese).

Yokota, Y. 2021. "The Meaning and Significance of International Human Rights"(Japanese title: *Kokusai Jinken no Imi to Igi*) in Yokota, Y. (ed.), *New Introduction to International Human Rights* (Japanese title: *Sin Kokusai Jinken Nyumon*), Horitsu Bunka Sha, pp. 8-25 (in Japanese).

Yoshimura, S. 2021. "Economic Activities and International Human Rights"(Japanese title: *Keizai Katsudo to Kokusai Jinken*) in Yokota, Y. (ed.), *New Introduction to International Human Rights* (Japanese title: *Sin Kokusai Jinken Nyumon*), Horitsu Bunka Sha, pp. 182-198 (in Japanese).

Part I

Part II

Part III

Part IV

## Section 5
# HOUSEHOLD DEBT AND THE HOUSING MARKET IN ASIA

*KARAVASILEV, Yani*

## 1. Introduction

### (1) Recent trends in household debt

According to the Institute of International Finance, total debt obligations globally reached an all-time high in 2022, breaking the $300 trillion threshold (three times the global GDP). Most of this increase in debt is due to a surge in public debt, which increased substantially as governments worldwide implemented sweeping policy interventions in response to the adverse impact of the COVID-19 pandemic. Public debt represents about 39% of total debt, the remainder being comprised of corporate debt (38%) and household debt (23%). Although the latter two did not expand at the same rate as public debt, they increased substantially, as well. In particular, the Asia-Pacific region saw a larger increase in the household debt-to-GDP ratio than any other world region. As a result, in some countries household debt is now at such a high level that it has raised concerns pertaining to debt sustainability and the stability of financial systems, especially in light of rising interest rates.

Table 1-5-1 shows that eight of the top 10 countries with the highest

| Table 1-5-1 | Changes in household debt levels during the Covid-19 pandemic |
|---|---|

| Country | Household debt in 2019, % of GDP | Household debt in 2021, % of GDP | Change 2019-2021, percentage points | Rate of change, global rank |
|---|---|---|---|---|
| Hong Kong | 81.7 | 93.1 | +11.4 | 1 |
| Korea | 95.0 | 105.8 | +10.8 | 2 |
| Thailand | 79.9 | 90.0 | +10.2 | 3 |
| Nepal | 29.9 | 37.8 | +7.9 | 4 |
| Vietnam | 58.5 | 66.2 | +7.7 | 5 |
| New Zealand | 91.7 | 98.8 | +7.1 | 6 |
| Japan | 62.5 | 68.8 | +6.3 | 7 |
| China | 55.8 | 62.1 | +6.3 | 8 |
| Switzerland | 126.3 | 131.9 | +5.6 | 9 |
| Malaysia | 68.1 | 73.1 | +4.9 | 10 |

Sources: Bank of International Settlements (2023). Data on Vietnam sourced from CEIC (2023) and Thuong & Minh (2022).

household debt growth are in Asia.[1] In light of this, this article aims to identify the risks to economic growth and financial stability posed by rising household debt in Asian countries, and to discuss policies on how these risks can be mitigated.

## (2) The impact of household debt on the economy

Since the ratio of household debt to GDP is positively correlated with GDP per capita, high-income countries naturally have higher household debt levels. This is due to three main factors, the first of which is that high-income countries have well-developed financial systems and an abundant supply of funds to meet demand for loans. Second, high-income countries have efficient institutions and frameworks for the protection of creditor rights and for insolvency resolutions, which allows financial institutions to lend without taking on significant risk. Third, loans are easier to obtain because customers have more assets that can serve as collateral. Even within high-income countries, most debt is held by wealthy households.

Only six countries in the world (Switzerland, Denmark, the Netherlands, Australia, Canada, and South Korea) have household debt exceeding 100% of GDP in 2021, and five of these are high-income Western countries with a long tradition of high levels of household debt. The ratio of household debt to GDP in these countries exceeds that in the U.S. just before the Global Recession (99.2% in 2007).

High household debt levels are not necessarily a cause for concern. Household debt is essential for economic growth because households take out loans to invest in housing, education, etc., which increases total domestic investment and boosts the economy (Punzi, 2022). However, many studies have shown that when the household debt level is too high, economic growth decelerates in the long run, and the negative impact of recessions is augmented.

For example, Cecchetti et al. (2011) found that a ratio of household debt to GDP exceeding 85% has a negative impact on economic growth. Additionally, based on data from 25 countries over the past 30 years, an IMF paper found

---

1) Only countries for which data is available, i.e. 70 countries, representing 84% of the world's population. Data on low-income countries is mostly unavailable. Cambodia, Laos, Myanmar, Nepal, and Bhutan, which are part of Asia, are classified as low-income countries by the IMF. These countries have very little household debt (less than 10% of GDP) due to the low level of development of their financial systems and the low penetration of bank lending. In addition to the scarcity of data, the proportion of the population living in urban areas in low-income countries is very low (less than one-third), making comparisons with middle- and high-income countries less valid. Therefore, low-income countries are not included in this analysis.

that when recessions occur when household debt levels are high, recessions are longer and more severe, and unemployment rates are higher (Leigh et al., 2012). The reason for this is that when household debt levels are high, much of the disposable income (income excluding taxes and social insurance premiums, i.e. the take-home pay that can be freely spent by the household) is directed toward debt repayment, leaving many households with insufficient funds to cope in an emergency. Thus, the economy as a whole becomes more vulnerable to shocks, the recession worsens, and the recovery may weaken (Zabai, 2017).

Despite the surge during the COVID-19 pandemic, household debt levels in Asian countries, with the exception of Korea, Hong Kong, and Thailand, are still below 85% of GDP, making it appear as if there should be no concerns about potential deceleration of economic growth. However, looking solely at the outstanding amount of household debt in order to determine the degree of risk debt poses to the economy and the financial system is far from sufficient. When such an analysis is conducted, four groups of factors should be considered:

(1) The income-adjusted level of household debt and its growth rate;
(2) The determinants of household debt (demand versus supply-side factors);
(3) The composition of household debt, collateral prices and interest rates;
(4) The likelihood of default as determined by changes in household assets and disposable income.

The following subsections examine these factors one by one.

## 2. The income-adjusted level of household debt and its growth rate

### (1) The income-adjusted level of household debt

When analyzing the impact of household debt on the economy, it is important to distinguish between the absolute ratio of household debt to GDP and its level relative to a country's income level. As mentioned above, the ratio of household debt to GDP is positively and strongly correlated with per capita GDP. Thus, it is natural for lower income countries to also have lower ratios of household debt to GDP. Most high-income countries have a household debt-to-GDP ratio of 60-120%, while most low-income countries have a ratio of less than 10%.

However, some middle-income Asian countries (China, Thailand, Vietnam, and Malaysia) already exceed the ratios of household debt to GDP of many high-income countries (e.g. Germany, Japan, and Italy). In other words, their income-adjusted debt ratios are higher than one would expect to see in countries with similar per-capita income levels. This is also true for Korea, which is a high-income economy. According to the IMF, the average nominal GDP

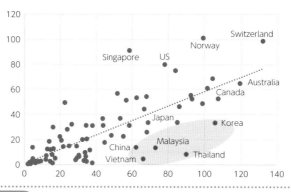

**Figure 1-5-1** The ratio of household debt to GDP (percent, horizontal axis) vs nominal GDP per capita (thousand USD, vertical axis) in 2021

Sources: IMF (2023), Bank of International Settlements (2023).

per capita in 2023 in those Western countries where household debt exceeds national GDP is about $70,000. Meanwhile, in Korea, where the ratio of household debt to GDP is the same as in these countries, the per capita GDP is about $30,000, demonstrating that Korea's income-adjusted household debt level is extremely high.

Figure 1-5-1 shows the ratio of household debt to GDP (horizontal axis) plotted against nominal GDP per capita (vertical axis) in countries for which data is available. The line of best fit shows the expected value of the ratio of household debt to GDP, i.e. the income-adjusted level of household debt. Countries above the line have a lower level of household debt relative to what would be expected at their income level, while countries below the line have relatively higher household debt ratios. Notably, those located furthest below the line of best fit are all East Asian countries, which illustrates the fact that their income-adjusted household debt levels in the region are the highest.

## (2) The growth rate of household debt

Regardless of whether household debt is high or low, the rate at which it increases does not seem to be any less relevant. In a recent panel VAR analysis using household debt data for nine Asian countries (Hong Kong, China, India, Indonesia, Japan, Korea, Malaysia, Singapore, and Thailand) from 2010 to 2017, Punzi (2022) found that a one-percentage-point increase in household debt to GDP ratio increases real GDP by +0.5% in the short run (two to three years), but this positive effect is reversed seven to eight years later, causing a real GDP decline of -1.5%.

In addition, a rapid increase in household debt is regarded as a leading

Part I

Part II

Part III

Part IV

indicator of economic recession and may pose various economic risks. For example, in the decade leading up to the Global Recession, the U.S. ratio of household debt to GDP rose from 69% to 99%, a 30-percentage-point increase. Consequently, close attention should be paid to the rate of increase in household debt.

Table 1-5-2 shows the growth of household debt as a percentage of GDP and the growth rate of outstanding household debt per adult from 2010 to 2021. As a reference, the U.S. and Western countries where household debt exceeds the GDP in 2021 are also shown.

It can be observed that the ratio of household debt to GDP has increased by more than 30 percentage points in five countries over the past decade: Korea, China, Hong Kong, Thailand, and Vietnam. This rate of increase is similar to that of the U.S. just before the Great Recession. Of these five countries, Korea, Hong Kong, and Thailand also exceed the 85% level, which, as mentioned above, is considered to have a negative impact on economic growth. It is also noteworthy

| Table 1-5-2 | Household debt as a percentage of GDP and household debt per adult in 2010 and 2021 | | | | | | | |
|---|---|---|---|---|---|---|---|---|
| Country | Household debt per adult (2021 USD) | | Change, percent | Change, USD | Household debt, percent of GDP | | Change, percent | Change, percentage points |
| | 2010 | 2021 | | | 2010 | 2021 | | |
| China | 679 | 8,991 | 1225% | +8,312 | 28% | 62% | 125% | +34.6 |
| Vietnam | 255 | 1,402 | 450% | +1,147 | 25% | 66% | 165% | +41.2 |
| Philippines | 262 | 1,206 | 360% | +943 | 5% | 10% | 106% | +5.2 |
| Thailand | 1,362 | 5,593 | 311% | +4,230 | 59% | 90% | 52% | +30.8 |
| Indonesia | 329 | 1,120 | 241% | +791 | 14% | 17% | 27% | +3.6 |
| Malaysia | 4,649 | 12,034 | 159% | +7,385 | 59% | 73% | 24% | +14.3 |
| Korea | 29,708 | 44,309 | 49% | +14,600 | 73% | 106% | 45% | +32.6 |
| Switzerland | 121,834 | 151,230 | 24% | +29,395 | 108% | 132% | 22% | +24.2 |
| Taiwan | 30,939 | 37,304 | 21% | +6,365 | 91% | 92% | 1% | +0.3 |
| Hong Kong | 46,591 | 53,928 | 16% | +7,337 | 59% | 93% | 57% | +33.9 |
| Singapore | 47,743 | 54,532 | 14% | +6,788 | 52% | 58% | 12% | +6.1 |
| Sweden | 69,070 | 73,759 | 7% | +4,688 | 76% | 92% | 22% | +16.5 |
| New Zealand | 52,922 | 52,957 | 0% | +34 | 90% | 99% | 9% | +8.6 |
| Canada | 71,376 | 69,323 | -3% | -2,053 | 95% | 107% | 13% | +12.6 |
| Australia | 105,800 | 102,558 | -3% | -3,241 | 111% | 119% | 7% | +8.3 |
| United States | 74,654 | 69,533 | -7% | -5,120 | 92% | 78% | -15% | -14.1 |
| Netherlands | 94,030 | 76,551 | -19% | -17,478 | 120% | 106% | -12% | -14.0 |
| Japan | 45,490 | 29,233 | -36% | -16,257 | 61% | 69% | 12% | +7.6 |
| Denmark | 142,283 | 89,476 | -37% | -52,807 | 134% | 104% | -22% | -29.5 |

Sources: Credit Suisse (2022) , IMF (2023), Bank of International Settlements (2023).

that in absolute terms, China's increase of over $8,000 is larger than that of almost any other country, including high-income ones (except for Switzerland and Korea).

To summarize the discussion in this subsection two characteristics stand out when looking at household debt in Asian countries (especially Korea, China, Thailand, and Vietnam). First, the income-adjusted level of household debt in Asia is the highest in the world. Second, household debt in Asia has consistently and significantly increased during the decade leading to the COVID-19 pandemic. These two characteristics represent a major difference from debt-ridden Western countries, and point to the existence of major risks to future economic growth in East Asia.

## 3. The determinants of household debt

In analyzing the rapid increase in household debt, it is important to determine why debt increases in the first place, i.e. whether it is due to the demand for loans or the supply of loans. If the main determinant of household debt is the demand for loans, that would indicate an increase in aggregate demand due to an increase in household consumption, which would boost economic growth. However, if the main determinant is an increase in the supply of loans, and that increase is not matched by a similar increase in demand, that can eventually cause deflationary pressures and slow economic growth.

### (1) Demand-side factors

The rapid increase in the ratio of household debt to GDP seen in many Asian countries is frequently attributed to an increasing demand for loans, which is traditionally driven by mortgages. While home ownership is essential in most societies, this is especially true in Asian countries. Although data is not available for all countries, a recent survey of home-ownership preferences shows that a much larger percentage of the population in Asian countries would like to own their own homes than in other regions. For example, 95% of respondents in Indonesia, 89% in Korea, 84% in Singapore, and 82% in China indicated that they would like to own their own homes. In contrast, only 68% of respondents in the U.S, 66% in Denmark, 62% in France, and 48% in Germany did so.

In Korea and China, as well as in other aging societies, the percentage of respondents who would like to own their own homes is even more pronounced among younger generations, due in part to concerns about old-age financial security. For example, according to a joint survey by JobKorea and Albamon (Korean employment websites), 95% of Koreans in their 20s want to own their own home, which is a higher percentage than the 89% figure for Koreans of all ages. Additionally, 78% of Koreans in their 20s answered that they plan to buy a home even if that requires a loan (Korea JoongAng Daily, 2020).

Despite the high demand for mortgages in Asian countries, household debt would not have increased without a sufficient supply of loans to meet this demand in the first place. In fact, some researchers argue that what drove the rapid increase in household debt is precisely the supply of loans and the abundance of bank assets, as discussed next.

## (2) Supply-side factors

In a recent study, Punzi (2022) has challenged the widespread assumption that household debt in Asia is driven by demand-side factors. Using data on nine Asian countries (Hong Kong, China, India, Indonesia, Japan, Korea, Malaysia, Singapore, and Thailand), the study argues that the large increase in household debt in recent years is mainly due to the increasing supply of loans.

The easing of lending constraints and deregulation of the banking sector in Asia in recent years has made it easier to obtain loans at low interest rates. This

**Table 1-5-3** Average annual growth rates of real GDP and household debt per person between 2010 and 2021

| Country | Average annual growth, 2010-2021 | | Difference |
|---|---|---|---|
| | Real GDP (A) | Household debt (B) | (A-B) |
| Vietnam | 6.6% | 15.7% | -9.0% |
| China | 6.5% | 13.9% | -7.5% |
| Philippines | 4.1% | 10.6% | -6.5% |
| Thailand | 3.2% | 6.9% | -3.7% |
| Korea | 3.9% | 7.1% | -3.2% |
| Hong Kong | 3.8% | 6.5% | -2.7% |
| Indonesia | 3.5% | 5.6% | -2.1% |
| Malaysia | 3.2% | 5.1% | -1.9% |
| Switzerland | 2.8% | 4.5% | -1.8% |
| Canada | 2.5% | 3.5% | -1.1% |
| Japan | 2.0% | 3.0% | -1.0% |
| Australia | 2.6% | 3.2% | -0.6% |
| Singapore | 3.9% | 4.3% | -0.4% |
| Taiwan | 4.2% | 4.2% | 0.0% |
| India | 4.9% | 4.7% | 0.1% |
| Netherlands | 2.8% | 1.7% | 1.1% |
| United States | 3.1% | 1.7% | 1.4% |
| Denmark | 3.4% | 1.3% | 2.1% |

Source: IMF (2023).

poses two major economic risks, one of which is that loans issued at low interest rates flow to households that are less likely to repay their debts, creating a risk of default. The second is that if the determinant of household debt is supply rather than demand, the risk of default and economic recession increases if the growth rate of debt is greater than that of income.

Table 1-5-3 shows the average annual growth rates of real GDP and household debt per person between 2010 and 2021. The growth in household debt has been outpacing GDP growth in virtually all East Asian countries, with the difference being around or over three percentage points in Vietnam, China, the Philippines, Thailand and Korea. As seen above, except for the Philippines, these are the countries with both the highest levels of, and the steepest increases in, household debt.

The reason for the abundance of loan supply in Asian countries is that banks in these countries have large assets. According to data from the Bank for International Settlements (BIS), Asian banks' lending to the private sector (i.e. households plus firms) as a percentage of GDP is the highest in the world, with Hong Kong, China and Korea topping the global ranking. Table 1-5-4 shows that bank lending exceeds GDP in almost all countries. Additionally, the

**Table 1-5-4**  Bank assets and bank credit to the private non-financial sector

| Country | Bank credit to the private non-financial sector in Q3 2022 | | Bank assets to GDP in 2021 | |
|---|---|---|---|---|
| | % of GDP | Globanl rank | % of GDP | Globanl rank |
| Hong Kong | 275% | 1 | 269% | 1 |
| China | 185% | 2 | 214% | 3 |
| Korea | 163% | 3 | 182% | 5 |
| Switzerland | 155% | 4 | NA | NA |
| New Zealand | 142% | 5 | 154% | 9 |
| Sweden | 137% | 6 | 146% | 13 |
| Singapore | 135% | 7 | NA | NA |
| Denmark | 135% | 8 | 170% | 6 |
| Australia | 134% | 9 | 148% | 12 |
| Malaysia | 126% | 10 | 153% | 10 |
| Thailand | 125% | 11 | 152% | 11 |
| Japan | 122% | 12 | 170% | 7 |
| Indonesia | 33% | 40 | 43% | 95 |
| United States | 51% | 35 | NA | NA |
| Vietnam | NA | NA | 136% | 14 |
| Philippines | NA | NA | 71% | 59 |

Note: Latest available data. Values within the global top 15 are highlighted.
Source: Bank of International Settlements (2023).

steepest increases in this ratio during the Covid-19 pandemic can be observed in Korea, China, and Thailand (no data is available for Vietnam).

The reason for this is that, until the latter half of the 20th century, mortgage loans were not available in Asia, and thus a large amount of savings was required to purchase a home. However, as economies developed, savings increased and financial institutions accumulated assets. Accordingly, lending increased, as well.

## 4. The composition of household debt and collateral prices

Having established the importance of home ownership in Asia, it is essential to discuss the role that mortgages play in household debt. Detailed data on the composition of household debt is needed for this purpose, and unfortunately, little information on the composition of household debt is available for Asian countries. It is well known, however, that most of the world's household debt is in the form of mortgages. In general, the higher the per capita income of a country, the larger the share of mortgage loans in household income. In OECD countries, this share is between 60% and 90% of total household debt, and in emerging economies it is between 30% and 50%. In other words, mortgages are the largest component of household debt, even if they account for only half or less of the total. Therefore, when analyzing collateral prices, it is best to focus on trends in housing prices.

### (1) Trends in housing prices

In the case of the U.S. and Europe, housing prices seemed unstoppable during the long boom after the Great Recession. Sales rose sharply due to intensifying competition for properties caused by ultra-low interest rates and a shortage of housing supply. However, this changed dramatically after the Covid-19 pandemic. In high-income countries, central banks have embarked on the most intensive monetary tightening in 40 years, making mortgages less accessible. This resulted in a sharp decline in sales and a sharp drop in home prices. For example, according to the OECD, prices have fallen 14% from their peak in Sweden and New Zealand, and about 9% in Australia.

In contrast, trends in housing prices in Asian countries have been quite different. As Figure 1-5-2 shows, real housing prices in Asian countries have grown only slightly over the past decade, with the exception of Malaysia and the Philippines. The temporary increase seen during the Covid-19 pandemic is also considerably smaller in Asia than in Europe and the U.S.

This seemingly favorable trend, however, conceals a structural problem.

**Figure 1 - 5 - 2**    Monthly changes in real housing prices (March 2010 = 100)

Source: Bank of International Settlements (2023).

The reason why housing prices in Asian countries (especially China) have not risen as much as in other regions is that housing prices in Asia are extremely high to begin with, and accordingly, there is not much room for further appreciation. Rather, there is a strong possibility that there will be a downward correction in housing prices, as is the case in high-income countries. As of the end of 2023, such a downward correction is becoming increasingly visible in China and Korea.

## (2) The high level of housing prices in Asia

As mentioned above, demand for housing has traditionally been high in Asian countries. Housing supply has not been able to keep up with this demand, and banks have been providing an abundance of loans, which is why housing prices in Asian countries, especially in urban areas, are extremely high even by global standards.

The most common indicator used to measure housing affordability (e.g. by the World Bank and the United Nations) is the 'median multiple.' This multiple (or ratio) is calculated by dividing the median housing price by the median gross annual household income. A ratio of three and below signals that the housing market of an area is affordable. A ratio of four or more signals an "unaffordable" market.

If average rather than median values are used, and/or if disposable income is used instead of gross income, these benchmarks might be up to twice higher. If the ratio is above 10, however, the housing market can be considered extremely unaffordable in any case. Table 1-5-5, based on Numbeo data, shows how this multiple has changed in the past decade using average urban housing prices and average individual disposable incomes. For reference, the U.S. and Western countries whose household debt exceeds their GDP are also shown.

The data in Table 1-5-5 suggests that urban housing in Asian countries is extremely unaffordable. An average apartment of 90 m² would require about 45 years' worth of an average disposable income in Hong Kong, and 30 years in China and the Philippines, to be completely saved (i.e. none of it consumed). This is followed by Korea, with 26 years, the highest of all high-income countries (the average for high-income countries is about 5 to 10 years). Thailand, Taiwan, Vietnam, and Indonesia are in a similar situation to Korea, with ratios ranging from 21 to 23 years. Malaysia and Japan are the only Asian countries with relatively affordable housing prices, with ratios in the 7 to 11-year range.

Since it is not possible to save all of one's disposable income, a single person with an average income in Hong Kong, China, the Philippines, or Korea would be unable to purchase an average urban home during their lifetime. Assuming an average income and zero interest rate, the minimum condition for purchasing

**Table 1-5-5**    Ratios of average housing prices to average disposable incomes

| Country | Price-to-Income Ratio | | |
|---|---|---|---|
| | 2011-13 average | 2021-23 average | 10-year change |
| Hong Kong | 25.5 | 45.7 | +20.2 |
| China | 28.1 | 30.9 | +2.7 |
| Philippines | 16.4 | 29.9 | +13.5 |
| Korea | 14.6 | 26.3 | +11.7 |
| Thailand | 18.4 | 22.6 | +4.2 |
| Taiwan | 17.8 | 21.8 | +4.1 |
| Vietnam | 15.9 | 21.5 | +5.6 |
| Indonesia | 24.7 | 20.8 | -3.9 |
| Singapore | 19.7 | 17.5 | -2.2 |
| Japan | 12.1 | 11.4 | -0.7 |
| Malaysia | 5.7 | 9.3 | +3.6 |
| Switzerland | 6.3 | 8.8 | +2.5 |
| New Zealand | 6.7 | 8.4 | +1.7 |
| Canada | 5.3 | 8.1 | +2.9 |
| Australia | 7.3 | 7.4 | +0.1 |
| Netherlands | 6.0 | 7.3 | +1.2 |
| Denmark | 7.1 | 6.7 | -0.4 |
| United States | 2.6 | 4.2 | +1.5 |

Note: The average price of a 90 m² apartment divided by the average individual disposable income in urban areas. Source: Based on data by Numbeo (2023)

an average urban residence is a double-income household whose saving rate is 45% in China and 30% or more in Korea, Thailand, and Vietnam over a 40-year working life.

## (3) Mortgage interest rates

The above simulation assumes that interest rates are zero. However, mortgages do have interest rates, making it even more difficult to own real estate, and rising interest rates pose a significant risk to debt sustainability.

In the decade before the Covid-19 pandemic, interest rates in Asian countries were quite low, contributing to the increase in household debt. However, Asian governments, like their Western counterparts, have started raising interest rates to control inflation. At present, most Asian countries have not raised interest rates as much as Western countries, but there is concern that this might change in the future.

Figure 1-5-3 juxtaposes the increase in household debt during the Covid-19 pandemic (2019 = 100) with mortgage interest rates in early 2023. The U.S. and Western countries whose household debt exceeds their GDP are also shown for reference. A risky combination of a rapid increase in household debt and relatively high interest rates can be observed in China, Vietnam, Korea, and Thailand, the four countries with the highest levels of income-adjusted levels of, and steepest increases in, household debt, which keep recurring in every subsection of this analysis. Although the Philippines also appears to be in a similar situation, the ratio of household debt to GDP there is very low (10% in 2021), suggesting that the overall risk is considerably lower.

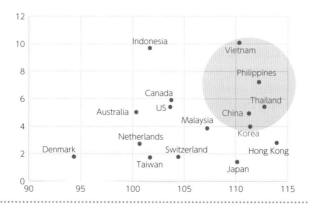

| Figure 1-5-3 | Increase in household debt during the Covid-19 pandemic (2019 = 100, horizontal axis) plotted against mortgage interest rates in early 2023 (vertical axis) |

Sources: Bank of International Settlements (2023), Numbeo(2023)

A related risk factor in Asian countries is the limited use of fixed interest rate loans. Whereas fixed interest rate loans are the norm in Europe and the U.S., the majority of housing loans in Asian countries (about 60% in the case of Korea) have variable interest rates, which means that rising policy interest rates pose serious risks to indebted households. As interest rates rise, household finances are squeezed, the worst-case scenario being that those who cannot service their mortgage debts might be forced to sell their mortgaged homes, causing a steep decline in housing prices to occur. A decline in housing prices would in turn increase the number of households whose household debt exceeds household assets, causing domestic consumption to decline and further increasing the risk of default. The possibility of such a negative scenario necessitates a deeper look into the composition and status of household assets.

## 5. The composition of household assets and disposable income

### (1) The composition of household assets

The inextricably linked phenomena of high housing prices and high household debt in Asia are reflected in the composition of household assets. Table 1-5-6 shows that household assets in Asian countries are mainly non-financial, i.e. real estate. For reference, the U.S. and Western countries whose household debt exceeds their GDP are also shown. It can be observed that in high-income Western countries, except Australia, non-financial assets account for 30-50% of total household assets, whereas in Asia, they account for an extremely high 60-80%.

Not only are households' assets in Asia highly illiquid, their financial assets (cash, savings, stocks, mutual funds, etc.) are also far below the average levels in high-income countries. Even in Korea, a high-income country, households' average net financial assets are only one-third to one-fourth of those in other high-income countries. This is problematic because the lack of net financial assets is linked to an increased economic vulnerability. As noted above, high household debt levels mean that much of the disposable income is directed toward debt repayment, so that many households might not have enough money to deal with an unexpected emergency, which can exacerbate an otherwise mild recession.

Asian countries have been the center of global economic growth in recent decades, and presumably their high economic growth and savings rates should have helped households accumulate financial assets. However, Asian

| Table 1-5-6 | | Financial vs non-financial household assets | | | | | | |
|---|---|---|---|---|---|---|---|---|

| Country | Share of non-financial wealth in total wealth | Financial wealth per adult | Change 2010-2021 | Non-finan-cial wealth per adult | Change 2010-2021 | Household debt per adult | Change 2010-2021 | Home ownership rate |
|---|---|---|---|---|---|---|---|---|
| Vietnam | 79% | 3,232 | 161% | 12,416 | 162% | 1,402 | 450% | 90% |
| Malaysia | 68% | 12,479 | -39% | 26,633 | 40% | 12,034 | 159% | 77% |
| Thailand | 67% | 10,027 | 89% | 20,205 | 334% | 5,593 | 311% | 80% |
| Korea | 66% | 97,177 | 49% | 184,775 | 234% | 44,309 | 49% | 56% |
| Indonesia | 65% | 6,883 | 175% | 12,770 | 11% | 1,120 | 241% | 84% |
| Philippines | 62% | 6,024 | 183% | 9,684 | 79% | 1,206 | 360% | 64% |
| Australia | 61% | 254,419 | 48% | 398,248 | 14% | 102,558 | -3% | 66% |
| China | 55% | 38,248 | 227% | 47,382 | 321% | 8,991 | 1225% | 90% |
| Canada | 49% | 241,785 | 19% | 236,835 | 47% | 69,323 | -3% | 69% |
| New Zealand | 48% | 272,410 | 345% | 252,700 | 47% | 52,957 | 0% | 65% |
| Netherlands | 46% | 257,224 | 22% | 220,155 | 117% | 76,551 | -19% | 71% |
| Switzerland | 44% | 475,140 | 27% | 372,694 | 39% | 151,230 | 24% | 36% |
| Singapore | 42% | 238,070 | 29% | 174,666 | 5% | 54,532 | 14% | 88% |
| Japan | 38% | 169,080 | -10% | 105,391 | -15% | 29,233 | -36% | 61% |
| Sweden | 36% | 292,931 | 83% | 162,796 | -23% | 73,759 | 7% | 65% |
| Hong Kong | 35% | 393,130 | 251% | 213,729 | 125% | 53,928 | 16% | 51% |
| Denmark | 32% | 350,452 | 51% | 165,517 | -8% | 89,476 | -37% | 59% |
| Taiwan | 31% | 232,920 | 63% | 102,249 | 26% | 37,304 | 21% | 84% |
| United States | 28% | 468,295 | 83% | 180,290 | 44% | 69,533 | -7% | 66% |

Source: Based on data by Credit Suisse (2022).

households' net financial assets remain low. Apart from the high homeowner-ship rates and the related elevated levels of household debt, the low level of net financial wealth can be attributed to three other factors. First, as discussed throughout this article, income-adjusted household debt levels in Asian coun-tries are unusually high, which automatically affects net assets. Second, with the exception of Japan, the high economic growth rates of Asian countries are a recent phenomenon. As a result, although GDP per person has registered impressive growth in places like China, Korea and Vietnam in the past two to three decades, financial assets will inevitably take much longer to accumulate. Third, GDP per person and disposable income per person in Asian countries tend to diverge more than in Western countries, and usually in the opposite direction. This point is examined in more detail below.

## (2) The discrepancy between GDP and disposable income

While most analyses of household debt tend to focus on household debt as a percentage of a country's GDP, others (especially analyses by the OECD) look at household debt as a percentage of household disposable income (i.e. the after-tax income per person, which is invariably lower than GDP per person).

Some researchers argue that using disposable income is more appropriate than GDP because income tax rates vary widely across countries. Additionally, the share of wages (labor income) in national income differs substantially from country to country. In countries where the share of labor income in the Gross Domestic Income (GDE, i.e. GDP as seen from the income distribution perspective) is relatively low, disposable income per person tends to be significantly lower than GDP per person. This is the case in many Asian countries.

Unfortunately, data on the ratio of household debt to disposable income is only available for high-income economies (in the case of Asia, only Korea and Japan). Since most countries in East Asia are not high-income, the current analysis measures household debt as a percentage of GDP. The implication is that the results presented here may be only a lower-bound estimate. In other words, the household debt problem in Asian countries might in reality be up to twice as severe. To illustrate, according to the OECD, Korea's household debt in 2021 was more than 206% of disposable income, while the ratio of household debt to GDP was only one-half of that (105%).

It is worth noting that neither the share of wages in national income nor the tax rate in a country are stationary variables. As they change over time, so does the ratio of disposable income to GDP. As a result, disposable income may increase or remain unchanged even when GDP decreases. Conversely, disposable income may not change much even if GDP increases. Consequently, GDP growth and growth in disposable income are not necessarily correlated.

Among OECD members, the largest discrepancy between per capita GDP growth and disposable income growth is observed in Korea: between 1995 and 2013, Korea's average per capita GDP growth rate was 3.8%, while its per capita disposable income growth rate was only about 2.0%. Under these conditions, debt growth in Korea is likely to have exceeded income growth at a much higher pace (over 5 percentage points) than the one seen in Table 1-5-3 (3.2 percentage points).

Considering the structural characteristics of other countries in East Asia (high share of invested earnings, lower share of labor income, etc.), the growth rate of household disposable income is likely to be significantly lower than the growth rate of the GDP in the other high-risk countries identified in this analysis (China, Thailand and Vietnam).

As a reference, in the U.S. and Western countries whose household debt exceeds their GDP, the growth rate of per capita disposable income was higher than the growth rate of per capita GDP over the same period. Thus, the significant discrepancy between per capita GDP and household disposable income in East Asia is a major difference from the West, and it suggests that East Asian economies might be more vulnerable to economic shock than previously thought.

## 6. Outlook and policies

### (1) The looming Japanification of East Asian economies?

This analysis has shown that the characteristics of household debt in Asian countries (e.g. its determinants, trends, and composition) are quite different from the characteristics of household debt in high-income Western countries, which raises serious concerns about debt sustainability and economic growth. As seen throughout this analysis, the countries facing the highest risks related to household debt seem to be Korea, China, Thailand and Vietnam. In these four countries, the risks posed by household debt could be significantly exacerbated by changes in interest rates and housing prices.

In the case of Korea, housing prices have been declining for seven consecutive quarters (likely eight, at the time of writing), registering a decline of over 11% between 2021 Q4 and 2023 Q2, the worst since the data has been available, and in the same period, the policy interest rate has spiked by 3 percentage points (from 0.5% to 3.5%), with the actual lending rate being at least one percentage point higher. In particular, condominium prices in Seoul have fallen by an impressive one-fourth from their peak in October 2009. A similar trend can be seen in urban China since 2020, triggered by the default of Evergrande, China's largest real estate developer, which resorted to temporarily selling all properties at a 30% discount as a result. As for Thailand and Vietnam, since these countries are at an earlier stage of urbanization and economic development, the decline in urban housing prices there is not as noticeable.

Given region-wide demographic factors, such as declining populations and low levels of immigration, the decline of housing prices in Asian countries is likely to continue. According to United Nations data, the populations of Korea and China are already declining, while Thailand's population is expected to begin declining by 2029 and Vietnam's by 2050. Unlike Western countries, immigration will not compensate for that decline, as most Asian countries receive little or no immigration, with most countries sending out more migrants than they receive. For instance, China and Vietnam have the lowest percentage of foreign-born people in the world (0.07%), which is a major difference from debt-ridden Western countries, where immigration is abundant: in Australia, Switzerland, and New Zealand, the foreign-born account for about 30% of the total population. The percentage in Canada is 25%, and in Denmark and the

Netherlands about 15%. These figures are much higher than the world average of 3.5%, indicating that immigrants are a major factor behind rising (urban) housing prices in Western countries.

Additionally, given the abnormally high housing prices in urban areas of Asian countries, and the fact that some countries (China and Korea) have approached the limit of urbanization, pressures for downward correction are likely to remain strong. The decline in housing prices will increase the number of households whose debts exceed their assets, and as household assets in Asia are highly illiquid, many households might become highly vulnerable to economic shocks such as unemployment and declining disposable income. As a result, social inequalities might worsen and economic growth might decelerate. Eventually, China, Korea, Thailand and Vietnam could end up in a situation similar to Japan's "lost decades." In 1989-90, stock and real estate (housing) prices in Japan began to slump, ending a decades-long economic boom. Uncertainty about the future permeated the economy, and economic growth stalled as consumers and businesses became increasingly thrifty.

Apart from the property market, another similarity between the experiences of Asian countries (especially China, Korea, Taiwan, Thailand, and Vietnam) and Japan's experience over the past three decades is the rapid aging of the population. Korea, a high-income country, is expected to be the most aged society in the world in 2044, with the share of the population over 65 years old reaching 45% around 2060. Similarly, China, Thailand, and Vietnam, middle-income countries, are aging more rapidly than other countries at similar stages of economic development. The percentage of Chinese above retirement age is projected to reach 40% of the total population in less than 50 years, and some Chinese banks have already extended the upper age limit for mortgage loans to 80-95 years. The extension of the upper age limit will make it possible to take out a mortgage loan for 30 to 40 years even past the age of 50, which may lead to higher debt burdens in the post-retirement age group, increasing the risk of default and undermining the sustainability of household debt in the future.

## (2) Demand- vs. Supply-side Policies

Considering the possibility of such a grim outlook, measures need to be taken in order to bring the increase in household debt as well as the exorbitant prices of urban housing under control. Similar to the determinants of household debt, which can be either demand-driven or supply-driven, measures required to address this issue can be divided into demand-side policies and supply-side policies.

Naturally, what kind of measures can best solve the issue of household debt and unaffordable housing is of great concern to governments in Asia. In recent years, a number of demand-side-oriented policies have been implemented in Asian countries, including a reduction of the loan-to-value (LTV) ratio of mortgages, and extending mortgage repayment terms. Policies implemented by the Moon administration in Korea have been particularly prominent. However, these have largely been regarded as a policy failure. In consideration of that, this section argues in favor of supply-side policies, such as the ones in those Western countries where household debt has been declining.

As mentioned above, home-ownership is relatively low in many Western countries, and renting is increasingly seen as the norm, especially in urban areas. Some of the reasons behind the low propensity for home-ownership in places like Germany, Switzerland, and the Scandinavian countries are high real estate taxes, the absence of mortgage interest deductions for owner-occupied homes, and most importantly, the abundant availability and use of public housing and public rental housing (a supply-side policy).

As shown in Table 1-5-7, in Asian countries, notably Korea, China, the

**Table 1-5-7**    Trends in housing price-to-rent ratios in urban areas

| Country | Price-to-Rent Ratio in Urban Areas | | |
|---|---|---|---|
| | 2011-13 average | 2021-23 average | 10-year change |
| Korea | 52.4 | 102.3 | +49.8 |
| China | 28.0 | 62.5 | +34.5 |
| Hong Kong | 31.8 | 61.3 | +29.5 |
| Philippines | 15.4 | 30.4 | +15.0 |
| Thailand | 17.8 | 30.4 | +12.6 |
| Taiwan | 50.6 | 63.1 | +12.6 |
| Vietnam | 12.3 | 24.4 | +12.2 |
| Japan | 31.9 | 40.4 | +8.5 |
| Switzerland | 24.7 | 32.9 | +8.2 |
| Singapore | 25.6 | 32.7 | +7.1 |
| Canada | 17.4 | 21.4 | +4.1 |
| Malaysia | 21.1 | 24.6 | +3.6 |
| Indonesia | 19.3 | 22.7 | +3.4 |
| United States | 8.8 | 11.1 | +2.3 |
| New Zealand | 20.2 | 22.2 | +2.0 |
| Netherlands | 17.7 | 19.2 | +1.6 |
| Australia | 21.0 | 22.5 | +1.5 |
| Denmark | 23.1 | 23.1 | -0.0 |

Note: The price-to-rent ratio is the average housing price divided by the average annual housing rent for a 90 m² apartment in urban areas. Countries with significant increases are highlighted.
Source: Numbeo (2023).

Part I

Part II

Part III

Part IV

Philippines, Thailand, and Vietnam, the average growth in rents over the past decade has been considerably lower than the average growth in housing prices. This trend indicates that affordability of home-ownership and renting have diverged, with rents having become relatively more affordable. On the other hand, in the high-income Western countries, where housing prices and rents have been increasing at about the same pace, a similar trend is not observed.

This suggests that Asian countries could benefit from promoting affordable renting as an alternative to home-ownership. Since renting in Asian countries is relatively affordable, an expansion in renting could reduce household debt and improve prospects for economic growth in the long run. Renting could also generate positive externalities in the rest of the economy. For example, it could increase labor market flexibility by making it easier for people to relocate.

A reference to countries in northern Europe suggests that the key to promoting renting as an alternative to home-ownership in Asia might be to increase the supply of affordable public housing. In fact, public housing projects in some Asian countries (notably Singapore and Japan) have a long history of public housing provision dating back to the postwar period. However, such projects remain extremely limited in scope in the high-risk countries identified in this analysis (Korea, China, Thailand and Vietnam).

Fortunately, this is gradually changing. In the case of China, in May 2021 the Ministry of Housing and Urban-Rural Construction called for an accelerated development of public rental housing, and less than two months later, the State Council declared a policy aimed at "accelerating the development of public rental housing." As a result, the development of public rental housing has become a priority during China's 14th Five-Year Plan. Similar trends can be seen in Korea, Thailand, Vietnam, and the Philippines, indicating that policies in Asian countries are moving in the right direction.

Nevertheless, according to the IMF, supply-side policies, such as public housing construction, take much longer to take effect than demand-side policies (Deb et al., 2022). In addition, the question of how to finance the construction of public housing without running fiscal deficits remains a major challenge. Since the construction of public housing is often insufficiently profitable from the perspective of private construction companies, governments are expected to play an important role in the provision of such housing. Bert Hofman (2022), a professor at the National University of Singapore, has suggested that utilizing state-run pension funds to accelerate the development of public housing might provide a sustainable solution. Whereas this may be feasible in China, many middle-income Asian countries, including Vietnam and Thailand, have few pension funds, making it difficult to raise funds for public housing projects. Therefore, a solution to this problem will necessitate an open discussion involving all relevant stakeholders.

Finally, the fact that many people in countries with aging populations purchase homes in order to secure rent-free housing for their retirement suggests that encouraging investment in housing for the elderly, such as nursing homes and assisted living facilities, could reduce demand for housing in general. To this end, however, the stigma related to the use of old-age homes that permeates many societies in Asia, needs to be eliminated.

On the positive side, there are signs that such social changes are already underway. According to Reuters, China's senior housing market is expected to boom around 2025-2028, and investment is accelerating to the extent that the sector is attracting foreign companies. For example, the Japanese Panasonic Corporation recently opened a 1,170-unit complex for the elderly in Jiangsu Province, China. Investment in affordable rental housing both for senior citizens and for the younger segments of the population is a win-win situation for both tenants and investors, which can create a virtuous cycle of lower household debt and higher economic growth.

## References

Allianz A.G. (2022) Allianz Global Wealth Report 2022. Allianz Research, 12 October 2022.

Bank of International Settlements (2023) Bank of International Settlement Statistics <https://www.bis.org/statistics/index.htm>

Cecchetti, S.G., M.S. Mohanty and F. Zampolli (2011) "The Real Effects of Debt," BIS Working Paper No. 352. Basel: Bank for International Settlements.

Credit Suisse (2022) Global Wealth Databook 2022. Credit Suisse Research Institute.

Deb, P., Finger, H., Kashiwase, K., Kido, Y., Kothari, S., Papageorgiou, E. (2022) "Housing Market Stability and Affordability in Asia-Pacific," IMF DP/2022/020. International Monetary Fund, Washington, DC.

Hofman, B. (2022) "How China can overcome its property crisis," Official Monetary and Financial Institutions Forum, 1 August 2022: <https://www.omfif.org/2022/08/how-china-can-overcome-its-property-crisis/>

International Institute of Finance (2023) "Global Debt Monitor: Cracks in the Foundation," 17 May 2023.

International Monetary Fund (2023) World Economic Outlook October 2023.

International Monetary Fund (2023) Global Debt Database.

Korean Herald (2022) "14 years a miser...to be a homeowner in Seoul," 21 December 2022: <https://www.koreaherald.com/view.php?ud=20221221000504>

Korea JoongAng Daily (2020) "95 percent of young Koreans think owning a home is essential," 6 October 2020: <https://koreajoongangdaily.joins.com/2020/10/06/business/economy/Realestate-house-apartment/20201006184600378.html>

Leigh, D., D. Igan, J. Simon and P. Topalova (2012) "Dealing with Household Debt," in IMF World Economic Outlook: Growth Resuming, Dangers Remain. Washington, DC.

Numbeo (2023) Property Prices Index by Country; Mortgage Interest Rate in Percentages: <https://www.numbeo.com/cost-of-living/>

OECD (2016) "Chapter 3. From GDP to average household income," in Economic Policy Reforms 2016.

Punzi, M.T. (2022) "Chapter 8: Household debt: supply-driven sugar rushes," in The Sustainability of Asia's Debt, edited by B. Ferrarini, M. M. Giugale, and J. J. Pradelli, Edward Elgar Publishing.

Reuters (2023) "Analysis: As China ages, investors bet they can beat retirement home stigma," 4 March 2023: <https://www.reuters.com/world/china/china-ages-investors-bet-they-can-beatretirement-home-stigma-2023-03-03/>

Thuong D.T.H. and Minh P.T.T. (2022) "The Effect of Household Debt on the Stability of the Banking System in Vietnam," South Asian Journal of Finance, 2(2), 86–97.

United Nations (2022) World Population Prospects 2022: <https://population.un.org/wpp/>

Zabai, A. (2017) "Household debt recent developments," Bank of International Settlement Quarterly Review, December 2017.

## Column B ( New Population Dynamics: From WPP2022

*YOSHIDA, Shigekazu; NOMURA, Ryosuke*

In July 2022, the United Nations released the World Population Prospects 2022 ("WPP2022")[1]. Comparing WPP2022 with the previous estimates ("WPP2019"), the world population will reach 8 billion earlier in the former than in the latter. The next milestone of 9 billion people is expected to be reached in 2037, 15 years to increase from 8 to 9 billion in WPP 2022 (medium estimate). Taking into consideration that it took 12 years for the world population to increase from 7 to 8 billion, this is due to a decline in the world's fertility rate. By region, there are signs of change in Asia, where previously the population increased significantly, the population of China has entered a phase of decline, while India's population is steadily increasing.

Column B presents the world demographic characteristics based on WPP 2022. Column B.1 identifies the demographic characteristics of the world's major regions, and Column B.2 identifies the demographic characteristics of the major countries. Column B.1 identifies demographic trends by major world region. Column B.2 identifies the demographic characteristics of major countries, and Column B.3 presents the implications of the analysis.

## 1. Demographics by Major Region

### (1) World Population

According to WPP2022, the world population will reach 8 billion in November 2022, and India is projected to overtake China as the most populous country in the world in 2023[2]. It is of great interest to see in which areas population growth has occurred so far and in which areas population decline will happen in the future. Before we conduct analysis by region, let us review the extent to which the world population projection

---

1) WPP2022 is a global population estimate based on 1,758 censuses and dynamics registration systems and 2,890 global sample surveys conducted between 1950 and 2022.
2) India conducts a national census every 10 years, but the survey scheduled for 2021 was postponed due to the COVID-19 pandemic, and the next census is scheduled for 2023. Therefore, it is still estimated that India's population will exceed that of China.

has changed from the previous report (Figure 1-CB-1). WPP 2019 projects a slight increase of the world population until 2100. However, this report estimates that the world population would peak at 10.43 billion in 2086 and begin declining subsequently. Population estimates for 2100 are 10.88 billion in WPP2019 and 10.35 billion in WPP2022, making a difference of 530 million people. This is due to the change in the estimated outlook for the world's fertility and mortality rates.

Figure 1-CB-2 shows the transition of crude birth rate and death

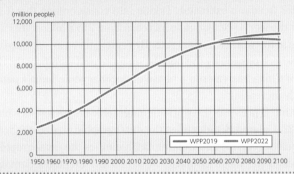

**Figure 1-CB-1**    Comparison of World Population Projections

Note: WPP2019 is actual data until 2020 and medium estimate afterwards
     WPP2022 is actual data until 2021 and medium estimate afterwards
Source: WPP2019 and WPP2022

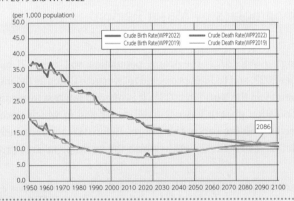

**Figure 1-CB-2**    World Crude Birth and Death Rates (estimated)

Note: Actual data until 2020, medium estimates after 2025
Source: WPP2019 and WPP2022

rate per thousand world population[3]. In the WPP2019 projection, the crude birth rate did not fall below the crude death rate until 2100. However, in the WPP2022 projection, the crude death rate was modified and projected to exceed the crude birth rate in 2086. The downward modification of the crude birth rate and upward modification of the crude death rate are probably due to the global expansion of COVID-19 in 2020.

## (2) Comparison of Population by Major Region

Next, let us look at the world population by region (Figure 1-CB-3). In 1950, 55.2% of the world population was from Asia, 22.0% from Europe, 9.1% from Africa, 6.7% from Latin America, 6.5% from North America, and 0.5% from Oceania, in descending order. In particular, Asia has consistently accounted for a large share, reaching a peak of 60.8% in 2003. Since then, however, its share has shown a declining trend, falling to 59.4% in 2021, and is projected to decrease to 54.5% in 2050, and 45.2% in 2100.

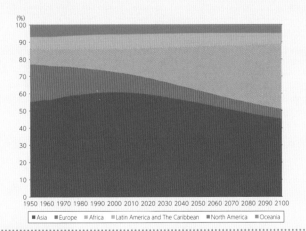

| Figure 1-CB-3 | Population Estimates by Region (Share) |

Note: Actual data until 2021, medium estimates after 2022
Source: Prepared by the author using WPP2022

---

3) Crude birth rate and crude death rate are calculated by dividing the number of births and deaths in a given year by the population in that year. In WPP, they are calculated as the number of births and deaths per 1,000 population in that year. For WPP2019, values are given every five years, and for WPP2022, values are given for each year.

The share of the Asian region will decline while that of the African region will increase. The share of the African region in 2021 was 17.6%, but it is expected to increase significantly to 25.6% by 2050 and to 37.9% by 2100.

Thus, the center of population growth is shifting from Asia to Africa. In the following subsections, we will review population dynamics in major regions (Asia, Europe, North America, and Africa).

[Asia]
Figure 1-CB-4 shows the population by age group and crude birth and death rates in the Asian region. The total population is 4,694.58 million in 2021, and will reach a peak of 5,305.28 million in 2055. However, the

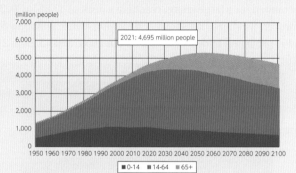

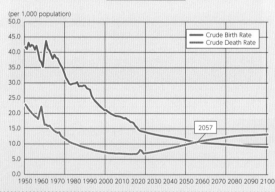

| Figure 1-CB-4 | Population in Asia (upper graph) and crude birth and death rates (lower graph) |

Note: Actual data until 2021, medium estimates after 2022
Source: Prepared by the author using WPP2022

population is expected to show a downward trend thereafter, reaching 4,674.25 million by 2100.

The working-age population (15-64 years old) is expected to increase steadily from the 1980s to the 2030s, but is projected to decline gradually after the 2040s. The population aged 0-14 (hereinafter referred to as the "juvenile population") has been gradually increasing since 1950, but after a slight increase in the 1990s, it began to decline in the 2000s, and is expected to increase slightly or remain almost flat in the 2010s before declining again after 2020. On the other hand, the population aged 65 and over (hereinafter referred to as "the elderly population") has been gradually increasing since the 2010s, and is expected to increase significantly from the 2030s onward. This is due to the declining birthrate and aging population in China, which will be discussed later.

The crude birth rate was 40 per 1,000 population between the 1950s and 1960s, but has shown a gradual downward trend since 1970. The crude death rate, excluding the effects of the Chinese famine and the spread of COVID-19 infection, has been declining from 1950 to 2020, but is expected to increase gradually after 2030, exceeding the crude birth rate by 2057.

[Europe]

Figure 1-CB-5 shows the population by age group and crude birth and death rates in the European region. The total population is expected to peak at 746.23 million in 2020, followed by a gradual decline. The total population in 2021 was 745.17 million, and it is expected to decrease to 586.52 million by 2100.

The working-age population has been steadily increasing since 1950, but is expected to decline after peaking at 501.96 million in 2010. The juvenile population peaked at 167.76 million in 1965 and has been declining since then. On the other hand, the elderly population has been increasing since 1950, and is expected to start declining after 2057.

The crude birth rate, which had been at about 20 per 1,000 population in the 1950s, showed a gradual downward trend after 1960, falling below the crude death rate in 1993 and temporarily exceeding the crude death rate in the early 2010s before declining again thereafter. The crude death rate, on the other hand, has shown an upward trend since

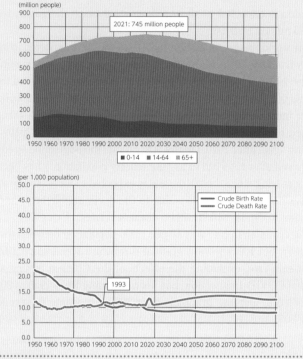

(million people)

2021: 745 million people

■ 0-14　■ 14-64　▩ 65+

(per 1,000 population)

Crude Birth Rate
Crude Death Rate

1993

**Figure 1 –CB- 5**　Population in Europe (upper graph) and crude birth and death rates (lower graph)

Note: Actual data until 2021, medium estimates after 2022
Source: Prepared by the author using WPP2022

the 1970s and has increased significantly from 2020 to 2022 due to the COVID-19 pandemic, and is expected to remain above the crude birth rate from 2023 onward.

[North America]
Figure 1-CB-6 shows trends in population by age group and crude birth and death rates in the North American region.

The total population has been on an upward trend since 1950, reaching 375.28 million in 2021, and is expected to increase gradually after 2022, reaching 448.03 million by 2100.

The working-age population has been increasing since 1950, as has

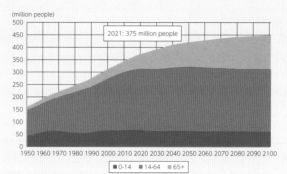

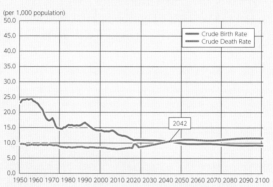

Figure 1 -CB-6    Population in North America (upper graph) and crude birth and death rates (lower graph)

Note: Actual data until 2021, medium estimates after 2022
Source: Prepared by the author using WPP2022

the total population, and is expected to peak at 256.07 million in 2053 before declining at a slower pace than in other regions. The juvenile population is expected to peak at 68.79 million in 2018 and then decline at a slower pace. On the other hand, the elderly population has been increasing since 1950 and is expected to exceed the juvenile population by 2023. The elderly population is expected to exceed 100 million by 2050, and the aging of the population is expected to continue.

The crude birth rate remained at around 20-24 per 1,000 population from the 1950s to the early 1960s, and showed a downward trend from the late 1960s to the 1970s, followed by a slight upward trend in the 1980s and 1990s. Since 1991, however, it has been on a gradual downward trend, and is expected to remain at an average of about 9 per 1,000 population after 2048. On the other hand, the crude death rate declined somewhat from 1950 to the 2000s, but has been gradually increasing since 2010. Although the crude death rate is expected to exceed the crude birth rate in 2042, the degree of increase will be lower than in other regions.

[Africa]
Figure 1-CB-7 shows population trends and crude birth and death rates in the African region. As shown in the figure, the total population of the African region has been rising steadily since 1950, reaching 1,393.68 million in 2021, and will be 3,924.42 million in 2100, which is characterized by the fact that the population is not expected to decline as in the North

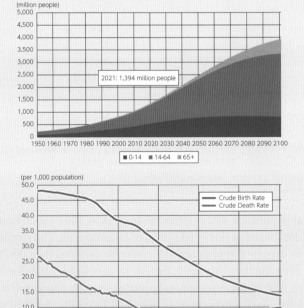

| Figure 1-CB-7 | Population in Africa (upper graph) and crude birth and death rates (lower graph) |
|---|---|

Note: Actual data until 2021, medium estimates after 2022
Source: Prepared by the author using WPP2022

America region.

By age group, the working-age population is steadily increasing and is expected to account for a large portion of the total population until the year 2100. The elderly population is expected to increase at a slower pace than the working-age population after 2040. On the other hand, the juvenile population is expected to gradually decline after 2080, although it has been on an increasing trend.

The crude birth rate remained at a high level of approximately 40 per 1,000 population from 1950 to the 1990s, and is expected to decline gradually after 2000. On the other hand, the crude death rate remained at about 20 per 1,000 population from the 1950s to the 1970s, but has shown a downward trend since 1980, and is expected to remain flat or increase slightly after the 2020s. Thus, the African region is characterized by the fact that the crude birth rate has consistently been higher than the crude death rate.

## 2. Population Trends in Major Countries

### (1) Population Trends in Major Asian Countries

As described in Column B.1, the world's population is expected to decline in the future, especially in the Asian region. In this subsection, we will focus on major countries in the Asian region and review the demographic trends of each country. We will also examine the demographics of Russia, which has close ties to the Asian region, including China and India, as well as to Europe.

[Japan]

Figure 1-CB-8 shows trends in population by age group, crude birth rate, and crude death rate in Japan.

The total population peaked at 128.12 million in 2009 and has been declining, reaching 124.61 million in 2021.

The working-age population peaked at 87.12 million in 1994 (69.6% of the total population) and has continued to decline, reaching 72.82 million (58.4%) in 2021. The working-age population is expected to halve from 2021 to 53.31 million (51.4%) in 2050 and 36.87 million (50.1%) in 2100. On the other hand, the ratio of the elderly population to the total population

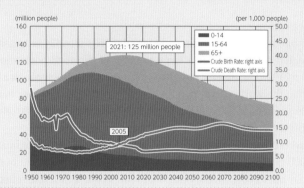

| Figure 1-CB-8 | Population in Japan (by age group) and crude birth and death rates |

Note: Actual data until 2021, medium estimates after 2022
Source: Prepared by the author using WPP2022

was 4.9% in 1950, but has increased significantly to 29.8% in 2021. The aging rate is projected to be 37.5% in 1950 and 38.7% in 2100, indicating that the aging of the population is expected to further progress.

The crude birth rate averaged 24 per 1,000 population in the first half of the 1950s after the so-called "First Baby Boom[4]" and showed a downward trend until 1961. It again showed an upward trend from 1962 to 1974, which included the period of the "second baby boom[5]," but turned to a downward trend after 1975. On the other hand, the crude death rate has been on an upward trend since 1980 and exceeded the crude birth rate in 2005.

[China]
Figure 1-CB-9 shows the trends of population by age group, crude birth rate, and crude death rate in China.

Although the total population has been on an increasing trend, it is

---

4) The term "first baby boom" refers to the phenomenon in which more than 2.6 million babies were born each year between 1947 and 1949.
5) The "second baby boom" is the term used to refer to the phenomenon in which the generation of children born during the "first baby boom," were born by more than 2 million each year from 1971 to 1974. The birth rate temporarily declined in 1966, which is believed to be due to the superstition that women born in the year of Hinoe-uma have a violent temperament, and many couples avoided having children in that year.

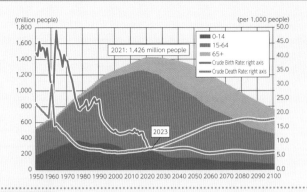

(million people)    (per 1,000 people)

**Figure 1 -CB- 9**  Population in China (by age group) and crude birth and death rates

Note: Actual data until 2021, medium estimates after 2022
Source: Prepared by the author using WPP2022

expected to peak at 1,425.89 million in 2021, and is expected to decline thereafter.

The working-age population peaked at 998.23 million (71.6%) in 2015 and began to decline, reaching 986.46 million (69.2%) in 2021. The population is expected to continue to decline thereafter, reaching 767.37 million (58.5%) in 2050 and 378.06 million (49.3%) in 2100. On the other hand, the aging rate is projected to be 5.0% in 1950, 13.1% in 2021, 30.1% in 2050, and 40.9% in 2100. The aging population is expected to be higher than that of Japan in 2100, and it will need to urgently cope with an aging society in the future.

The crude birth rate averaged about 40 per 1,000 population in the 1950s and 1960s, excluding the effects of the great famine in China[6]. After 1970, the crude birth rate showed a gradual downward trend, but increased somewhat in the 1980s. Since 1990, however, it has again been on a downward trend, and is expected to fall below the crude death rate by 2023.

[Korea]
Figure 1-CB-10 shows trends in population by age group, crude birth rate, and crude death rate in Korea.

---

6) In addition to the occurrence of natural disasters, China experienced a large-scale famine in 1959-1961 due to the "Great Leap Forward" policy of that time.

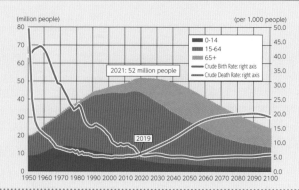

**Figure 1-CB-10** Population in Korea (by age group) and crude birth and death rates

Note: Actual data until 2021, medium estimates after 2022
Source: Prepared by the author using WPP2022

As the figure shows, the total population is projected to peak at 51.85 million in 2020 and decline to 24.1 million by 2100.

The working-age population peaked at 37.64 million (73.1%) in 2017 and has been on a downward trend since, reaching 37.04 million (71.5%) in 2021. The working-age population is expected to further decrease to 23.98 million (52.4%) in 2050 and 11.16 million (46.3%) in 2100. On the other hand, the aging rate, which was 2.7% in 1950, is expected to increase significantly to 16.7% in 2021. The aging rate will further increase to 39.4% in 2050, peaking at 47.5% in 2081, and continuing at a high level thereafter. As approximately half of the population of Korea will be elderly within the next 60 years, it will be necessary to take more urgent measures to cope with an aging society than in Japan and China.

The crude birth rate, which had remained at about 40 per 1,000 population in the 1950s, declined rapidly from 1960 onward. The crude death rate, on the other hand, was very high during the Korean War (1950-1953), but declined rapidly thereafter, and began to rise again in the 2000s, exceeding the crude birth rate in 2019.

[India]
Figure 1-CB-11 shows trends in population by age group, crude birth rate, and crude death rate in India.

The total population has been steadily increasing since 1950, and

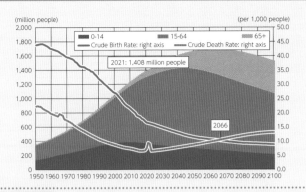

**Figure 1 -CB-11**    Population in India (by age group) and crude birth and death rates

Note: Actual data until 2021, medium estimates after 2022
Source: Prepared by the author using WPP2022

is expected to reach 1,407.56 million in 2021, surpassing China as the world's most populous country by 2023.

The working-age population is expected to peak at 1,119.4 million (67.4%) in 2048, followed by a downward trend. The aging rate in 1950 was 3.1%, and it will be 6.8% in 2021, still in the single-digit range. This rate would increase by 29.8% in 2100, which is still lower than in Japan, China, and Korea.

The crude birth rate remained at about 40 per 1,000 population from 1950 to 1970, and has shown a gradual downward trend since then. On the other hand, the crude death rate, which had been gradually declining since 1950, is expected to rise again after 2018 and to exceed the crude birth rate in 2066.

[Russia]

We have looked at the demographics of major Asian countries, so let us now examine the demographics of Russia, a country with close ties to Asia. Figure 1-CB-12 shows the population by age group, crude birth rate, and crude death rate in Russia.

The total population peaked at 148.9 million in 1993 and has been on a declining trend, increasing somewhat since 2010, but then declining again in 2020, reaching 145.1 million in 2021. The population of Russia is expected to decrease to 133.13 million in 2050 and to 112.07 million in 2100.

Part I

Part II

Part III

Part IV

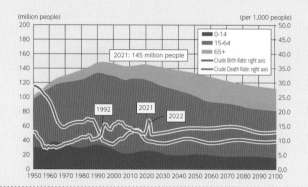

| Figure 1-CA-12 | Population in Russia (by age group) and crude birth and death rates |

Note: Actual data until 2021, medium estimates after 2022
Source: Prepared by the author using WPP2022

The crude birth rate has been higher than the crude death rate since the establishment of the Russian Federation in 1991[7]. Although the crude birth rate increased somewhat after 2010[8], it is expected to decline again after 2020, remaining at about 10 per 1,000 population. The crude death rate was high in 2022, partly due to the invasion in Ukraine, but it had already risen sharply in the previous year.

## (2) Comparative analysis of total fertility rates

We have looked at population by age group and crude birth and death rates in major countries and regions. Here, we focus our analysis on the

---

7) According to Kumo (2022), the "sharp decline in the birth rate since the 1990s is due to the abolition and fee-charging of social childcare support facilities such as nursery schools and kindergartens, which were extremely inexpensive in the Soviet era, and the sharp decline in income following the systemic change, which has darkened future prospects." The increase in the mortality rate was attributed to "increased social stress, increased alcohol consumption, worsening social unrest, and the spread of accidents and crimes."

8) Kumo (2022) points out that the "Maternity Capital," launched in 2007, has had an impact on the temporary increase in the birth rate. The fund was established to provide 250,000 rubles (about JPY 1.2 million at the time) to parents with two or more children to subsidize either the cost of purchasing a house, the cost of their children's education, or the accumulation of funds in a pension fund. Considering that the average monthly income in Russia was 12,000 rubles as of September 2007, its benefit is considered to be very large.

total fertility rate[9], an important variable for population projections.

According to the WPP2022 medium projection, the global total fertility rate is 2.31 in 2022 (Figure 1-CB-13), falling below the replacement-level fertility rate (2.07) in 2059, and is projected to decrease to 1.84 by 2100. The population of Europe fell below the replacement-level as early as 1975, while the population of Asia will fall below the replacement level in 2019, and the population of Africa fell below the replacement-level in 2091. There are major differences by region, so let's take a look at the total fertility rates in major Asian countries (Figure 1-CB-14).

First, the total fertility rate in Japan has been on a downward trend since 1950, and although it fell far below the replacement-level fertility rate in 1966 due to the aforementioned "Hinoe-uma" superstition, it rose again and remained near 2.00. In 1974, it fell below the replacement-level fertility rate at 2.06, and has remained below 2.00 since then. The replacement-level fertility rate is projected to be 1.31 in 2022, 1.47 in 2050, and 1.55 in 2100.

Next, China's total fertility rate remained at an average level of 6.00 from 1950 to 1970, excluding the effects of the famine mentioned

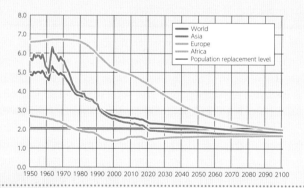

**Figure 1-CB-13**    Total Fertility Rates in Major World Regions

Note: Actual data until 2021, medium estimates after 2022
Source: Prepared by the author using WPP2022

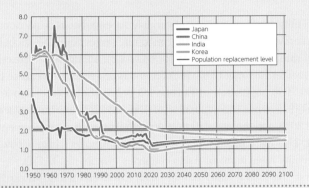

Figure 1-CB-14    Total Fertility Rate in Asian Countries

Note: Actual data until 2021, medium estimates after 2022
Source: Prepared by the author using WPP2022

above. However, since 1970, partly due to the introduction of the "one-child policy," the rate has been on a downward trend, and by 2020 it was projected to be 1.28, below the level of Japan.[10] Although the rate is projected to rise somewhat to 1.39 by 2050 and to 1.48 by 2100, it is still below the replacement-level fertility rate.

Korea's total fertility rate averaged 6.06 in the 1950s. However, since the 1960s, it has been on a downward trend and recorded 1.93, which is below the replacement-level fertility rate. In 2001, it was 1.30, which was lower than that of Japan (1.33) during the same period, and in 2021, it was as low as 0.88. It is expected to increase somewhat to 1.17 in 2050 and to 1.43 in 2100, but it is still below the replacement-level fertility rate.

India's total fertility rate averaged 5.66 between the 1950s and 1970s, and remained above the population replacement level until 2019, although it showed a gradual downward trend after 1980. In 2021, the birthrate fell below the replacement-level fertility rate at 2.03, and has shown a declining trend since then, but remains above the levels of Japan, China, and South Korea.

---

10) Trends in China's total fertility rate are also discussed in Chapter 1 Section 1.

## 3. Summary

To demonstrate the future prospects of the world economy, it is important to analyze the growth of the whole-element productivity, population, and capital in growth accounting. Column B presents the future world population and dynamics, by region and major country, based on new population estimates. The following are some of the important points obtained from WPP2022.

The center of future world population growth is shifting from Asia to Africa.

This is due to the fact that in Asia, China, which has had the world's largest population to date, is expected to decline, while India's population is projected to grow steadily. Population growth in Asia as a whole will slow down.

In Japan and Korea, the working-age population is expected to decline due to the further development of the aging society with a declining birth rate.

One of the new issues emerging from global population dynamics is the need to address labor shortages. This is a major challenge for the Japanese economy in particular. In addition to increasing productivity, it is important to increase the labor participation rate of women and the elderly. Establishment of well-balanced work styles is important for this purpose.

### References

Japan Research Institute, Economic & Policy Report, "How Asia's Demographic Outlook Has Changed After the COVID-19 Pandemic" (Japanese title: *Koronaka wo Hete Ajia no Jinko Dotai no Mitoshi ha Do Kawattaka*), (November 11, 2022) (https://www.jri.co.jp/page.jsp?id=103853)

JETRO, Regional and Analytical Report, "China's Population to Decline, India to Lead the World in 2023: UN Prediction" (Japanese title: *Chugoku no Jinko ga Gensho, 2023nen niha Indo ga Sekai Shui: Kokuren Yosoku*), (September 27, 2022) (https://www.jetro.go.jp/biz/areareports/2022/db12433a352ecc90.html)

Kumo, K. (2022), "Russia's Declining Population and Acceptance of

Foreign Labor: Migration Policy from Russian Perspective" (Japanese title: *Roshia no Jinko Gensho to Gaikokujin Rodo no Juyo Roshia Kara Mita Imin Seisaku*), (https://www2.jiia.or.jp/kokusaimondai_archive/2020/2022-08_004.pdf?noprint, last viewed on July 9, 2023) (August 2022, No. 708), Japan Institute of International Affairs.

Sumitomo Mitsui Trust Bank, Research Monthly Report, November 2022, No. 127, "Future as Seen in 'World Population Estimates' by the United Nations" (Japanese title: *Kokuren 'Sekai Jinko Suikei' Kara Mieru Mirai*), (https://www.smtb.jp/-/media/tb/personal/useful/report-economy/pdf/127.pdf)

United Nations Department of Economic and Social Affairs, Population Division (2019), "World Population Prospects 2019," (https://population.un.org/wpp2019/Publications/, last viewed on July 10, 2023)

United Nations Department of Economic and Social Affairs, Population Division (2022), "World Population Prospects 2022," (https://population. un.org/wpp/Publications/, last viewed on July 10, 2023)

# Part II

## Topics in Kansai: A Crossroads for its Economic Turnaround

*INADA, Yoshihisa; NOMURA, Ryosuke*

In Part II, we shift our focus from the world and the Asia-Pacific to the Kansai region. Our analysis was conducted from various angles based on the theme of 'Kansai's role and future challenges as revealed by the COVID-19 pandemic. The following is a summary of the chapters in Part II.

### Chapter 2

Chapter 2 presents a macroeconomic analysis of the economies of Japan and Kansai, including both retrospective analyses and forecasts.

For the Japanese economy to grow sustainably in the future, a virtuous cycle of rising prices and wages is indispensable. This process was especially noteworthy in 2022. Section 1 presents a theoretical framework of the virtuous cycle mechanism for later analysis.

Section 2 focuses on the Japanese economy, which in FY 2022 showed a gradual recovery mainly in service consumption expenditures due to the normalization of socioeconomic activities. However, the economic recovery has been slow due to downward pressure on external demand caused by the stagnation of world trade and the deteriorating income environment caused by soaring domestic prices. Our latest forecasts for the Japanese economy in FY 2023-25 presented here (+1.7% for FY 2023, +1.4% for FY 2024, and +1.1% for FY 2025) incorporate the second advance estimate of GDP for Q3 2023 as well as our new assumptions about exogenous variables. With the normalization of socioeconomic activities, the forced savings accumulated due to the COVID-19 pandemic are spent in service consumption expenditures. However, since the acceleration and persistence of high consumer price inflation suppresses the growth of real disposable income, spending on goods consumption becomes selective. For this reason, growth in real disposable income is essential for a continuous recovery in household consumption.

In Section 3, we analyze the Kansai economy. In FY 2022, the economy in the Kansai region generally recovered as socioeconomic activities normalized. The current situation can be summarized by sector as follows. (1) The household sector showed a moderate recovery. However, real wages continued to deteriorate as households faced rising consumer prices due to price hikes in many items. (2) In the corporate sector, the manufacturing sector was weak, while the non-manufacturing sector generally recovered, especially in face-to-face services, as economic activity resumed. (3) In the external sector, both exports and imports of goods increased for the second consecutive year, while exports of services showed a remarkable recovery due to the easing of border control measures. (4) The public sector (public works) remained steady compared to the nation as a whole. Incorporating each economic indicator, real GRP growth in the Kansai is forecasted to be +1.3% in FY 2023, +1.6% in FY 2024, and +1.4% in FY 2025. Advance estimates of FY 2020-23 GRP for the six prefectures in Kansai are also presented, and a comparison of the recovery process from the COVID-19 pandemic is made for each prefecture.

In Section 4, we analyzed the impact of accelerated inflation in 2022, focusing on households in the Kansai region. The results showed that the high prices were mainly caused by basic expenses such as food and energy, and that low-income households, which have a high rate of these expenses, bore a large burden. We also estimated the effects of sudden fluctuations in electricity and gas prices.

Column C discusses the regional economic ripple effects of the 2023 Hanshin-ORIX championship. Specifically, the economic impact of the league championship, the Climax Series, the Japan Series, and the subsequent victory-related sales and the victory parade were analyzed using the APIR interregional input-output table.

## Chapter 3

In Chapter 3, the industrial structure of the Kansai economy is summarized based on basic data, growth industries (profitable industries) are identified, and the future industrial structure is examined.

Section 1 identifies growth industries using basic data in order to identify profitable industries. Specifically, we used the Economic Census of Japan to compare the industrial structure and productivity of the Kansai region with those of other regions in order to clarify the characteristics of the Kansai economy.

In Section 2, based on the analysis in Section 1, we examined strategies for attracting investment and human resources, and considered industries that will become new strengths of the Kansai region. In doing so, we identified "profitable businesses" that do not match existing industry classifications by combining problem-solving businesses and industries in the Kansai region with the DX business concept.

Section 3 discusses the current state of the labor market in the Kansai region and the challenges it faces. The labor market in the Kansai region, which was hit hard by the COVID-19 pandemic, is slowly recovering, but the degree of recovery differs by gender and age group. A recent issue is a growing labor shortage in the non-manufacturing sector, and there are concerns that supply constraints may be occured in the future due to labor shortages. The introduction of new technologies is important to overcome these issues, and improvements in the working environment can increase the employment rate and retention rate in the industry.

## Chapter 4

In Chapter 4, we review the past tourism strategies, shed light on the rapid recovery of inbound tourism demand since the COVID-19 pandemic and the recovery of the tourism industry as a whole, including domestic tourism, and analyze the issues that have become apparent.

In section 1, we review tourism strategies in 10 years from the viewpoints of the national government and the private sector, and clarifies the challenges of tourism strategies for the future. Specifically, we clarified the characteristics of the past strategies based on the past budget trends of the Japan Tourism Agency and organized the trends of large-scale hotel construction in the Kansai region on a micro basis.

In section 2, we analyze the rapidly recovering inbound tourism demand and domestic travel demand using the latest major statistics. The section points out that the following issues must be addressed in future tourism strategies: (1) increasing and sustaining per capita consumption, (2) attracting more visitors to local regions and promoting sightseeing tours, and (3) improving the profitability of the tourism industry and improving labor supply constraints.

## Chapter 5

In Chapter 5, we analyzed the economic impact of the Greater EXPO and the development of DX at the Osaka-Kansai Expo.

Section 1 updates the economic impact of the Greater EXPO estimated last year and introduces specific initiatives being undertaken by local governments in line with the concept of the Greater EXPO, and estimates the economic impact of highly value-added trips around regions.

Section 2 discusses the use of DX in Kansai and Osaka from two aspects: "quantitative improvement effects" and "qualitative business transformation." It examines the economic effects of DX, taking up the case of "MaaS" such as Yumeshima Construction and Virtual Space (Metaverse).

# INTRODUCTION

*INADA, Yoshihisa*

The year 2022 was a historic year in which attention was focused on the virtuous cycle between prices and wages.

During the global financial crisis known as the Lehman Shock, both nominal and real wages fell due to the substantial expansion of the supply-demand gap, and the two did not diverge. During the recovery process after the COVID-19 pandemic, nominal wages rose only moderately, and the decline in real wages expanded due to the price hikes that exceeded them.

To clarify the situation during this period, Figure 2-0-1 shows the movements of the Core CPI and the import price index (in both contract currency and JPY terms) during the Lehman shock period and after the COVID-19 pandemic.

In both periods, the surge in crude oil prices led to a sharp increase in import prices. During the Lehman shock period, the import price index in contract currency terms peaked in July 2008 (+34.7% YoY), while the import price index in JPY terms peaked in August 2008 (+27.2% YoY). However, due to the rapid appreciation of the JPY in the exchange rate, the Core CPI turned downward in January 2009. During the recovery process after the COVID-19 pandemic, on the other hand, the import price index in contract currency terms peaked in November 2021 (+34.0%), while the import price index in JPY terms

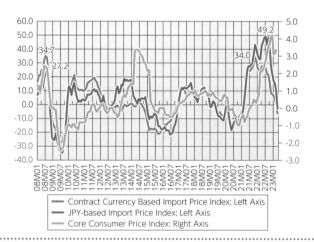

| Figure 2-0-1 | Contract Currency-Based Import Price Index, JPY-Based Import Price Index, and Core CPI: YoY (%) |
|---|---|

Source: Author's calculations based on the Bank of Japan's "Domestic corporate goods price index" and the Ministry of Internal Affairs and Communications' "National Consumer Price Index"

peaked in July 2022 (+49.2%). During this period, the yen depreciated rapidly against the U.S. dollar from 114.13 yen to 136.63 yen, so the peak of the yen-based import price index was delayed by eight months relative to the contract currency-based index. With a time lag, import price inflation propagated to domestic corporate prices (peak in December 2022) and was passed on to consumer prices (peak in January 2023). As a result, real wages in Q1 2023 declined YoY for the fourth consecutive quarter. This rapid deterioration in the income environment drew national attention to the need for wage increases and to the virtuous cycle between prices and wages. Chapter 2, Section 1 presents the theoretical and empirical frames of the price-wage virtuous cycle. First, in order for wages to rise sustainably, it is fundamental to first increase the level of activity in the economy as a whole before raising prices. For this to happen, strong growth in private demand, mainly household consumption and private capital investment, is indispensable. Second, an increase in labor productivity is essential for wages to rise, the key to which is the expansion of production facilities through capital investment.

Japan's capital equipment growth has lacked momentum. However, supported by the accommodative financial environment that has prevailed over the past decade, the performance of large companies in particular has improved, and capital investment has remained strong. The key will be for this to spread to small and medium-sized enterprises (SMEs), leading to a further increase in capital equipment and productivity in the macroeconomy as a whole. The source of robust capital investment will be sustained growth in household consumption. Wage increases are indispensable for this purpose.

A virtuous cycle between prices and wages is a mechanism by which the demand and supply sides of the macroeconomy mutually exert a positive influence on each other. In Japan, capital investment is currently growing against the backdrop of a labor shortage and the digital transformation (DX) accompanying improvements in artificial intelligence (AI). This situation, coupled with a recovery in consumption following the COVID-19 pandemic, should continue to generate sustained increases in productivity and wages, creating a virtuous cycle between prices and wages. In addition, the creation of high-value-added products and the premiumization of value-added products are important when considering the improvement of productivity.

# Chapter 2

# THE ECONOMIES OF JAPAN AND KANSAI: A RETROSPECTIVE AND OUTLOOK

FY 2022 was a year in which the virtuous cycle between prices and wages attracted attention, as the effects of the yen's depreciation and soaring import prices, which had been conspicuous since the summer of 2021, were greatly reflected in domestic corporate prices and consumer prices with a time lag from the beginning of FY 2022. The speed of change was significant for firms and households that had been accustomed to low or zero inflation. In an environment where nominal wages did not grow, the rapid increase in consumer prices caused real wages to fall, suppressing household consumption. Firms faced the problem of soaring import prices, which squeezed their earnings and were passed on to domestic prices[1]. In this fiscal year, we focus on the mechanisms behind these large changes.

Section 2 presents a retrospective and current status of the Japanese and Kansai economies in FY 2022 in the first half, and their respective economic outlooks (forecasts) for FY 2023-2024 in the second half. Section 3 describes the impact of high prices on Kansai households.

## Section 1
## VIRTUOUS CYCLE MECHANISM OF PRICES AND WAGES

*MATSUBAYASHI, Yoichi; INADA, Yoshihisa*

## 1. Introduction

Section 1 outlines the mechanism of the virtuous cycle and examines in detail the points at which this virtuous cycle is established. Subsection 1.2 outlines the basic framework of the virtuous cycle, Subsection 1.3 discusses the mechanism of price increases, and Subsection 1.4 examines the mechanism of wage

---

1) For this point, refer to the description in Chapter 3, Section 2.

increases. Subsection 1.5 introduces the factors that cause consumption to increase, Subsection 1.6 examines in detail the increase in labor productivity, and Subsection 1.7 describes the increase in capital equipment, which is closely related to labor productivity. Subsection 1.8 builds on the discussion in Section 1 and summarizes the key points regarding the mechanism by which the virtuous cycle between prices and wages is realized.

## 2. Basis of virtuous cycle mechanism

It is essential that aggregate supply and demand have balanced growth for the macroeconomy to expand steadily and sustainably. It is also important that household consumption, the largest demand item, grows steadily. The basic factors that determine consumption are current and future income, and wages, which represent the base of the income level.

What factors cause wages to fluctuate? The key is that prices must rise in line with sustained economic growth, and that firms' sales and compensation of employees must continue to increase. These mechanisms can be summarized as follows.

Step ①: Prices rise due to an increase in aggregate demand based on consumption.

Step ②: Wages rise as sales and profits increase with rising prices.

Step ③: Income increases through higher wages.

Step ④: Consumption increases as income increases.

Step ⑤: The economy continues to boom due to increased consumption.

A virtuous cycle is created in the macroeconomy by repeating the mechanism from Step ① to Step ②. The mechanism of this virtuous cycle can be expressed as shown in Figure 2-1-1. The key elements in this mechanism are the increase in prices in Step ① and the increase in wages in Step ②. The phrase "virtuous cycle of prices and wages" was created in response to this circumstance[2].

Figure 2-1-1 is the basic form of the virtuous cycle mechanism. However, in the real economy, this mechanism needs to be modified. By carefully examining these modifications, the problems facing the Japanese economy now should be able to be emphasized. In the following, we will discuss these issues using

---

2) If we focus on Step ⑤ and Step ③ in Figure 2-1-1, it is called a "virtuous cycle of growth and distribution." If we focus on Step ⑤ and the wage increase in Step ②, it is called a "virtuous cycle of wage hikes and growth" (Nihon Keizai Shimbun (2023a)). In both cases, the mechanism shown in Figure 2-1-1 is used as the basis for the terminology.

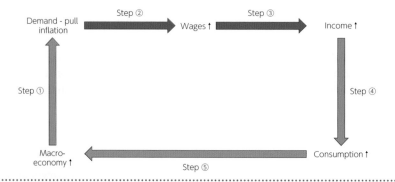

**Figure 2-1-1**　Virtuous Cycle Mechanism of Prices and Wages (Basic Form)

Source: Prepared by the author

various data[3].

## 3. Mechanism of price increase

First, we examine the mechanism of price increases in Step ①.

Figure 2-1-2 shows the rate of change in the CPI (Consumer Index, excluding fresh food and energy (Core-core CPI)) from January 2000 to April 2023[4].

From 2000 to 2012, consumer prices generally trended downward, with the exception of some years, and a deflationary trend continued.[5] Since 2013, the price inflation rate has generally remained positive, indicating an inflationary trend. As of April 2023, the composite index has increased by 3.5% and the core-core index by 4.1%.

The main mechanisms by which prices rise are summarized here.

The first is price inflation caused by an increase in demand throughout the economy, which is called "demand-pull inflation."

The second type of inflation is the rise in prices accompanying the increase in the cost of production by firms, such as the price of raw materials, and is

---

3) The following summary is based on previous studies of theory and empirical analysis of the various channels that comprise the mechanism, as well as various reports and articles on the state of affairs.

4) The composite index of consumer prices is an index using all items covered by the survey. The composite index excluding fresh food and energy excludes fresh food and energy-related items, which are considered to be subject to extreme fluctuations due to weather and market conditions and is also referred to as the core-core index.

5) The rapid increase in the composite index from the end of 2007 to 2008 (+2.3% (July 2008)) was largely due to the sharp rise in fuel prices during the same period, with the core-core index rising by +1.0% over the same period.

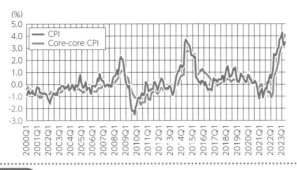

**Figure 2-1-2**    Change in Consumer Prices: YoY

Source: National Consumer Price Index, Statistics Bureau, Ministry of Internal Affairs and Communications

called "cost-push inflation." Since the main cause is the rise in the cost of raw materials, Section 1 will refer to this as "raw material inflation."

The third type of inflation is a rise in prices accompanying a rise in wages, or labor costs (costs), and is called "cost-push inflation" in the same way as the second mechanism. However, since the rise in wages is the main cause, it will be referred to as "wage inflation" in Section 1.

The fourth is a mechanism whereby higher expectations of future price increases held by households and firms (usually referred to as "inflation expectations") cause actual prices to rise[6].

For the virtuous cycle between prices and wages to be sustained, the key point is whether or not price hikes due to demand-pull inflation, the process in Step ① of Figure 2-1-1, will occur. Figure 2-1-3 depicts the relationship between the overall macroeconomic activity (indicated by the GDP gap) and the rate of price inflation[7].

There appears to be a moderately positive correlation between the GDP gap and the rate of price increases. Although the price inflation rate has been rising rapidly since 2021, the GDP gap has been negative, and it is difficult to say that the current price increases are primarily the result of the overall level of economic activity. As shown in Figure 2-1-4, this is largely due to soaring energy prices, especially for mineral fuels, and there are strong signs of raw

---

6) When households and firms have higher inflation expectations and anticipate that the prices of goods they intend to purchase in the future will rise, they will bring forward consumption and investment, resulting in a rise in current prices. This mechanism stimulates demand through a fall in the real interest rate (= nominal interest rate - expected inflation rate).

7) The GDP gap is the degree of divergence between overall macroeconomic demand (aggregate demand) and potentially achievable supply (called potential supply or potential GDP) and is published periodically by the Cabinet Office.

Figure 2-1-3    GDP Gap and Consumer Price Inflation: YoY Transfers

Source: National Consumer Price Index, Statistics Bureau, Ministry of Internal Affairs and Communications; Monthly Economic Report, Cabinet Office

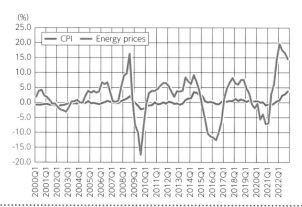

Figure 2-1-4    Changes in Consumer Prices and Energy Price Increases: YoY

Source: National Consumer Price Index, Statistics Bureau, Ministry of Internal Affairs and Communications

material inflation[8].

## 4. Mechanism of wage increase

As we pointed out, the current rise in prices is primarily due to the surge in energy prices, rather than being driven by a booming economy as a whole.

---

8) Cabinet Office (2023) uses regression analysis to break down the price inflation factors shown in the main text into factors to determine the extent to which they affect the actual price inflation rate.

Next, let's look at Figure 2-1-1, Step 2: Mechanism of wage increase. The factors that cause wages to rise can be summarized as follows.

Factor (1): This is a case in which labor supply (households providing labor to earn income) and labor demand (firms hiring labor) do not match, resulting in a tight labor market and higher wages.

Factor (2): This is the case where prices rise as the economy booms (occurrence of demand-pull inflation) and wages, which are payments to workers, rise as firms' sales and profits increase.

Factor (3): This is a case in which wages, the compensation of workers, increase as a result of an increase in the labor productivity of the company, which is expressed as value added per worker (gross profit).

Factor (4): Real income may decrease due to a sharp rise in prices caused by raw material inflation (see Subsection 2.1 for the process of shifting from raw material inflation to consumer prices). In these conditions, worker demand for wage hikes may intensify and nominal salaries may rise as a result of labor-management negotiations (annual wage negotiations in Japan) between workers (households) and management (firms).

Figure 2-1-5 shows the nominal wage growth rate in Japan[9].

Nominal wages have not grown since 2000 and will not turn positive until 2014. However, the growth rate is extremely slow, barely +1.1% in 2022[10].

According to the Japanese Trade Union Confederation survey conducted on May 10, the rate of increase in annual wage negotiations in 2023 was +3.67%, the highest since 1993 (+3.90%). Therefore, a relatively high increase in the predetermined salary is expected in FY 2023. The fact that wages, which have not been rising for a long time, are showing signs of rising is largely due to factor (4) among those discussed above. In other words, households' real incomes have been forced to decline due to raw material inflation caused by high resource

---

9) The nominal wage growth rate series is YoY for "fixed wages per worker" (total of 5 or more workers).

10) The growth in 2022 is attributable in part to the sample replacement in the Monthly Labor Survey and the benchmark update. Saito (2023) provides a detailed explanation of these statistical characteristics and the current state of wage increases. Various factors have been pointed out to explain the long period of sluggish nominal wage growth in Japan. For example, Okubo et al. (2023) point out: 1) the dual structure of the labor market, 2) wage-setting behavior of firms, and 3) industry-specific factors (especially in the non-manufacturing industry) and employment mobility among industries and firms. In relation to the wage-setting behavior of firms, in Japan, firms may prioritize an increase in the number of employees over a wage increase when earnings increase (Hamada and Adachi (2015)).

**Figure 2-1-5**    Nominal Wage Growth: YoY

Source: Ministry of Health, Labour and Welfare, Monthly Labor Survey.

prices and a weak JPY, forcing wages to rise[11].

In any case, as shown in Figure 2-1-1, the mechanism (factor (2) of pay hikes) from price hikes to wage raises is unlikely to have developed. The current price hikes are strongly reminiscent of raw material inflation, which means that the precondition for Step ② in Figure 2-1-1 is not yet in place. The key to increasing wages in Japan from a medium- to long-term perspective is to realize the mechanism of factor (3).

Here, the basic form of firm labor productivity is shown in equation (1).

Labor productivity = amount of value added by the company
                    / number of employees
        = gross profit / number of employees
        = (Net sales - Cost of sales) / Number of employees
        = (Personnel expenses + Net operating income + Other)
        / Number of employees                                    (1)

Equation (1) indicates that if the ratio of labor costs to gross profit (labor's

---

11) Factor (1) is also considered to exist as a medium- to long-term factor. Factor (2) and Factor (1) can occur simultaneously because a tight labor market is brought about by a booming economy. However, in Japan, due to the aging of the population and a mismatch of human resources, the labor supply does not meet the labor demand, and the labor shortage is becoming a structural factor, and factor (1) is becoming apparent as a medium- to long-term factor. Genda (2017) comprehensively examines the relationship between labor shortages and wages.

share) does not change significantly, wages, which are labor costs per employee, will increase as labor productivity increases. Therefore, an efficient way to raise salaries in the medium to long term is to increase labor productivity. A more detailed study of the mechanism that raises labor productivity is needed and will be discussed later[12].

## 5. Mechanism of consumption increase

Next, we will look at the mechanism of rising consumption, which is essential to understanding how rising wages are correlated with rising prices. (Figure 2-1-1 Steps ③ and ④).

Figure 2-1-6 shows the evolution of real household consumption expenditures (2007=100) from 2007 to 2022 for Japan, the United States, and Germany.

The United States and Germany have shown a steady increase for about 15 years, with the exception of a temporary drop due to the COVID-19 pandemic.

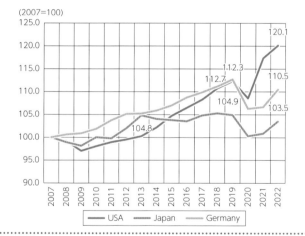

| Figure 2-1-6 | Real Household Consumption Expenditures |

Source: Compiled from OECD

---

12) In equation (1), there are two ways to increase productivity: 1) increase value added (gross profit) in the numerator, and 2) reduce the number of employees in the denominator. If a drastic reduction in the number of employees is not realistic, the key to increasing productivity may be an increase in value added, or more simply put, the ability of a company to generate more profit. Thus, the expression "higher productivity raises wages" might be more suitably understood as "a marked increase in value-added results in higher productivity and higher wages." This point was also discussed at the Asia Pacific Institute of Research (2022).

In other words, in 2022, the U.S. and Germany are 120.1 and 110.5, respectively, while Japan's figure is 103.5, which is low.

Disposable income is the main factor influencing household consumption. Figure 2-1-7 depicts changes in real household disposable income (2007=100) for the three countries.

While consumption in the U.S. and Germany has been growing at a steady pace, the rate of growth in Japan has been extremely slow, standing at 108.8 in 2021, an increase of less than 10% over the past 15 years. Thus, it is clear that the fundamental factor behind sluggish consumption in Japan is the slow growth of disposable income or wages.

Consumption behavior depends not only on income in the current period but also on lifetime income that can be earned in the future. For example, when purchasing a car or durable consumer goods, or when spending on education, consumption decisions should be made based on the income profile during the employment period and the expected future income.

Although lifetime income is a variable that cannot be observed, it is possible to create an observable series with econometric technique[13].

Figure 2-1-8 shows lifetime earnings in Japan and the U.S. from 2010 to 2021. 2010 lifetime earnings in Japan were approximately 130 million yen, while lifetime earnings in the U.S. were approximately 220 million yen in terms of JPY,

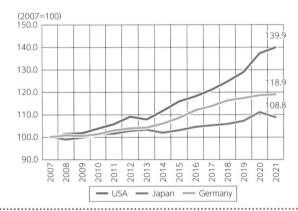

**Figure 2-1-7**    Real Household Disposable Income

Source: Compiled from OECD

---

13) The measurement is made possible by specifying a stochastic process of real per capita labor income in each period and assuming rational expectation formation with respect to the expected income profile of households. The details of the measurement are explained in Ogawa (1992) and Matsubayashi (2007).

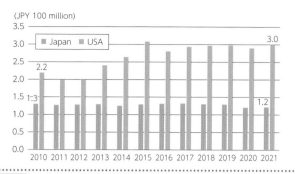

**Figure 2-1-8**   Japan-U.S. Comparison of Lifetime Income

Source: Prepared by the author

a difference of approximately 1.7 times. While lifetime earnings in the U.S. have been increasing since then, they have remained stagnant in Japan. As a result, in 2021, the lifetime income in the U.S. will be approximately JPY 300 million, while the lifetime income in Japan will be JPY 120 million, resulting in a gap of more than two times.  This is the result of households' expectations for their lifetime income being low because salaries in Japan have not improved significantly.

As outlined above, the main reason for the sluggish household consumption in Japan is the slow growth of income in each period and future income[14].

## 6. Mechanism of productivity increase

In these conditions, when wage growth is uncertain, a significant boost in consumption cannot be expected. Therefore, we will again carefully examine the possibility of an increase in labor productivity (factor (3), which we have already discussed) as a mechanism for a sustained increase in wages.

(The labor productivity shown in equation (1) can be rewritten as in equation (2).)

$$\frac{\text{labor}}{\text{productivity}} = \frac{\text{capital equipment}}{\text{Number of Employees}} \times \frac{\text{Net sales}}{\text{capital equipment}} \times \frac{\text{gross profit}}{\text{Net sales}} \quad (2)$$

---

14) Household consumption, which had fallen sharply due to the COVID-19 shock, showed signs of recovery from early spring to summer of 2022. Based on the discussion in Section 1, if households perceive the price hikes to be prolonged and wage increases to be temporary, they will have pessimistic expectations about their lifetime income, which may lead to a medium- to long-term slump in consumption. A detailed analysis based on the diachronic household behavior theory (life-cycle hypothesis), including these points, has been conducted, for example, by Unayama (2023).

The first term on the right-hand side of equation (2) expresses how much production equipment is equipped per employee and is called the "capital equipment ratio." The higher the capital equipment ratio, the better the capital equipment and the higher the labor productivity. The second term on the right-hand side is the sales per unit of production equipment and is called the "capitalization coefficient." The higher the capital coefficient, the more efficiently production is carried out, and labor productivity increases[15]. The third term on the right-hand side is the profit to sales ratio, which is called the "return on sales." The higher the return on sales, the higher the labor productivity.

We will now look at the changes in labor productivity in Japan since 2000, breaking it down into three items[16].

Labor productivity (Figure 2-1-9) is consistently lower for small and medium-sized firms than for large firms. Although labor productivity of large firms

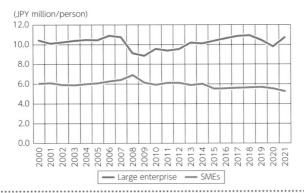

(JPY million/person)

Legend: — Large enterprise    — SMEs

**Figure 2-1-9**    Labor Productivity

Source: Compiled from "Corporate Statistics," Ministry of Finance

---

15) When capital investment is made, the machinery and equipment installed is often accompanied by new technology (referred to as "embodied technology"). Therefore, the capital equipment ratio and capital coefficient increase not only with the size of the capital equipment but also with the quality of the equipment.

16) Based on the "Annual Report of Corporate Statistics of Japan," each variable is measured as follows: labor productivity = value added / total number of employees; total number of employees = number of employees + number of directors; capital equipment ratio = tangible fixed assets / total number of employees; capital coefficient = net sales / tangible fixed assets; and profit to net sales ratio = value added / net sales. Large firms are classified by capitalization of JPY 100 million or more, while small and medium-sized firms are classified by capitalization of less than JPY 100 million. The Japan Productivity Center (2020) provides a more detailed measurement based on the same method as in this paper. Chapter 6, Section 1 of the white paper provides a detailed analysis of the characteristics of labor productivity in Kansai firms, using a simplified version of equation (2).

has been on a gradual upward trend since the Lehman shock, it has not reached a level exceeding that of the 2000s. On the other hand, the labor productivity of small and medium-sized firms has been on a downward trend since the 1960s.

Next, the capital equipment ratio (Figure 2-1-10), capital coefficient (Figure 2-1-11), and return on sales (Figure 2-1-12) demonstrate that all of these ratios have either remained almost flat or declined gradually. The decline in the capital equipment ratio is particularly clear for large firms, suggesting that the lack of sufficient accumulation of production equipment has contributed to the sluggishness of labor productivity.

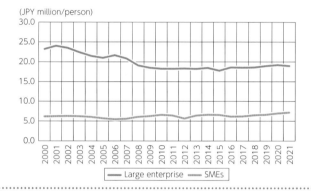

**Figure 2-1-10**    Capital Equipment Ratio

Source: Compiled from "Corporate Statistics," Ministry of Finance

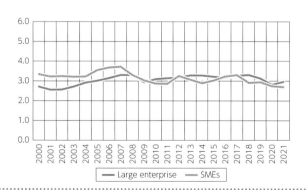

**Figure 2-1-11**    Capital Coefficients

Source: Compiled from "Corporate Statistics," Ministry of Finance

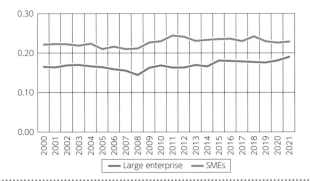

**Figure 2-1-12**    Profit Margin on Sales

Source: Compiled from "Corporate Statistics," Ministry of Finance

## 7. Mechanism of capital equipment increase

Increases in labor productivity are the driving force behind medium- and long-term wage increases, and the key to these increases is an increase in capital equipment.

There are many factors that influence capital investment, but the key factor is a company's expected future earnings. If future earnings are expected to increase in the medium to long term, firms will increase capital investment with the intention of enhancing their existing capital facilities. The basis for forecasting future earnings is a long-term forecast of economic growth. Specifically, the forecast of how much the Japanese economy will grow in the next three or five years is important information for capital investment decisions that require large amounts of capital, unlike short-term sales forecasts[17].

The Cabinet Office has published a questionnaire in the form of a "Questionnaire Survey on Corporate Behavior" on the medium- to long-term prospects for the economic growth rate of firms[18].

Figure 2-1-13 shows the relationship between the real economic growth

---

[17] Keynes (1936) classified expectations, which are the basis of corporate management, into two categories: short-term expectations and long-term expectations. Short-term expectations are those related to sales when production takes place. On the other hand, long-run expectations are expectations of future earnings when a firm purchases and installs new production equipment. The outlook for the growth of the Japanese economy over the next three to five years is a key factor in the formation of firms' long-term expectations. This point is also identified in Ogawa (2021).

[18] The survey asked respondents about their outlook for economic growth, as well as the growth rate of capital investment, the number of employees, the ratio of overseas local production, and the profitable JPY rate.

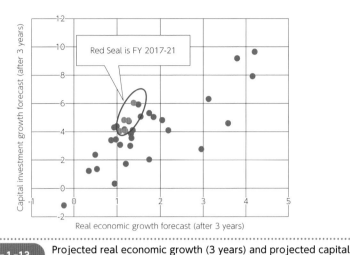

**Figure 2-1-13**  Projected real economic growth (3 years) and projected capital investment growth (3 years); unit: %

Source: Cabinet Office, "Questionnaire Survey on Corporate Behavior."

rate forecast from 1983 to 2021 (three years later) and the capital investment growth rate forecast (three years later).

As the figure shows, the higher the medium- to long-term economic growth expectations, the higher the projected growth rate of capital investment[19]. Looking at the past five years (2017-2021), while economic growth expectations are not high, capital investment expectations have risen somewhat.

Here, we discuss some of the key factors in the outlook for economic growth. Household consumption is the largest demand item in terms of total spending. GDP, and the impact of real consumption growth on medium- and long-term economic growth prospects are expected to be extremely large.

To confirm this point, Figure 2-1-14 shows the actual growth rate of household consumption and the projected economic growth rate three years from now. As the figure clearly shows, the economic growth forecast held by firms is strongly related to the actual growth of household consumption. In other words, a medium- to long-term slump in consumption will lower the economic growth forecast held by firms and lead to a slowdown in capital investment growth[20].

---

19) This point is also explained in detail in Cabinet Office (2023).
20) The economic growth forecasts held by firms should be affected not only by household consumption but also by various other factors. However, over the medium to long term, trends in household consumption, which accounts for the largest share of total domestic expenditures (i.e. trends in domestic demand), are expected to have a large impact on the economic growth forecasts of firms. This point is also identified in Ogawa (2021).

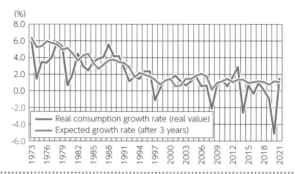

**Figure 2-1-14**    Real household consumption growth (real value) and real economic growth forecast (3 years)

Source: Cabinet Office, "Questionnaire Survey on Corporate Behavior."

In order to examine Japan's capital investment situation in more detail, a comparison with Germany and Korea follows. Germany and Korea, like Japan, are manufacturing-driven economies, making them suitable for comparison examining trends in capital investment.

Figure 2-1-15 depicts the capital investment rate (ratio of capital investment to capital stock) from 2005 to 2020 based on financial data for individual firms[21]. The measured values for each year represent the median.

Compared to Germany and Korea, Japan has consistently lower investment rates for both large and small firms over the sample period. While the investment rates in Germany and Korea have been gradually increasing since the late 2000s, the upward trend in Japan has not been as strong[22].

Figure 2-1-16 shows the expected rate of return (Tobin's marginal q is a proxy variable for the expected rate of return, which is the main factor in capital investment decisions[23]).

As Figure 2-1-16 shows, the level of marginal q in Japan is lower than in Germany and Korea, and this characteristic may be reflected in the sluggish

---

21) The details of the measurement method from Figures 2-1-15 to 2-1-17 are organized in Hagiwara (2023) and Hagiwara and Matsubayashi (2019). The database used for the measurements is based on "Orbis" (global financial data) provided by Bureau van Dijk. Hagiwara and Matsubayashi (2019) also examined the embodied technology process described in footnote 15.

22) The medium- to long-term trends of capital investment in Japan are also discussed in detail in Cabinet Office (2022).

23) Tobin's q is a variable that contains all the information on the expected rate of return, and is statistically called sufficient statistics. Therefore, the information on the expected growth rate of firms based on the Cabinet Office's questionnaire survey shown above is also considered to be included in Tobin's q.

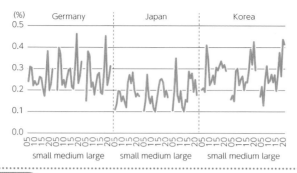

| Figure 2-1-15 | Comparison of capital investment rates between Japan, the U.S., and Germany[24] |
| --- | --- |

Source: Compiled from Hagiwara (2023).

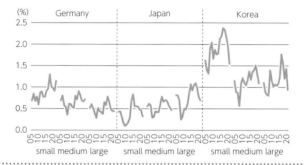

| Figure 2-1-16 | Comparison of Expected Rates of Return between Japan, the U.S. and Germany |
| --- | --- |

Source: Compiled from Hagiwara (2023).

investment rate in Figure 2-1-15.

Figure 2-1-17 shows the average age of capital equipment, the Vintage Index. The smaller the value of the index, the younger the age of the capital equipment, meaning that the capital equipment is being actively renewed. In general, new technology is embodied in new capital equipment, and a smaller vintage index is desirable from the viewpoint of productivity improvement.

As Figure 2-1-17 shows, Japan's vintage index is nearly twice as high as those of Germany and Korea, confirming that capital renewal is stagnant. This can be attributed to the stagnation of the investment rate, which is accompanied by a decline in the expected rate of return, as seen in Figures 2-1-15 and 2-1-16.

24) "Large," "medium," and "small" in Figs. 2-1-15 through 2-1-17 indicate respective firm size.

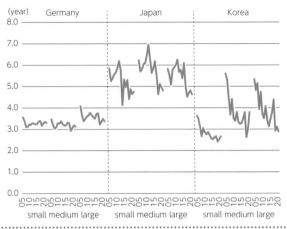

**Figure 2-1-17**     Comparison of Vintage Indexes between Japan, the U.S., and Germany

Source: Compiled from Hagiwara (2023).

## 8. To realize a virtuous cycle mechanism between prices and wages

In this subsection, we have examined the mechanisms that allow the virtuous cycle between prices and wages to persist.

The model (basic form) of the mechanism shown in Figure 2-1-1 can be modified as shown in Figure 2-1-18 through previous considerations. The three main points are as follows:

First, it is essential to raise prices and boost macroeconomic activity to ensure sustainable growth in salaries. Strong growth in private demand—primarily in the form of household consumption and private capital investment—is necessary for this to occur. Second, an increase in labor productivity is necessary for wages to rise, the key mechanism of which is to increase labor productivity through capital investment.

Third, capital investment not only increases demand in the macroeconomy, but also increases productivity and supply capacity through an increase in production facilities[25]. In other words, it plays an important role in stimulating the economy from both the demand and supply sides.

As shown earlier, in comparison with other countries, Japan's capital equipment growth has lacked momentum. However, supported by the large easing

---

25) The accumulation of not only tangible fixed assets but also intangible fixed assets (software, goodwill, etc.) is important for increasing productivity.

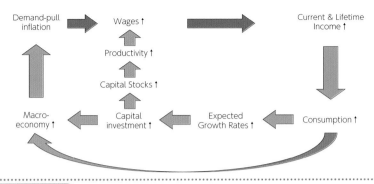

**Figure 2-1-18** Mechanism of the Virtuous Cycle between Prices and Wages (Modified Form)

Source: Prepared by the author

of the financial environment over the past decade, earnings and capital investment have remained strong, especially among large firms[26]. As shown in Figure 2-1-9, labor productivity is rising among large firms. The key to the future is for these improving trends to spread to small and medium-sized enterprises (SMEs), leading to a further increase in capital equipment and productivity in the macroeconomy. Consistently rising household consumption will be the source of strong, robust capital investment.

The above summary confirms that a virtuous cycle between prices and wages is nothing more than a mechanism in which the demand side and supply side of the macroeconomy are interlinked and exert a positive influence on each other. With a workforce scarcity and the digital transformation (DX) that comes with advancements in artificial intelligence (AI), capital investment is currently rising in Japan[27]. This situation, coupled with a recovery in consumption following the COVID-19 pandemic, is expected to continue to generate sustained increases in productivity and wages, and to create a virtuous cycle between prices and wages.

Based on the mechanisms outlined in Section 1, more detailed analyses of the Japanese and Kansai economies are presented in the following sections and thereafter.

---

26) This point can be seen in Figures 2-1-5 and 2-1-12, and in Figures 2-1-15 through 2-1-17.

27) For example, the most recent situation is presented in Nihon Keizai Shimbun (2023b). The current surge in capital investment is mainly based on the abundant cash flow of companies. In the future, however, a sustained increase is expected based on the medium- and long-term factors (expected economic growth and expected earnings) described in Section 1.

# References

Asia Pacific Institute of Research (2022), "Economic Debate 2022 (Japanese Economy)"

Cabinet Office (2022), Annual Report on the Japanese Economy and Public Finance 2022, Chapter 3.

Cabinet Office (2023), "Japanese Economy 2022-2023: Toward Full-Scale Growth under Rising Prices."

Genda, Y. (ed.) (2017), "Why Wages Do Not Rise Despite Human Resource Shortages," (Japanese title: *Hitode Busoku Nanoni Naze Chingin ga Agaranai Noka*), Keio University Press.

Hagiwara, T. (2023), "Tobin's Marginal q and Productivity in Japan, Germany and Korea," (Japanese title: *Tobin no Genkai q to Seisansei ni Kansuru Nichi-Doku-Kan Hikaku*), Journal of National Economy, Vol. 227, No. 1, pp. 1-11.

Hagiwara, T. and Matsubayashi, Y. (2019), "Capital Accumulation, Vintage, and Productivity: The Japanese Experience," The Singapore Economic Review, 64(3), pp. 747-771.

Hamada, K. and Adachi, S. (2015), "The Day the World Envies the Japanese Economy," (Japanese title: *Sekai ga Nihon Keizai wo Urayamu Hi*), Gentosha.

Japan Productivity Center (2020), "Report on Factor Analysis of Labor Productivity Trends," (Japanese title: *Rodo Seisansei no Suii ni Kakawaru Yoin Bunseki no Hokoku*).

Keynes, J.M. (1936), "The General Theory of Employment, Interest and Money," Harcourt Brace, London, translated by Shionoya, Y. (1995), Toyo Keizai Shinposha.

Matsubayashi, Y. (2007), "Validity and Limitations of the Asset Effect: A Reexamination of Japanese and U.S. Consumption Behavior," (Japanese title: *Shisan Koka no Yukosei to Genkai: Nichibei Shohi Kodo no Saikensho*) National Economic Journal, Vol. 196, No. 3, pp. 17-35.

Nihon Keizai Shimbun (2023a), "Accelerate Reforms for a Virtuous Cycle of Wage Increases and Growth," (Japanese title: *Chinage to Seicho no Kojunkan he Kaikaku wo Kasoku Seyo*), Editorial, March 16, 2023.

Nihon Keizai Shimbun (2023b), "Capital Investment Up to JPY 31 Trillion," (Japanese title: *Setsubi Toshi Saiko 31 Choen*), June 22, 2023.

Ogawa, K. (1992), "An Empirical Analysis of Household Behavior in Japan," (Japanese title: *Waga Kuni ni Okeru Kakei Kodo no Jissho Bunseki*), Financial Review, No.25, pp.112-134.

Ogawa, K. (2021), "Long-Term Stagnation in the Japanese Economy: The Mechanism Revealed by Empirical Analysis," (Japanese title: *Nihon Keizai no Choki Teitai: Jissho Bunseki ga Akirakanisuru Mekanizumu*), Nikkei

Publishing Inc.

Okubo, T., Kido, Y., Suita, K., Takatomi, K., Hada, S., Fukunaga, I., Furukawa, K., and Hogen, Y. (2023), "Discussion Paper on Wage Trends in Japan," (Japanese title: *Waga Kuni no Chingin Doko ni Kansuru Ronten Seiri*), Bank of Japan Working Paper Series 23-J-1.

Saito, T. (2023), "Annual wage negotiations to reach the highest level in 30 years: The future focus will be on the sustainability of wage increases and the pace of service price increases," (Japanese title: *Shunto Chinageritsu ha 30nen Buri no Kosuijun he -Kongo no Shoten ha Chinage no Jizokusei to Sabisu Kakaku no Josho Pesu-*), Nissay Research Institute, Weekly Economist Letter, 2023-4-14.

Unayama, T. (2023), "Contemporary Japanese Consumption Analysis: The Current State of Life Cycle Theory," (Japanese title: *Gendai Nihon no Shohi Bunseki: Raifu Saikuru Riron no Genzaichi*), Keio University Press.

Part I    Part II    Part III    Part IV

## Section 2
## THE JAPANESE ECONOMY: RECENT DEVELOPMENTS AND SHORT-TERM FORECASTS

*INADA, Yoshihisa; SHIMODA Mitsuru*

## 1. Recent Developments in the Japanese economy: FY 2022 through mid-FY 2023

### (1) Global trade will take some time to recover

World trade is increasingly showing signs of stagnation: according to the CPB World Trade Monitor, world trade (in volume terms, 2010=100) increased MoM +0.7% in September 2023, marking the second consecutive month of growth. Although on a monthly basis there are signs of recovery, on a quarterly basis that is not the case. World trade in Q3 2023 declined by -0.4% QoQ, marking the fourth consecutive quarterly decline. It will take some time for global trade to bottom out. Compared to the previous quarter, trade in advanced economies declined -0.4% in Q3, the fourth consecutive quarterly decline, while trade in emerging economies fell -0.4%, marking the first decline in three quarters (Figure 2-2-1). The reason behind the stagnation of trade in advanced economies is the decline in industrial production.

According to the CPB, the global industrial production index rose +0.8% QoQ in Q3, marking the first increase in two quarters. Therein, industrial production

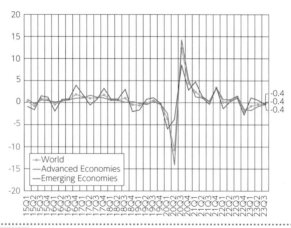

| Figure 2-2-1 | QoQ changes in world trade volume (2010=100, %). |

Source: CPB World Trade Monitor, 24 November 2023

in advanced economies declined -0.1% QoQ for the fourth consecutive quarter, while it rose +1.5% QoQ in emerging economies, marking the first increase in two quarters. Industrial production in advanced economies kept declining from Q4 2022 to Q3 2023, and the situation remains difficult for the Japanese economy, which depends heavily on exports to other advanced economies.

According to the IMF (World Economic Outlook -Navigating Global Divergences-, October 2023), the global economy in 2023-24 will be "resilient, with a moderate recovery but widening growth gaps." The forecast for the global economy has been revised downward by -0.1 %pt for 2023 and -0.1 %pt for 2023-24, respectively. The U.S. economy is projected to grow +2.1% in 2022 and 2023, and to accelerate to +1.5% in 2024, while the EU economy is expected to slump from +3.6% in 2022 to +0.7% in 2023 and then recover slightly to +1.5% in 2024. Meanwhile, the Chinese economy is projected to recover from +3.0% in 2022 to +5.0% in 2023, but then to slow to +4.2% in 2024. While the U.S. forecast has been revised upward from the previous forecast, China and the EU have been revised downward. Interest rate hikes by central banks as a counter-inflationary measure continue to be a drag on economic activity. As a result, a slowdown in world trade volume (goods and services) in 2023 (+0.9%) is inevitable. However, a reversal is likely in 2024 (+3.5%).

According to the Global Semiconductor Market Statistics, global semiconductor sales in September (3-month moving average) fell -4.5% YoY, marking the 14th consecutive monthly decline, although the decline margin has been decelerating for five consecutive months after bottoming out in June (-21.3% YoY). By region, sales in Asia were down 7.7% YoY, marking the 14th consecutive monthly decline. Those in the U.S. were down 2.0% YoY, marking the first decline in two months. Although the decline in semiconductor demand has bottomed out, it will take some time before it recovers to the previous peak level (Figure 2-2-2).

## (2) The current state of the Japanese economy
### Second Preliminary Estimate of Q3 2023 GDP

According to the second official advance GDP estimate for Q3 2023, released on December 8, Japan's real GDP growth was -0.7% QoQ, or an annualized -2.9%. This represents a downward revision from the first advance estimate (-0.5% QoQ, or an annualized -2.1%). However, since Q1 2023 growth was revised upward to positive growth, Q3 2023 effectively marked the first negative quarterly growth in four quarters.

Past values were revised retroactively due to seasonal adjustments and revisions in basic statistics. Comparing previous second versus first advance estimates, the growth rate for Q1 2021 was revised upward by +2.2 %pt, the one

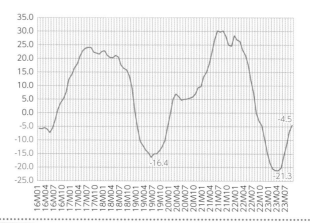

**Figure 2-2-2** Global Semiconductor Sales: 3-month moving average (YoY, %)

Source: World Semiconductor Trade Statistics, September 2023

for Q4 2022 by +1.2 %pt, and the one for Q1 2023 by +1.3 %pt. All of these are substantial upward revisions. On an annual basis, real GDP growth for FY 2022 was revised upward from +1.3% to +1.5%, and from +2.6% to +2.8% for FY 2021.

Looking at contributions to real GDP growth (-0.7% QoQ) in Q3 2023, domestic demand made a negative contribution for the second consecutive quarter at -0.6%pt. Therein, private demand made a negative contribution for the second consecutive quarter (-0.6%pt). Household final consumption expenditure, private residential investment, private non-residential investment, and changes in private inventories all declined. Public demand made a negligible positive contribution for the sixth consecutive quarter (+0.0 %pt). Net exports made a slight negative contribution for the first time in two quarters, (-0.1%pt).

Real gross domestic income (GDI) growth, which includes GDP plus trading gains resulting from changes in the terms of trade, was -0.4% QoQ, exceeding real GDP growth for the fourth consecutive quarter. This was due to the terms of trade improving for the fourth consecutive quarter. Income outflows from households and firms to foreign countries have decelerated (Table 2-2-1).

## Trends in GDP components in Q3 2023

Household final consumption expenditure fell for the second consecutive quarter in 2023 (-0.2% QoQ), and while spending on face-to-face services continued to recover with the end of the pandemic, spending on goods remained sluggish due to a decline in real income caused by inflation.

Looking at the components of household final consumption expenditure (-0.3% QoQ), spending on durable goods, such as passenger cars and household

**Table 2-2-1**  QoQ changes in real GDP and its demand-side components (units: %, % points)

| | Annualized GDP | GDP | Domestic demand | Private demand | Private final consumption expenditure | Private residential investment | Private non-residential investment | Private inventory changes | Public demand | Government final consumption expenditure | Public investment | Public inventory changes | Net exports | Exports | Imports | GDI |
|---|---|---|---|---|---|---|---|---|---|---|---|---|---|---|---|---|
| | | | Contribution | Contribution | | | | Contribution | Contribution | | | | Contribution | Contribution | | |
| 19Q4 | -10.6 | -2.7 | -2.9 | -3.0 | -3.5 | -2.0 | -7.2 | 0.2 | 0.1 | 0.3 | -0.1 | 0.0 | 0.1 | -1.6 | -2.3 | -2.6 |
| 20Q1 | 2.1 | 0.5 | 0.6 | 0.6 | 0.9 | -4.7 | 4.5 | -0.4 | 0.0 | 0.0 | 0.1 | 0.0 | -0.1 | -4.4 | -3.8 | 0.6 |
| 20Q2 | -27.6 | -7.8 | -4.9 | -5.2 | -8.1 | 0.1 | -6.9 | 0.4 | 0.3 | 0.2 | 4.5 | 0.0 | -2.8 | -17.3 | -0.5 | -6.8 |
| 20Q3 | 24.0 | 5.5 | 2.7 | 2.1 | 5.3 | -4.8 | 0.0 | -0.6 | 0.5 | 2.3 | -0.4 | 0.0 | 2.9 | 9.9 | -7.4 | 5.4 |
| 20Q4 | 7.6 | 1.9 | 1.3 | 1.2 | 1.7 | 0.0 | 1.8 | -0.1 | 0.2 | 0.8 | 1.3 | 0.0 | 0.5 | 9.1 | 5.5 | 1.9 |
| 21Q1 | 1.1 | 0.3 | 0.2 | 0.2 | -1.3 | 1.7 | 1.1 | 0.6 | 0.0 | -0.1 | -0.1 | 0.0 | 0.1 | 3.0 | 2.3 | -0.5 |
| 21Q2 | 1.5 | 0.4 | 0.6 | 0.3 | 0.3 | 1.7 | 1.2 | -0.1 | 0.3 | 1.7 | -1.3 | 0.0 | -0.3 | 3.3 | 5.1 | -0.1 |
| 21Q3 | -1.7 | -0.4 | -0.7 | -0.7 | -1.2 | -1.1 | -1.7 | 0.2 | 0.1 | 1.3 | -3.3 | 0.0 | 0.2 | -0.5 | -1.9 | -1.1 |
| 21Q4 | 4.6 | 1.1 | 1.1 | 1.5 | 2.9 | -0.8 | 0.3 | 0.0 | -0.4 | -1.2 | -3.3 | 0.0 | 0.0 | 0.0 | -0.3 | 0.5 |
| 22Q1 | -2.4 | -0.6 | -0.1 | 0.0 | -1.1 | -1.2 | 0.0 | 0.6 | -0.1 | 0.7 | -4.5 | 0.0 | -0.5 | 1.5 | 4.3 | -1.0 |
| 22Q2 | 4.4 | 1.1 | 1.0 | 0.9 | 2.0 | -2.6 | 2.1 | -0.4 | 0.1 | 0.7 | -2.0 | 0.0 | 0.1 | 2.2 | 1.5 | 0.2 |
| 22Q3 | -0.4 | -0.1 | 0.4 | 0.4 | 0.1 | 0.4 | 1.8 | 0.0 | 0.0 | 0.2 | 1.1 | -0.1 | -0.5 | 2.2 | 4.9 | -0.7 |
| 22Q4 | 1.0 | 0.2 | -0.2 | -0.4 | 0.0 | 0.7 | -0.8 | -0.2 | 0.2 | 0.5 | -0.1 | 0.1 | 0.4 | 1.5 | -0.7 | 0.7 |
| 23Q1 | 5.0 | 1.2 | 1.6 | 1.5 | 0.9 | 0.3 | 1.8 | 0.7 | 0.1 | 0.2 | 1.9 | 0.0 | -0.4 | -3.6 | -1.5 | 1.8 |
| 23Q2 | 3.6 | 0.9 | -0.7 | -0.8 | -0.6 | 1.7 | -1.3 | -0.3 | 0.0 | -0.1 | 1.5 | 0.0 | 1.6 | 3.8 | -3.3 | 1.6 |
| 23Q3 | -2.9 | -0.7 | -0.6 | -0.6 | -0.2 | -0.5 | -0.4 | -0.5 | 0.0 | 0.3 | -0.8 | 0.0 | -0.1 | 0.4 | 0.8 | -0.4 |

Note: Domestic demand, private demand, private inventory change, public demand and net exports are contributions. Others are QoQ changes.

Source: National Accounts, Economic and Social Research Institute, Cabinet Office; "Preliminary Quarterly GDP Estimate for Q3 2023 (2nd Preliminary Figures)

durables, declined for the second consecutive quarter (-2.9% QoQ). Spending on semi-durable goods, such as clothing, fell for the first time in two quarters (-3.2% QoQ). Spending on non-durable goods, such as food, also declined for the second consecutive quarter (-0.3% QoQ), partly due to inflation. Meanwhile, spending on services increased for the sixth consecutive quarter (+0.4% QoQ), but growth remained sluggish (less than 1%) for the third consecutive quarter.

Within fixed capital formation, real private residential investment fell for the first time in five quarters(-0.5% QoQ). Real private non-residential investment fell for the second consecutive quarter(-0.4% QoQ). The BOJ's short-term economic survey of Japan (Tankan) shows that companies have a strong appetite for capital investment, but the recovery has been moderate over the past three quarters (January-September).

The contribution of real private inventory changes to real GDP growth was -0.5%pt QoQ, marking the second consecutive quarter of negative growth.

Within public demand, real government final consumption expenditure increased for the first time in two quarters (+0.3% QoQ). Real public fixed capital formation declined for the first time in three quarters (-0.8% QoQ). This is due to the impact of the round of the national land consolidation and supplementary budgets.

The real exports of goods and services increased +0.4% QoQ, marking the second consecutive quarter of positive growth. Therein, the exports of goods increased +0.5% QoQ, marking the second consecutive quarter of positive growth, but the underlying tone was weak. On the other hand, services exports (including direct domestic purchases by non-resident households) fell for the first time in six quarters (-0.3% QoQ). Demand by inbound tourism, i.e. direct domestic purchases by non-resident households, fell -5.0% QoQ, marking the first decline in five quarters. On the other hand, the real imports of goods and services increased for the first time in three quarters, +0.8% QoQ. Therein, goods imports fell for the third consecutive quarter(-0.4% QoQ). On the other hand, the imports of services (including direct purchases abroad by resident households) increased +5.1% QoQ, marking the third consecutive quarterly increase.

Looking at deflators, the domestic demand deflator increased for the 11th consecutive quarter (+0.3% QoQ). Therein, the household final consumption expenditure deflator rose for the 11th consecutive quarter at +0.5%, accelerating somewhat from the previous quarter. The effect of high consumer prices continues to be felt. The private non-residential investment deflator also rose for the 11th consecutive quarter (+0.9%). On the other hand, the private residential investment deflator fell for the fourth consecutive quarter (-0.2%). In terms of external demand deflators, the deflator for exports of goods and services rose for the second consecutive quarter (+2.8%), while the deflator for imports of goods and services rose for the first time in four quarters (+1.9%). The terms of trade improved for the fourth consecutive quarter, but the extent of improvement decelerated. Overall, the GDP deflator rose for the fourth consecutive quarter (+0.5%).

As a result, although real GDP fell -0.7% QoQ (or annualized -2.9% QoQ), while nominal GDP fell by a negligible -0.0% QoQ (or annualized -0.2% QoQ), marking the first decline in four quarters.

## Three consecutive quarters above the pre-pandemic peak

The second official advance estimate of Japan's GDP is characterized by a significant upward revision of the growth rate for the second half of FY2022. As a result, real GDP (JPY 557.4 trillion) in Q1 2023 recovered its pre-pandemic peak (JPY 557.3 trillion in Q3 2019) for the first time, and it has exceeded that peak for three consecutive quarters. Nominal GDP also exceeded its pre-pandemic peak (JPY 561.5 trillion) for the fourth consecutive quarter (Table 2-2-2).

Household final consumption expenditure (-2.3%) and private investment (-4.5%) are still lagging behind, but service exports (+6.7%) have exceeded their pre-pandemic peak for the third consecutive quarter, partly due to a sharp recovery in demand by inbound tourism. Meanwhile, goods imports (-0.9%) fell below their peak for the second consecutive quarter, reflecting weak domestic demand (Table 2-2-2). Although a recovery in household final consumption expenditure is expected, driven by service consumption and the normalization of socioeconomic activities, the real compensation of employees (non-seasonally adjusted) has declined for eight consecutive quarters (YoY), partly due to persistently high inflation. A recovery in consumption will require a turnaround in real wages.

**Table 2-2-2** Adjustment process from the COVID-19 pandemic: Real GDP and its components (pre-pandemic peak=100)

| | GDP | Goods imports | Services imports | Private final consump-tion expen-diture | Private invest-ment | Govern-ment spend-ing | Goods exports | Services exports | Nominal GDP |
|---|---|---|---|---|---|---|---|---|---|
| **19Q3** | 100.0 | 100.0 | 100.0 | 100.0 | 100.0 | 100.0 | 100.0 | 100.0 | 100.0 |
| 19Q4 | 97.3 | 98.2 | 96.1 | 96.5 | 94.9 | 100.2 | 97.9 | 100.3 | 98.0 |
| 20Q1 | 97.7 | 93.7 | 94.7 | 97.4 | 95.4 | 100.3 | 95.6 | 88.7 | 98.7 |
| 20Q2 | 90.2 | 94.8 | 89.4 | 89.5 | 91.8 | 101.3 | 78.1 | 76.7 | 91.5 |
| 20Q3 | 95.1 | 87.2 | 84.7 | 94.2 | 88.5 | 103.1 | 88.9 | 73.3 | 96.3 |
| 20Q4 | 96.9 | 93.7 | 84.3 | 95.9 | 89.4 | 103.9 | 98.3 | 75.1 | 97.8 |
| 21Q1 | 97.2 | 96.1 | 85.4 | 94.6 | 93.7 | 103.8 | 100.8 | 79.1 | 98.1 |
| 21Q2 | 97.5 | 99.4 | 94.6 | 95.0 | 94.4 | 105.0 | 104.7 | 79.7 | 98.6 |
| 21Q3 | 97.1 | 98.3 | 90.7 | 93.9 | 93.8 | 105.4 | 103.9 | 80.6 | 98.1 |
| 21Q4 | 98.2 | 98.1 | 90.0 | 96.6 | 93.7 | 103.8 | 103.9 | 80.3 | 98.9 |
| 22Q1 | 97.6 | 102.7 | 92.3 | 95.6 | 96.3 | 103.5 | 106.4 | 78.3 | 98.8 |
| 22Q2 | 98.7 | 105.0 | 91.6 | 97.5 | 95.6 | 103.8 | 107.8 | 83.3 | 99.7 |
| 22Q3 | 98.6 | 106.6 | 107.6 | 97.6 | 97.2 | 103.9 | 109.4 | 88.1 | 99.3 |
| 22Q4 | 98.8 | 107.2 | 102.3 | 97.6 | 95.6 | 104.6 | 109.3 | 95.5 | 101.0 |
| 23Q1 | 100.0 | 103.8 | 107.7 | 98.4 | 99.9 | 105.1 | 102.9 | 101.1 | 103.3 |
| 23Q2 | 100.9 | 99.5 | 107.8 | 97.8 | 98.0 | 105.2 | 106.3 | 107.0 | 106.0 |
| 23Q3 | 100.2 | 99.1 | 113.3 | 97.7 | 95.5 | 105.4 | 106.8 | 106.7 | 106.0 |

Source: Authors' calculations based on the National Accounts, Economic and Social Research Institute, Cabinet Office, Government of Japan, and the "Preliminary Estimate of Quarterly GDP (Second Preliminary Estimate) for Q3 2023."

## 2. Forecasts for Japan's Economy: FY 2023-2025

### (1) Assumption about exogenous variables

Regarding our assumptions about domestic policy (exogenous variables), we estimate that real public fixed capital formation in Q3 2023 declined -0.8% QoQ, the first decline in three quarters. Based on data by the Ministry of Land, Infrastructure, Transport and Tourism's General Construction Statistics (volume basis), we estimate that public works in September (seasonally adjusted) increased for the first time in two months(+0.4% MoM). As a result, Q3 is estimated to have seen a small but consecutive three-quarter increase of +0.3% QoQ. In virew of these trends, we assume real public fixed capital formation growth of +3.0% in FY 2023, +1.7% in FY 2024, and +0.9% in FY 2025.

On November 10, 2023, the Cabinet approved the FY 2023 supplementary budget. Reflecting these and other current developments, we assume that real government consumption expenditures will grow by +0.9% in FY 2023, +0.3% in FY 2024, and +0.2% in FY 2025.

Of the overseas environment (exogenous variables), the most important are the assumptions concerning crude oil prices, world trade, and exchange rates. The crude oil price (average price of WTI, Dubai, and North Sea Brent) peaked in the Q2 2022 ($109.41) and then declined to $76.54 in the Q2 2023. We expecte the price to reach $80.58 in Q1 2024, $73.08 in Q1 2025, and $78.30 in Q1 2026. The annual average is assumed to be $82.15 in FY 2023, $81.48 in FY 2024, and $75.77 in FY 2025.

The outlook for real world trade is based on S&P Global's Global Economic Outlook, November 2023. In real terms, global exports of goods and services will slow sharply from +6.7% in 2022 to +0.9% in 2023 and will recover to +3.7% in 2024 and +4.5% in 2025.

The U.S. central bank (the Fed) shifted to a tighter monetary stance after March 2022, and maintained its tightening bias at the November 2023 FOMC meeting, although the policy rate range was not raised from the previous meeting to 5.25-5.50%. Investors reacted by assuming that the tightening cycle was over, resulting in lower interest rates and a rebound in equity prices. Meanwhile, at the July Monetary Policy Meeting, the BOJ maintained its current accommodative monetary policy (YCC) but made the long-term interest rate range more flexible, raising the cap to 1.0%. Furthermore, it decided to make another revision in October, but this has not had any impact on the JPY exchange rate. The difference in the monetary policy stance between Japan and the U.S. is likely to keep the JPY weak in the short term. However, the JPY is likely to appreciate gradually. Therefore, we assume exchange rates of 144.0 JPY/USD for FY 2023, 139.8 JPY/USD for FY 2024, and 132.3 JPY/USD for FY 2025 (Table 2-2-3).

| Table 2-2-3 | Summary of APIR's Forecast Results | | | |
|---|---|---|---|---|

| | 2022 | 2023 | 2024 | 2025 |
|---|---|---|---|---|
| Real GDP (%) | 1.5 | 1.7 | 1.4 | 1.1 |
| Private demand (contribution) | 2.0 | -0.0 | 0.9 | 0.9 |
| Private final consumption expenditure (%) | 2.7 | 0.0 | 0.9 | 0.8 |
| Private residential investment (%) | -3.4 | 2.5 | 1.6 | 0.3 |
| Private non-residential investment (%) | 3.4 | -0.1 | 2.1 | 2.9 |
| Private inventory changes (contribution) | 0.1 | -0.3 | 0.1 | 0.0 |
| Public demand (contirbution) | 0.0 | 0.4 | 0.1 | 0.1 |
| Government final consumption expenditure (%) | 1.4 | 0.9 | 0.3 | 0.2 |
| Public investment expenditure (%) | -6.1 | 3.0 | 1.7 | 0.9 |
| Public inventory changes (contribution) | 0.0 | -0.0 | 0.0 | 0.0 |
| External demand (contribution) | -0.5 | 1.4 | 0.4 | 0.1 |
| Exports of goods and services (%) | 4.7 | 4.1 | 3.8 | 2.4 |
| Imports of goods and services (%) | 7.1 | -2.7 | 1.9 | 1.9 |
| Nominal GDP (%) | 2.3 | 5.1 | 1.8 | 2.3 |
| GDP deflator (%) | 0.8 | 3.3 | 0.4 | 1.2 |
| Domestic corporate price index (%) | 9.5 | 2.1 | -0.5 | -0.0 |
| Core consumer price index (%) | 3.1 | 2.8 | 2.0 | 1.4 |
| Industrial production index (%) | -0.3 | -0.5 | 1.1 | 1.6 |
| New housing starts (%) | -0.6 | -5.7 | 0.1 | -0.1 |
| Unemployment rate (%) | 2.6 | 2.6 | 2.5 | 2.4 |
| Current account balance (JPY trillion) | 8.3 | 23.6 | 24.3 | 25.2 |
| % of nominal GDP | 1.5 | 4.0 | 4.0 | 4.1 |
| Crude oil price (USD/barrel) | 92.5 | 82.2 | 81.5 | 75.8 |
| USD/JPY exchange rate | 135.4 | 144.0 | 139.8 | 132.3 |
| USA real GDP (%, calendar year) | 1.9 | 2.5 | 1.5 | 1.5 |

Note: % change from the previous year, others are notes.

## (2) Projected real GDP growth rate: +1.7% in FY 2023, +1.4% in FY 2024, +1.1% in FY 2025

We have revised our outlook for the Japanese economy, incorporating the second official advance GDP estimate for 2023 Q3 as well as our new assumptions concerning exogenous variables (fiscal and monetary policy and variables related to overseas economies). We now forecast real GDP growth of +1.7% in FY 2023, +1.4% in FY 2024, and +1.1% in FY 2025 (Table 2-2-3). On a calendar-year basis, this translates to +2.1% in 2023, +1.3% in 2024, and +1.2% in 2025.

Looking at the contributions to real growth by GDP components, the contribution of private demand will slow down significantly to -0.0%pt in FY 2023 from +2.0%pt in FY 2022. The contribution of public demand, on the other hand, will accelerate to +0.4%pt from -0.0%pt in the previous year. In FY 2024, private demand, public demand, and net exports will prop up the economy by +0.9%pts, +0.1%pts, and +0.4%pts, respectively. In FY 2025, private demand, public demand, and net exports will contribute +0.9%pt, +0.1%pt, and +0.1%pt, respectively (Figure 2-2-3).

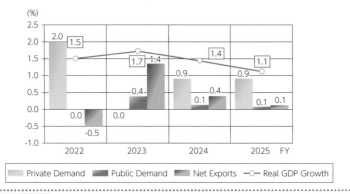

**Figure 2-2-3**    Real GDP Growth Rate and Contribution by Item: %.

Looking at private demand, in FY 2023, real private final consumption expenditure and real private residential investment are expected to make small positive contributions of +0.0%pt and +0.1%pt, respectively. In contrast, real private non-residential investment and real private inventory changes are expected to make negative contributions of -0.0%pt and -0.3%pt. In FY 2024, real household final consumption expenditure, real private residential investment, real private non-residential investment, and real private inventory changes will all make positive contributions of +0.5%pt, +0.1%pt, +0.3%pt, and 0.1%pt, respectively. In FY 2025, real private final consumption expenditure will contribute +0.4 %pt, real private residential investment +0.0%pt, real private non-residential investment +0.5 %pt, and real private inventory changes +0.0%pt (Figure 2-2-4).

In the second official advnace estimate, the second half of FY 2022 was revised upward, and the carry-over effect in the growth rate for FY 2023 was raised. Therefore, looking at real GDP (actual and forecast) on a quarterly basis, the level will be raised, but the growth rate pattern will not change significantly compared to the previous forecast (Figure 2-2-5).

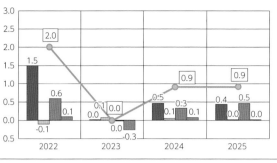

**Figure 2-2-4**  Contributions to GDP growth by the components of private demand (units: %pt).

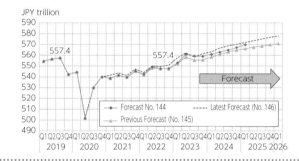

**Figure 2-2-5**  Quarterly GDP: Actual and Forecast (units: JPY trillion)

Note: Actual figures through Q3 2023, projected figures thereafter.

## (3) Household Sector: Zero growth in FY 2023 household consumption due to delayed growth in real wages.

With the normalization of socioeconomic activities, the forced savings accumulated during the COVID-19 pandemic were gradually directed toward service consumption expenditures. However, the acceleration and elevation of CPI inflation suppresses the growth of real disposable income, making spending on goods consumption selective. In fact, real household final consumption expenditure declined for the second consecutive quarter in Q3 2023. Growth in real disposable income is essential for a sustained recovery in household consumption.

According to the Monthly Labor Survey by the Ministry of Health, Labor and Welfare's (final, all industries, establishments of 5 or more employees), nominal wages in October increased YoY for the 22nd consecutive month (+1.5%). However, real wages declined for the 19th consecutive month, falling -2.3% YoY (Figure 2-2-6). As a result, nominal wages in Q3 increased +0.9% YoY for the 10th consecutive quarter, while real wages declined -2.8% YoY for the 6th consecutive quarter.

In the wage hikes resulting from the 2023 annual wage negotiations was +3.60% (+2.20% in 2022), the highest since 1993 (+3.90%) (Ministry of Health, Labor and Welfare's "Status of Spring Wage Increase Demands and Compromises by Major Private Corporations"). Although wage hikes exceeding this level are expected next year, on an all-industry and all-size basis, scheduled salaries have grown in the 1% YoY range since May 2023.

Since consumer price inflation will slow only moderately from the second half of FY 2023 onward, a positive reversal in real wage growth is not expected until FY 2025 or later. As a result of these trends, we forecast that real household final consumption expenditure will grow +0.0% in FY 2023, +0.9% in FY2024, and +0.9% in FY 2025.

According to the Ministry of Land, Infrastructure, Transport and Tourism, new housing starts in September decreased by -6.8% YoY, marking the fourth consecutive monthly decline. The seasonally adjusted figure was -1.5% MoM, the first decline in two months. As a result, Q3 starts fell -2.2% QoQ for the second consecutive quarter. On the other hand, planned construction expenditure (1 x residential construction + 0.7 x combined residential-industrial construction), which well explains GDP-based private residential investment, increased YoY by 3.1% in September, marking the fifth consecutive month of growth. The seasonally adjusted figure (APIR estimate) was -3.1% MoM, the first decline in two

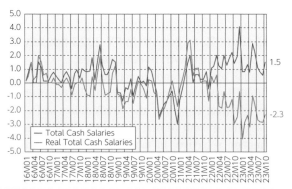

**Figure 2-2-6**    Total Wages: % change from the same month last year

Source: "Monthly Labor Survey," Ministry of Health, Labor and Welfare months. As a result, the Q3 fuigure is likely to have decreased -1.2% QoQ, the first decline in three quarters.

Reflecting the current peak-out of housing construction cost inflation, real private residential investment in FY2023 will turn positive at +2.5% but will not recover from the previous year's decline (-3.4%.) We forecast a moderate recovery at +1.6% in FY2024 and +0.3% in FY2025.

## (4) Corporate Sector: Despite strong potential for investment growth, actual growth likely to be moderate due to supply constraints

According to the Ministry of Economy, Trade and Industry's (METI), the Indicex of Industrial Production (seasonally adjusted; 2020=100) rose +1.3% MoM in October, reaching 104.9, and marking the second consecutive month of increase (Figure 2-2-7). As a result, the October value rose +1.4% over the Q3 average. METI maintained the underlying tone of production at "steady" for the third consecutive month. According to the Survey of Production Forecasts for Manufacturers (preliminary basis), manufacturing output in November is expected to decline -0.3% MoM, but it is expected to rise +3.2% MoM in December. If the forecast is accurate, Q4 production will rise +1.9% QoQ.

Factoring in these current conditions, we forecast the Index of Industrial Production for FY 2023 to decline -0.5% YoY, and then to increase +1.1% in FY 2024, and +1.6% in FY 2025.

The Tertiary Industry Activity Index (seasonally adjusted, 2015 average=100) fell for the second consecutive month in October to -0.8% MoM. As a result, in October the index was -1.3% lower than the Q3 average (Q3: +0.8% QoQ). METI revised its assessment of the economy downward from the

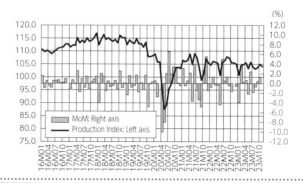

**Figure 2-2-7**    Indices of Industrial Production (seasonally adjusted, 2020=100)

Source: "Indices of Industrial Production," Ministry of Economy, Trade and Industry previous month, stating that the economy "appears to have stalled" (Figure 2-2-8). Therein, the index for the face-to-face service industry (2015 average=100) fell -0.5% MoM in October, marking the third consecutive monthly decline. As a result, in October the index was -2.6% lower than the Q3 average (Q3: +3.7% QoQ).

According to the Q2 2023 Survey of Corporate Business Enterprises released by the Ministry of Finance, ordinary profits (seasonally adjusted, excluding the financial and insurance sectors) for all industries increased by 9.5% QoQ for the second consecutive quarter (Q1: +7.4% QoQ). This was the record-high profits. In the manufacturing sector, the increase was +12.5% QoQ, the second consecutive quarterly increase. In the non-manufacturing, it was +8.0%, the third consecutive quarterly increase.

Corporate earnings remain at high levels, and there is strong potential for expansion, especially in response to labor shortages and investment in digital technologies (DX). Downside risks are the growing uncertainty about the economic outlook due to the slowdown in overseas economies and supply constraints for capital goods.

Looking at investment-related indicators, the capital goods shipments index rose for the second consecutive month in October, by +3.7% MoM (Figure 2-2-9). As a result, October saw an increase of +3.0% over the Q3 average.

According to the Cabinet Office, Core Machinery Orders (private demand excluding ships and power: seasonally adjusted), a leading indicator of private

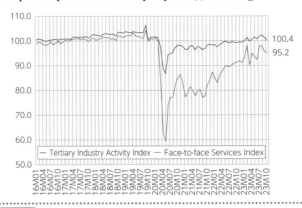

**Figure 2-2-8**    Face-to-face Services vs. Tertiary Industry Activity Index (2015=100)

Note: The face-to-face services index is a weighted average of the transportation, accommodation, restaurants, food services, other lifestyle-related services, and entertainment industry indexes; the tourism-related index is a weighted average of the tourism-related index of the face-to-face services index. 2015 average =100.

Source: Tertiary Industry Activity Index, Ministry of Economy, Trade and Industry

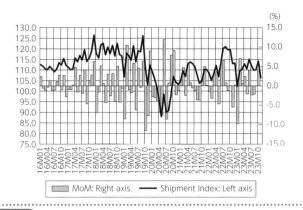

**Figure 2-2-9**    Capital Goods Shipment Index (seasonally adjusted, 2020=100)

Source: "Indices of Industrial Production," Ministry of Economy, Trade and Industry

capital investment, increased for the second consecutive month in October (+0.7% MoM). As a result, October saw an increase of +1.5% over the Q3 average (Q3: -1.8% QoQ).

According to the outlook survey conducted at the end of Q3, private-sector demand for Q4 is expected to decrease for the first time in two quarters (-4.7% QoQ). Public-sector demand (+7.6% QoQ) and demand by public-sector agencies (+1.5% QoQ) are expected to increase, while external demand is expected to decline for the first time in three quarters (-3.8% QoQ). Potential investment demand is strong, but the actual state of current capital investment is highly uncertain.

Real private non-residential investment in FY 2023 is projected to decline -0.1% YoY, but to then recover by +2.1% in FY 2024 and +2.9% in FY 2025.

## (5) External Sector: FY 2023 net exports revised upward due to improved terms of trade and recovery of inbound tourism demand

According to preliminary Trade Statistics released by the Ministry of Finance, the November trade balance was -776.9 billion yen, a deficit for the second consecutive month despite a contraction of -62.2% YoY over last year's deficit. The seasonally adjusted figure was -408.9 billion yen, the 30th consecutive monthly deficit, although the deficit margin narrowed by -18.4% MoM (the first negative figure in two months). As a result, the October-November average trade deficit contracted by -12.6% from the Q3 average.

Exports (seasonally adjusted) in November fell by -1.8% MoM for the second consecutive month, while imports (seasonally adjusted) shrank by -2.7% MoM, also for the second consecutive month. Comparing the October-November average with the Q3 average, however, both exports and imports increased by +1.2% and +0.4%, respectively.

On a volume basis (seasonally adjusted, APIR estimates), the export volume index fell for the second consecutive month in November (-4.2% MoM), while the import volume index declined for the first time in three months (-3.4% MoM). Compared to the Q3 average, the October-November average of the export volume index fell by -4.4% and the import volume index fell by -0.1%. The October-November average contribution of real net goods exports of to GDP growth was negative.

By region, November exports (seasonally adjusted by APIR) to Asia shrank by -2.8% MoM, to China by -0.4% MoM, to the U.S. by -5.1% MoM, and to the EU by -9.6% MoM. Comparing the October-November average to the Q3average, the decline rate was -5.1% to Asia, -1.6% to China, -3.3% to the US, and -7.9% to the EU. Exports to the U.S. have been strong so far due to the pickup in the U.S. economy, but exports to key regions are in a general decline at present (Figure 2-2-11). On the other hand, in November, imports from Asia declined by -4.6%, from China by -5.7%, from the U.S. by -3.7%, and from the EU by -0.7% MoM. Compared to the Q3 average, the October-November average was -1.7% lower for imports from Asia, but +3.1% higher for imports from China, +2.8% higher for imports from the U.S., and +5.3% higher for imports from the EU (Figure 2-2-10).

Considering these factors, real exports of goods and services in FY2023 are projected to grow by +4.1% YoY in FY 2023, by +3.8% YoY in FY 2024, and by +2.4 YoY in FY2025. Real imports of goods and services are projected to decline by

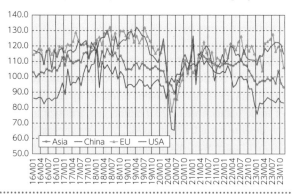

**Figure 2-2-10**    Export Volume Index by Region (2020=100)

Source: Trade Statistics, Ministry of Finance; seasonally adjusted values are APIR estimates.

-2.7% YoY in FY 2023, but then to increase by +1.9% YoY in FY 2024, and by +1.9% YoY in FY 2025.

In value terms, the trade deficit margin is likely to narrow as the terms of trade improve. A sharp recovery in inbound tourism demand will contribute to a narrowing of the deficit margin in the services balance. As the primary income balance is expected to remain positive and large, the current account balance is projected to be +JPY 23.6 trillion in FY 2023, +JPY 24.3 trillion in FY 2024, and +JPY 25.2 trillion in FY 2025,

---

## (6) Price trends: Goods prices down, services prices up

According to the Bank of Japan, the domestic corporate goods price index (2020 average=100) rose YoY for the 33rd consecutive month in November (+0.3%) but has slowed for 11 consecutive months. The figure remained below 1% for the second consecutive month (Figure 2-2-11).

The dollar-yen exchange rate (monthly average) for November was 149.83 yen, up 5.2% YoY, marking the 33rd consecutive month of yen depreciation. As a result, the JPY-based export price index (2020 average=100) rose +4.7% YoY, marking for the fourth consecutive month of increase. The JPY-based import price index (2020 average=100) fell -6.1%, marking the eighth consecutive month of decline. As a result, the terms of trade index (export price index/import price index*100) stood at 81.7 (2020 average=100) in November, up 8.4 points from the same month last year, marking the eighth consecutive month of improvement (Figure 2-2-12).

According to the Ministry of Internal Affairs and Communications, the

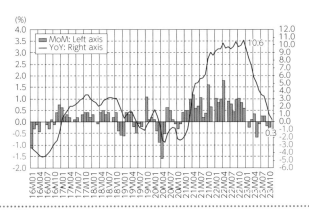

**Figure 2-2-11**    Domestic Corporate Goods Price Index (2020=100)

Source: Bank of Japan, Domestic corporate goods price index

National Consumer Price Index (2020 average=100) rose YoY for the 27th consecutive month in November (+2.8%). The core index excluding volatile fresh food rose for the 27th consecutive month (+2.5%), and inflation remained in the 2% range for the third consecutive month. The core-core index excluding fresh food and energy rose for the 20th consecutive month (+3.8%). Inflation also slowed for the third consecutive month (Figure 2-2-13).

Looking at the components of the National Consumer Price Index in November YoY, energy prices declined YoY for the 10th consecutive month, falling -10.1%. Their contribution to the index was -0.87%. This is due to government measures to curb electricity and gas prices, as a result of which electricity bills

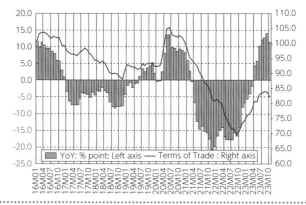

Figure 2-2-12    Terms of Trade (2020=100)

Source: Authors' calculations based on Bank of Japan, Domestic corporate goods price index.

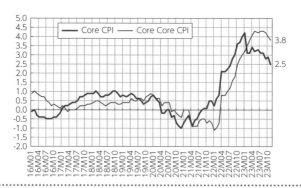

Figure 2-2-13    National Consumer Price Index (2020=100; % change from the same month last year)

Source: Authors' calculations based on "National Consumer Price Index," Ministry of Internal Affairs and Communications

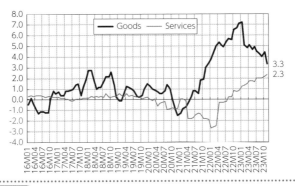

**Figure 2-2-14**    National Consumer Price Index by Cetegory (% change from the same month last year)

Source: Authors' calculations based on "National Consumer Price Index," Ministry of Internal Affairs and Communications

fell for the 10th consecutive month (-18.1% YoY), and gas bills in urban areas fell for the sixth consecutive month (-16.8% YoY). According to the Ministry of Internal Affairs and Communications, the impact (contribution) of the "sudden fluctuations in electricity and gas prices" was -0.49%. Non-energy prices increased for the 20th consecutive month at +4.1%. The contribution to overall CPI inflation was +3.67%. Therein, food prices (excluding fresh food) rose for the 29th consecutive month (+6.7%). Food inflation, however, decelerated for the third consecutive month. Its contribution to overall CPI inflation was +1.56%.

By category, goods prices increased YoY for the 31st consecutive month (+3.3%). The contribution of goods prices to total inflation was 1.76%. Goods prices peaked in January 2023 (+7.2% YoY) and have been on a decelerating trend. Services prices rose for the 16th consecutive month (+2.3%). The contribution to total inflation was +1.08%. Among service expenditures, the increase in hotel rates was impressive (+62.9% YoY). Hotel rates kept rising for the eighth consecutive months due to strong inbound travel. The contribution to total inflation was +0.45%.

Considering the current situation, the domestic corporate goods price index is projected to increase by +2.1% in FY 2023, but then decline by -0.5% in FY 2024, and -0.0% in FY 2025.

Although goods prices turned to a downtrend due to the fall in import prices, due to the rise in service prices, consumer price inflation is expected to remain high, in the 3% range, in the first half of FY 2023 but it is likely to decelerate in the second half of the year. As a result, we forecast core CPI inflation to be +2.8% in FY 2023, +2.0% in FY 2024, and +1.4% in FY 2025.

The GDP deflator is projected to be +3.3% in FY 2023, +0.4% in FY 2024,

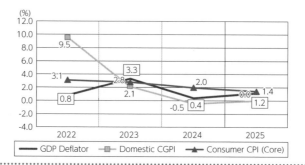

**Figure 2-2-15**    Trends in Prices (% change from the previous year)

and +1.2% in FY 2025, with a slowdown in FY 2024-25 as the terms of trade are expected to improve (Figure 2-2-15).

## Section 3
# THE KANSAI ECONOMY:
## RECENT DEVELOPMENTS AND SHORT-TERM FORECASTS

*IRIE, Hiroaki; INADA, Yoshihisa*

## 1. Retrospective of the Kansai economy in FY 2022 and the first half of FY 2023

In FY 2022, the Kansai economy generally picked up as socioeconomic activities normalized, and although the number of new COVID-19 infections reached the sixth and seventh waves during FY 2022, no emergency declarations or other strict behavioral restrictions were imposed. In May 2023, the handling of COVID-19 was shifted to category 5, and economic and social activities have returned to normal and become more active. FY 2023 also saw a continued pickup, but the pace of recovery was slow, and some signs of deterioration were evident.

Below is a sector-by-sector retrospective of the Kansai economy in FY 2022 and beyond, focusing on monthly economic indicators.

### (1) Household sector

The household sector in the Kansai region picked up moderately in FY 2022. Sentiment, large retail sales, the employment environment, and the housing market all held up well, partly due to more relaxed action restrictions on the COVID-19 infection expansion compared to the previous year. However, households were faced with higher consumer prices for a wide range of items, particularly food and energy. As a result, real wages continued to deteriorate. In FY 2023, the gradual recovery continued, but growth remained sluggish due to weak trends in income and employment conditions and sentiment.

### Consumer Sentiment

The FY 2022 Consumer Confidence Index was 31.6, down 4.4 points from the previous year, marking the first deterioration in two years (Figure 2-3-1). Although the level was higher than in FY 2020 (29.7), when the COVID-19 pandemic began, sentiment deteriorated as the number of new positives increased in the 6th and 7th waves. However, it subsequently began to recover, mainly due to the government's emphasis on maintaining economic and social activities and not imposing behavioral restrictions; it reached 38.3 in May 2023, the highest level since the COVID-19 pandemic, but has remained weak and sluggish ever since.

**Figure 2-3-1**    Consumer Confidence Index

Source: Cabinet Office, "Survey of Consumption Trends"

## Income environment

The income environment continued to show steady growth in nominal terms but continued to decline in real terms due to high prices (Figure 2-3-2), with gross nominal wages in Kansai in FY 2022 (APIR estimate) averaging JPY 318,361 per month. This was an increase of 2.2% YoY, marking the second consecutive year of year-on-year growth. Real wages (i.e. excluding the effect of price fluctuations based on the consumer price index) were down 1.4% from the previous year. The Kansai region is also facing rising consumer prices, and wage growth is not keeping pace with the growth in prices.

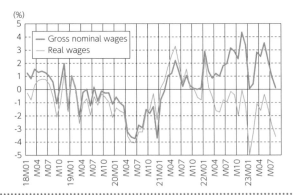

**Figure 2-3-2**    Gross Nominal Wages and Real Wages (% change from the same month of the previous year)

Source: Ministry of Health, Labour and Welfare, "Monthly Labor Survey," etc.

## Employment environment

The employment environment picked up as socioeconomic activities normalized (Figure 2-3-3), and the ratio of job offers to applicants in the Kansai region in FY 2022 was 1.19, up 0.11 points from the previous year, marking the first improvement in two years. The national ratio for FY 2022 was 1.31. On a monthly basis, the Kansai region had been improving for 14 consecutive months since November 2021, but since the beginning of 2023, the number of job openings has remained almost unchanged. While job openings in the accommodation/restaurant and retail sectors are increasing, those in the manufacturing and construction sectors, which are facing cost increases, are being held down, with the trend differing somewhat by industry sector.

## Large retailers' sales

Large- retailers' sales recovered due in part to a recovery in customer traffic and higher prices (Figure 2-3-4). The overall sales of large retailers in the Kansai region in FY 2022 totaling JPY 3,744.8 billion, up 7.2%, the second consecutive year of YoY growth and above the FY 2019 level. The growth is higher than that of the nation as a whole (+4.5% YoY).

Therein, department store sales (on an all-store basis) totaled JPY 1,429.8 billion, up 20.5% from the previous year, marking the second consecutive year of year-on-year growth, and have been recovering steadily since 2023 on the back of a recovery in customer traffic. In addition, supermarket sales totaled JPY 2,307.4 billion. YoY, sales increased for the first time in seven years, up 0.3%.

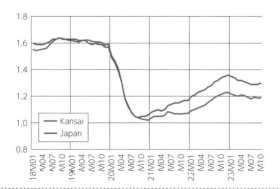

| Figure 2-3-3 | Effective Job Openings to Applicants Ratio (Seasonally Adjusted) |

Source: Ministry of Health, Labour and Welfare, "General Job Placement Situation"

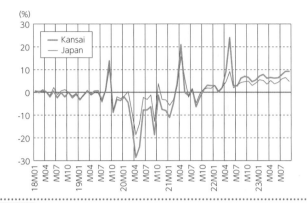

**Figure 2-3-4**    Department store and supermarket sales (YoY: %)

Note: Based on all stores
Source: Kansai Bureau of Economy, Trade and Industry, "Department Store and Supermarket Sales"

## (2) Corporate Sector

In FY 2022, the corporate sector in the Kansai region showed different trends among industries. In the manufacturing sector, both production and business confidence were weak due to soaring raw material prices and a slowdown in overseas economies. On the other hand, the non-manufacturing sector generally recovered with the resumption of economic activity, especially in face-to-face services such as lodging, food services, and retail.

### Business confidence

According to the Bank of Japan's Osaka Branch Tankan survey, the Diffusion Index (DI) for business conditions in Kansai (firms of all sizes in all industries) was positive for the eighth consecutive quarter as of the December 2023 survey (Figure 2-3-5). Compared to the nation as a whole, there is no significant difference. By industry, the manufacturing sector has been in and out of the vicinity of zero since 2022. The non-manufacturing sector recovered steadily, especially in face-to-face services.

### Industrial production

The production index has been sluggish due to the global shortage of semiconductors and soaring raw material prices (Figure 2-3-6). The production index for FY 2022 was 93.5 (2015=100, seasonally adjusted). This was -2.2% from the previous year, the first decline in production in two years. The trend is similar to the national level. The electronic components/devices industry, ceramic/soil

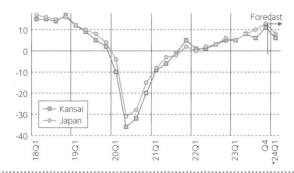

**Figure 2-3-5** DI for business conditions in the Bank of Japan's Tankan survey (all sizes, all industries)

Note: * denotes that it is a forecast.
Source: Bank of Japan, Osaka Branch, "Tankan: Short-term Economic Survey of Enterprises"

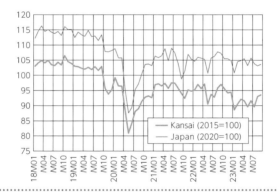

**Figure 2-3-6** Indices of Industrial Production (seasonally adjusted)

Source: Kansai Bureau of Economy, Trade and Industry, "Kansai Region Industrial Production Trends"

and stone products industry, and plastic products industry contributed to the overall decline in production, which has continued to fluctuate since 2023.

## Capital investment

According to the Bank of Japan's December 2023 Tankan survey, capital investment by companies in the Kansai region in FY 2022 (all sizes and all industries) was up 8.7% from the previous year (Table 2-3-1). Growth was high, especially in the manufacturing sector. The planned investment in FY 2023 is +6.0% over the previous year, which is a modest increase compared to the previous year's growth, but still shows an aggressive stance.

| Table 2-3-1 | | BOJ Tankan: Planned Capital Investment | | | | |

| | Kansai | | | Japan | | |
|---|---|---|---|---|---|---|
| | All indus-tries | Manufac-turing | Non-manu-facturing | All indus-tries | Manufac-turing | Non-manu-facturing |
| FY 2022 | **8.7** | 14.4 | 5.1 | **9.2** | 9.0 | 9.3 |
| FY 2023 | **6.0** | 7.0 | 5.4 | **12.8** | 14.6 | 11.7 |

Source: Bank of Japan, Osaka Branch, "Tankan: Short-term Economic Survey of Enterprises (Kansai Region)"

## (3) External Sector

For the external sector, we focus on trade in goods and exports of services (inbound tourism demand). Both exports and imports of goods increased for the second consecutive year. As for exports of services, a remarkable recovery was seen as a result of the increase in the number of foreign visitors to Japan following the substantial easing of waterfront measures such as the removal of the cap on the number of people entering Japan.

### Trade in goods

Both imports and exports in FY 2022 set new FY records for the second year in a row (Figure 2-3-7). The price changes for both imports and exports were significant due to rising resource prices and the depreciation of the yen. Exports totaled JPY 21,729.1 billion, up 13.0% from the previous year, marking the second consecutive year of growth. Mineral fuels and steel contributed to the increase. However, this growth was modest compared to that in exports for the nation as a whole (+15.5% YoY). Exports to China were higher in the Kansai region than in the nation as a whole, and the impact of the zero-COVID policy is thought to

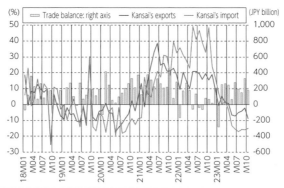

| Figure 2-3-7 | | Exports, imports, and trade balance |

Source: Osaka Customs, "The Summary Report on Trade of Kansai"

have had a large impact. Exports to the U.S., the EU, and China respectively increased YoY by 29.4%, 16.1%, and 4.0% (Figure 2-3-8). While exports to Europe and the U.S. were relatively firm, those to China gradually declined due to the impact of the zero-COVID policy lockdown. Since FY 2023, the trend has been weak due to the contraction of world trade.

Imports totaled JPY 20,958.7 billion, up 26.2% YoY, marking the second consecutive year of year-on-year increase, as did exports. Crude oil, natural gas, and manufactured gas increased, and imports have been declining since the second half of FY 2022, as the sharp rise in crude oil prices has subsided.

The trade balance was +JPY 771 billion, the eighth consecutive year of surplus, but the surplus was smaller than that of the previous year (+JPY 2.6 trillion).

## Inbound tourism demand

A remarkable recovery was seen in the number of international visitors to Japan due to the significant relaxation of border control measures, including the removal of the cap on the number of visitors to Japan.

According to the Ministry of Justice, the number of international visitors to Japan in FY 2022 was 9,029,000 nationwide, of which 2,042,000 entered Japan from Kansai International Airport (Figure 2-3-9). Since October 2022, the number of international visitors to Japan have increased rapidly due to the significant relaxation of the COVID-19 border control measures by the Japanese government. The number of visitors reached 656,000 in October 2023, surpassing for the first time the level of the same month in 2019 (652,000), the month before the COVID-19 pandemic.

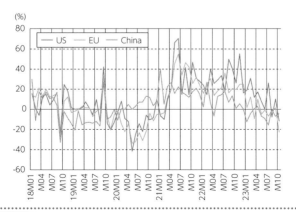

| Figure 2-3-8 | Exports by region (YoY) |

Source: Osaka Customs, "The Summary Report on Trade of Kansai"

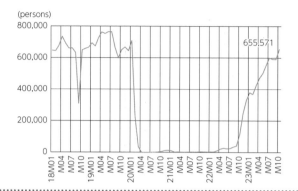

Figure 2-3-9  Number of foreign visitors to Japan via Kansai International Airport

Source: Ministry of Justice, "Immigration Statistics"

Department store duty-free sales also continue to pick up (Figure 2-3-10). According to the Osaka branch of the Bank of Japan, duty-free sales at department stores in the Kansai region almost tripled in FY 2022, up 201.8% from the previous year. The depreciation of the yen boosted sales of cosmetics and high-end products, etc. Duty-free sales exceeded the same month in 2019, which was before the COVID-19 pandemic, in June 2023, and reached a record single month in October of the same year.

## (4) Public sector

The public sector (public works) in the Kansai region remained steady compared to the nation as a whole.

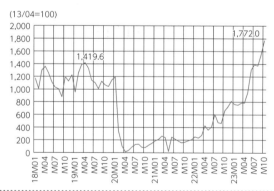

Figure 2-3-10  Department store duty-free sales (April 2013=100)

Source: Bank of Japan, Osaka Branch, "Department Store Duty Free Sales (Kansai Region)"

In FY 2022, the value of the completed public works in the Kansai region totaled JPY 3,016.5 billion, a YoY increase of 9.4% (Figure 2-3-11). This is the fourth consecutive year of YoY increase since FY 2019, when retroactive data became available. On a monthly basis, the Kansai region posted year-on-year growth for 21 consecutive months from July 2021 to March 2023. Large-scale public investment projects, such as the development of land on Yumeshima, the site of the Osaka-Kansai Expo, the Shinmeishin Expressway, and the Yodogawa Left Bank Route, have been progressing, and in FY 2023, the region continued to show steady growth, exceeding the previous year's level. The value of completed public works in nationwide was JPY 21,783.7, an increase of 1.1% YoY.

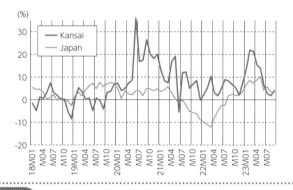

**Figure 2-3-11**    Public works output (YoY)

Source: Ministry of Land, Infrastructure, Transport and Tourism, "General Construction Statistics"

## 2. Kansai Economic Forecast: FY 2023-25

The forecast of the Kansai economy for FY 2023-25, reflecting the latest economic indicators in and out of the Kansai region, including the second preliminary GDP report for Q3 2023, and the forecast results of the Japanese economy.

### (1) Kansai GRP growth forecast: FY 2023 +1.3%, FY 2024 +1.6%, FY 2025 +1.4%.

We forecast that Kansai's real GRP growth will be +1.3% in FY 2023, +1.6% in FY 2024, and +1.4% in FY 2025 (Table 2-3-2, Figure 2-3-12). Actual forecasts for past years are +2.5% for FY 2021 and +1.4% for FY 2022, with moderate growth in the 1% range from FY 2022 onward, recovering to pre-COVID-19 pandemic levels in FY 2023.

**Table 2-3-2**    Results Table of Kansai Economic Forecast

| FY | 2021 | 2022 | 2023 | 2024 | 2025 |
|---|---|---|---|---|---|
| Private final consumption expenditure | 1.6 | 2.6 | 0.4 | 1.1 | 0.8 |
| Private residential investment | ▲ 1.5 | 3.6 | 1.2 | 0.1 | 1.3 |
| Private non-residential capital investment | 1.2 | 1.6 | 2.1 | 2.3 | 2.8 |
| Government final consumption expenditure | 3.0 | 1.1 | 0.7 | 0.3 | 0.4 |
| Public fixed capital formation | ▲ 1.5 | 0.8 | 4.0 | 2.9 | 2.4 |
| Exports | 8.4 | 2.7 | 0.7 | 2.1 | 3.4 |
| Imports | 4.1 | 6.0 | 0.1 | 1.3 | 3.2 |
| Real GRP | 2.5 | 1.4 | 1.3 | 1.6 | 1.4 |
| Private demand (contribution) | 1.0 | 2.1 | 0.6 | 1.1 | 1.0 |
| Public demand (contribution) | 0.4 | 0.2 | 0.4 | 0.3 | 0.2 |
| Net exports (contribution) | 1.0 | ▲ 0.9 | 0.3 | 0.2 | 0.2 |
| Nominal GRP | 2.3 | 2.0 | 4.3 | 1.9 | 2.9 |
| GRP deflator | ▲ 0.1 | 0.5 | 3.0 | 0.3 | 1.4 |
| Consumer Price Index | 0.0 | 2.8 | 2.8 | 2.1 | 1.6 |
| Industrial Production Index | 5.2 | ▲ 2.2 | ▲ 0.0 | 1.1 | 1.6 |
| Unemployment rate | 3.0 | 2.9 | 3.0 | 2.9 | 2.8 |

Note: Unit %, except for Unemployment rate, is the growth rate from the previous year; FY 2021-22 is the actual forecast; FY 2023-25 is the forecast.
Source: Prepared by the author

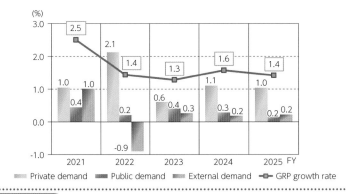

**Figure 2-3-12**    GRP Forecast Results and Contribution to Growth

Source: Prepared by the author

Let us look at the contribution of each demand item to growth. Private demand will be the driver of growth with +0.6 %pts in FY 2023, +1.1 %pts in FY 2024, and +1.0 %pts in FY 2025. Public demand will also support growth by +0.4 %pts in FY 2023, +0.3 %pts in FY 2024, and +0.2 %pts in FY 2025. External demand will be weak, at +0.3 %pts in FY 2023, +0.2 %pts in FY 2024, and +0.2 %pts in FY 2025.

Comparing the Kansai and Japan economic forecasts, the growth rate for FY 2023 will be lower in Kansai than in the nation as a whole but will be higher in Kansai in FY 2024-25 (Figure 2-3-13). Private demand and public demand, especially capital investment, will be stronger than in the nation as a whole.

## (2) Forecasts by sector
## (1) Private sector

The breakdown of the contribution of private demand to GRP growth will be +0.2 %pts in FY 2023, +0.6 %pts in FY 2024, and +0.5 %pts in FY 2025 for the household sector. The corporate sector will be +0.4 %pts in FY 2023, +0.5 %pts in FY 2024, and +0.5 %pts in FY 2025.

In the household sector, real private final consumption expenditures is projected to grow by 0.4% in FY 2023, +1.1% in FY 2024, and +0.8% in FY 2025. Real private residential investment is projected to increase by 1.2% in FY 2023, +0.1% in FY 2024, and +1.3% in FY 2025. Both household consumption and housing investment are expected to recover at a slower pace, due to the thriftiness associated with high prices and sluggish growth in real wages.

Real private capital investment, which accounts for the bulk of the corporate sector, is forecast to grow by 2.1% in FY 2023, 2.3% in FY 2024, and 2.8% in FY 2025. Private capital investment plans continue to be on the rise, and this will continue to support growth in the future.

## (2) Public sector

The contribution of public demand to real GRP growth is forecast to be +0.4 %pts

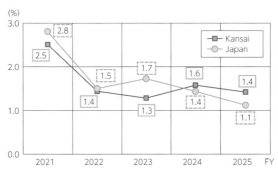

**Figure 2-3-13**    Economic Growth Rates in Kansai and Nationwide

Source: Prepared by the author

in FY 2023, +0.3 %pts in FY 2024, and +0.2 %pts in FY 2025.

Real Government final consumption expenditure growth is expected to be +0.7% in FY 2023, +0.3% in FY 2024, and +0.4% in FY 2025. And, real public fixed capital formation is expected to grow by +4.0% in FY 2023, +2.9% in FY 2024, and +2.4% in FY 2025. From FY 2024 onward, public investment growth in the Kansai region is expected to exceed that of the nation as a whole in preparation for the hosting of the World Exposition.

### (3) External sector

The contribution of extraterrestrial demand to real GRP growth is expected to be small, at +0.3 %pts in FY 2023, +0.2 %pts in FY 2024, and +0.2 %pts in FY 2025.

Real export growth is projected to be +0.7% in FY 2023, +2.1% in FY 2024, and +3.4% in FY 2025. The Japanese Economic forecasts export growth of +4.1% in FY 2023 and +3.8% in FY 2024, which is lower than the Kansai Economic forecast. Kansai's exports to China were below the previous year's level in the first half of FY 2023, reflecting the large weight of exports to China in the Kansai region, which has a large impact, both positive and negative. Real import growth is projected to be +0.1% in FY 2023, +1.3% in FY 2024, and +3.2% in FY 2025, reflecting current performance and weak domestic demand. As a result, the contribution of net exports to real GRP growth will be +0.2 %pts in FY 2023, +0.3 %pts in FY 2024, and +0.1 %pts in FY 2025.

The contribution of real domestic net exports is projected to be +0.1 %pts in FY 2023, -0.1 %pts in FY 2024, and +0.1 %pts in FY 2025.

### (4) Employment and income environment

The Unemployment rate is projected to gradually improve to 3.0% in FY 2023, 2.9% in FY 2024, and 2.8% in FY 2025.

Growth in per capita employment income is expected to be moderate, at +1.3% in FY 2023, +1.4% in FY 2024, and +1.9% in FY 2025. Growth in the CPI is expected to slow gradually, to +2.7% in FY 2023, +2.1% in FY 2024, and +1.5% in FY 2025. As a result, real wage growth will be -1.5% in FY 2023, -0.7% in FY 2024, and +0.3% in FY 2025. It will take until FY 2025 for real wages to turn positive.

## 3. Recovery process from COVID-19 pandemic in Kansai prefectures: GRP advance estimation

In Japan, official prefectural GRP figures are released about two years later than the release of the national GDP figure. For that reason, APIR has been making its own advance estimates of the actual GRPs for the six prefectures in

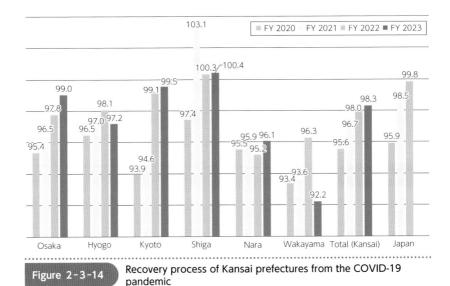

FY 2020   FY 2021   FY 2022   FY 2023

**Figure 2-3-14** Recovery process of Kansai prefectures from the COVID-19 pandemic

Source: APIR "Kansai Economic Insight Quarterly," No. 66

the Kansai region for previous years that have not yet been published.

Figure 2-3-14 shows the change from FY 2020-23 when the FY 2019 GRP for each prefecture is set at 100.

In FY 2020, when the COVID-19 pandemic began, the largest decrease in GRP was seen in Wakayama Prefecture (-6.6 points), followed by Kyoto (-6.1 points), Osaka (-4.6 points), Nara (-4.5 points), Hyogo (-3.5 points), and Shiga (-2.6 points). The Kansai region (six prefectures) saw a decline of -4.4 points.

Looking at the next two years, FY 2021-22, when the COVID-19 pandemic continued, Hyogo, Kyoto, Osaka, and Wakayama prefectures reversed their positive trend. Shiga Prefecture recovered to its pre-COVID-19 level in FY 2021. On the other hand, unlike other prefectures, Nara Prefecture is not on a recovery track and has been slow to recover from the COVID-19 pandemic.

FY 2023 is also entering a new phase for each prefecture. Osaka and Kyoto prefectures will maintain their recovery pace, and Shiga will also maintain its pre-COVID-19 level. Hyogo and Wakayama prefectures will deteriorate from the previous year, and recovery from the COVID-19 pandemic will be delayed. Nara Prefecture has been stagnant since the COVID-19 pandemic and shows little signs of recovery.

Finally, the contribution of each prefecture to the growth rate of the Kansai economy in FY 2020-23 is shown in Figure 2-3-15. In FY 2020, under the economic impact of COVID-19, the negative contribution of each Kansai prefecture

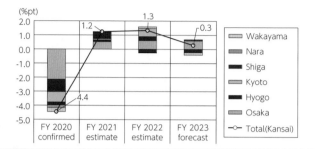

**Figure 2-3-15**    Kansai's contribution to real growth by prefecture

Source: APIR "Kansai Economic Insight Quarterly," No. 66

increased significantly, and the real GRP growth rate of the entire Kansai region was -4.1%, close to the negative growth rate of the nation as a whole. in FY 2021, the growth rate of the entire Kansai region was +1.2%. In FY 2022, Osaka and Kyoto prefectures boosted the growth of the Kansai region, resulting in a real GDP growth rate of +1.3%, similar to that of the nation as a whole. In FY 2023, growth in the Kansai region is expected to remain flat, mainly due to a slump in the manufacturing sector. While Osaka Prefecture will continue to show strong growth as it did in FY 2021 and FY 2022, all other prefectures will see either modest or negative growth.

## Column C　Economic Impact of Hanshin-Orix Championships by Region in 2023

*TAKABAYASHI, Kikuo; IRIE, Hiroaki; SHIMOYAMA, Akira; SHIMODA, Mitsuru; INADA, Yoshihisa; NOMURA, Ryosuke*

## Introduction

In 2023, the Central League championship was won by the Hanshin Tigers (Hanshin) and that of the Pacific League by the Orix Buffaloes (Orix), with both of these professional baseball teams based in the Kansai region. In the Climax Series, the league champions of both the Central and Pacific League won the series, making it the first time in 59 years that two teams from the Kansai region faced off in the so-called "Kansai Derby." Finally, Hanshin won the Japan Series for the second time in 38 years.

In Column C, in addition to the analysis of the Hanshin and Orix championships, the economic ripple effects of the Climax Series, Japan Series, subsequent victory-related sales, and victory parades are measured using the APIR-Kansai interregional input-output tables.[1] The procedure for measuring economic ripple effects is shown in Figure 2-CC-1.

First, we estimate the new demand generated by winning the championship. New demand is estimated by dividing it into three categories:

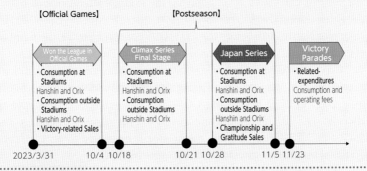

| [Official Games] | [Postseason] | | |
|---|---|---|---|
| **Won the League in Official Games** | **Climax Series Final Stage** | **Japan Series** | **Victory Parades** |
| · Consumption at Stadiums Hanshin and Orix · Consumption outside Stadiums Hanshin and Orix · Victory-related Sales | · Consumption at Stadiums Hanshin and Orix · Consumption outside Stadiums Hanshin and Orix | · Consumption at Stadiums Hanshin and Orix · Consumption outside Stadiums Hanshin and Orix · Championship and Gratitude Sales | · Related-expenditures Consumption and operating fees |

2023/3/31　　10/4 10/18　　10/21 10/28　　11/5 11/23

**Figure 2-CC-1**　Procedure for estimating economic ripple effects

Source: Prepared by the author

---

1) For a detailed analysis, see APIR-Kansai Interregional Input-Output Tables Project Team (2023).

1) consumption by spectators at the stadium; 2) consumption outside the stadium during official games and the postseason; and 3) the league championship, the Japan championship, and the "Gratitude Sale" (hereinafter referred to as "victory-related sale"), and victory parades. New demand is assumed by region and industry, and is refined to reflect the actual situation as much as possible. The 2015 Interregional Input-Output Table for the Kansai Region were used to calculate the economic ripple effects of the estimated new demand on the entire nation and the Greater Kansai region.

## 1. Consumption at stadiums

Consumption by stadium-visitors is calculated by multiplying the number of stadium visitors by per capita consumption price. By assuming the case where a team does not win the championship (hereafter referred to as "a normal situation") and the case where a team did so this year, the difference between the two is considered as the new demand generated by the championship.

### (1) Number of spectators at stadiums

Hanshin's average number of spectators per game in normal conditions is 2,901,110, calculated by multiplying the average attendance of 40,861 per game during the 15 years from 2006, the subsequent year of its last championship to 2019 before the COVID-19 pandemic, by 71, the number of games hosted in 2023. The total attendance in 2023 was 2,915,528.

Orix's average number of spectators per game in normal conditions is calculated in the same way, using the average number of spectators from 2006 to 2019 before the COVID-19 pandemic as in the case of Hanshin, i.e., 20,939. Multiplying this by 72, the number of games conducted in 2023, Orix's average attendance is estimated to be 1,507,583. The total number of spectators in 2023 was 1,947,453.

Therefore, the increased attendance due to the 2023 championship would be 14,418 for Hanshin and 439,870 for Orix.

Next, let's look at postseason attendance. Since post-season games are a net increase compared to normal conditions, the number of spectators thus motivated is directly attributable to the incremental increase due to the holding of post-season games. In the Climax Series, Hanshin held three games and Orix four games at their home stadiums, with respectively attendance totaling 127,913 and 141,311. In the Japan Series, three games were held at Hanshin Koshien Stadium and four games at Kyocera Dome Osaka. The attendance for the three games at Koshien Stadium totaled 123,075, while that for the four games at Kyocera Dome Osaka totaled 134,323. In addition, public viewing of the 6th and 7th games in the Japan Series was held at Hanshin Koshien Stadium, totaling 25,887 people over the two days.

## (2) Assumed unit consumption price at stadiums

We then identified the following four items of consumption for stadiums games: tickets, transportation, food and beverages, and merchandise purchases, and assumed unit consumption of these items in normal conditions and in 2023 for each team.

## (3) Result: Consumption Expenditures by Spectators at stadiums

Multiplying the number of stadium spectators in 1.(1) by the assumed unit consumption price in 1.(2), the respective amounts of consumption expenditures by stadium spectators in normal conditions and during this year, can be calculated. The calculation results are summarized in Table 2-CC-1.

# 2. Consumption outside stadiums

Next, we consider consumption outside stadiums. The estimation here is the multiplication of the number of fans and additional unit consumption prices outside stadiums, which is the amount of additional consumption that occurs in the league championship and postseason.

## (1) Assumption of fan population

Population estimates are made for the number of people who will additionally spend money outside stadiums as a result of the Hanshin-Orix victories, i.e., the fan populations of the two teams. Using the results of the annual "Popular Sports Survey" conducted by Central Research

| Table 2-CC-1 | Spectator Attendance, Consumption Prices, and Spending by Spectators at Ballparks |

Number of People

| | Hanshin | | | Orix | | |
|---|---|---|---|---|---|---|
| | Normal Year | 2023 | Difference | Normal Year | 2023 | Difference |
| Average Number of Visitors to a Official Game | 40,861 | 41,064 | 203 | 20,939 | 27,048 | 6,109 |
| Total Number of Visitors to Official Games | 2,901,110 | 2,915,528 | 14,418 | 1,507,583 | 1,947,453 | 439,870 |
| Climax Series | 0 | 127,913 | 127,913 | 0 | 141,311 | 141,311 |
| Japan Series | 0 | 123,075 | 123,075 | 0 | 134,323 | 134,323 |
| Public Viewing | 0 | 25,887 | 25,887 | 0 | 0 | 0 |

| | Hanshin | | | | | Orix | | | | |
|---|---|---|---|---|---|---|---|---|---|---|
| | Average Unit Price per Game in Yen | | Annual Expenditure in a Million Yen | | | Average Unit Price per Game in Yen | | Annual Expenditure in a Million Yen | | |
| | Normal Year | 2023 | Normal Year | 2023 | Difference | Normal Year | 2023 | Normal Year | 2023 | Difference |
| Ticket | 3,653 | 3,653 | 10,597 | 10,650 | 53 | 3,441 | 3,441 | 5,188 | 6,701 | 1,514 |
| Transportation | 2,825 | 2,927 | 8,196 | 8,533 | 337 | 2,825 | 2,927 | 4,259 | 5,700 | 1,441 |
| Food and beverage | 2,064 | 2,171 | 5,988 | 6,331 | 343 | 2,064 | 2,171 | 3,112 | 4,229 | 1,117 |
| Goods | 1,429 | 2,245 | 4,147 | 6,545 | 2,398 | 1,918 | 3,012 | 2,892 | 5,866 | 2,975 |
| Total | 9,971 | 10,996 | 28,927 | 32,058 | 3,131 | 10,248 | 11,551 | 15,450 | 22,496 | 7,046 |

| | Hanshin | | Orix | |
|---|---|---|---|---|
| | Average Unit Price per Game in Yen | Total Expenditure in a Million Yen | Average Unit Price per Game in Yen | Total Expenditure in a Million Yen |
| Ticket | 4,373 | 559 | 3,666 | 518 |
| Transportation | 2,927 | 810 | 2,927 | 807 |
| Food and beverage | 2,171 | 601 | 2,171 | 598 |
| Goods | 748 | 207 | 753 | 208 |
| Total | 10,220 | 2,178 | 9,517 | 2,131 |

Source: Prepared by the author

Services, Inc and the Mitsubishi UFJ Research and Consulting (2022), we estimated the Hanshin fan total to be 4.04 million and the Orix fan total to be 673,333 in Japan.

## (2) Assumed unit consumption price: Official games and post-season

Next, for consumption outside stadiums, we assumed the unit price for food and beverages and other consumption such as team merchandise. We assumed that an additional JPY 10,000 per person a year would be spent on food and beverages when a favorite team wins the league championship. In addition, we assume that each fan spends JPY 1,000 a year for the purchase of merchandise and other items. There is no difference between teams in this assumption.

As for Hanshin, additional expenditures will be incurred due to their achievement of the first Japanese championship in 38 years. The unit price of the additional expenditures is assumed to be JPY 2,000 for food and beverages and JPY 200 for the purchase of team merchandise. The predicted expenditures for the purchase of merchandise, etc. is assumed to be the same as for the league championship. For Orix, additional expenditures are not calculated.

### (3) Result: Consumption Expenditures outside stadiums

Multiplying fan population by region and the assumed unit consumption price, we calculated the amount of consumption expenditures by fans in each region outside stadiums associated with the league championship and the Japan championship. The calculation results are summarized in Table 2-CC-2.

## 3. Victory-related Sales and Victory Parades

This subsection illustrates the new demand generated by victory-related sales at department stores to commemorate the Hanshin and Orix championships and by the victory parades held in Kobe and Osaka on November 23 to celebrate the two teams' victories.

### (1) Victory-related Sales

Regarding victory-related sales, we limited our estimates to the Hanshin Department Store Umeda main store and the Kintetsu Department Store Abeno Harukas Kintetsu main store, and compared sales from May to August 2023, as well as sales in September and November 2023 for both stores.

Regarding the league championship sales, the figures for the Hanshin Umeda main store and the Kintetsu Abeno Harukas store were estimated at JPY 1.799 billion and JPY 506 million, respectively, for a total of JPY 2.305 billion.

The combined sales figures in the Hanshin Umeda main store and the Kintetsu Abeno Harukas store were estimated at JPY 1.496 billion, comprising JPY 1.43 billion and JPY 66 million for the Kintetsu Abeno Harukas store for the Japan Championship sale and the gratitude sales, respectively.

**Table 2-CC-2　Fan population and consumption expenditures outside stadiums**

Hanshin in League Chanmpionship / Hanshin in Postseason

| Prefecture | Fan Population (Number of People) | Food and Beverage (In a Million Yen) | Other Consumption (In a Million Yen) | Food (In a Million Yen) | Cloth and Texitile (In a Million Yen) | Industrial Goods (In a Million Yen) | Books and DVDs (In a Million Yen) | Food and Beverage (In a Million Yen) | Other Consumption (In a Million Yen) | Food (In a Million Yen) | Cloth and Texitile (In a Million Yen) | Industrial Goods (In a Million Yen) | Books and DVDs (In a Million Yen) |
|---|---|---|---|---|---|---|---|---|---|---|---|---|---|
| Fukui | 8,843 | 88 | 9 | 1 | 4 | 4 | 1 | 18 | 2 | 0 | 1 | 1 | 0 |
| Mie | 14,243 | 142 | 14 | 1 | 6 | 6 | 1 | 28 | 3 | 0 | 1 | 1 | 0 |
| Shiga | 186,242 | 1,862 | 186 | 19 | 74 | 74 | 19 | 372 | 37 | 4 | 15 | 15 | 4 |
| Kyoto | 338,743 | 3,387 | 339 | 34 | 135 | 135 | 34 | 677 | 68 | 7 | 27 | 27 | 7 |
| Osaka | 1,189,686 | 11,897 | 1,190 | 119 | 476 | 476 | 119 | 2,379 | 238 | 24 | 95 | 95 | 24 |
| Hyogo | 734,280 | 7,343 | 734 | 73 | 294 | 294 | 73 | 1,469 | 147 | 15 | 59 | 59 | 15 |
| Nara | 179,500 | 1,795 | 180 | 18 | 72 | 72 | 18 | 359 | 36 | 4 | 14 | 14 | 4 |
| Wakayama | 126,140 | 1,261 | 126 | 13 | 50 | 50 | 13 | 252 | 25 | 3 | 10 | 10 | 3 |
| Tottori | 14,008 | 140 | 14 | 1 | 6 | 6 | 1 | 28 | 3 | 0 | 1 | 1 | 0 |
| Tokushima | 29,499 | 295 | 29 | 3 | 12 | 12 | 3 | 59 | 6 | 1 | 2 | 2 | 1 |
| Other Areas | 1,218,815 | 12,188 | 1,219 | 122 | 488 | 488 | 122 | 2,438 | 244 | 24 | 98 | 98 | 24 |
| Total | 4,040,000 | 40,400 | 4,040 | 404 | 1,616 | 1,616 | 404 | 8,080 | 808 | 81 | 323 | 323 | 81 |

Orix in League Championship

| Prefectures | Fan Population (Number of People) | Food and Beverage (In a Million Yen) | Other Consumption (In a Million Yen) | Food (In a Million Yen) | Cloth and Texitile (In a Million Yen) | Industrial Goods (In a Million Yen) | Books and DVDs (In a Million Yen) |
|---|---|---|---|---|---|---|---|
| Fukui | 2,279 | 23 | 2 | 0 | 1 | 1 | 0 |
| Mie | 5,352 | 54 | 5 | 1 | 2 | 2 | 1 |
| Shiga | 24,031 | 240 | 24 | 2 | 10 | 10 | 2 |
| Kyoto | 43,709 | 437 | 44 | 4 | 17 | 17 | 4 |
| Osaka | 153,508 | 1,535 | 154 | 15 | 61 | 61 | 15 |
| Hyogo | 94,746 | 947 | 95 | 9 | 38 | 38 | 9 |
| Nara | 23,161 | 232 | 23 | 2 | 9 | 9 | 2 |
| Wakayama | 16,276 | 163 | 16 | 2 | 7 | 7 | 2 |
| Tottori | 1,641 | 16 | 2 | 0 | 1 | 1 | 0 |
| Tokushima | 2,199 | 22 | 2 | 0 | 1 | 1 | 0 |
| Other Areas | 306,431 | 3,064 | 306 | 31 | 123 | 123 | 31 |
| Total | 673,333 | 6,733 | 673 | 67 | 269 | 269 | 67 |

Source: Prepared by the author

## (2) Victory Parade

On November 23, victory parades were held simultaneously in Sannomiya, Kobe, and Midosuji, Osaka, to celebrate the league championships of Hanshin and Orix, with the teams switching places in the morning and afternoon. Blessed with fine weather, the parades attracted a total of 1 million spectators, comprising 300,000 in Kobe and 200,000 in Osaka in the morning, and 150,000 in Kobe and 350,000 in Osaka in the afternoon, according to an organizer's estimate. Consumption expenditures by parade spectators, such as food, drink, and transportation costs, as well as operating expenses spent on the parades, also had economic ripple effects.

Total consumption expenditures associated with the victory parade are estimated at JPY 1.06 billion for Osaka and Hyogo prefectures, comprising JPY 150 million for transportation and JPY 410 million for food and beverages in Osaka Prefecture, and JPY 150 million for transportation and JPY 340 million for food and beverages in Hyogo Prefecture. In addition to the consumption expenditures, the parade also generated new demand of JPY 500 million in operating expenses such as security at associated parade sites and parade operation expenses.

## 4. Economic Ripple Effects of Hanshin-Orix Victory

Based on the assumptions in subsections 1, 2 and 3, the economic ripple effects of the Hanshin-Orix league championship, postseason, and victory parades were calculated using the 2015 Interregional Input-Output Table for the Kansai Region.

### (1) New demand

We estimated the new demand generated by the Hanshin and Orix championships by dividing it into consumption by spectators in and outside of stadiums during the league championships and postseason, as well as by victory-related sales and victory parades. New demand generated by the league championships was JPY 62.02 billion, 13.20 billion for postseason, JPY 3.80 billion for the victory-related sales, and JPY 1.56 billion for victory parades, for a total of JPY 80.58 billion. Table 2-CC-3 shows these figures broken down by expenditure item and region.

By item, the final demand of the league championship was JPY 47.57 billion for Hanshin and JPY 14.45 billion for Orix, for a total of JPY 62.02 billion. Final postseason demand was JPY 11.07 billion for Hanshin and JPY 2.13 billion for Orix, for a total of JPY 13.20 billion. Final total demand from victory-related sales was JPY 3.80 billion, comprising JPY 2.31 billion from the league championship and JPY 1.50 billion from the Japan championships and gratitude sales. The final demand for the victory parades totaled JPY 1.56 billion.

By region, both Hanshin and Orix were highest in Osaka Prefecture, with JPY 17.04 billion and JPY 8.29 billion, respectively. Although Hanshin had the larger amount, the ratio of Osaka Prefecture in total final demand (excluding victory parades) was 29% for the Hanshin region and 51% for the ORIX region. The rates for other regions were 28% for Hanshin and 26% for Orix, indicating that the final total demand generated by championships by Kansai teams is not limited to the Kansai region.

**Table 2-CC-3    Assumed Final Demand**

By Item

| In a Million Yen | League Championship | | | Postseason | | | Sales | | | Parades | Total |
|---|---|---|---|---|---|---|---|---|---|---|---|
| | Hanshin | Orix | Total | Hanshin | Orix | Total | Victory-related Sales | Japan Championship and Gratitde Sales | Total | | |
| Consumption at Stadiums | 3,131 | 7,046 | 10,177 | 2,178 | 2,131 | 4,309 | - | - | - | | 14,486 |
| Tickets | 53 | 1,514 | 1,566 | 559 | 518 | 1,077 | - | - | - | | 2,644 |
| Transportation | 337 | 1,441 | 1,778 | 810 | 807 | 1,617 | - | - | - | | 3,395 |
| Food and Beverage | 343 | 1,117 | 1,460 | 601 | 598 | 1,200 | - | - | - | | 2,659 |
| Goods | 2,398 | 2,975 | 5,373 | 207 | 208 | 415 | - | - | - | | 5,788 |
| Additional Consumption outside Stadiums | 44,440 | 7,407 | 51,847 | 8,888 | 0 | 8,888 | - | - | - | | 60,735 |
| Food and Beverage | 40,400 | 6,733 | 47,133 | 8,080 | 0 | 8,080 | - | - | - | | 55,213 |
| Goods and Other Consumption | 4,040 | 673 | 4,713 | 808 | 0 | 808 | - | - | - | | 5,521 |
| League Championship, Japan Championship, and Victory Sales | - | - | - | - | - | - | 2,305 | 1,496 | - | | 3,801 |
| Victory Parades | - | - | - | - | - | - | - | - | - | 1,564 | 1,564 |
| Total | 47,571 | 14,452 | 62,023 | 11,066 | 2,131 | 13,197 | 2,305 | 1,496 | 1,564 | | 80,584 |

By Region

| | Final Demand in a Million Yen | | | | | Share in Prefectures | | | | |
|---|---|---|---|---|---|---|---|---|---|---|
| | Hanshin | Orix | Sales | Parades | Total | Hanshin | Orix | Sales | Parades | Total |
| Fukui | 152 | 71 | 40 | 0 | 264 | 0.3 | 0.4 | 1.1 | 0.0 | 0.3 |
| Mie | 192 | 71 | 19 | 0 | 283 | 0.3 | 0.4 | 0.5 | 0.0 | 0.4 |
| Shiga | 2,496 | 325 | 23 | 0 | 2,844 | 4.3 | 2.0 | 0.6 | 0.0 | 3.5 |
| Kyoto | 4,534 | 584 | 158 | 0 | 5,277 | 7.7 | 3.5 | 4.2 | 0.0 | 6.5 |
| Osaka | 17,043 | 8,286 | 2,827 | 844 | 29,000 | 29.1 | 50.0 | 74.4 | 54.0 | 36.0 |
| Hyogo | 13,000 | 2,397 | 139 | 719 | 16,255 | 22.2 | 14.5 | 3.7 | 46.0 | 20.2 |
| Nara | 2,415 | 324 | 39 | 0 | 2,778 | 4.1 | 2.0 | 1.0 | 0.0 | 3.4 |
| Wakayama | 1,694 | 224 | 29 | 0 | 1,948 | 2.9 | 1.4 | 0.8 | 0.0 | 2.4 |
| Tottori | 201 | 39 | 23 | 0 | 263 | 0.3 | 0.2 | 0.6 | 0.0 | 0.3 |
| Tokushima | 402 | 39 | 16 | 0 | 458 | 0.7 | 0.2 | 0.4 | 0.0 | 0.6 |
| Other Areas | 16,506 | 4,223 | 487 | 0 | 21,215 | 28.1 | 25.5 | 12.8 | 0.0 | 26.3 |
| Total | 58,637 | 16,583 | 3,801 | 1,564 | 80,584 | 100.0 | 100.0 | 100.0 | 100.0 | 100.0 |

Source: Prepared by the author

## (2) Economic ripple effects of the Hanshin-Orix Japan Series: Impact on the Kansai economy

The economic ripple effects were measured based on the new demand shown in Table 2-CC-3. Here, we looked at the effect of the new demand generated (direct effects) and the additional indirect effect generated to meet this demand (indirect effects). Indirect effects include first-order spillovers from induced production of intermediate goods as well as second-order spillovers from increased incomes. The sum of the direct and indirect effects is the total economic ripple effect.

The total economic impact of the league championship, postseason, victory-related sales, and the victory parades is JPY 160,733 million, comprising JPY 71,999 million for direct impacts and JPY 88,733 million for indirect impacts.

While the aforementioned economic ripple effects are on a national basis, they are important to the impacts on regional economies. Since our analysis used the 2015 Interregional Input-Output Table for the Kansai Region, it is possible to determine in which regions economic ripple effects occur.

As Figure 2-CC-2 shows, by region, the economic ripple effect in the Greater Kansai region was JPY 93,557 million (58.2%), and JPY 67,176 million (41.8%) in other regions excluding Greater Kansai. Looking at the economic ripple effects for the Kansai prefectures (Figure 2-CC-3),

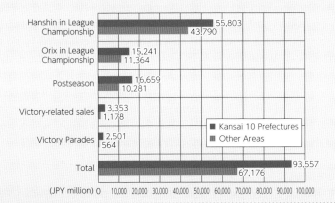

| Figure 2-CC-2 | Economic ripple effects by region: 10 prefectures in Greater Kansai and other regions |

Source: Prepared by the author

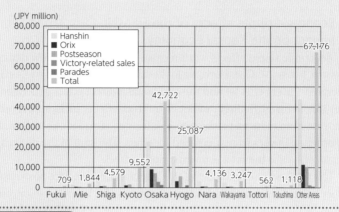

**Figure 2-CC-3**    Economic ripple effects by region

Source: Prepared by the author

Osaka and Hyogo prefectures accounted for JPY 42.722 billion (26.6%) and JPY 25.087 billion (15.6%), respectively.

Regarding the economic ripple effects of victory-related sales, Osaka Prefecture accounted for the overwhelming majority with 62.8%, while Osaka Prefecture (42.1%) and Hyogo Prefecture (35.4%) comprised 77.5% of the ripple effects of the victory parades.

Although we have examined economic ripple effects based on induced production prices, the economic ripple effects of the league championships, postseason, victory-related sales, and victory parades in the six prefectures in terms of added value were estimated to be JPY 44.076 billion. According to APIR's latest prediction, in 2023, the nominal GRP of the six prefectures of the Kansai region was JPY 9,337,600 billion, with these effects expected to boost the nominal GRP of the Kansai region by about 0.05%. On a national scale, the economic ripple effects on a value-added inducement basis would be JPY 79.3 billion, which would boost the national nominal GDP (JPY 588.5 trillion) by about 0.01%.

## References

APIR Kansai Interregional Input-Output Tables Project Team (2023), "Final Report: Economic Effects of the 2023 Hanshin-Orix Championship by Region - Comprehensive Analysis of the League Cham-

pionship, Postseason, Victory-related Sales, and victory Parades,"
APIR Trend Watch No. 91, (Japanese title: *Ketteiban: 2023nen Hanshin Orix yusyo no chiikibetsu keizai kouka -ri-gu yusyo, posutoshizun,
yusyo kanrense-ru oyobi yusyopare-do no sougoubunseki-*), (https://
www. apir.or.jp/research/13218/; last viewed on December 4, 2023).

Central Research Services, Inc, "Popular Sports Survey," (Japanese title:
*Ninki supo-tsu chosa*), (https://www.crs.or.jp/data/; last viewed on
September 14, 2023).

Mitsubishi UFJ Research and Consulting Co., Ltd. (2022), "[Prelimi-
nary Report] 2022 Basic Sports Marketing Survey," (Japanese title:
*[Sokuhou] 2022nen Supo-tuma-kethingu kiso chosa*), (https://www.
murc.jp/news/news_release/news_release_221027/; last viewed on
September 14, 2023).

Part I

Part II

Part III

Part IV

## Section 4
## INFLATION, ITS BURDEN ON HOUSEHOLDS, AND THE EFFECTS OF GOVERNMENT MEASURES

*LU, Zhaoying; INADA, Yoshihisa*

Section 4 examines the impact of accelerated inflation in 2022 on households in the Kansai region. Subsection 4.1 analyzes the movement in the consumer price index by category of expenditure to identify the characteristics of inflation in 2022. Considering that inflation was significant in food, fuel and light, the estimate of the household burden is limited to these two expense items. Since the proportion of expenses for these items differs by income quantile class, the extent of the burden should also vary. Therefore, the burden amount and the burden ratio were estimated for each income group. In addition, Subsection 4.3 examines the regional characteristics of the increase in the household burden due to inflation. And Subsection 4.4 assesses government measures to mitigate sharp fluctuations in electricity and gas prices from February 2023.

## 1. Inflation Trends in 2022

All index items of national consumer prices in 2022 reached 102.3 (2020=100), up 2.5% from the previous year. This is the highest growth since the 2014 consumption tax hike (+2.7% YoY). A characteristic of the recent price increases is that while the service price increase rate remains low, the rate of price increase for goods, particularly food and energy, is high. As explained in Subsection 2.2.1, there are several factors contributing to the acceleration of consumer price inflation in 2022. First, the surge in crude oil prices spilled over into resource prices and food prices, leading to a sharp increase in import prices (contract currency basis). Behind this lies Russia's invasion of Ukraine. Russia's geopolitical instability led to a sharp rise in energy prices. Moreover, Russia and Ukraine are major exporters of wheat, and the conflict has resulted in a rise in global food prices. The increase in import prices pushed up the production costs for companies and spread to domestic corporate prices. As a result, transferring these costs to consumers led to an increase in consumer prices.

In addition, the rapid depreciation of the JPY has been an additional factor pushing up consumer prices. In previous economic cycles, the coexistence of rising import prices and a weakening JPY had never occurred, however, this time the coexistence had a significant impact on consumers.

The National Consumer Price Index is a representative cost-of-living index that measures price changes in goods and services purchased by households nationwide. The rate of change in the overall index reflects the movement of consumer prices as a whole, and to understand the specific details, it is necessary to examine the trends in prices by expense item.

Table 2-4-1 displays the 2022 average trend in the National Consumer Price Index. It shows the growth rate (YoY) and contribution levels of the overall index and the 10 major expense items.[1] Food rose +4.5% YoY, while fuel, light and water charges rose +14.8% YoY. On the other hand, transportation and communication fell -1.5% YoY, and medical care fell -0.3% YoY. However, when considering the contribution levels weighted by each expense item's significance, they are 1.17%, 1.04%, -0.22%, and -0.01%, respectively.

Figure 2-4-1 shows the monthly contribution level of the 10 major expense items to the growth rate of the National Consumer Price Index. Although fuel, light and water charges account for less than 7% of total consumption expenditures, the surge in the price of fuel, light and water had been a major factor in driving up the overall consumer price index since the fall of 2021. On the other hand, the price of food (excluding fresh food) gradually increased, and it became the main driving factor, overtaking fuel, light and water charges from October 2022. Looking at the contribution to the overall consumer price index in 2022, food, fuel, light and water charges accounted for nearly 90%

| Table 2-4-1 | Price Index Change YoY and Contribution of the 10 Major Expense Category Indices (2022 Average) | | | | |
|---|---|---|---|---|---|
| | National YoY Change (%) | National Contribution (% points) | Kansai YoY Change (%) | Kansai Contribution (% points) | Weight |
| All items | 2.5 | — | 2.3 | — | 10,000 |
| Food | 4.5 | 1.17 | 4.6 | 1.22 | 2,626 |
| Housing | 0.6 | 0.14 | 0.5 | 0.10 | 2,149 |
| Fuel, Light and Water | 14.8 | 1.04 | 11.7 | 0.83 | 693 |
| Furniture and Household Utensils | 3.8 | 0.15 | 4.5 | 0.18 | 387 |
| Clothing and Footwear | 1.6 | 0.06 | 1.4 | 0.05 | 353 |
| Medical Care | -0.3 | -0.01 | -0.3 | -0.01 | 477 |
| Transportation and Communication | -1.5 | -0.22 | -2.1 | -0.31 | 1,493 |
| Education | 0.9 | 0.03 | 0.5 | 0.01 | 304 |
| Culture and Recreation | 1.1 | 0.10 | 1.0 | 0.10 | 911 |
| Miscellaneous | 1.1 | 0.07 | 1.1 | 0.07 | 607 |

1) For details, see "How the Consumer Price Index Works and How to Read it - Consumer Price Index for the Base Year 2020 -," by the Statistics Bureau of the Ministry of Internal Affairs and Communications.

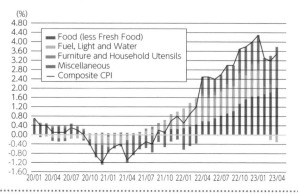

| Figure 2-4-1 | Contribution Breakdown of the National Consumer Price Composite Index (January 2020 to April 2023) |
| --- | --- |

Note: Weights are based on the year 2020 when calculating contributions.
Source: Authors' estimates based on the "Consumer Price Index" from the Statistics Bureau, Ministry of Internal Affairs and Communications.

((1.17+1.04)/2.5*100=88.4) of the increase. In other words, the rise in consumer prices in 2022 can be primarily attributed to the price increases in food, fuel, light and water. The following subsections will consider the burden on household budgets due to the price increases in food, fuel, light and water.[2]

## 2. Inflation and the Burden on Households

### (1) Increased Burden on Households Due to Inflation by Income Quantile Group

Before examining the impact of rising prices on household budgets, it is necessary to explain the "Family Income and Expenditure Survey." The survey is conducted by the Statistics Bureau of the Ministry of Internal Affairs and Communications, which samples approximately 9,000 households nationwide every month to investigate household income and expenditure by category. In this paper, data from the survey on two-or-more-person households (of which workers' households), which have disposable income available, is used.

Even if the rate of price increase is the same, it does not affect all households equally. By using data from the Consumer Price Index and the Family Income and Expenditure Survey, this study examines the burden caused by price fluctuations in food, fuel and light on households, categorized by annual income quantile. All households are sorted from lowest to highest annual income and

---

2) Since the growth rate of water prices is almost zero, the following subsections are limited to fuel and light only.

| Table 2-4-2 | | Income and Consumption Expenditures in 2021 (in JPY) | | | | |

| | Income (Annual) | Consumer Expenditures (Monthly) | Food Expenditures (Monthly) | Fuel and Light Expenditures (Monthly) | Food/Total Expenditures (%) | Fuel and Light/Total Expenditures (%) |
|---|---|---|---|---|---|---|
| National Average | 7,263,789 | 309,469 | 78,576 | 15,844 | 25.4 | 5.1 |
| Quantile I | 4,089,008 | 221,435 | 61,718 | 15,039 | 27.9 | 6.8 |
| Quantile II | 5,420,871 | 258,599 | 70,361 | 15,226 | 27.2 | 5.9 |
| Quantile III | 6,567,262 | 288,274 | 77,706 | 15,698 | 27.0 | 5.4 |
| Quantile IV | 8,208,987 | 338,708 | 82,990 | 16,203 | 24.5 | 4.8 |
| Quantile V | 12,032,814 | 440,328 | 100,102 | 17,052 | 22.7 | 3.9 |

Source: Created based on "Family Income and Expenditure Survey" by the Statistics Bureau of the Ministry of Internal Affairs and Communications.

divided into five quantile groups: Quantile I, Quantile II, Quantile III, Quantile IV, and Quantile V. Table 2-4-2 shows the average actual income, food, fuel and light expenditure amounts for all households and by annual income quantile in 2021, before inflation accelerated. As can be seen from the table, while households with higher incomes spend more on food, fuel and light, the proportion of these expenditures in their total spending is lower for higher-income households.

Since there is no data on the quantity of consumption by income group, it is not possible to grasp the changes in household consumption patterns. Therefore, based on the assumption that the consumption patterns of 2022 are the same as those of 2021, the burden on households due to the rise in prices has been estimated. The following formula is used to calculate how much the cost-of-living expenses for households has increased each month due to the rise in prices.

Increase in burden for expense item i in the current period
= Expenditure on expense item i in the previous period
× YoY change in price index of expense item i in the current period

For example, the increase in the food burden for January 2022 is calculated based on the amount spent on food in January 2021 and multiplied by the rate of increase in food prices.

Figure 2-4-2 sums up the monthly increase in burden due to the rise in prices in 2022 for 12 months and calculates it for each income quantile. To maintain the same standard of living as in 2021, the average household burden for food increased by JPY 42,491, and the burden for fuel and light increased by

Part I    Part II    Part III    Part IV

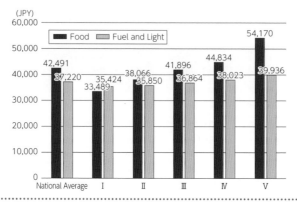

**Figure 2-4-2**  Increase in Food, Fuel and Light Costs Due to Price Rises in 2022 (by Income Quantile Group)

Source: Authors' estimates based on "Consumer Price Index" and "Family Income and Expenditure Survey" by the Statistics Bureau of the Ministry of Internal Affairs and Communications.

JPY 37,220. As Table 2-4-2 and Figure 2-4-2 show, higher-income households spend more on food, fuel and light, resulting in a larger increase in the burden due to rising prices. From Quantile I to Quantile V, the increase per household in food expenses was JPY 33,489, JPY 38,066, 41,896, JPY 44,834, and JPY 54,170, respectively. The increase in the burden of fuel and light was JPY 35,424, JPY 35,850, JPY 36,864, JPY 38,023, and JPY 39,936 from Quantile I to Quantile V, respectively.

## (2) Percentage of Households Burdened Due to Inflation by Income Quantile Group

In Subsection 4.2.(1), we estimated the increased burden due to rising prices. However, when examining the impact of price increases on household budgets, the additional burden alone is insufficient. Even with the same increase in burden, higher-income households feel less of an impact than lower-income households. To more accurately capture the effects on households, various household attributes such as income level and number of household members must also be considered. Here, the proportion of the increase in household burden due to price rises to disposable income is calculated separately for each income group as follows:

Burden ratio for expense item i in the current year (%)

$$= \frac{\text{Increase in burden for expense item i in the current year}}{\text{Total disposable income in the previous year}}$$

For example, the burden ratio for food in 2022 is the increase in the food burden for 2022, as calculated in Subsection 4.2.(1) divided by the disposable income in 2021.

Figure 2-4-3 shows the ratio of the increased burden for two-or-more-person households (of which workers' households) to disposable income due to price increases in 2022, calculated for each income group. On national average, the increased burden for food due to higher prices accounted for 0.72% of the total disposable income. The increase in the burden for fuel and light was 0.63% of the total disposable income. As Table 2-4-2 shows, the lower the income class, the larger the proportion of food, fuel and light expenses in total consumption expenditures. As a result, the ratio of the burden due to the increase in food, fuel and light prices is larger for lower-income households than for higher-income households. In Figure 2-4-3, the respective food burden ratio for Quantiles I to V was 0.95%, 0.83%, 0.77%, 0.67%, and 0.58%. The burden ratio for fuel and light expenses also decreased from 1.00% in Quantile I to 0.43% in Quantile V as the income class increased. Since the price increase in 2022 was primarily due to rises in food, fuel and light prices, it is confirmed that the ratio of the burden is higher for households (lower-income quantile groups) that spend a larger proportion of their budget on food, fuel and light.

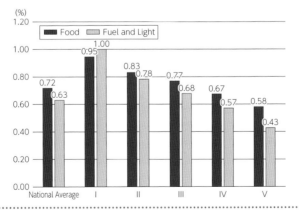

**Figure 2-4-3**    Proportion of Increased Burden on Food, Fuel and Light Costs to Disposable Income (by Income Quantile Group)

Source: Authors' estimates based on "Consumer Price Index" and "Family Income and Expenditure Survey" by the Statistics Bureau of the Ministry of Internal Affairs and Communications.

## 3. Inflation and Household Burden by Region

### (1) Inflation and Household Burden (by Region)

In Subsection 4.2, we calculated the increased burden of national average consumer price inflation. However, the combination of goods and services people consume has regional characteristics. Because the mix of consumption varies by region and the price increase rate for each category is not the same, the actual burden felt due to price increases also varies.

This subsection attempts to estimate the increase in household burden due to inflation by region. Table 2-4-3 shows the income, consumer spending, and the rate of increase in food, fuel and light prices for each of the 10 national regions. From Table 2-4-3, while there is not much regional variation in the rate of increase in food prices, the rate of increase in fuel and light prices varies significantly. For instance, in Kyushu, fuel and light prices rose by 9.2% YoY in 2022, whereas in Tokai, they increased by 18.6% YoY. As in the previous subsection, we first calculated the increased burden due to price hikes as follows:

| Table 2-4-3 | Income, Consumption Expenditures and Price Increases by Region (JPY, %) | | | | | | | | |
|---|---|---|---|---|---|---|---|---|---|
| | Income (Annual) | Consumer Expenditures (Monthly) | Food Expenditures (Monthly) | Fuel and Light Expenditures (Monthly) | Food/ Total Expenditures (%) | Fuel and Light/ Total Expenditures (%) | Food Price YoY Change (%) | Fuel and Light Price YoY Change (%) | Number of Households |
| National Average | 7,263,789 | 309,469 | 78,576 | 15,844 | 25.4 | 5.1 | 4.5 | 14.8 | 10,000 |
| Hokkaido | 6,530,397 | 277,611 | 68,917 | 21,301 | 24.8 | 7.7 | 5.3 | 13.6 | 419 |
| Tohoku | 6,404,911 | 276,346 | 72,910 | 18,816 | 26.4 | 6.8 | 4.5 | 13.0 | 636 |
| Hokuriku | 7,526,233 | 320,353 | 77,698 | 18,998 | 24.3 | 5.9 | 4.4 | 11.4 | 432 |
| Kanto | 7,907,560 | 331,623 | 85,172 | 14,927 | 25.7 | 4.5 | 4.6 | 17.9 | 3,719 |
| Tokai | 7,298,845 | 320,332 | 79,105 | 15,799 | 24.7 | 4.9 | 4.2 | 18.6 | 1,220 |
| Kansai | 7,095,559 | 300,294 | 77,823 | 15,072 | 25.9 | 5.0 | 4.6 | 11.7 | 1,585 |
| Chugoku | 6,434,141 | 284,646 | 71,462 | 16,171 | 25.1 | 5.7 | 4.5 | 14.1 | 606 |
| Shikoku | 6,986,485 | 285,062 | 67,175 | 16,046 | 23.6 | 5.6 | 3.9 | 9.4 | 296 |
| Kyushu | 6,530,397 | 277,611 | 71,049 | 14,726 | 24.8 | 5.2 | 4.5 | 9.2 | 970 |
| Okinawa | 5,224,277 | 253,374 | 70,486 | 15,734 | 27.8 | 6.2 | 5.2 | 12.4 | 118 |

Source: Authors' estimates based on "Consumer Price Index" and "Family Income and Expenditure Survey" by the Statistics Bureau of the Ministry of Internal Affairs and Communications.

Note: Income and consumer expenditures are based on 2021 data, while the year-over-year inflation rate for food, fuel and light prices is based on 2022 data.

Increase in burden for expense item i in region A for the current period
    = Expenditure on expense item i in region A for the previous period
        × YoY change in price index for expense item i in region A for the
        current period

For example, the increase in the food burden for Hokkaido in 2022 is based on the amount spent on food in Hokkaido one year earlier (on a monthly basis), multiplied by the monthly rate of increase in food prices in Hokkaido for each month of 2022, and then totaled.

Figure 2-4-4 sums up the respective monthly increase in burden due to price rises in 2022 for 12 months by region. Kanto saw the highest total increase in food expenditures due to price inflation in 2022, amounting to an additional JPY 44,923, despite the average rate of increase in food prices in Kanto being the same as the national average (+4.5%), and lower than the rate of increase in Hokkaido (+5.3%). However, since Kanto originally had the highest food expenditure in 2021, it has resulted in the highest increase in the food burden nationwide. In contrast, Shikoku had the lowest increase in food burden due to its lower food expenditure and the lowest average rate of increase in food prices, resulting in an increase of JPY 31,474. Kansai saw an increase in food burden of JPY 43,487, which is roughly the national average, due to similar levels of food expenditure and average rate of increase in food prices.

Next, let's look at the increase in the burden of fuel and light charges. As

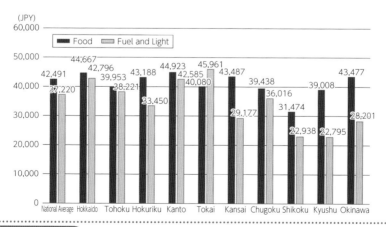

| **Figure 2-4-4** | Increase in Food and Electricity and Light Costs Due to Price Increases in 2022 (by Region) |

Source: Authors' estimates based on "Consumer Price Index" and "Family Income and Expenditure Survey" by the Statistics Bureau of the Ministry of Internal Affairs and Communications.

shown in Table 2-4-3, northern regions originally had higher expenditures for fuel and light. However, the average rate of increase in prices of fuel and light in 2022 was the highest in Tokai at 18.6%. As a result, the burden in Tokai increased by JPY 45,961, the largest in the country. In contrast, the lowest increase of fuel and light burden was in Kyushu at 22,795, about half that of Tokai. This is due to Kyushu's lower costs and the lowest average rate of increase in prices. In Kansai, the burden increased by 29,177. Since the fuel and light expenditure in Kansai in 2021 was at the same level as the national average, and the rate of increase in prices of fuel and light in Kansai in 2022 was lower at 11.7%, the burden was about JPY 8,000 less than the national average. Kansai Electric Power and Kyushu Electric Power, having operational nuclear power plants, managed to keep electricity costs relatively low, and as a result, the increase in the burden in Kansai and Kyushu was lower than the national average.

## (2) Inflation and the Share of Household Burden (by Region)

In this subsection, we will examine the ratio of the increased household burden due to inflation by region. Since income levels vary by region, the same increase in burden can feel more substantial in areas with lower incomes. For this analysis, disposable income is used as the basis for regional income, and the proportion of the increased burden on households due to inflation is estimated for each region as follows:

Burden ratio of expense i in region A for the current year (%)

$$= \frac{\text{Burden increase of expense i in region A for the current year}}{\text{Total disposable income in region A for the previous year}}$$

Figure 2-4-5 calculates the ratio of the increased burden for 2022 to the disposable income of 2021 for each region. In Okinawa, the increased burden for food due to higher prices was the highest, accounting for 0.98% of the total disposable income. Although Okinawa was the fourth-highest in terms of the increase in burden, the burden ratio was the highest because of its lower disposable income. On the other hand, the highest ratio of the increase in burden of fuel and light was in Hokkaido, where the increase accounted for 0.79% of the total disposable income. Due to the lower disposable income in Hokkaido, the ratio of fuel and light burden was also the highest. In Kansai, the ratio of the food burden increase was 0.75%, and for fuel and light, it was 0.50%. Compared to the national average, the food burden ratio in Kansai was slightly higher (national average: 0.72%, Kansai: 0.75%), while the burden of fuel and light was significantly lower (national: 0.63%, Kansai: 0.50%).

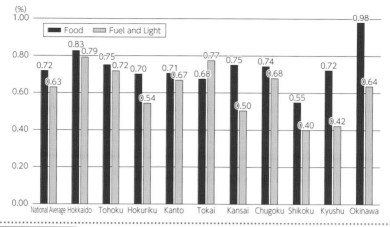

**Figure 2-4-5** Increased Food and Fuel and Light Costs as a Percentage of Disposable Income (by Region)

Source: Authors' estimates based on "Consumer Price Index" and "Family Income and Expenditure Survey" by the Statistics Bureau of the Ministry of Internal Affairs and Communications.

## 4. Estimation of the Government Measures to Mitigate Sharp Fluctuations in Electricity and Gas Prices

Up to this point, we have examined the impact of the price surge on households in 2022. It has been clarified that the sharp rise in the cost of food, fuel and light imposed a significant burden on households. Although fuel and light account for only about 5% of household consumption, the surge in their prices led the inflationary trend. Entering 2023, the effects of high international crude oil prices and the weakening JPY were expected to further burden households with increased costs for fuel and light. Against this backdrop, the government introduced the measures to mitigate sharp fluctuations in electricity and gas prices in February 2023, which provides a discount on electricity and gas bills according to usage (hereinafter referred to as "measures"). This initiative was implemented to alleviate the impact of significant increases in electricity and gas costs on household budgets.[3]

Evaluating the extent to which the government measures have had a mitigating effect on households is an important issue. Given that lower-income households bear a heavier burden for electricity and gas, as observed, it is necessary to examine the impact of the measures in more detail. However, it is not

---

3) The discount is applied only to manufactured and piped gas, not for liquefied propane gas. In this paper, the manufactured and piped gas is called as "gas" for convenience.

possible to directly determine the electricity and gas price indices in the absence of the measures. Nevertheless, using the contribution level to the price index published every month by the Ministry of Internal Affairs and Communications from February 2023, it is possible to estimate the electricity and gas price indices if the measures were not in place.

For example, looking at the impact on the overall price index for electricity costs in September 2023, the contribution degree is -1.01, and the contribution degree due to the measures as published by the Ministry is -0.82. This means that the contribution degree due to electricity price fluctuations alone is -0.19. The formula for calculating the contribution degree is as follows:

Contribution degree due to electricity prices fluctuations alone at time t

$$= \frac{\text{Electricity price index without measures at time t - Electricity price index at time t-12}}{\text{Composite consumer price index at time t-12}}$$

$\times$ weight of electricity costs

The electricity price index and the overall consumer price index one year ago, as well as the weight of electricity costs in overall consumption items, are known. Therefore, using the above formula, it is possible to derive the monthly electricity price index in the absence of the measures. The same approach applies to gas price.

Figure 2-4-6 shows the actual trend of the electricity and gas price indices with measures and the trend of these indices in the absence of measures. If the measures had not been implemented starting February 2023, the electricity price index would have fluctuated between 118.9 to 131.2, and gas between 120.8 to 149.2. In a scenario without measures, there would likely have been a gradual decline from the peak in February 2023, yet the prices would have remained at a high level.

Next, we will estimate the household expenditure on electricity and gas without the measures using the monthly expenditure data of households with two or more persons (of which workers' households) from the Family Income and Expenditure Survey. The ratio of the expenditure amount with the measures to the amount without them is equal to the ratio of the electricity price index with the measures to the index without them. We can therefore derive the expenditure amount without the measures using the following relationship, and

**Figure 2-4-6**   Electricity and Gas Price Indexes, Comparing Scenarios With and Without Government Measures

Note: The year 2020 is set as 100.
Source: Compiled by the authors based on "Consumer Price Index" from Statistics Bureau, Ministry of Internal Affairs and Communications

similar calculations can be performed for gas:[4]

$$\frac{\text{Expenditures with measures at time t}}{\text{Expenditures without measures at time t}}$$

$$= \frac{\text{Electricity price index with measures at time t}}{\text{Electricity price index without measures at time t}}$$

Lastly, we will estimate the amount of burden alleviation for electricity and gas provided by the measures. This is defined as the difference between the expenditure amount without the measures and the amount with them. Table 2-4-4 aggregates the monthly alleviation amount per household from February to October 2023, categorized by income quantile group. Due to the measures, the average expenditure amount decreased by JPY 25,288 for electricity and JPY 4,056 for gas. By income group, electricity bills per household were respectively reduced by JPY 23,570, JPY 25,785, JPY 26,333, JPY 27,873, and 29,141 per household from Quantile I to V. The higher the income of the households, the greater the amount of electricity used, and thus the greater the burden reduction due to the measures. The amount of the burden reduction for gas bills from Quantile I to V was JPY 4,226, JPY 3,943, JPY 4,044, JPY 4,208, and JPY 4,521,

---

4) Assuming that gas accounts for 62.25% of the total gas category, an estimated expenditure amount was calculated for a scenario without measures.

respectively.

On the right side of Table 2-4-4, the proportion of the alleviation amount from February to October 2023 to disposable income during the same period is shown for each income class. On national average, the alleviation amount for electricity costs due to the measures accounted for 0.60% of the total disposable income, and for gas cost, it was 0.10%. The respective proportion of alleviation for electricity costs ranging from Quantile I to V was 0.91%, 0.76%, 0.67%, 0.59%, and 0.50%, indicating that the percentage reductions are smaller for households with higher incomes. A similar trend was observed for the respective burden reduction ratio for gas bills, with 0.16%, 0.12%, 0.10%, 0.09%, and 0.08% from Quantile I to V.

As indicated by the previous analysis, the price inflation of 2022 was primarily due to essential expenses such as food, fuel and light, and the burden was higher for low-income groups with a higher proportion of these expenses. It was also observed that the degree of burden due to price increases varies significantly by region. Although the burden of food costs due to price inflation remains significant through 2023, the measures have provided a certain level of relief for households. Specifically, while high-income households experienced a larger amount of burden alleviation due to the measures, the proportion of alleviation was relatively larger for low-income households when viewed as a percentage of their income. According to the Monthly Labour Survey, real wages have declined for 19 consecutive months, underscoring the persistent economic pressures on households. Nonetheless, the government's measures to mitigate the burden of rising electricity and gas prices are anticipated to lessen household financial strains and boost consumption, which is likely to foster a positive impact on the overall economy.

**Table 2-4-4**    Amount and Percentage of Burden Reduction

| | Amount of Burden Reduction with Measures (in JPY) | | | Proportion of Burden Reduction in Disposable Income (%) | | |
|---|---|---|---|---|---|---|
| | Electricity | Gas | Total | Electricity | Gas | Total |
| National Average | 25,288 | 4,056 | 29,344 | 0.60 | 0.10 | 0.70 |
| Quantile I | 23,570 | 4,226 | 27,796 | 0.91 | 0.16 | 1.07 |
| Quantile II | 25,785 | 3,943 | 29,728 | 0.76 | 0.12 | 0.88 |
| Quantile III | 26,333 | 4,044 | 30,377 | 0.67 | 0.10 | 0.77 |
| Quantile IV | 27,873 | 4,208 | 32,081 | 0.59 | 0.09 | 0.68 |
| Quantile V | 29,141 | 4,521 | 33,661 | 0.50 | 0.08 | 0.58 |

Source: Authors' estimates based on "Consumer Price Index" and "Family Income and Expenditure Survey" by the Statistics Bureau of the Ministry of Internal Affairs and Communications.

# References

Bank of Japan (2023), "Outlook for Economic and Price Conditions (April 2023)," April 28, 2023, (https://www.boj.or.jp/en/mopo/outlook/gor2304a.pdf, last viewed on June 20, 2023).

HIDEO, Kumano (2022), "Energy Engel's Coefficient Shows Rising Burden on Households," (Japanese title: *Enaji Engeru Keisu ga Shimesu Kakei no Futan Zo*), August 5, 2022, (https://www.dlri.co.jp/report/macro/200547.html, last viewed on May 16, 2023).

NAKATA, Kazuyoshi (2022), "Characteristics of Personal Consumption by Income Group," (Japanese title: *Shotoku Kaiso Betsu ni Mita Kojin Shohi no Tokucho*), October 20, 2022, (https://www.murc.jp/wp-content/uploads/2022/11/report_221020_01.pdf, last viewed on June 12, 2023).

Nihon Keizai Shimbun (2023), "Electricity prices to rise next month, further burden on households ahead of summer," (Japanese title: *Denryoku Raigetsu Neage, Natsu Hikae Kakei Futan Sarani*), May 17, 2023 (https://www.nikkei.com/article/DGKKZO71067470X10C23A5EA2000/, last viewed on May 30, 2023).

SAITO, Taro (2022), "Burden of High Prices and Excess Savings by Household Attributes," (Japanese title: *Setai Zokusei Betsu ni Mita Bukka Daka no Futan to Kajo Chochiku*), July 15, 2022, (https://www.nli-research.co.jp/report/detail/id=71802?site=nli, last viewed on May 16, 2023).

SAITO, Taro (2023), "Problems with Subsidy Policies: The Higher the Income, the Greater the Burden Reduction," (Japanese title: *Hojokin Seisaku no Mondai Ten, Koshotokusha hodo Futan Keigen Gaku ga Okiku naru*), September 19, 2022, (https://www.nli-research.co.jp/report/detail/id=76103?site=nli, last viewed on December 19, 2023).

SAKAI, Saisuke and RIKUTO, Minami (2023), "How Long Will Japan's High Inflation Last?," (Japanese title: *Nihon no Infure ha Itsumade Tsuzuku noka*), January 25, 2023, (https://www.mizuho-rt.co.jp/publication/report/research/express/2023/express-jp 230125.html, last viewed on May 30, 2023).

Statistics Bureau, Ministry of Internal Affairs and Communications (2021), "How the Consumer Price Index Works and How to Read it - Consumer Price Index for the Base Year 2020 -," (Japanese title: *Shohisha Bukka Shisu no Shikumi to Mikata -2020nen Kijun Shohisha Bukka Shisu-*), August 2021, (https://www.stat.go.jp/data/cpi/2020/mikata/index.html, last viewed on May 16, 2023).

# Chapter 3

# EXPLORING KANSAI'S PROFITABLE INDUSTRIAL STRUCTURE

In "Kansai and the Asia Pacific Economic Outlook 2022-23," Chapter 4, Section 1, the lack of investment was identified as the cause of the subsidence of the Kansai economy[1]. The report also pointed out that, now that the environment for infrastructure facilities is being prepared for the economic turnaround of the Kansai economy, the challenge is how to attract and foster profitable industries. In this chapter, we first reviewed the industrial structure of the Kansai economy using basic data, identify growth industries, and examine the future industrial structure. The Osaka-Kansai Expo will be an extremely important milestone in the development of industries that will become new strengths of the Kansai region. The development of Chapter 3 is as follows.

In Section 2, based on the analysis in Section 1, strategies for attracting investment and human resources are discussed, and industries that will become new strengths of the Kansai region are considered. In doing so, it selects fields that will solve global issues from a long-term perspective and combines them with the DX business perspective to examine which industries will become the new strengths of the Kansai region.

In Section 3, the current state of the labor market in Kansai is reviewed, issues are identified, and future responses to labor supply constraints are discussed.

---

1) This point is analyzed in detail in Asia Pacific Institute of Research (2022) and Inada (2022).

## Section 1

# CHARACTERISTICS OF KANSAI'S INDUSTRIAL STRUCTURE: THE RELATIONSHIP BETWEEN VALUE-ADDED SHARE AND PRODUCTIVITY

*NOMURA, Ryosuke; INADA, Yoshihisa*

## 1. Basic data

The basic data used in this analysis is from the "2016 Economic Census for Business Activity" conducted by the Statistics Bureau of the Ministry of Internal Affairs and Communications. Specifically, the value added and the number of business employees are sorted by industry, and the value added per worker is calculated as an indicator of a "profitable industry." Using this index, we compare indices in Southern Kanto, Tokai, Kansai, and Kyushu in 2015[2] and clarify the characteristics of the industrial structure[3].

The "Economic Census for Business Activity" is a survey conducted every five years covering all establishments and companies located in Japan in order to grasp economic activities in all industrial fields at the same point in time. The survey covers 19 major, 97 medium, 598 minor, and 742 suvsectors of industries. It has a wider scope than Prefectural Accounts, which analyze regional value added, and has the advantage of providing detailed information on the number of employees, sales, and value added by industry[4]. The definitions of the three indicators in the Economic Census of Activity are shown in Table 3-1-1. Using this basic data, let's check the economic position of each region and examine its characteristics.

---

2) The regional divisions here are as follows.
   Southern Kanto: Saitama, Chiba, Tokyo, Kanagawa; Tokai: Gifu, Shizuoka, Aichi, Mie; Kansai: Osaka, Kyoto, Hyogo, Shiga, Nara, Wakayama, Fukui; Kyushu: Fukuoka, Saga, Nagasaki, Kumamoto, Oita, Miyazaki, Kagoshima. The data for Kansai are based on the data for the seven prefectures.
3) The most recent Economic Census of Japan (2021 Census) was released on June 27, 2023, but at the time of writing this report, cross-sectional data was not available for this survey. Therefore, the analysis in Section 1 is based on the 2016 Census of Activity. However, for the manufacturing industry subcategories described below, a portion of the results of the 2021 Survey had already been published (in December 2022) and is used in this analysis.
4) In the "Economic Census - Activity Survey, 2016," accounting items such as the value of manufactured goods shipped, value added, and total investment are actual results for the period from January to December 2015. The number of establishments and employees are as of June 1, 2016.

| Table 3-1-1 | Economic Census for Business Activity |
|---|---|

**Definition of Business Establishments**

A unit for each location where economic activity takes place, which in principle has the following requirements
1. An establishment is a unit of place which occupies a certain space(1 plot) and in which business activities are performed under a single management agency.
2. having employees and facilities to produce, sell and provide services on a continuous basis

**Definition of Employee**

"Persons engaged" refers to all those who belong to the establishments and work. Therefore, persons engaged include employees loaned or dispatched to the separately operated establishments such as other companies.
Conversely, loaned or dispatched employees from the separately operated establishments such as other companies, who do not receive their wage/salary (including wages in kind) from the establishments concerned, are not included in persons engaged, even if they work at the establishments.
However, family workers working at establishments of individual proprietorships are regarded as persons engaged, even if they do not receive any wage/salary.

**Definition of value added**

Value added = sales value - total cost + total wages and salaries + taxes and public imposition
Total cost = cost of goods sold + selling cost and administrative expenses
This survey does not include some of the gross domestic product items included in national accounts of Japan, mainly: Consumption of fixed capital, employer's share of social insurance premiums, imputed rent for owner-occupied homes, research and development costs, added value for farmers, foresters and fishermen, public enterprises, and government service producers

Source: Ministry of Internal Affairs and Communications, Economic Census for Business Activity.

## 2. Industrial structure of Kansai: analysis based on economic census

### (1) Comparison of industrial structure of each region

Reference Table 3-1-1 below shows the value added, the number of employee, and the value added per employee for the entire country, Southern Kanto, Tokai, Kansai, and Kyushu. The following analysis focuses on value added and the number of workers.

Figure 3-1-1 compares the national share of value added for all industries in the above regions. As the figure shows, the Southern Kanto region has the highest share at 35.0%, followed by Kansai at 16.4%, Tokai at 13.2%, and Kyushu at 7.9%. In order to clarify the industrial structure of each region, the top five industries in terms of value added by major industry category are listed below:[5]

---

5) As shown in Reference Table 3-1-1, "Mining, quarrying, and gravel extraction" and "Electricity, gas, heat supply, and water supply" have by far the highest value added per capita. Since these are equipment industries with a high capital equipment ratio, the value added per worker is high. For this reason, Tables 3-1-2 and 3-1-3 below compare value added per worker excluding these two industries.

Part I
Part II
Part III
Part IV

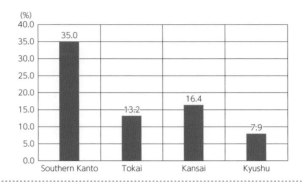

Figure 3-1-1    Comparison of national share of value added: 2015

Source: Ministry of Internal Affairs and Communications, Economic Census and Survey of Economic Activity, 2016

[Comparison of industrial structure of each region]

Figure 3-1-2 compares the shares of the top five industries in terms of value added in each region[6]. The top five industries in Japan in terms of value added are "Wholesale and Retail trade" at 21.2%, followed by "Manufacturing" at 20.3%, "Medical, health care and welfare" at 7.7%, "Construction" at 7.2%, and "Finance

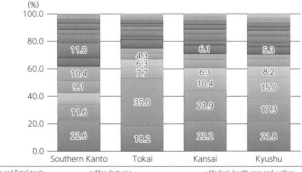

Figure 3-1-2    Share of value added by industry (top 5 industries) in each region: 2015

Source: Prepared by the author using the "2016 Economic Census - Activity Survey," Statistics Bureau, Ministry of Internal Affairs and Communications

6) See Reference Table below for detailed shares for all industries.

and Insurance" at 6.5%.

<Southern Kanto>
In the Southern Kanto region, the industry with the highest share of value added was "Wholesale and Retail trade" (22.6%), followed by "Manufacturing" (11.6%), "Information and communications" (11.0%), "Scientific research, professional and technical services" (10.4%) and "Finance and Insurance" (9.1%).

The above shows that the share of value added in the "Information and communications," "Scientific research, professional and technical services," and "Finance and Insurance" industries is higher in the Southern Kanto region than in other regions, with the "Information and communication" and "Finance and Insurance" industries in particular having overwhelmingly high shares.

<Tokai>
In Tokai, the industry with the highest share of value added was "Manufacturing" (35.0%), followed by "Wholesale and Retail trade" (18.2%), "Medical, health care and welfare" (7.7%), "Construction" (6.3%), and "Transportation and postal services" (6.0%).

As shown above, the share of value added in the "Manufacturing" sector is overwhelmingly higher in the Tokai region than in other regions.

<Kansai>
In Kansai, the industry with the highest share of value added was "Wholesale and Retail trade" (22.2%), followed by "Manufacturing" (21.9%), "Medical, health care and welfare" (10.4%), "Construction" (6.3%) and "Transportation and postal services" (6.1%).

The above shows that the share of value added in the "Wholesale and Retail trade" and "Manufacturing" sectors is high in Kansai, similar to that of the nation as a whole.

<Kyushu>
In Kyushu, the industry with the highest share of value added was "Wholesale and Retail trade" (21.8%), followed by "Manufacturing" (17.3%), "Medical, health care and welfare" (15.0%), "Construction" (8.2%), and "Transportation and postal services" (5.3%), Construction" (8.2%) and "Transportation and postal services" (5.3%) followed.

The industrial structure of Kyushu is similar to that of Kansai, but the share of "Medical, health care and welfare" is higher than that of other regions.

## (2) Comparison of Industrial Structure in Kansai Prefectures

Following Section 1.2 (1), we compare and analyze the industrial structure of the prefectures in Kansai[7]. In this section, the definition of Kansai is based on seven prefectures for comparisons among regions. When comparisons are made among prefectures in the Kansai region, they are made on the basis of ten prefectures (Fukui, Mie, Shiga, Kyoto, Osaka, Hyogo, Nara, Wakayama, Tottori, and Tokushima prefectures), which are wider economic zones.

Before examining the characteristics of the industrial structure of the prefectures in the Kansai region, we must first look at the national market share. As Figure 3-1-3 shows, Osaka Prefecture has the highest share at 8.3%, followed by Hyogo Prefecture at 3.6%, Kyoto Prefecture at 1.7%, Mie Prefecture at 1.3%, Shiga Prefecture at 1.0%, Nara Prefecture at 0.6%, Fukui Prefecture at 0.6%, Wakayama Prefecture at 0.5%, Tokushima Prefecture at 0.5% and Tottori Prefecture at 0.3%.

[Comparison of Industrial Structure in Kansai Prefectures]
Figure 3-1-4 compares the shares of the top five value-added industries in each of the prefectures in the Kansai region.

As shown in the figure, the characteristics of the industrial structure of each prefecture indicate that the top three industries are "Wholesale and Retail trade," "Manufacturing," and "Medical, health care and welfare". Of these, Shiga (43.1%) and Mie (36.5%) prefectures have higher shares of the "Manufacturing"

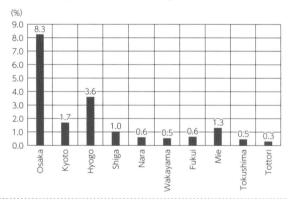

| Figure 3-1-3 | Comparison of national share of value added: Greater Kansai (2015) |

Source: Prepared by the author using the "2016 Economic Census - Activity Survey," Statistics Bureau, Ministry of Internal Affairs and Communications

---

7) See Reference Table 3-1-2 below for detailed figures.

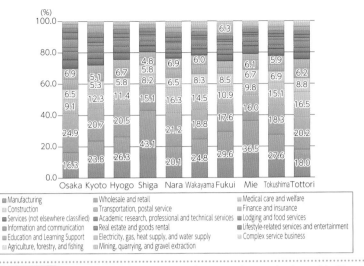

**Figure 3-1-4** Comparison of Kansai prefectures' shares of value added by industry (top 5 industries): 2015

Source: Ministry of Internal Affairs and Communications, Economic Census and Survey of Economic Activity, 2016

industry than the average share in the Kansai region (21.9%), which is a characteristic of both prefectures. In the "Wholesale and Retail trade" category, Osaka Prefecture's share (24.9%) is higher than that of the other prefectures and above the Kansai average (22.2%). In the third category, "Medical, health care and welfare", the share is higher than the Kansai average (10.4%) in all prefectures except Osaka, Shiga, and Mie.

Looking at other industries, "Construction" occupies the fourth-largest share (6.3%) in Kansai. It exceeds the Kansai average in all prefectures except Hyogo (5.8%), Shiga (5.8%), and Kyoto (5.3%). Only Hyogo Prefecture (6.7%) has a higher percentage than the Kansai average (6.1%) in the "Transportation, postal service" category.

The share of "Finance and Insurance" was higher than the Kansai average (6.0%) in Osaka (6.9%) and Nara (6.9%) prefectures. In "Electricity, gas, heat supply, and water supply," Fukui Prefecture's share of 6.3% is overwhelmingly higher than that of the other prefectures (Kansai average: 1.5%). This is a characteristic of the energy supply structure in Kansai.

Section 1.3 calculates the value added per business employee (hereinafter referred to as "value added per capita") and analyzes the characteristics of each region and prefecture.

# 3. Analysis of profitable industries: comparison of value added per capita

## (1) Comparison of regional value added per capita

This section compares the ranking of the share of value added (Figure 3-1-2) and that of value added per capita (Table 3-1-2) to see whether the industrial structure of each region has a "profitable structure."

As shown in Table 3-1-2, the top five industries nationwide in terms of value added per capita are "Finance and Insurance" at JPY12.27 million, followed by "Information and communications" at JPY9.76 million, "Scientific research, professional and technical services" at JPY9.63 million, "Real estate and goods rental and leasing" at JPY6.79 million and "Manufacturing" at JPY6.60 million.

In the Southern Kanto region, the industries with the highest value added per capita are "Finance and Insurance" (JPY15.68 million), "Scientific research, professional and technical services" (JPY14.16 million), "Information and communications" (JPY10.92 million), "Real estate and goods rental and leasing" (JPY8.85 million) and "Construction" (JPY7.04 million). The top three industries exceeded JPY10 million.

The top five industries in terms of value added share include "Finance and Insurance," "Scientific research, professional and technical services," and

| Table 3-1-2 | Comparison of the top five industries in terms of value added per capita:2015: Unit: JPY ten thousands |

|  | Nationwide | Southern Kanto | Tokai | Kansai | Kyushu |
|---|---|---|---|---|---|
| 1st | Finance and Insurance | Finance and Insurance | Finance and Insurance | Finance and Insurance | Finance and Insurance |
|  | 1,227 | 1,568 | 1,028 | 1,181 | 907 |
| 2nd | Information and communications | Scientific research, professional and technical services | Information and communications | Information and communications | Information and communications |
|  | 976 | 1,416 | 789 | 836 | 789 |
| 3rd | Scientific research, professional and technical services | Information and communications | Manufacturing | Scientific research, professional and technical services | Manufacturing |
|  | 963 | 1,092 | 730 | 743 | 565 |
| 4th | Real estate and goods rental and leasing | Real estate and goods rental and leasing | Scientific research, professional and technical services | Manufacturing | Scientific research, professional and technical services |
|  | 679 | 885 | 709 | 668 | 549 |
| 5th | Manufacturing | Construction | Transport and postal activities | Construction | Compound services |
|  | 660 | 704 | 609 | 637 | 539 |

Source: Ministry of Internal Affairs and Communications, Economic Census and Survey of Economic Activity, 2008

"Information and communications." These industries have by far the highest value added per capita compared to other regions. Therefore, it can be said that the Southern Kanto region has a profitable industrial structure.

In Tokai, the industries with the highest value added per capita are "Finance and Insurance" (JPY10.28 million), "Information and communications" (JPY7.89 million), "Manufacturing" (JPY7.3 million), "Scientific research, professional and technical services" (JPY7.09 million) and "Transportation and postal services" (JPY6.09 million).

Two of the top five industries in terms of value added share are included here: "Manufacturing" and "Transportation and postal services." In particular, the manufacturing industry is characterized by a higher share of value added and value added per capita than the other regions.

In Kansai, the industries with the highest value added per capita are "Finance and Insurance" (JPY11.81 million), "Information and communications" (JPY8.36 million), "Scientific research, professional and technical services" (JPY7.43 million), "Manufacturing" (JPY6.68 million) and "Construction" (JPY6.37 million).

Of the top five industries in terms of value added share, only two industries, "Manufacturing" and "Construction," have high value added per capita. "Wholesale and Retail trade" which has the largest share of value added, is not included in the top five industries in terms of value added per capita. This suggests that the Kansai region does not have a more profitable industrial structure than the Southern Kanto region.

Finally, in Kyushu, the industries with the highest per capita added value are "Finance and Insurance" (JPY9.07 million), "Information and communications" (JPY7.89 million), "Manufacturing" (JPY5.65 million), "Scientific research, professional and technical services" (JPY5.49 million) and "Compound services" (JPY5.39 million).

Of the top five industries in terms of value added share, only "Manufacturing" has a high value added per capita. As described below, Kyushu has by far the highest value added in the semiconductor industry on the basis of subsections of industries (see box).

---

**Box** ) Comparison of Semiconductor Related Industries in Kansai and Kyushu Based on Economic Census

As shown in Table 3-1-2, on major indutries basis, the value added per capita in Kyushu is lower than that in Kansai in almost all industries. However, the situation is different in the manufacturing industry related to the semiconductor industry (on a subsectors basis). Figure 3-1-5 compares the electronic parts, devices and circuits manufacturing industry in Kansai and Kyushu[8]. As the figure shows, in Kyushu, the value added per capita of "integrated circuit manufacturing" and "semiconductor device manufacturing" is high, with many industries exceeding JPY10 million. On the other hand, in Kansai, "resistors, capacitors, transformers and composite parts" and "electronic circuit board manufacturing" are high. Thus, it can be said that Kyushu is mainly engaged in the manufacture of integrated circuits, while Kansai is strong in the manufacture of circuit boards on which the integrated circuits are mounted. By reviewing the semiconductor-related industries into subsectors, the characteristics of each region can be observed.

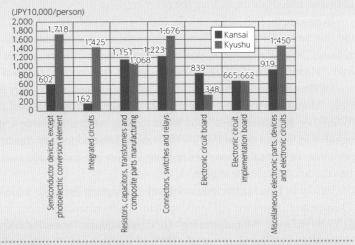

| Figure 3-1-5 | Comparison of value added per capita in the electronic parts, devices and circuits manufacturing industry subsector subcategory: Kansai vs. Kyushu |

Source: Prepared by the author using the "2016 Economic Census - Activity Survey," Statistics Bureau, Ministry of Internal Affairs and Communications

## (2) Comparison of value added per capita in Kansai prefectures

Next, let us examine the characteristics of the top five industries in each of the prefectures in the Kansai region in terms of value added per capita. See Figure 3-1-4 for the top five industries in terms of share of value added in each prefecture.

---

8) The regional classification of Kansai is based on Shiga, Kyoto, Osaka, Hyogo, Nara, and Wakayama prefectures.

As Table 3-1-3 shows, the per capita value added in the "Finance and Insurance" is the highest in each of the prefectures in the Kansai region. In particular, Osaka, Hyogo, and Nara Prefectures have more than JPY10 million, but only Osaka Prefecture has more than the national average (JPY12.27 million).

**Table 3-1-3** Comparison of top 5 industries in value added per capita: 2015: in JPY million

| | Kansai | Osaka | Kyoto | Hyogo | Shiga | Nara |
|---|---|---|---|---|---|---|
| 1st | Finance and Insurance | Finance and Insurance | Finance and Insurance | Finance and Insurance | Finance and Insurance | Finance and Insurance |
| | 1,145 | 1,319 | 945 | 1,134 | 886 | 1,177 |
| 2nd | Information and communications | Information and communications | Information and communications | Information and communications | Manufacturing | Compound services |
| | 830 | 894 | 678 | 695 | 744 | 781 |
| 3rd | Scientific research, professional and technical services | Scientific research, professional and technical services | Manufacturing | Manufacturing | Compound services | Information and communications |
| | 724 | 843 | 655 | 665 | 650 | 688 |
| 4th | Manufacturing | Construction | Scientific research, professional and technical services | Scientific research, professional and technical services | Scientific research, professional and technical services | Construction |
| | 663 | 740 | 653 | 664 | 648 | 551 |
| 5th | Construction | Real estate and goods rental and leasing | Real estate and goods rental and leasing | Construction | Information and communications | Scientific research, professional and technical services |
| | 619 | 717 | 589 | 578 | 590 | 534 |
| | **Wakayama** | **Fukui** | **Mie** | **Tokushima** | **Tottori** | |
| 1st | Finance and Insurance | Finance and Insurance | Finance and Insurance | Finance and Insurance | Finance and Insurance | |
| | 944 | 868 | 858 | 981 | 809 | |
| 2nd | Manufacturing | Information and communications | Information and communications | Information and communications | Information and communications | |
| | 644 | 707 | 667 | 844 | 696 | |
| 3rd | Information and communications | Manufacturing | Manufacturing | Manufacturing | Manufacturing | |
| | 564 | 668 | 640 | 717 | 479 | |
| 4th | Construction | Scientific research, professional and technical services | Scientific research, professional and technical services | Compound services | Transport and postal activities | |
| | 513 | 549 | 594 | 544 | 477 | |
| 5th | Transport and postal activities | Compound services | Construction | Scientific research, professional and technical services | Scientific research, professional and technical services | |
| | 462 | 544 | 560 | 469 | 469 | |

Source: Ministry of Internal Affairs and Communications, Economic Census and Survey of Economic Activity, 2016

Next, the per capita value added of the "Information and communications" is ranked second in Osaka, Kyoto, Hyogo, Fukui, Mie, Tokushima and Tottori prefectures, and third in Nara and Wakayama prefectures. However, the value added per capita is in the range of 5-8 million JPY, while that in the southern Kanto region is more than JPY10 million.

The value added per capita in the "Scientific research, professional and technical services "industry is ranked third in Osaka and Shiga Prefectures, and fourth in Kyoto, Hyogo, Fukui, and Mie Prefectures, in the range of JPY4-8 million, below the national average (JPY9.63 million).

Shiga and Wakayama prefectures rank second, respectively, in value added per capita in the "Manufacturing", while Kyoto, Hyogo, Fukui, Mie, Tokushima, and Tottori prefectures all rank third. Osaka and Nara prefectures are not included in the top five industries. Value added in Fukui, Shiga, Hyogo and Tokushima prefectures is higher than the national average (JPY6.6 million).

Finally, the per capita value added of the "construction industry" ranks fourth in Osaka, Nara, and Wakayama prefectures, and fifth in Hyogo, Shiga, and Mie prefectures.

## (3) Analysis of value added per capita by manufacturing industry subsector basis

In order to discover the industries that are Kansai's strengths, more detailed data will be needed, not only on the major categories.

Figure 3-1-6 compares the share of value added in each region in the manufacturing medium classification. The share of the manufacturing industry in the Kansai region is 18.5% of the national total. The following industries were also classified into the manufacturing industry by above 20% share: Other Manufacturing (34.2%), Machinery and equipment for general trade (32.7%), Tanning and Leather Products and Furs (29.9%), Textile Industry (28.6%), Iron and steel products (27.1%), Metal products (22.0%), Machinery and equipment for production (21.5%), Chemical industry (20.9%), Beverage, Tobacco and Feed (20.6%), Printing and related industries (20.1%), and Electric machinery (19.9%).

Below, we focus on "Electrical machinery," "Machinery and equipment for general trade," "Machinery and equipment for production," and "Metal products," and examine the value added per capita for each of these industry subsectors.

First, let's look at the "Electrical machinery, equipment and supplies" (Table 3-1-4). The "Miscellaneous electrical machinery equipment and supplies" accounted for the largest share (47.3%), followed by the "Kitchen ware" (46.3%), "Power and distribution transformers, except electronic appliances

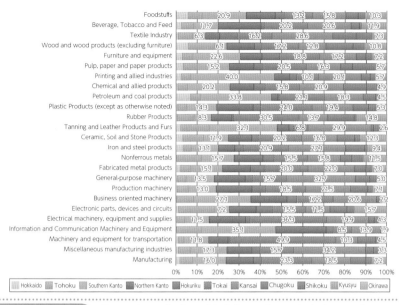

**Figure 3-1-6**    Comparison of value-added share of manufacturing medium classification: 2020

Source: Ministry of Internal Affairs and Communications Statistics Bureau, 2021 Economic Census for Business Activity

**Table 3-1-4**    Value added per capita by manufacturing industry subsector: Electrical machinery, equipment and supplies: Kansai: 2020

| Industry medium classification | Industry subsectors | National share: %. | Value added per capita: 10,000 yen |
|---|---|---|---|
| Electrical machinery, equipment and supplies | Miscellaneous electrical machinery equipment and supplies | 47.3 | 2,593 |
| | Kitchen ware | 46.3 | 2,320 |
| | Power and distribution transformers, except electronic appliances transformers | 38.0 | 1,464 |
| | Industrial process controlling instruments | 31.5 | 1,923 |
| | Miscellaneous industrial electrical apparatus, including those for vehicles and vessels | 29.0 | 976 |
| | Generators, motors and other rotating electrical machinery | 26.5 | 2,065 |
| | Miscellaneous household electric appliances | 25.8 | 1,296 |
| | Home comfort | 21.2 | 2,391 |
| | Clothes treatment and cleaner | 17.7 | 2,380 |

Source: Ministry of Internal Affairs and Communications Statistics Bureau, 2021 Economic Census for Business Activity

transformers" (38.0%), and "Industrial process controlling instruments" (31.5%). Half of the industries listed in the subsectors have a per-capita value-added of more than 20 million yen, far exceeding the average for the manufacturing industry in the Kansai region (6.63 million yen).

Next, let's look at the "General-purpose machinery"[9]. As shown in Table 3-1-5, the industries with particularly high shares are "Steam engines, turbines and water wheels, except marine engines" (65.5%), "Fire extinguishing equipment and its apparatus" (64.6%), and "Miscellaneous engines and turbines" (64.0%). The top three industries with the highest value added per capita were "Boiler manufacturing" (JPY51.28 million), "Refrigerating machines and air conditioning apparatus" (JPY30.75 million), and "Elevator and escalators" (JPY30.27 million).

Next, let's look at the "Production machinery." As shown in Table 3-1-6, the industries with particularly high shares are "Molds and dies, parts and accessories for nonmetal products" (55.4%), "Machinery for fabrication of plastic and its equipment" (47.9%), and "Dyeing and finishing machinery" (42.9%). The top three industries with the highest value added per capita were "Molds and dies, parts and accessories for nonmetal products"(JPY33.58 million), "Machinery for fabrication of plastic and its equipment" (JPY27.17 million), and "Packing machines" (JPY16.05 million).

Finally, we look at the "Fabricated metal products." As shown in Table 3-1-7, the industries with particularly high shares are "hand saw and saw blades

| Table 3-1-5 | Value added per capita by manufacturing industry subsector: General-purpose machinery: Kansai: 2020 | | |
|---|---|---|---|
| Industry medium classification | Industry subsectors | National share: %. | Value added per capita: 10,000 yen |
| General-purpose machinery | Steam engines, turbines and water wheels, except marine engines | 65.5 | 2,331 |
| | Fire extinguishing equipment and its apparatus | 64.6 | 2,303 |
| | Miscellaneous engines and turbines | 64.0 | 2,523 |
| | Refrigerating machines and air conditioning apparatus | 50.3 | 3,075 |
| | Elevators and escalators | 44.3 | 3,027 |
| | Boilers | 33.4 | 5,128 |
| | Pumps and pumping equipments | 33.0 | 1,440 |

Source: Ministry of Internal Affairs and Communications Statistics Bureau, 2021 Economic Census for Business Activity

9) The "General-purpose machinery" is engaged in the manufacture of general machinery and apparatus that are widely used when assembled or installed in various types of machinery.

**Table 3-1-6**  Value added per capita by manufacturing industry subsectors: Production machinery: Kansai: 2020

| Industry medium classification | Industry subsectors | National share: %. | Value added per capita: 10,000 yen |
|---|---|---|---|
| Production machinery | Molds and dies, parts and accessories for nonmetal products | 55.4 | 3,358 |
| | Machinery for fabrication of plastic and its equipment | 47.9 | 2,717 |
| | Dyeing and finishing machinery | 42.9 | 445 |
| | Machinery and equipment for construction and mining | 34.9 | 1,394 |
| | Textile machinery parts, attachments and accessories | 33.7 | 674 |
| | Chemical machinery and its equipment | 29.0 | 1,280 |
| | Packing machines | 28.9 | 1,605 |
| | Sewing machinery and equipment | 26.8 | 761 |

Source: Ministry of Internal Affairs and Communications Statistics Bureau, 2021 Economic Census for Business Activity

**Table 3-1-7**  Value added per capita by manufacturing industry subsectors: Fabricated metal products: Kansai: 2020

| Industry medium classification | Industry subsectors | National share: %. | Value added per capita: 10,000 yen |
|---|---|---|---|
| Fabricated metal products | Hand saws and saw blades | 62.9 | 1,198 |
| | Work tools | 52.5 | 1,137 |
| | Nails | 42.6 | 831 |
| | Gas and oil appliances | 35.0 | 1,888 |
| | Tin cans and other plated sheet products | 31.9 | 976 |
| | Plumbers' supplies, except valves and cocks | 31.4 | 1,350 |
| | Constructional metal products, except iron framework | 29.2 | 2,363 |
| | Bolts, nuts, rivets, machine screws and wood screws | 28.6 | 1,035 |
| | Fabricated metal products, n.e.c. | 28.4 | 969 |
| | Miscellaneous hardware | 27.2 | 976 |
| | Edge tools, artisans' tools and hand tools, except files, saws and knives for kitchen use | 26.9 | 1,078 |
| | Coating metal products | 26.2 | 769 |
| | Heat treated metal | 25.3 | 936 |
| | Miscellaneous fabricated wire products | 25.2 | 1,002 |
| | Galvanized and other hot-dip coated metal products, except coated steel | 23.4 | 830 |
| | Edge tools for machinery | 22.3 | 757 |

Source: Ministry of Internal Affairs and Communications Statistics Bureau, 2021 Economic Census for Business Activity

manufacturing" (62.9%), "working tool manufacturing" (52.5%), and "nail manu-facturing" (42.6%).

The top three industries with the highest per capita value added were "Constructional metal products, except iron framework" (JPY23.63 million), "Gas and oil appliances" (JPY18.88 million), and "Plumbers' supplies, except valves and cocks" (JPY13.5 million).

## 4. Summary

As we have seen, in Sections 1.2 and 1.3, we have compiled basic data for the creation of profitable industries in the Kansai region. The results of this analysis are summarized as follows.

(1) Share of value added by region: In the Southern Kanto region, the shares of "Information and communications," "Scientific research, professional and technical services," and "Finance and Insurance" are higher than those of other regions. In Tokai, the share of "Manufacturing" is overwhelmingly high. The industrial structure of Kansai and Kyushu is similar to that of the entire nation, with "Wholesale and Retail trade," "Manufacturing," and "Medical, health care and welfare" at the center.

(2) Looking at value added per capita by region, three of the top five indus-tries in the southern Kanto region match the top five industries in terms of market share. Therefore, it can be said that the Southern Kanto region has a profitable industrial structure. In Tokai, two of the top five industries in terms of value added are "Manufacturing" and "Transportation and postal services." In particular, the value added per capita in the "Manufacturing" industry is higher than in other regions. In the Kansai region, only two of the top five industries in terms of value added per capita are the "Manufacturing" and "Construction" industries. "Wholesale and Retail trade," which has the largest share of value added, is not among the top five industries in terms of value added per capita. This indicates that Kansai does not have a profitable industrial structure.

(3) In terms of manufacturing subsectors, the per capita value added in the Kansai region is high for "Boiler manufacturing" and "Molds and dies, parts and accessories for nonmetal products." Similarly, in Kyushu, the value added per capita is high in the "Integrated circuit" and "Semiconductor device" industries. This is due to Kyushu's efforts to become the so-called "Silicon Island Kyushu," where high-value-added semiconductor-related industries have been steadily

concentrated[10].

In terms of major industry categories, the industrial structure of the Kansai region cannot be said to be profitable. However, when looking at the manufacturing industry on subsectors basis, there are some industries that have a high market share and high value added per capita. Based on the results of this analysis, Section 2 discusses industries that will become the new strengths of the Kansai region.

## References

Asia Pacific Institute of Research (2022), Kansai and the Asia Pacific Economic Outlook 2022, October 2022, Nikkei Printing Inc.

Inada, Y. (2022), "Toward a Reversal of the Kansai Economy: Osaka-Kansai Expo and IR as Leverage," (Japanese title: *Kansaikeizai no hanten ni mukete: Osaka-kansai banoaku, IR wo tekoni*), APIR Trend Watch No. 81, June 21, 2022, (https://www.apir.or.jp/research/11106/, last viewed on June 29, 2023.)

Kyushu Bureau of Economy, Trade and Industry (2022), "Toward the Revival of Silicon Island Kyushu: How Kyushu Can Continue to Support Japanese Society in 2030," (Japanese title: *Shirikonairando Kyushu no Potensharu to mirai*), (https://www.kyushu.meti.go.jp/seisaku/jyoho/oshirase/220520_1_3.pdf, last viewed June 29, 2023).

Kyushu Economic Research Institute (2023), "The Potential and Future of Silicon Island Kyushu," (Japanese title: *Shirikonairando Kyushu no hukkatu ni mukete ~2030nen no nihonshakai wo sasaeru Kyushu de aritsudukerutameni~*), (https://www.kerc.or.jp/sp/semicon/20230303-02.pdf, last viewed June 29, 2023).

---

10) For more information on recent semiconductor-related activity in Kyushu, see Kyushu Bureau of Economy, Trade and Industry (2022) and Kyushu Economic Research Institute (2023).

**Reference Table 3-1-1**    Comparison of value added, number of business employees,

| Industry | Nationwide | | | Southern Kanto | | |
|---|---|---|---|---|---|---|
| | vlaue added | Number of business employees | Value added per capita | vlaue added | Number of business employees | Value added per capita |
| Unit | JPY million | person | JPY ten thousands | JPY million | person | JPY ten thousands |
| Wholesale and Retail trade | 61,407,746 | 11,362,022 | 540.5 | 22,912,727 | 3,491,739 | 656.2 |
| Manufacturing | 58,881,864 | 8,923,721 | 659.8 | 11,788,316 | 1,698,847 | 693.9 |
| Medical, health care and welfare | 22,366,210 | 7,025,613 | 318.4 | 1,886,899 | 1,807,111 | 104.4 |
| Construction | 20,763,296 | 3,564,232 | 582.5 | 6,457,792 | 917,775 | 703.6 |
| Finance and Insurance | 18,830,881 | 1,535,224 | 1,226.6 | 9,182,347 | 585,645 | 1,567.9 |
| Scientific research, professional and technical services | 17,228,871 | 1,789,444 | 962.8 | 10,531,999 | 743,617 | 1,416.3 |
| Transport and postal activities | 16,959,527 | 3,093,342 | 548.3 | 6,180,019 | 994,691 | 621.3 |
| Information and communications | 16,023,415 | 1,642,108 | 975.8 | 11,118,275 | 1,017,878 | 1,092.3 |
| Services, N.E.C | 15,232,647 | 4,038,313 | 377.2 | 6,291,205 | 1,408,928 | 446.5 |
| Accomodations, eating and drinking services | 10,137,119 | 4,705,392 | 215.4 | 3,406,164 | 1,445,600 | 235.6 |
| Real estate and goods rental and leasing | 9,205,138 | 1,355,286 | 679.2 | 4,695,639 | 530,546 | 885.1 |
| Living-related and personal services and amusement services | 7,851,378 | 2,183,576 | 359.6 | 2,769,757 | 644,826 | 429.5 |
| Education, learning support | 6,513,183 | 1,729,974 | 376.5 | 2,441,235 | 596,591 | 409.2 |
| Electricity, Gas, Heat supply and Water | 3,782,707 | 179,274 | 2,110.0 | 664,267 | 38,363 | 1,731.5 |
| Compound services | 2,543,621 | 481,331 | 528.5 | 474,793 | 90,337 | 525.6 |
| Agriculture, forestry and fishing | 1,175,186 | 346,292 | 339.4 | 93,111 | 25,230 | 369.0 |
| Mining and quarrying of stone and gravel | 632,731 | 19,138 | 3,306.2 | 487,825 | 3,440 | 14,181.0 |

| Industry | Nationwide | | Southern Kanto | |
|---|---|---|---|---|
| | vlaue added | Number of business employees | vlaue added | Number of business employees |
| Unit | % | % | % | % |
| Wholesale and Retail trade | 21.2 | 21.1 | 22.6 | 21.8 |
| Manufacturing | 20.3 | 16.5 | 11.6 | 10.6 |
| Medical, health care and welfare | 7.7 | 13.0 | 1.9 | 11.3 |
| Construction | 7.2 | 6.6 | 6.4 | 5.7 |
| Finance and Insurance | 6.5 | 2.8 | 9.1 | 3.7 |
| Scientific research, professional and technical services | 6.0 | 3.3 | 10.4 | 4.6 |
| Transport and postal activities | 5.9 | 5.7 | 6.1 | 6.2 |
| Information and communications | 5.5 | 3.0 | 11.0 | 6.3 |
| Services, N.E.C | 5.3 | 7.5 | 6.2 | 8.8 |
| Accomodations, eating and drinking services | 3.5 | 8.7 | 3.4 | 9.0 |
| Real estate and goods rental and leasing | 3.2 | 2.5 | 4.6 | 3.3 |
| Living-related and personal services and amusement services | 2.7 | 4.0 | 2.7 | 4.0 |
| Education, learning support | 2.2 | 3.2 | 2.4 | 3.7 |
| Electricity, Gas, Heat supply and Water | 1.3 | 0.3 | 0.7 | 0.2 |
| Compound services | 0.9 | 0.9 | 0.5 | 0.6 |
| Agriculture, forestry and fishing | 0.4 | 0.6 | 0.1 | 0.2 |
| Mining and quarrying of stone and gravel | 0.2 | 0.0 | 0.5 | 0.0 |

Source: Compiled by Ministry of Internal Affairs and Communications, Statistics Bureau, from "Economic Census

and value added per capita: Southern Kanto, Tokai, Kansai, and Kyushu, 2015

| Tokai | | | Kansai | | | Kyusyu | | |
|---|---|---|---|---|---|---|---|---|
| vlaue added | Number of business employees | Value added per capita | vlaue added | Number of business employees | Value added per capita | vlaue added | Number of business employees | Value added per capita |
| JPY million | person | JPY ten thousands | JPY million | person | JPY ten thousands | JPY million | person | JPY ten thousands |
| 6,955,599 | 1,317,976 | 527.7 | 10,538,174 | 1,959,273 | 537.9 | 5,001,492 | 1,110,761 | 450.3 |
| 13,376,745 | 1,831,761 | 730.3 | 10,390,054 | 1,555,843 | 667.8 | 3,969,178 | 702,865 | 564.7 |
| 2,944,875 | 723,547 | 407.0 | 4,918,594 | 1,251,953 | 392.9 | 3,438,520 | 911,462 | 377.3 |
| 2,426,381 | 415,314 | 584.2 | 3,003,398 | 471,183 | 637.4 | 1,875,882 | 384,023 | 488.5 |
| 1,631,794 | 158,672 | 1,028.4 | 2,842,764 | 240,774 | 1,180.7 | 1,228,668 | 135,438 | 907.2 |
| 1,376,805 | 194,109 | 709.3 | 2,006,929 | 270,265 | 742.6 | 718,531 | 130,839 | 549.2 |
| 2,305,041 | 378,803 | 608.5 | 2,909,563 | 507,139 | 573.7 | 1,229,568 | 279,687 | 439.6 |
| 877,315 | 111,248 | 788.6 | 1,605,828 | 191,991 | 836.4 | 668,022 | 84,694 | 788.7 |
| 1,716,309 | 477,766 | 359.2 | 2,243,198 | 654,675 | 342.6 | 1,156,946 | 354,232 | 326.6 |
| 1,213,330 | 580,893 | 208.9 | 1,658,896 | 813,061 | 204.0 | 919,597 | 450,583 | 204.1 |
| 732,162 | 132,534 | 552.4 | 1,527,890 | 244,857 | 624.0 | 577,902 | 108,673 | 531.8 |
| 880,029 | 265,436 | 331.5 | 1,354,265 | 347,604 | 389.6 | 683,054 | 218,061 | 313.2 |
| 680,800 | 183,186 | 371.6 | 1,230,201 | 327,522 | 375.6 | 557,558 | 156,814 | 355.6 |
| 689,017 | 25,125 | 2,742.4 | 730,375 | 25,046 | 2,916.1 | 393,054 | 20,013 | 1,964.0 |
| 308,087 | 55,277 | 557.4 | 368,557 | 67,917 | 542.7 | 322,579 | 59,824 | 539.2 |
| 111,319 | 30,281 | 367.6 | 66,154 | 26,324 | 251.3 | 223,699 | 60,833 | 367.7 |
| 10,654 | 1,629 | 654.0 | 6,780 | 905 | 749.2 | 22,993 | 2,634 | 872.9 |

| Tokai | | Kansai | | Kyusyu | |
|---|---|---|---|---|---|
| vlaue added | Number of business employees | vlaue added | Number of business employees | vlaue added | Number of business employees |
| % | % | % | % | % | % |
| 18.2 | 19.1 | 22.2 | 21.9 | 21.8 | 21.5 |
| 35.0 | 26.6 | 21.9 | 17.4 | 17.3 | 13.6 |
| 7.7 | 10.5 | 10.4 | 14.0 | 15.0 | 17.6 |
| 6.3 | 6.0 | 6.3 | 5.3 | 8.2 | 7.4 |
| 4.3 | 2.3 | 6.0 | 2.7 | 5.3 | 2.6 |
| 3.6 | 2.8 | 4.2 | 3.0 | 3.1 | 2.5 |
| 6.0 | 5.5 | 6.1 | 5.7 | 5.3 | 5.4 |
| 2.3 | 1.6 | 3.4 | 2.1 | 2.9 | 1.6 |
| 4.5 | 6.9 | 4.7 | 7.3 | 5.0 | 6.8 |
| 3.2 | 8.4 | 3.5 | 9.1 | 4.0 | 8.7 |
| 1.9 | 1.9 | 3.2 | 2.7 | 2.5 | 2.1 |
| 2.3 | 3.9 | 2.9 | 3.9 | 3.0 | 4.2 |
| 1.8 | 2.7 | 2.6 | 3.7 | 2.4 | 3.0 |
| 1.8 | 0.4 | 1.5 | 0.3 | 1.7 | 0.4 |
| 0.8 | 0.8 | 0.8 | 0.8 | 1.4 | 1.2 |
| 0.3 | 0.4 | 0.1 | 0.3 | 1.0 | 1.2 |
| 0.0 | 0.0 | 0.0 | 0.0 | 0.1 | 0.1 |

for Business Activity, 2016

## Reference Table 3-1-2　Comparison of value added, number of business employees,

| Industry | Kansai | | | Osaka | | |
|---|---|---|---|---|---|---|
| | vlue added | Number of business employees | Value added per capita | vlue added | Number of business employees | Value added per capita |
| Unit | JPY million | person | JPY ten thousands | JPY million | person | JPY ten thousands |
| Manufacturing | 12,290,053 | 1,854,919 | 662.6 | 3,903,126 | 580,642 | 672.2 |
| Wholesale and Retail trade | 11,563,646 | 2,204,808 | 524.5 | 5,951,964 | 954,966 | 623.3 |
| Medical, health care and welfare | 5,635,262 | 1,433,653 | 393.1 | 2,167,982 | 540,276 | 401.3 |
| Construction | 3,425,756 | 553,648 | 618.8 | 1,563,572 | 211,267 | 740.1 |
| Transport and postal activities | 3,251,630 | 575,162 | 565.3 | 1,558,366 | 245,452 | 634.9 |
| Finance and Insurance | 3,126,717 | 273,101 | 1,144.9 | 1,656,966 | 125,658 | 1,318.6 |
| Services, N.E.C | 2,519,080 | 734,053 | 343.2 | 1,291,641 | 339,041 | 381.0 |
| Scientific research, professional and technical services | 2,154,120 | 297,334 | 724.5 | 1,188,402 | 140,926 | 843.3 |
| Accomodations, eating and drinking services | 1,887,246 | 923,530 | 204.4 | 721,746 | 353,704 | 204.1 |
| Information and communications | 1,679,250 | 202,218 | 830.4 | 1,264,057 | 141,430 | 893.8 |
| Real estate and goods rental and leasing | 1,619,731 | 267,200 | 606.2 | 960,697 | 133,967 | 717.1 |
| Living-related and personal services and amusement services | 1,491,643 | 400,321 | 372.6 | 700,924 | 148,695 | 471.4 |
| Education, learning support | 1,334,978 | 360,517 | 370.3 | 539,189 | 135,560 | 397.7 |
| Electricity, Gas, Heat supply and Water | 842,426 | 29,895 | 2,817.9 | 333,988 | 12,130 | 2,753.4 |
| Compound services | 440,794 | 83,431 | 528.3 | 104,164 | 21,132 | 492.9 |
| Agriculture, forestry and fishing | 109,729 | 39,975 | 274.5 | 7,514 | 2,100 | 357.8 |
| Mining and quarrying of stone and gravel | 10,638 | 1,466 | 725.6 | 915 | 109 | 839.4 |

| Industry | Wakayama | | | Fukui | | |
|---|---|---|---|---|---|---|
| | vlue added | Number of business employees | Value added per capita | vlue added | Number of business employees | Value added per capita |
| Unit | JPY million | person | JPY ten thousands | JPY million | person | JPY ten thousands |
| Manufacturing | 385,792 | 59,951 | 643.5 | 552,886 | 82,733 | 668.3 |
| Wholesale and Retail trade | 292,504 | 77,054 | 379.6 | 328,485 | 72,470 | 453.3 |
| Medical, health care and welfare | 226,279 | 60,953 | 371.2 | 203,855 | 46,777 | 435.8 |
| Construction | 128,911 | 25,143 | 512.7 | 159,289 | 31,495 | 505.8 |
| Transport and postal activities | 93,146 | 20,182 | 461.5 | 69,790 | 15,962 | 437.2 |
| Finance and Insurance | 94,081 | 9,965 | 944.1 | 79,347 | 9,144 | 867.7 |
| Services, N.E.C | 61,037 | 21,330 | 286.2 | 76,474 | 23,405 | 326.7 |
| Scientific research, professional and technical services | 33,232 | 7,233 | 459.4 | 52,036 | 9,475 | 549.2 |
| Accomodations, eating and drinking services | 57,538 | 32,824 | 175.3 | 62,954 | 30,114 | 209.1 |
| Information and communications | 16,378 | 2,902 | 564.4 | 37,518 | 5,305 | 707.2 |
| Real estate and goods rental and leasing | 25,443 | 8,104 | 314.0 | 24,493 | 4,947 | 495.1 |
| Living-related and personal services and amusement services | 37,214 | 15,188 | 245.0 | 42,623 | 13,619 | 313.0 |
| Education, learning support | 33,234 | 9,722 | 341.8 | 27,938 | 8,277 | 337.5 |
| Electricity, Gas, Heat supply and Water | 38,296 | 1,201 | 3,188.7 | 117,947 | 3,543 | 3,329.0 |
| Compound services | 24,783 | 5,468 | 453.2 | 26,431 | 4,857 | 544.2 |
| Agriculture, forestry and fishing | 8,953 | 3,347 | 267.5 | 6,373 | 4,372 | 145.8 |
| Mining and quarrying of stone and gravel | 1,279 | 128 | 999.2 | 446 | 84 | 531.0 |

| Industry | Kansai | | Osaka | |
|---|---|---|---|---|
| | vlue added | Number of business employees | vlue added | Number of business employees |
| Unit | % | % | % | % |
| Manufacturing | 23.0 | 18.1 | 16.3 | 14.2 |
| Wholesale and Retail trade | 21.7 | 21.5 | 24.9 | 23.4 |
| Medical, health care and welfare | 10.6 | 14.0 | 9.1 | 13.2 |
| Construction | 6.4 | 5.4 | 6.5 | 5.2 |
| Transport and postal activities | 6.1 | 5.6 | 6.5 | 6.0 |
| Finance and Insurance | 5.9 | 2.7 | 6.9 | 3.1 |
| Services, N.E.C | 4.7 | 7.2 | 5.4 | 8.3 |
| Scientific research, professional and technical services | 4.0 | 2.9 | 5.0 | 3.4 |
| Accomodations, eating and drinking services | 3.5 | 9.0 | 3.0 | 8.7 |
| Information and communications | 3.1 | 2.0 | 5.3 | 3.5 |
| Real estate and goods rental and leasing | 3.0 | 2.6 | 4.0 | 3.3 |
| Living-related and personal services and amusement services | 2.8 | 3.9 | 2.9 | 3.6 |
| Education, learning support | 2.5 | 3.5 | 2.3 | 3.3 |
| Electricity, Gas, Heat supply and Water | 1.6 | 0.3 | 1.4 | 0.3 |
| Compound services | 0.8 | 0.8 | 0.4 | 0.5 |
| Agriculture, forestry and fishing | 0.2 | 0.4 | 0.0 | 0.1 |
| Mining and quarrying of stone and gravel | 0.0 | 0.0 | 0.0 | 0.0 |

| Industry | Wakayama | | Fukui | |
|---|---|---|---|---|
| | vlue added | Number of business employees | vlue added | Number of business employees |
| Unit | % | % | % | % |
| Manufacturing | 24.8 | 16.6 | 29.6 | 22.6 |
| Wholesale and Retail trade | 18.8 | 21.4 | 17.6 | 19.8 |
| Medical, health care and welfare | 14.5 | 16.9 | 10.9 | 12.8 |
| Construction | 8.3 | 7.0 | 8.5 | 8.6 |
| Transport and postal activities | 6.0 | 5.6 | 3.7 | 4.4 |
| Finance and Insurance | 6.0 | 2.8 | 4.2 | 2.5 |
| Services, N.E.C | 3.9 | 5.9 | 4.1 | 6.4 |
| Scientific research, professional and technical services | 2.1 | 2.0 | 2.8 | 2.6 |
| Accomodations, eating and drinking services | 3.7 | 9.1 | 3.4 | 8.2 |
| Information and communications | 1.1 | 0.8 | 2.0 | 1.4 |
| Real estate and goods rental and leasing | 1.6 | 2.2 | 1.3 | 1.3 |
| Living-related and personal services and amusement services | 2.4 | 4.2 | 2.3 | 3.7 |
| Education, learning support | 2.1 | 2.7 | 1.5 | 2.3 |
| Electricity, Gas, Heat supply and Water | 2.5 | 0.3 | 6.3 | 1.0 |
| Compound services | 1.6 | 1.5 | 1.4 | 1.3 |
| Agriculture, forestry and fishing | 0.6 | 0.9 | 0.3 | 1.2 |
| Mining and quarrying of stone and gravel | 0.1 | 0.0 | 0.0 | 0.0 |

Source: Compiled by Ministry of Internal Affairs and Communications, Statistics Bureau, from "Economic Census

## and value added per capita: 2015, based on 2 prefectures in the Kansai region

| Kyoto vlaue added JPY million | Kyoto Number of business employees person | Kyoto Value added per capita JPY ten thousands | Hyogo vlaue added JPY million | Hyogo Number of business employees person | Hyogo Value added per capita JPY ten thousands | Shiga vlaue added JPY million | Shiga Number of business employees person | Shiga Value added per capita JPY ten thousands | Nara vlaue added JPY million | Nara Number of business employees person | Nara Value added per capita JPY ten thousands |
|---|---|---|---|---|---|---|---|---|---|---|---|
| 1,161,752 | 177,493 | 654.5 | 2,746,998 | 412,892 | 665.3 | 1,287,526 | 173,029 | 744.1 | 351,974 | 69,103 | 509.3 |
| 1,010,254 | 231,489 | 436.4 | 2,133,266 | 428,327 | 498.0 | 449,455 | 105,913 | 424.4 | 372,246 | 89,054 | 418.0 |
| 603,709 | 155,585 | 388.0 | 1,187,219 | 307,252 | 386.4 | 243,881 | 66,413 | 367.2 | 285,669 | 74,697 | 382.4 |
| 257,265 | 46,987 | 547.5 | 608,592 | 105,226 | 578.4 | 172,134 | 30,435 | 565.6 | 113,635 | 20,630 | 550.8 |
| 251,652 | 50,623 | 497.1 | 699,237 | 128,217 | 545.4 | 141,870 | 28,155 | 503.9 | 95,502 | 18,548 | 514.9 |
| 250,324 | 26,493 | 944.9 | 531,244 | 46,855 | 1,133.8 | 109,411 | 12,350 | 885.9 | 121,368 | 10,309 | 1,177.3 |
| 200,197 | 69,772 | 286.9 | 441,955 | 138,610 | 318.8 | 114,063 | 37,957 | 300.5 | 57,831 | 24,560 | 235.5 |
| 187,662 | 28,751 | 652.7 | 420,992 | 63,411 | 663.9 | 87,018 | 13,426 | 648.1 | 37,587 | 7,043 | 533.7 |
| 219,696 | 106,928 | 205.5 | 422,203 | 200,966 | 210.1 | 99,105 | 49,192 | 201.5 | 75,654 | 39,333 | 192.3 |
| 92,353 | 13,617 | 678.2 | 159,121 | 22,897 | 694.9 | 22,775 | 3,860 | 590.0 | 13,626 | 1,980 | 688.2 |
| 159,917 | 27,130 | 589.4 | 257,570 | 50,890 | 506.1 | 53,456 | 11,011 | 485.5 | 46,314 | 8,808 | 525.8 |
| 139,354 | 40,078 | 347.7 | 307,456 | 87,529 | 351.3 | 70,898 | 22,255 | 318.6 | 55,796 | 20,240 | 275.7 |
| 243,402 | 60,760 | 400.6 | 265,496 | 75,841 | 350.1 | 68,699 | 20,272 | 338.9 | 52,243 | 17,090 | 305.7 |
| 57,695 | 1,980 | 2,913.9 | 139,346 | 4,435 | 3,142.0 | 18,389 | 806 | 2,281.5 | 24,714 | 951 | 2,598.7 |
| 45,351 | 7,969 | 569.1 | 87,175 | 17,195 | 507.0 | 37,622 | 5,789 | 649.9 | 43,031 | 5,507 | 781.4 |
| 9,509 | 3,979 | 239.0 | 20,985 | 6,695 | 313.4 | 8,072 | 4,660 | 173.2 | 4,748 | 1,171 | 405.5 |
| 756 | 144 | 525.0 | 1,940 | 275 | 705.5 | 531 | 102 | 520.6 | 913 | 63 | 1,449.2 |

| Mie vlaue added JPY million | Mie Number of business employees person | Mie Value added per capita JPY ten thousands | Tokushima vlaue added JPY million | Tokushima Number of business employees person | Tokushima Value added per capita JPY ten thousands | Tottori vlaue added JPY million | Tottori Number of business employees person | Tottori Value added per capita JPY ten thousands |
|---|---|---|---|---|---|---|---|---|
| 1,374,563 | 214,691 | 640.3 | 365,875 | 51,063 | 716.5 | 159,561 | 33,322 | 478.8 |
| 604,120 | 140,098 | 431.2 | 242,309 | 59,001 | 410.7 | 179,043 | 46,436 | 385.6 |
| 370,199 | 93,764 | 394.8 | 200,122 | 50,631 | 395.3 | 146,347 | 37,305 | 392.3 |
| 252,614 | 45,089 | 560.3 | 91,935 | 20,341 | 452.0 | 77,809 | 17,035 | 456.8 |
| 231,686 | 43,348 | 534.5 | 55,445 | 13,151 | 421.6 | 54,936 | 11,524 | 476.7 |
| 154,147 | 17,961 | 858.2 | 77,826 | 7,937 | 980.5 | 51,980 | 6,429 | 808.5 |
| 180,104 | 49,948 | 360.6 | 57,851 | 16,240 | 356.2 | 37,927 | 13,190 | 287.5 |
| 96,318 | 16,215 | 594.0 | 27,711 | 5,912 | 468.7 | 23,162 | 4,942 | 468.7 |
| 137,333 | 66,815 | 205.5 | 51,260 | 23,896 | 214.5 | 39,757 | 19,758 | 201.2 |
| 33,593 | 5,038 | 666.8 | 21,203 | 2,511 | 844.4 | 18,626 | 2,678 | 695.5 |
| 51,840 | 12,447 | 416.5 | 23,388 | 6,130 | 381.5 | 16,613 | 3,766 | 441.1 |
| 89,084 | 31,989 | 278.5 | 27,121 | 11,813 | 229.6 | 21,173 | 8,915 | 237.5 |
| 47,445 | 15,630 | 303.6 | 31,560 | 9,750 | 323.7 | 25,772 | 7,615 | 338.4 |
| 80,085 | 3,102 | 2,581.7 | 21,169 | 1,054 | 2,008.4 | 10,797 | 693 | 1,558.0 |
| 40,786 | 8,276 | 492.8 | 22,297 | 4,097 | 544.2 | 9,154 | 3,141 | 291.4 |
| 22,198 | 6,892 | 322.1 | 8,531 | 3,217 | 265.2 | 12,846 | 3,542 | 362.7 |
| 2,829 | 337 | 839.5 | 915 | 189 | 484.1 | 114 | 35 | 325.7 |

| Kyoto vlaue added % | Kyoto Number of business employees % | Hyogo vlaue added % | Hyogo Number of business employees % | Shiga vlaue added % | Shiga Number of business employees % | Nara vlaue added % | Nara Number of business employees % |
|---|---|---|---|---|---|---|---|
| 23.8 | 16.9 | 26.3 | 19.7 | 43.1 | 29.5 | 20.1 | 16.9 |
| 20.7 | 22.1 | 20.5 | 20.4 | 15.1 | 18.1 | 21.2 | 21.8 |
| 12.3 | 14.8 | 11.4 | 14.6 | 8.2 | 11.3 | 16.3 | 18.3 |
| 5.3 | 4.5 | 5.8 | 5.0 | 5.8 | 5.2 | 6.5 | 5.0 |
| 5.1 | 4.8 | 6.7 | 6.1 | 4.8 | 4.8 | 5.4 | 4.5 |
| 5.1 | 2.5 | 5.1 | 2.2 | 3.7 | 2.1 | 6.9 | 2.5 |
| 4.1 | 6.6 | 4.2 | 6.6 | 3.8 | 6.5 | 3.3 | 6.0 |
| 3.8 | 2.7 | 4.0 | 3.0 | 2.9 | 2.3 | 2.1 | 1.7 |
| 4.5 | 10.2 | 4.0 | 9.6 | 3.3 | 8.4 | 4.3 | 9.6 |
| 1.9 | 1.3 | 1.5 | 1.1 | 0.8 | 0.7 | 0.8 | 0.5 |
| 3.3 | 2.6 | 2.5 | 2.4 | 1.8 | 1.9 | 2.6 | 2.2 |
| 2.8 | 3.8 | 2.9 | 4.2 | 2.4 | 3.8 | 3.2 | 4.9 |
| 5.0 | 5.8 | 2.5 | 3.6 | 2.3 | 3.5 | 3.0 | 4.2 |
| 1.2 | 0.2 | 1.3 | 0.2 | 0.6 | 0.1 | 1.4 | 0.2 |
| 0.9 | 0.8 | 0.8 | 0.8 | 1.3 | 1.0 | 2.5 | 1.3 |
| 0.2 | 0.4 | 0.2 | 0.3 | 0.3 | 0.8 | 0.3 | 0.3 |
| 0.0 | 0.0 | 0.0 | 0.0 | 0.0 | 0.0 | 0.1 | 0.0 |

| Mie vlaue added % | Mie Number of business employees % | Tokushima vlaue added % | Tokushima Number of business employees % | Tottori vlaue added % | Tottori Number of business employees % |
|---|---|---|---|---|---|
| 36.5 | 27.8 | 27.6 | 17.8 | 18.0 | 15.1 |
| 16.0 | 18.2 | 18.3 | 20.6 | 20.2 | 21.1 |
| 9.8 | 12.2 | 15.1 | 17.6 | 16.5 | 16.9 |
| 6.7 | 5.8 | 6.9 | 7.1 | 8.8 | 7.7 |
| 6.1 | 5.6 | 4.2 | 4.6 | 6.2 | 5.2 |
| 4.1 | 2.3 | 5.9 | 2.8 | 5.9 | 2.9 |
| 4.8 | 6.5 | 4.4 | 5.7 | 4.3 | 6.0 |
| 2.6 | 2.1 | 2.1 | 2.1 | 2.6 | 2.2 |
| 3.6 | 8.7 | 3.9 | 8.3 | 4.5 | 9.0 |
| 0.9 | 0.7 | 1.6 | 2.1 | 2.1 | 1.2 |
| 1.4 | 1.6 | 1.8 | 2.1 | 1.9 | 1.7 |
| 2.4 | 4.1 | 2.0 | 4.1 | 2.4 | 4.0 |
| 1.3 | 2.0 | 2.4 | 3.4 | 2.9 | 3.5 |
| 2.1 | 0.4 | 1.6 | 0.4 | 1.2 | 0.3 |
| 1.1 | 1.1 | 1.7 | 1.4 | 1.0 | 1.4 |
| 0.6 | 0.9 | 0.6 | 1.1 | 1.5 | 1.6 |
| 0.1 | 0.0 | 0.1 | 0.1 | 0.0 | 0.0 |

Part I

Part II

Part III

Part IV

## Section 2
# EXPECTATIONS FOR KANSAI'S INDUSTRIAL STRUCTURE: ATTRACTING INVESTMENT AND HUMAN RESOURCES

*TERADA, Kenji; INADA, Yoshihisa*

## 1. Identification of industries with new strengths

In Section 2, based on the analysis in Section 1, strategies for attracting investment and human resources are discussed, and industries that will become new strengths in the Kansai region are considered.

What is important in this process is the perspective of "sustainable development" of the Kansai economy, and based on this viewpoint, it is necessary to work on the development of industries that can solve global challenges.

For example, the Osaka-Kansai Expo will focus on long-term, global issues such as carbon neutrality and the SDGs. This section therefore attempts to identify "industries that will become new strengths" of the Kansai region by referring to these issues.

### (1) Desirable Industrial Structure of Kansai
### [1] Problem-solving business

In order to achieve sustainable development, it is important to focus on areas that are considered long-term and global challenges and to solve those challenges as a business-based practice.

As for long-term global issues, in addition to "carbon neutrality" with a target year of 2050, "SDGs" has a target year of 2030.

If we look at the SDGs, common issues include "climate change," "energy," "health and welfare," "food," "disaster," "population," "poverty," "peace," and "education" (left side in Table 3-2-1).

On the other hand, the "Future Society Showcase Project[1]" to be held at the Osaka-Kansai Expo is attracting worldwide attention. If these projects are conducted on a business-base and lead to solutions to problems, they will contribute to the sustainable development of the Kansai economy (right side in Table 3-2-1).

Comparing long-term and global issues with the themes to be demonstrated

---

1) The Expo site will be regarded as a showcase in the society of the future, and the project aims to realize a part of the future society by introducing advanced technologies and systems.

| Table 3-2-1 | Long-term and global issues compared with demonstration projects at the Osaka-Kansai Expo |
|---|---|

| Long-term and global challenges | Osaka-Kansai Expo Future Society Showcase Project |
|---|---|
| Carbon Neutral | Green (Carbon Neutral) |
| Climate Change | |
| Energy | Green (Energy) |
| Health & Wellness | Future Life (Healthcare) |
| Food (Zero Hunger) | Future Life (Food and Agriculture) |
| Disaster | Future Life (Urban & Residential) |
| Population | Smart Mobility |
| Poverty | Digital |
| Peace | Virtual |
| Education, etc. | Art, etc. |

Source: Right side of the Table is based on the "Future Society Showcase Project" prepared by the Japan Association for the 2025 World Exposition.

at the Osaka-Kansai Expo, "carbon neutrality," "energy," "healthcare," and "food" are corresponding promising problem-solving business fields.

## [2] Osaka-Kansai Expo Themes and Problem-Solving Businesses

In the previous subsection, we listed promising problem-solving business fields for the Kansai region, and in this subsection, we will look at them again referring to more concrete businesses.

On December 24, 2021, the Japanese government released the "Osaka-Kansai Expo 2025 Action Plan Ver. 1" to help realize the concept of the Osaka-Kansai Expo as a "People's living lab," in which the Action Plan includes demonstration projects in a variety of fields. In preparation for the Action Plan (Ver. 4) to be released in June 2023, the local Kansai governments, the business society, and the Expo Association jointly requested the Japanese government to prioritize promotion and financial support for the host city. Table 3-2-2 lists the requested topics by area.

Table 3-2-2 includes promising problem-solving businesses such as carbon neutrality, which was discussed in the previous subsection. The table lists "the development and practical implementation of storage batteries, hydrogen, $CO_2$ capture, and next-generation solar cells." In life science and healthcare, actual projects include "industrialization of regenerative medicine using iPS cells and human somatic stem cells" and "promotion creating next-generation healthcare services toward the realization of a society with longevity and good health."

| Table 3-2-2 | Osaka-Kansai Expo-related projects requested of the Japanese government by local governments, business society, and the Expo Association in the Kansai region |
|---|---|
| **Areas related to Osaka-Kansai Expo Action Plan Ver. 4** | **Major Osaka-Kansai Expo-related projects requested by the Japanese government, the business society, and the Expo Association in the Kansai region** |
| Realization of carbon neutrality and the "Osaka Blue Ocean Vision" | Development and practical implementation of storage batteries, hydrogen, $CO_2$ capture, next-generation solar cells, etc.<br>Acceleration of behavioral change among businesses and local residents<br>Realization of the "Osaka Blue Ocean Vision" |
| Promoting life science and next-generation healthcare | Industrialization of regenerative medicine using iPS cells and human somatic stem cells<br>Promotion of creating next-generation healthcare services toward the realization of a healthy and long-lived society. |
| Realization of "smart cities" using advanced technology and creation of startups | Realization of smart cities using cutting-edge technology (promotion of "Yumeshima Construction" etc.)<br>Utilization of digital ID and digital Local Currency<br>Social implementation of "Common Ground," a next-generation urban spatial information platform<br>Creation and development of startups |
| Promoting Smart Mobility | Realization of commercial operation of flying cars at the Expo<br>Realization of automatic driving in the Expo site and on roads to the Expo site<br>Provision of stress-free mobility services (MaaS) in the wide Kansai region.<br>Utilization of zero-emission mobility (EV/FC buses, EV/FC boats) to access the Expo site. |
| Creation and dissemination of diverse attractions and promotion of further communication | Creation and dissemination of Osaka/Kansai's urban attractions<br>Construction of water transportation network<br>Utilization of urban space to communicate and experience the attractions of Osaka and the Kansai region.<br>Establishment and operation of Kansai Pavilion<br>International cultural exchange and promotion of culture and arts |
| Creating a welcoming environment for visitors | Promotion of the use of universal design taxis<br>Improvement of Kansai International Airport's Acceptance Capacity<br>Creation of an environment respecting the diversity of food |

Note: Areas in red are those of long-term and global challenges listed in the previous subsection.
Source: Osaka Prefecture, Osaka City, Union of Kansai Governments, Kansai Chamber of Commerce and Industry, Osaka Chamber of Commerce and Industry, Kansai Association of Corporate Executives, Japan Association for the 2025 World Exposition (2023), "Requests for Projects Related to the 2025 Japan International Exposition (Osaka-Kansai Expo) Toward the Revision of the Japanese Government's '2025 Osaka-Kansai Expo Action Plans, Ver 3.0'"

## [3] Startups and venture companies in Kansai

Table 3-2-3 is based on the list of 1,387 venture businesses in the Kansai region and the "Survey of Kansai Venture Businesses 2021" published by the Kansai Bureau of Economy, Trade and Industry (METI-Kansai). As the table shows, start-ups and venture companies in the Kansai region are concentrated in the areas related to the themes in the Osaka-Kansai Expo.

The table shows that "medical care" is the most common industry, and IT-related services such as "web," "application," "platform," and "system development" are also mainstream (refer to Fukuoka City as a good example of this industry concentration; see Box). In addition, "advertisement, " "marketing," "food," and "bio-technology" are also common.

| Table 3-2-3 | | Industries and Number of Companies in Kansai Venture Businesses | | | |

| Area | Number of companies | Area | Number of companies | Area | Number of companies |
|---|---|---|---|---|---|
| Medical care | 106 | Robot | 24 | Arts | 9 |
| Web | 88 | Health | 23 | Sightseeing | 9 |
| Application | 61 | IOT | 22 | Hardware | 9 |
| Software | 51 | Semiconductor | 21 | Data Analysis | 7 |
| Platform | 49 | Environment | 20 | Artificial Intelligence (AI) | 7 |
| Human Resource Services | 43 | Drug Discovery | 20 | Education | 7 |
| System Development | 41 | Energy | 16 | Social | 7 |
| Advertisement | 39 | Product Development | 16 | Inbound | 6 |
| Marketing | 37 | Game | 14 | Digital Content | 5 |
| Food | 37 | AR/VR | 13 | Recycle | 5 |
| Bio-technology- | 34 | Agriculture | 13 | Apparel | 5 |
| EC | 26 | Sport | 11 | Community revitalization | 4 |

Source: Compiled by the author based on the "List of Kansai Venture Businesses," Kansai Bureau of Economy, Trade and Industry (2022)

## Box ) Trends in Industrial Agglomeration in Fukuoka City

We held an interview with Fukuoka City, which has been successful in attracting many IT-related service companies, about its success factors (June 23, 2023).

Looking at the topography of the city, it is the only ordinance-designated city that has no first-class rivers and is poor in industrial water supply, making it difficult to build factories. Therefore, since the 1960s, the city has developed its industrial structure mainly in the tertiary industry, and currently the tertiary industry accounts for 91% of the city's gross regional product (in real terms) (based on the 2021 Basic Economic Census).

The city has a lower probability of earthquakes with seismic intensity of 6 or higher than other large cities. In addition, the proximity of the airport to the city center is uniquely favorable. This makes the city an ideal geographic location for companies that value backup functions.

In 2014, the city was selected as a "Special Zone for Global Startups and Job Creation," a national strategic zone, and has focused on startups early on, promoting various initiatives. Since then, 801 companies have been created obtaining funds totaling JPY36.5 billion. In order to attract companies to the city, the city has supported the location of 571 companies between 2013 and

2022, 58% of which were in the IT and creative industries. Currently, the city ranks fourth among ordinance-designated cities in terms of the number of business locations in the information and telecommunications industry. The concentration of many IT and creative companies in the city has led to the establishment of many science and technology universities and technical colleges, and this virtuous cycle of matching human resources and companies has encouraged companies to expand into the local area.

Japan's first industry-academia-government-affiliated organization specializing in games, the Fukuoka Game Industry Promotion Organization, and an e-sports organization were established ahead of other cities, and the public and private sectors are working together to develop human resources and promote the entire industry.

In addition, after the aforementioned approval as a national strategic special zone, the Tenjin district was deregulated in terms of height restriction under the Civil Aeronautics Act, and tall buildings up to 115 meters high are now being constructed at a rapid pace. As a result, the city is now able to attract companies more aggressively than ever before, as office space can be increased or occupy an entire floor due to large-scale developments.

The "Tenjin Big Bang" redevelopment project in the Tenjin area involves the reconstruction of 70 buildings with an economic impact of JPY850 billion, while the "Hakata Connected" redevelopment project around the Hakata Station entails the reconstruction of 20 buildings with an economic impact of JPY500 billion.

## (2) What is DX Business?

In Subsection 2.1 (1), we identified possible areas and businesses as promising industries in the Kansai region. Subsection 2.1 (2) presents a new perspective on DX business, which effectively utilizes goods and services and brings diverse values to the society, in order to link the insight in the previous subsection to profitable businesses in the future.

According to Onozuka Seishi (2022), DX businesses can be broadly classified into the following four categories, which exercise various effects on the transaction of goods and services.

   (i)   Businesses that "expand supply and demand"
       Match people who want to offer unused time and space with people who want to use it.
   (ii)  Businesses that "create places"
       Provide and share goods and services that were never traded.

(iii) Businesses that "eliminate inefficiencies"

Eliminate "tasks that are essentially unnecessary" in transactions of goods and services.

(iv) Businesses that "expand profit-earning opportunities"

Utilize data obtained from various media to create new value and expand profit-earning opportunities.

## (3) Profitable Businesses: Finding businesses that will become new strengths of the Kansai region

It is difficult for the Kansai economy to escape from long-term stagnation if new businesses are examined as an extension of existing industry classifications. It is necessary to develop new businesses based on differing ideas and transform them into "profitable industries." We tried to find "profitable businesses" without relying on existing industrial classifications by combining the problem-solving businesses and industries in Kansai identified in Subsection 2.1 (1) with the DX business concept described in Subsection 2.1 (2) (Figure 3-2-1).

This "multiplication" can be done in a variety of combinations. In this report, we have identified potential new businesses by combining the businesses and industries discussed in Tables 3-2-2 and 3-2-3 above with DX businesses. Based on this, "healthy life extension support service," "support service to increase the number of tourists," and "athlete meal catering service" were identified as examples of businesses that combine desirable industries and businesses in the Kansai region with DX businesses (Figure 3-2-2).

The business environment is constantly changing, and the pace of change is expected to accelerate even more. It is therefore necessary to continue discovering new businesses through "multiplication." As an example of how new businesses can be found through "multiplication," the METI-Kansai Greater EXPO "Let's Expand Osaka-Kansai EXPO: Recommendations for Expo Activities Outside the Expo Site, Utilizing the Power (Geographical Advantage) of Hosting the Expo" is a good reference.

The theme of the report is "Future New Industry Chain," and it introduces a conceptual method to the development of new businesses. The concept is not an extension of industry classification, but rather the combination of existing

**Figure 3-2-1**    The method of finding businesses that will become new strengths of the Kansai region

Source: Prepared by the author

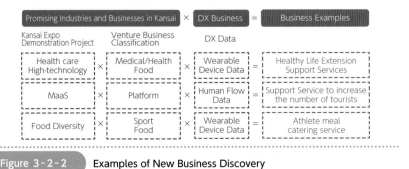

**Figure 3-2-2**    **Examples of New Business Discovery**

Source: Prepared by the author

industries with IT and other fundamental technologies to create a broad range of new businesses that have never existed before and that will expand widely.

## 2. Examination of new developments in existing industries

In Subsection 2.1, we discussed new industries (profitable industries) that can solve long-term and global issues by taking advantage of Kansai's strengths.

In order for the industry as a whole to become more profitable, existing industries must also be transformed into profitable entities. In particular, small and medium-sized enterprises (SMEs), which account for the majority of all Japanese companies, need to improve their profitability.

Many SMEs in the Kansai region are manufacturers, and "improving productivity and added value" is critically important for increasing their profits.

Subsection 2.2 introduces some examples of such efforts.

### (1) From the Economic Debate

At the "APIR Forum Economic Debate (Kansai Economy)" held in March 2023, discussions focused on the efforts of SMEs under the theme of "Toward a Shin-Economic Virtuous Circle in the Kansai Region." Three representatives from top-level companies in the Kansai region with proven track records of increasing productivity and added value were invited to discuss the relationship between "increase of productivity and added value" and a "virtuous circle of growth." (See Figure 3-2-3 for an overview of the forum.) The following is a brief summary of the results obtained from this discussion.

In the discussion session, we first asked whether productivity improvements have been able to increase wages in SMEs, which account for the overwhelming share of the manufacturing industry in the Kansai region, and found that they not only allocate the increased profits generated by productivity improvements

[Reference] APIR Forum, Economic Debate 2022 <Kansai Economy> Theme: Toward a Shin-Economic Virtuous Circle in the Kansai region

March 13, 2023 (Monday) 15:00-16:30
Face-to-face: Grand Front Osaka, North Bldg. Tower C, 8F
    Knowledge Capital Conference Room C01 +C02 /Online: Live Webcast via Zoom
Part 1: Keynote Speech "Short-term Outlook for the Kansai Economy"
Hiroaki Irie, Professor, Department of Business and Economics, Kindai University Junior College
    2: Discussions (in no particular order)
    Ms. Hiroko Kusaba, Representative Director, Seiko SCM Co.
    Mr. Takenosuke Yasufuku, President and Representative Director, Kobe Shushinkan Breweries Co. Mr. Yuki Yamamoto, President and Representative Director, HILLTOP Co.
    Moderator: Yoshihisa Inada, Professor Emeritus, Konan University, APIR Research Director/ Directorate and Center for Quantitative Economic Analysis

**Figure 3-2-3**    Outline of the Economic Debate <Kansai Economy>

Source: Excerpted from Asia Pacific Institute of Research (2023)

to wage increases, but also tend to focus on investment in human resources (reskilling) for the future.

Next, three companies introduced their efforts to "increase productivity and added value" as follows.

The speakers pointed out that the key points are "improvement of productivity and added value" through DX and premium products, "market globalization," and "employee reskilling." Each company seems to be actively working on a virtuous cycle for their own growth.

## <Increasing productivity and added value>

In terms of "increasing productivity and added value," companies focused on moving away from being a subcontractor, increasing its independence as a company, and creating a risk tolerance that would not be affected by the fluctuation of the economy. Specifically, they aimed to become a global niche company, which will be discussed in a later subsection.

## <Globalization>

In the area of "globalization," companies sought to increase their corporate value and further expand their business in overseas markets, which were expected to grow even more in the future since domestic demand decreases due to a shrinking population.

## <Reskilling >

Regarding reskilling, companies worked to expand their business by shifting highly skilled craftsmen who became redundant as a result of increased productivity through DX to upstream businesses (design and development) and new businesses with high productivity.

### <Proposals>

Finally, as a result of the discussion toward an economic virtuous circle in the Kansai region, the following were proposed.

It is important to create an enabling environment in which SMEs can be independent business entities and become equal partners with large enterprises in value-added manufacturing.

In addition, it was proposed that mass production and consumption are outdated and that it is important for companies and governments to work together to actively promote consumption behavior that respects people, society, community, and the environment. In this economic discussion, it was suggested that large corporations and SMEs should work together to create new value-added products by taking advantage of their respective strengths and by creating new value-added products with keywords such as "SDGs" and "environment," thereby creating a "virtuous cycle of growth" for corporations and ultimately leading to the realization of an economic virtuous circle in the Kansai region.

## (2) Global Niche Perspectives

The "premium products" mentioned in the discussion of "increase of productivity and added value" described in Subsection 2.2 (1), are those that increase the value of the products and differentiate them from other products, and can increase profitability through high profit margins even without increasing sales volume.

On the other hand, by occupying an overwhelming share, even if it is only a part of the supply chain, a company can minimize the impact of price competition and increase profitability. From this perspective, a new development could be the pursuit of "global niche" products that leverage company strengths.

The Ministry of Economy, Trade and Industry (METI) selected 113 companies for the "2020 Global Niche Top 100 Companies)," which selects companies that are succeeding in niche fields in the global market and excellent companies with enterprises such as functional-materials that are becoming increasingly important in the supply chain amid the changing international situation.

(Hereafter, global niche top 100 companies are referred to GNTs.) Of these, 27 were located in the Kansai region (see Reference Table 3-2-1 below).

The net profit margins (FY 2019 and beyond) of SMEs in the Kansai GNT show that many companies have remained stable and profitable during the FY

2020-22 COVID-19 pandemic (Table 3-2-4).

According to the results of the interview survey conducted on GNT companies selected by METI, many of the interviewees responded that the strategy they should take is to "utilize their core technologies to expand into other fields" and "expand transactions with new customers and build a business structure that is not influenced by the management of the buyers to whom they deliver their products" (Figure 3-2-4).

In this way, SMEs can ensure business stability by creating global niche products that take advantage of their strengths, and can also look to develop

| Table 3-2-4 | Performance of SMEs as global niche in the Kansai region (Ratio of net income to net sales) | | | |
|---|---|---|---|---|
| Company Name | FY 2019 | FY 2020 | FY 2021 | FY 2022 |
| Nisshin Kogyo Co. | 4.7% | 0.6% | 5.2% | 4.6% |
| Okamura Engineering Co. | 10.3% | 6.5% | 8.6% | 10.1% |
| Futa-Q Co. | 0.2% | 2.0% | 2.6% | 2.3% |
| Nabel Co. | 1.6% | 18.0% | 18.7% | 14.9% |
| Kataoka Co. | 1.2% | 1.0% | 0.8% | 1.3% |
| Riko Float Technology Co. | 13.5% | 13.7% | -2.1% | 35.0% |
| Fukui Seisakusho Co. | 12.3% | 11.0% | 12.8% | 7.1% |
| Itoh Denki Co. | 11.2% | 9.1% | 14.9% | 17.4% |
| Shiraishi Kogyo Kaisha Co. | 2.2% | 2.4% | 3.5% | 3.3% |
| Kohoku Kogyo Co. | 18.4% | 24.0% | 38.8% | 35.8% |
| Optex, Co. | 11.2% | 7.5% | 16.0% | 13.0% |
| Figaro Engineering Co. | 9.2% | 4.6% | 7.6% | 15.4% |
| Patlite Co. | 7.4% | 3.6% | 4.4% | 5.1% |

Note: Calculated based on public information of each company and data from Teikoku Databank and Tokyo Shoko Research. Shaded years are the three fiscal years during the COVID-19 pandemic.
Source: Ministry of Economy, Trade, and Industry (2020), "The 100 Top Global Niche Companies in 2020."

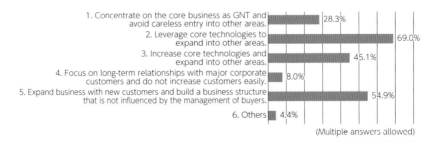

| 1. Concentrate on the core business as GNT and avoid careless entry into other areas. | 28.3% |
| 2. Leverage core technologies to expand into other areas. | 69.0% |
| 3. Increase core technologies and expand into other areas. | 45.1% |
| 4. Focus on long-term relationships with major corporate customers and do not increase customers easily. | 8.0% |
| 5. Expand business with new customers and build a business structure that is not influenced by the management of buyers. | 54.9% |
| 6. Others | 4.4% |

(Multiple answers allowed)

| Figure 3-2-4 | Strategies to be taken by GNT |
|---|---|

Source: Ministry of Economy, Trade and Industry (2020) "2020 Global Top 100 Niche Companies."

new businesses that utilize their technologies. This could also lead to the creation of a virtuous growth cycle as a company.

## 3. Summary

The key points of the "Expected Industrial Structure of Kansai" discussed in Section 2 can be summarized as follows.

(1) To find industries that will become new strengths, we looked at businesses and industries such as "carbon neutral" and "healthcare" as promising industries in the Kansai region, based on the theme of the Osaka-Kansai Expo and from the perspective of problem-solving businesses. In addition, we classified startups and venture companies in Kansai and identified "profitable businesses" by combining them with DX businesses.

(2) To scrutinize potential new development of existing industries, many SMEs in the Kansai region are in the manufacturing industry, and "increasing productivity and added value" is critically important to improving their profitability. In the discussion in this economic debate, the key points were "increasing productivity and added value" through DX and premium products, "market globalization," and "reskilling of employees." In addition, creating global niche products that leverage the company's strengths also leads to a virtuous cycle of corporate growth.

## References

Asia Pacific Institute of Research (2023), "APIR Symposium Economic Debate Report 2022," (https://www.apir.or.jp/wp/wp-content/uploads/apir_Economic_Debate_2022.pdf, last viewed on July 4, 2023).

Cabinet Secretariat (2023), "2025 Osaka-Kansai Expo Action Plan Ver. 4," (https://www.cas.go.jp/jp/seisaku/expo_suisin_honbu/pdf/Action_Plan_Ver.4.pdf, last viewed July 4, 2023)

Japan Association for the 2025 World Exposition (2023), "Future Society Showcase Project," (https://www.expo2025.or.jp/sponsorship/#sec03, last viewed on July 4, 2023)

Kansai Bureau of Economy, Trade and Industry (2022), "List of Kansai Venture Businesses" (December 9, 2022 edition), (https://www.kansai.meti.go.jp/3-3shinki/supporters/181129venturelist.html, last viewed on March 31, 2023).

Kansai Bureau of Economy, Trade and Industry, 2025 NEXT Kansai Planning Office (2023), "Let's Extend Osaka-Kansai Expo: Recommendations for Expo Activities Outside the Expo Site, Utilizing the Power (Geographical

Advantage) of Hosting the Expo," (Japanese title: *Osaka-Kansai Banpaku wo Kakucho Shiyo ~Banpaku Kaisai no Pawa [Chinori] wo Ikasita Banpaku Renkei Kaijogai Katsudo no Susume~*).

Ministry of Economy, Trade and Industry (2020), "The 100 Top Global Niche Companies," (https://www.meti.go.jp/policy/mono_info_service/mono/gnt100/index.html, last viewed on March 31, 2023).

Onozuka, S. (2022), "DX Business Models: Learning from 80 Cases of Aggressive Strategies to Generate Profits (Dekiru Business)," (Japanese title: *DX Bijinesu Moderu 80 Jirei ni Manabu Rieki wo Umidasu Seme no Senryaku [Dekiru Bijinesu]*).

Osaka Prefecture, Osaka City, Union of Kansai Governments, Kansai Economic Federation, Osaka Chamber of Commerce and Industry, Kansai Association of Corporate Executives, Japan Association for the 2025 Osaka-Kansai Expo (2023), "Requests for Projects Related to the 2025 Japan International Exposition (Osaka-Kansai Expo,) Toward Revision of the Government's '2025 Osaka-Kansai Expo Action Plan Ver. 3,'" (https://www.pref.osaka.lg.jp/attach/205/00454661/230706.pdf, last viewed on July 4, 2023).

Yamamoto, Y. (2021), "Five Technologies to Change the World: The Frontiers of SDGs and ESG," (Japanese title: *Sekai wo Kaeru 5tsu no Tekunoroji -SDGs, ESG no Saizensen-*).

| Reference Figure 3-2-1 | List of Kansai Companies Selected as One of the Top 100 Global Niche Companies in 2020 |
| --- | --- |

| Sector | Company Name | Location | Business Scale | Global niche top products and services |
| --- | --- | --- | --- | --- |
| Machinery & Processing | NIDEC MACHINE TOOL, Co. | Shiga Pref. | Large enterprise | Gear machine tools (hobbing machines, gear shaping machines, shaving machines, gear grinding machines) |
| | HORIZON Inc. | Shiga Pref. | Second-tier company | 4-Clamp automatic radio binding machine BQ-480 |
| | Nisshin Kogyo Co. | Shiga Pref. | SME | Stainless steel caps and cases for lithium-ion coin batteries, cases for automotive ABS solenoid valves |
| | Okamura Engineering, Co. | Shiga Pref. | SME | Butterfly valve for marine exhaust gas treatment equipment |
| | Ishida Co. | Kyoto Pref. | Large enterprise | Automatic weighing and packaging valuing machine (WM-AI Super, Dtop-UNI, Wmini-UNI) |
| | Kanken Techno Co. | Kyoto Pref. | Second-tier company | Semiconductor manufacturing exhaust gas abatement equipment |
| | FUTA-Q Co. | Kyoto Pref. | SME | 6 mm or less inner small-diameter pipes made of beta-titanium alloy |
| | Nabel Corporation | Kyoto Pref. | SME | Automatic chicken egg washing, sorting and packaging machine |
| | Kataoka Co. | Kyoto Pref. | SME | Charge-discharge inspection equipment for lithium-ion secondary batteries |
| | Torishima Pump Mfg. Co. | Osaka Pref. | Large enterprise | Large pumps for desalination plants |
| | Riko Float Technology Co. | Osaka Pref. | SME | Floats for industrial |
| | Fukui Seisakusho Co. | Osaka Pref. | SME | Safety valves for LNG carriers |
| | Kanzaki Kokyukoki Mfg. Co. | Hyogo Pref. | Large enterprise | World standardized integrated hydraulic continuously variable speed axle drive (IHT) |
| | Kawasaki Heavy Industries, Ltd. | Hyogo Pref. | Large enterprise | Gearbox products for aviation |
| | Ito Denki Co. | Hyogo Pref. | SME | Motor rollers for conveyor drive |
| Materials & Chemicals | JTEC Corporation | Osaka Pref. | Second-tier company | X-ray mirrors for synchrotron radiation used in large synchrotron radiation facilities and X-ray free electron laser facilities |
| | Daiichi KIGENSO KAGAKU KOGYO. Co. | Osaka Pref. | Second-tier company | Materials for automotive exhaust gas purification catalysts |
| | Shiraishi Kogyo Kaisha. Co. | Osaka Pref. | SME | Calcium carbonate for sealant and adhesive industry |
| | Osaka Titanium Technologies Co. | Hyogo Pref. | Large enterprise | Sponge titanium |
| Electricity & Electronics | Kohoku Kogyo Co. | Shiga Pref. | SME | Highly reliable optical device for submarine cable |
| | Optex Co | Shiga Pref. | SME | Automatic door sensor |
| | SCREEN Graphic Solutions Inc. | Kyoto Pref. | Large enterprise | Roll-type high-speed full-color inkjet printing press |
| | ESPEC Corporation | Osaka Pref. | Large enterprise | Environmental testing equipment that artificially reproduces environmental factors such as temperature, humidity, and pressure to ensure the reliability of industrial products. |
| | Tayca Corporation | Osaka Pref. | Large enterprise | Ceramic transducer for medical ultrasound imaging |
| | Figaro Engineering Co. | Osaka Pref. | SME | Carbon monoxide (CO) gas sensor |
| | Patlite Corporation | Osaka Pref. | SME | Audible & Visual Signaling Devices |
| | Furuno Electric Co. | Hyogo Pref. | Large enterprise | Radar for Merchant Marine |

Source: Ministry of Economy, Trade and Industry (2020), quoted from the "2020 Global Top 100 Niche Companies."

# Section 3
## LABOR SHORTAGES CONFRONTED BY KANSAI

*KUO, Chiu-Wei; NOMURA, Ryosuke*

Since the latter part of 2022, economic and social activities have systematically returned to a state of normalcy following the repercussions of the COVID-19 pandemic. Nonetheless, the economic ramifications stemming from the pandemic have been profound, with the labor market recovery experiencing considerable delays, notably within the non-manufacturing sector. Furthermore, over the medium to long term, Japan faces a demographic decline, contributing to a persistent labor scarcity due to diminishing working-age demographics. Specifically, the anticipated future contraction of the population in the Kansai region surpassing the national average accentuates the urgency in addressing the imminent labor shortage.

In Section 3, we ascertain the prevailing condition of the labor market in Kansai, pinpoint associated challenges, and contemplate strategic responses to potential disruptions in the labor supply. Subsection 3.1 employs statistical data to scrutinize the existing state and obstacles of the labor market in Kansai. Subsection 3.2 provides illustrations of private enterprises that are proactively addressing impending labor shortages, and Subsection 3.3 consolidates the outcomes derived from the analysis presented in Section 3.

## 1. Current situation and issues in the Kansai labor market

### (1) Current situation

Assessing the trajectory of key labor statistical indicators in the Kansai region from 2019 onward, it is evident that the labor market has substantially rebounded from the adverse effects induced by the COVID-19 pandemic. Examining aggregate figures (Table 3-3-1), the employment landscape experienced a downturn in 2020, marked by a decline in the employment rate and an increase in the unemployment rate compared to 2019 – the year preceding the pandemic. However, a recovery ensued in 2021 and 2022. On average, the employment rate in 2022 surpassed the 2019 level, and while the unemployment rate remained elevated compared to 2019, it decreased from the prior year. Notably, in the first quarter of 2023, the employment rate exhibited a decline from the previous year, and the unemployment rate persisted at a level above that of 2019, hinting at a potential interruption in the ongoing recovery. Despite the setbacks induced

**Table 3-3-1**    Trends in Major Labor Market Indicators in Kansai

| total | | | | |
|---|---|---|---|---|
| | labor force participation rate | employment rate | unemployment rate | average monthly working hours |
| 2019 | 59.8 | 58.3 | 2.6 | 37.3 |
| 2020 | 60.0 | 58.2 | 3.0 | 36.1 |
| 2021 | 60.4 | 58.5 | 3.1 | 36.0 |
| 2022 | 60.9 | 59.1 | 2.9 | 36.0 |
| 2023Q1 | 60.5 | 58.8 | 2.9 | 35.7 |

| male | | | | |
|---|---|---|---|---|
| | labor force participation rate | employment rate | unemployment rate | average monthly working hours |
| 2019 | 69.2 | 67.3 | 2.8 | 42.4 |
| 2020 | 69.7 | 67.5 | 3.2 | 40.7 |
| 2021 | 70.0 | 67.8 | 3.2 | 40.6 |
| 2022 | 70.3 | 68.2 | 3.1 | 40.7 |
| 2023Q1 | 70.0 | 67.8 | 3.1 | 40.2 |

| female | | | | |
|---|---|---|---|---|
| | labor force participation rte | employment rate | unemployment rate | average monthly working hours |
| 2019 | 51.5 | 50.2 | 2.3 | 30.9 |
| 2020 | 51.2 | 49.8 | 2.8 | 30.1 |
| 2021 | 51.7 | 50.2 | 2.9 | 30.2 |
| 2022 | 52.4 | 51.0 | 2.6 | 30.4 |
| 2023Q1 | 52.0 | 50.6 | 2.6 | 30.1 |

Note: Figures for 2019-2022 are annual averages of quarterly data. Average monthly working hours is in hours; all other units are in percent.
Source: Labour Force Survey, Statistics Bureau, Ministry of Internal Affairs and Communications

by the COVID-19 pandemic, the number of labor force participation rates has consistently exhibited an upward trajectory from 2019 through the most recent 2023Q1.

When disaggregated by gender, during the peak impact of the COVID-19 pandemic on economic activity in 2020, both the labor force participation rate and employment rate experienced a decline among women, constituting the majority of non-regular workers in the service industry—predominantly engaged in face-to-face interactions with clients. This downturn was notably pronounced within the 15-24 age cohort, where temporary part-time employment (*arubaito*) predominates. While not explicitly detailed in the table, it is noteworthy that the labor force participation rate and employment rate for this demographic decreased by 1.8 and 2.1 percentage points, respectively, from their 2019 levels. Conversely, for men, both the labor force participation rate and the employment rate exhibited an increase, underscoring that the detrimental impacts of the COVID-19 pandemic on the labor market were comparatively less severe for men than for women.

Nevertheless, the unemployment rate witnessed an increment of 0.4 to 0.5 percentage points above the 2019 baseline for both men and women, signifying a deteriorating employment landscape for both genders. Among men, the most substantial surge in the unemployment rate occurred within the 35-44 age cohort, manifesting an increase of 0.8 percentage points from the 2019 level. Conversely, for women, the steepest rise in the unemployment rate occurred within the 25-34 age cohort, constituting the majority of regular workers (29.2%), with a noteworthy uptick of 1.4 percentage points. Subsequently, the 15-24 age cohort and the 55-64 cohort group experienced respective increases of 0.7 percentage points (Table 3-3-2).

In both 2021 and 2022, the labor force participation rates and employment rates demonstrated an upward trajectory for both men and women, rebounding to levels surpassing those of 2019 (excluding women aged 15-24).[1] However, despite a decline in the unemployment rate for both genders in 2022 compared to the previous year, it persisted above the 2019 benchmarks. Among men, the most significant deviation from the 2019 benchmark in the unemployment rate is observed in the 45 to 54 age cohort, registering a +0.5 percentage point

| Table 3-3-2 | Changes in Unemployment Rates Relative to 2019 levels Across Gender and Age Categories (Kansai) |

| male | | | | | | |
| --- | --- | --- | --- | --- | --- | --- |
|  | 15~24 | 25~34 | 35~44 | 45~54 | 55~64 | 65 and over |
| 2020 | +0.5 | -0.1 | +0.8 | +0.4 | +0.7 | +0.0 |
| 2021 | +0.4 | +0.2 | +0.3 | +0.7 | +0.9 | +0.2 |
| 2022 | +0.3 | +0.3 | +0.4 | +0.5 | +0.2 | +0.0 |
| 2023Q1 | -1.2 | +2.0 | +0.5 | +0.5 | +0.1 | -0.8 |
| female | | | | | | |
|  | 15~24 | 25~34 | 35~44 | 45~54 | 55~64 | 65 and over |
| 2020 | +0.7 | +1.4 | +0.0 | +0.3 | +0.7 | -0.2 |
| 2021 | +1.4 | +1.0 | -0.3 | +0.4 | +1.1 | +0.3 |
| 2022 | +1.2 | +0.5 | +0.2 | +0.0 | +0.6 | -0.2 |
| 2023Q1 | +0.3 | +0.8 | -0.1 | +0.1 | +0.5 | -0.1 |

Note: The figures are derived from the annual average of quarterly data on the unemployment rate, with units expressed in percentage points.
Source: Labour Force Survey, Statistics Bureau, Ministry of Internal Affairs and Communications

---

1) In 2022, both the labor force participation rate and employment rate for women aged 15-24 continue to trail the 2019 levels, registering -0.1 percentage points and -0.6 percentage points below, respectively.

difference. Conversely, for women, the divergence from the 2019 benchmark in the unemployment rate was particularly pronounced, recording +1.2 percentage points for those aged 15-24, and +0.5 percentage points and +0.6 percentage points for those aged 25-34 and 55-64, respectively.

In the first quarter of 2023, both the labor force participation rate and the employment rate exhibit a decline from the previous year for both men and women, while the unemployment rate remains unchanged from the previous year's average, persisting at a level surpassing that of 2019. This pattern suggests a halt in the ongoing recovery of the employment situation. Notably, for men, this trend is particularly pronounced within the prime working age cohorts (25-34, 35-44, and 45-54), whereas recovery continues in the older age cohorts (55-64 and 65 and over). In contrast, for women, noticeable declines in both the labor force participation rates and employment rates are apparent in the 15-24 age cohort and the 65 and over age group.

The average monthly working hours for both men and women experienced a notable decline in 2020 compared to 2019. Men's average working hours hovered around 40.7 hours since 2020, further decreasing to 40.2 hours in the first quarter of 2023. Conversely, the average monthly hours worked for women exhibited recovery in 2021 and 2022 but saw a decline again in the first quarter of 2023. This reduction in working hours, despite improvements in the employment situation, can be attributed to two primary factors. First, there was a substantial increase in the number of workers forced to take temporary leave in 2020, coinciding with the onset of the COVID-19 pandemic. Although this number declined post-2020, it remained significantly higher than the 2019 level (refer to Table 3-3-3). Second, as part of the workstyle reform, the overtime work limit was imposed on small and medium-sized enterprises (SMEs) starting from April 2020. The upper limit for overtime work was set at 45 hours per

| Table 3-3-3 | The number of workers forced to take temporary leave and its proportion relative to the employed workforce (Kansai) |

| | total | | male | | female | |
|---|---|---|---|---|---|---|
| | number of workers | proportion | number of workers | proportion | number of workers | proportion |
| 2019 | 27.8 | 2.6 | 10.5 | 1.8 | 17.3 | 3.6 |
| 2020 | 42.3 | 4.0 | 15.8 | 2.7 | 26.3 | 5.6 |
| 2021 | 33.8 | 3.2 | 13.0 | 2.3 | 20.5 | 4.3 |
| 2022 | 33.5 | 3.2 | 13.8 | 2.4 | 19.5 | 4.0 |
| 2023Q1 | 36.0 | 3.4 | 13.0 | 2.3 | 22.0 | 4.6 |

Note: Figures for 2019 to 2022 are annual averages of quarterly data. The number and rate of absences are expressed in thousands and percentages, respectively.
Source: Labour Force Survey, Statistics Bureau, Ministry of Internal Affairs and Communications

month and 360 hours per year, as a general rule.

## (2) Issues

While employment has rebounded from the impact of the COVID-19 pandemic, novel challenges have surfaced. One such challenge is the escalating labor shortage within the non-manufacturing sector. The second challenge is anticipated constraints on labor supply stemming from the continual decline in the working-age population.

## 1) Increased labor shortage within the non-manufacturing sector

Figure 3-3-1 illustrates the employment conditions D.I., an index quantifying the disparity between "Excessive employment" and "insufficient employment," thereby reflecting the evaluative perspective on employment conditions in the Kansai region across various industries. A positive D.I. signifies that a higher percentage of firms perceive their workforce to be in surplus, whereas a negative D.I. suggests that a higher percentage of firms perceive their workforce to be in shortage. As illustrated, both the manufacturing and non-manufacturing industries are exhibiting a declining trend, with the exception of the year 2020, when the COVID-19 pandemic exerted its impact. Particularly noteworthy is the non-manufacturing sector, where the perception of a labor shortage

| Figure 3-3-1 | Employment conditions D.I. by Sector (Mar. 2010-Mar. 2023, Kansai) |

Source: "Short-term Economic Survey of Enterprises in the Kinki Region," Osaka Branch, Bank of Japan

has heightened since 2012, and the disparity with the manufacturing sector has expanded. In the March 2023 survey, the D.I. for the non-manufacturing sector stood at -36, significantly lower than the -21 recorded for the manufacturing sector.

To pinpoint industries in the non-manufacturing sector experiencing a substantial increase in labor demand, we analyzed trends in the number of new job openings by industry. Recognizing the influence of the labor market's size within each industry on the number of new job openings, we calculated the ratio of new job openings by industry to the number of workers in that industry. The trends based on these ratios are visually depicted in Figure 3-3-2.

From 2016 to 2019, prior to the COVID-19 pandemic, the top six industries based on the ratio of new job openings to the number of workers were medical care and welfare, other services, accommodations, eating and drinking services, information and communications, transportation and postal services, and living-related services and entertainment. Notably, only the medical and welfare and construction industries exhibited a sustained upward trend during this period.

In 2020, the impact of the COVID-19 pandemic prompted companies to curtail or suspend their hiring activities, leading to a substantial decline in the ratio of new job openings to the number of workers throughout nearly all industries

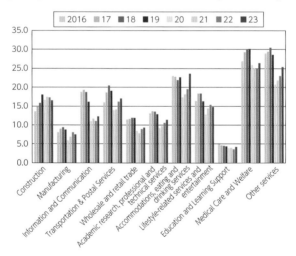

Figure 3-3-2    Ratio of new job openings by industry to the number of workers in that industry (Kansai)

Note: The number of new job openings by industry is the annual average of monthly data (January 2016-April 2023), and the number of workers by industry is the annual average of quarterly data.
Source: "Employment Security Service Statistics," Ministry of Internal Affairs and Communications; "Labour Force Survey," Statistics Bureau, Ministry of Internal Affairs and Communications

(year on year: -11% to -33%). The sole exception was observed in the construction industry, where the year-on-year decline was comparatively modest at -8%.

Following 2020, numerous industries witnessed a gradual recovery in the number of job openings. Notably, the accommodations, eating and drinking services industry experienced a substantial increase in the ratio of new job openings to the number of workers in 2023 (+21.0% year on year). This resurgence can be attributed, in part, to the swift rise in the number of foreign visitors to Japan following the easing of border control measures in October 2022. Consequently, the accommodations, eating and drinking services industry stands as the only sector to have fully recuperated to the 2019 level by 2023.

As of the first quarter of 2023, the six leading industries, based on the ratio of new job openings to the number of workers, comprise medical care and welfare; other services; accommodations, eating and drinking services; construction; transportation and postal services; and lifestyle-related services and entertainment.

In summary, robust labor demand characterized medical care and welfare, service industries involved in face-to-face interactions with clients, and transportation and postal services even before the advent of the COVID-19 pandemic. Notably, the accommodations, eating and drinking services sector exhibited notably robust growth in job openings in the most recent period. Additionally, the construction industry has displayed a consistent and resilient increase in labor demand, maintaining its upward trajectory and avoiding significant decline even during the COVID-19 pandemic.

## 2) Current and anticipated future conditions regarding constraints in labor supply

Although the population aged 15 and over in the Kansai region reached its zenith in 2012 and has since been on a downward trajectory, the count of the labor force has demonstrated a converse trend, experiencing growth since 2023 (refer to Figure 3-3-3). This shift can be primarily attributed to the heightened participation of women and the elderly in the labor market.

Table 3-3-4 illustrates the disparity in the number of labor force participants at each specific point in time (by sex and age cohort) relative to the count five years prior.

The labor force participation rates within the age cohort of 25 to 64 have consistently displayed an upward trajectory over the past two decades. Notably, the engagement of women aged 25-34 in the labor market has exhibited a notable surge since the early 2000s, with their participation rate in 2005 being 7.3 percentage points higher than that of five years earlier. This surge is attributed

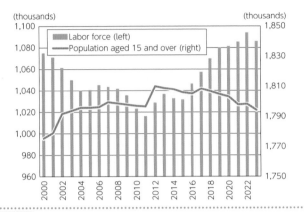

Figure 3-3-3    Population aged 15 and over and labor force (Kansai)

Note: Figures spanning from 2019 to 2022 represent annual averages derived from quarterly data, whereas
      figures for 2023 specifically pertain to the first quarter of that year.
Source: Labour Force Survey, Statistics Bureau, Ministry of Internal Affairs and Communications

Table 3-3-4    Comparison of Labor Force Participation Rates at each specific point in time relative to the count five years prior (by sex and age cohort) (Kansai)

| | male | | | | | |
|---|---|---|---|---|---|---|
| | 15~24 | 25~34 | 35~44 | 45~54 | 55~64 | 65 and over |
| 2005 | -10.1 | -2.9 | -0.7 | -0.4 | -2.1 | -16.5 |
| 2010 | -1.2 | +1.2 | -0.4 | -0.4 | +0.1 | +0.2 |
| 2015 | +1.8 | -1.9 | -1.1 | -0.7 | +3.1 | +8.5 |
| 2020 | +17.1 | +1.1 | -0.6 | -0.6 | +6.8 | +13.1 |
| | female | | | | | |
| | 15~24 | 25~34 | 35~44 | 45~54 | 55~64 | 65 and over |
| 2005 | -5.8 | +7.3 | +2.5 | +1.5 | +0.8 | -8.3 |
| 2010 | -4.3 | +6.9 | +5.2 | +6.7 | +5.9 | +4.4 |
| 2015 | +0.5 | +4.6 | +7.1 | +6.7 | +14.2 | +21.3 |
| 2020 | +16.8 | +9.9 | +8.8 | +4.9 | +19.5 | +15.0 |

Note: Figures used in the calculations are annual averages of quarterly data. All figures are in percentages.
Source: Labour Force Survey, Statistics Bureau, Ministry of Internal Affairs and Communications

to the implementation and amendment of the Child Care and Family Care Leave Law commencing in the 1990s, coupled with the establishment of daycare centers (Higuchi et al., 2016; Yamaguchi, Asai, and Kambayashi, 2018). The concerted efforts to encourage women to remain in the workforce post-child-birth, aided by developments such as the revision of the Child Care and Family Care Leave Law, the enforcement of the Women's Advancement Promotion Law, and a growing understanding of women's roles by companies, have contributed to a substantial increase in the labor force participation rates for women aged

35-44 and 45-54 since the late 2000s. Consequently, the upward trend in labor force participation rates persists for women aged 25-54, driven in part by further amendments to the Child Care and Family Care Leave Law, the enforcement of the Women's Advancement Promotion Law, and improved corporate understanding of women's roles and contributions.

Females aged 55-64 and 65 and above exhibited a discernible upward trajectory in their engagement in the labor market during the latter part of the 2000s, marking a notably steep ascent in the 2010s. This pattern was likewise discerned among males aged 55-64 and 65 and over. The impetus behind this trend appears rooted in the overhauls of the pension system in 1994 and 2000, coupled with the amendment of the Act on Stabilization of Employment of Elderly Persons in 2012 (Yamada, 2017; Kondo and Shigeoka, 2017). Following the pension system revision, the initiation age for the fixed-rate segment of Old-age Employees' Pension special benefits underwent incremental elevation from 60 to 65 between 2001 and 2013, with a subsequent increase for the remuneration-proportional segment spanning from 2013 to 2025. The rise in the commencement age for benefit receipt is anticipated to stimulate employment, given the diminishing pension income until that age. Moreover, the 2012 amendment to the Act on Stabilization of Employment of Elderly Persons mandated companies to retain employees up to the age of 65, affording workers the option to continue working until that age.

However, as depicted in Figure 3-3-3, the pace of the increment in the labor force has decelerated since 2020. In the most recent first quarter of 2023, the female labor force participation rate rebounded to surpass the 2019 level, but only by a marginal +1.1%. The resurgence of women's labor force participation following the impact of the COVID-19 pandemic has been sluggish. Similarly, the growth in the rates of labor force participation for the 55-64 and the 65 and over age cohorts has attenuated, signaling a plateau in the engagement of the elderly in the labor market (Figure 3-3-4).

Beyond the stagnation in the labor participation of women and the elderly, the anticipated acceleration in the future decline of the working-age population is attributed to both a low birthrate and an aging society. Consequently, it is highly probable that labor shortages will exert an impact on supply regulations in the future. To discern the industries susceptible to such effects, we analyzed the age structure within each sector.

Table 3-3-5 shows the demographic composition of the workforce in each industry for the first quarter of 2023. The industries with the lowest share of individuals aged 15-34 were other services, construction, and transportation and postal services, all registering below 20%. Conversely, the top three industries in terms of the proportion of workers aged 65 and over are other services,

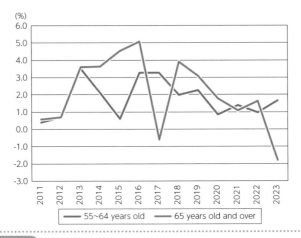

**Figure 3-3-4**    Year-on-year change in the labor force (Kansai)

Note: Figures for 2011 through 2022 represent annual averages derived from quarterly data, while figures for 2023 pertain specifically to the first quarter of the year.
Source: Labour Force Survey, Statistics Bureau, Ministry of Internal Affairs and Communications

**Table 3-3-5**    Demographic composition of the workforce in each industry (Q1 2023, Kansai)

| | 15-34 years old | 35-64 years old | 65 years old and over |
|---|---|---|---|
| Construction | 15.9 | 66.7 | 17.4 |
| Manufacturing | 27.3 | 64.2 | 8.6 |
| Information and Communication | 35.7 | 60.7 | 3.6 |
| Transportation & Postal Services | 17.2 | 72.4 | 10.3 |
| Wholesale and retail trade | 26.2 | 62.2 | 11.6 |
| Academic research, professional and technical services | 22.9 | 62.9 | 14.3 |
| Accommodations, eating and drinking services | 43.1 | 44.8 | 12.1 |
| Lifestyle-related services and entertainment | 30.3 | 48.5 | 21.2 |
| Education and Learning Support | 31.0 | 58.6 | 10.3 |
| Medical Care and Welfare | 23.1 | 65.3 | 11.6 |
| Other services | 13.7 | 63.0 | 23.3 |

Note: Units are expressed in percentages.
Source: Labour Force Survey, Statistics Bureau, Ministry of Internal Affairs and Communications

lifestyle-related services and entertainment, and construction.[2] The percentage of elderly workers in the other services and lifestyle-related services industry, it exceeds 20%, while in the construction industry, it is at 17.4%.

The social infrastructure established during the high-growth period is rapidly aging, and the construction industry anticipates a swift surge in the demand for labor to construct and uphold this infrastructure (Ministry of Land, Infrastructure, Transport and Tourism 2021a). With an aging workforce in the industry and a deficit of younger individuals to inherit and sustain these skills, there exists a shortage of human resources poised to carry the industry forward. This scenario implies imminent supply constraints for services and public investments crucial to maintaining the essential functions of daily life.

Currently, the transportation and postal service industries exhibit a high proportion of middle-aged workers. Consequently, the retirement of older workers is anticipated to have a minimal impact. However, the scarcity of young workers is projected to result in a substantial reduction in the workforce two decades from now.

## 2. Addressing the anticipated labor shortage problem in the future

As mentioned above, the sectors of medical care and welfare, accommodations, eating and drinking services, construction, as well as transportation and postal services presently confront labor shortages attributable to heightened demand, with certain industries inevitably encountering labor supply constraints due to a decline in the working-age population. To surmount these challenges, it is imperative to augment the labor force by enhancing the working environment, encompassing work styles. Equally crucial is the adoption of novel technologies to enhance labor productivity.

[2]   To discern the industries witnessing a progression in population aging, data from the 2020 National Census on the number of workers by industry (industry group, 4-digit) is employed, specifically focusing on the other services and lifestyle-related services and entertainment sectors. Within the other services industry, specifically in building maintenance services and guard services, employing 35.5% of the workforce, the percentages of workers aged 65 and over are notably high at 42.8% and 38.3%, respectively. Likewise, in the laundry, beauty, and bath services, encompassing approximately 50% of the workforce, 20.7% of the workers fall into the 65 and over age category.

Part I

Part II

Part III

Part IV

## (1) Enhancing the accession rate and attachment through the improvement of the work environment.

Figure 3-3-5 illustrates the accession and separation rates by industry for the first half of 2022 at the national level. Despite a considerable number of new job openings, the construction and transportation and postal services exhibit the lowest accession rates. Conversely, service industries involving face-to-face interactions with clients, such as accommodations, eating and drinking services (20.3%), lifestyle-related services and entertainment (14.2%), and other services (11.3%), continue to recover from the COVID-19 pandemic, securing the top three positions in employment rates. Nevertheless, these industries also demonstrate high separation rates (15.0%, 10.0%, and 11.1%, respectively), indicating a low level of worker attachment. Additionally, medical care and welfare rank among the top five in terms of separation rate, suggesting similarly low attachment levels.

The primary factor contributing to the diminished accession and separation rates in these sectors is the challenging working environment. Firstly, suboptimal working conditions are highlighted. As depicted in Figure 3-3-6, which illustrates the average number of paid vacations taken per worker and the average weekly working hours in each industry, construction, transportation and postal services, medical care and welfare, and service-oriented industries involving

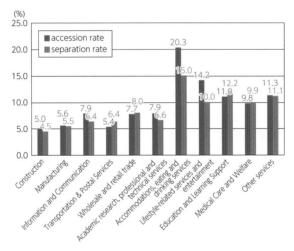

| Figure 3-3-5 | Accession and separation rates by industry (first half of 2022, Japan) |

Note: Figures for 2023 through 2022 are annual averages of quarterly data; figures for 2023 are for the first quarter of 2023.

Source: "Survey on Employment Trends in the First Half of 2022," Ministry of Health, Labor and Welfare

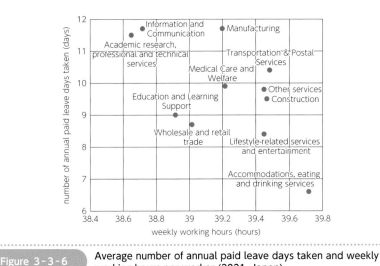

Figure 3-3-6    Average number of annual paid leave days taken and weekly working hours per worker (2021, Japan)

Source: Ministry of Health, Labour and Welfare, 2022 Comprehensive Survey of Working Conditions

face-to-face interactions with clients such as accommodations, eating and drinking services tend to exhibit extended working hours coupled with fewer days of paid leave taken compared to other sectors. This phenomenon is attributed to the prevalent practice of "nakanuke" in the medical, accommodations, eating and drinking services, and transportation industries, where workers experience prolonged work periods with extended breaks during periods of low activity in the middle of the day. Although workers are granted lengthy breaks during these low-demand periods, they are often tethered to work for an extended duration on the same day, making it challenging for them to avail themselves of leave. Furthermore, the construction industry has adopted a norm of working on holidays and maintaining prolonged working hours to meet construction deadlines.[3]

Low wages constitute another contributing factor. Illustrated in Figure 3-3-7 are the earnings of ordinary employees, predominantly regular workers, and part-time employees, primarily non-regular workers. Throughout accommodation, eating and drinking services, lifestyle-related services and entertainment, other services, as well as transportation and postal services, wages fall below

---

3) As per the Ministry of Land, Infrastructure, Transport, and Tourism (2021b), the aggregate annual working hours for construction workers in FY 2020 exceeded those of all industries by 364 hours, constituting an approximately 20% increase. Furthermore, around 40% of engineers engaged in construction activities operate on a schedule that allows for only four or fewer days off within a four-week period.

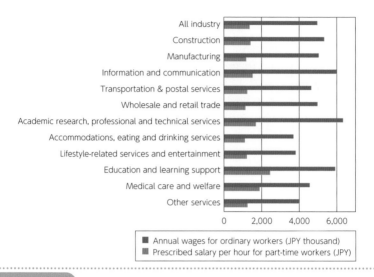

**Figure 3-3-7**    Wages by Employment Type by Industry (2022, Japan)

Note: "Part-time workers" are workers who have shorter prescribed working hours per day or the same pre-scribed working hours per day but fewer prescribed working days per week than ordinary workers at the same establishment. The annual wage of an ordinary worker is calculated as "cash paid on time" x 12 + "annual bonus and other special salary."
Source: "Basic Survey on Wage Structure," Ministry of Health, Labour and Welfare

the industry-wide average for both types of employment. Notably, wages in the accommodations and eating and drinking services industry rank as the lowest among both regular and part-time employment. Although wages in service industries with face-to-face interactions experienced a significant increase in 2022 due to a heightened labor shortage following the post-COVID-19 economic normalization (Nishioka, 2022), they remain relatively low compared to other sectors.

In summary, improvements in the working environment, including work-styles and wages, are essential to improve the job accession rate and attachment in these industries.

## (2) Improving productivity by introducing new technologies

The incorporation of new technologies holds the potential to enhance productivity and mitigate labor shortages by elevating work efficiency and diminishing the need for manpower. Historically, the advent of microelectronics (ME) technology in the 1980s catalyzed the widespread adoption of industrial robots and machine tools in manufacturing settings. Concurrently, the introduction of office computers, word processors, and other office automation (OA) machines revolutionized office work. This technological advancement led to significant labor savings, particularly in the manufacturing sector, where numerous production processes witnessed a reduction in personnel, accompanied by advancements in unmanned operations (Nakayama, 1987). Consequently, this transition resulted in heightened production volume and efficiency, all achieved without a corresponding increase in the workforce (New Energy and Industrial Technology Development Organization 2014).

In recent years, the advancement of Information and Communication Technology (ICT) has broadened the application of information devices, Local Area Networks (LANs), and the Internet. This evolution is exemplified by the systemization of diverse tasks, the automation of office work through Robotic Process Automation (RPA), and the emergence of smart factories leveraging Artificial Intelligence (AI) and the Internet of Things (IoT). A noteworthy trend involves the pursuit of new business models and enhanced customer value by optimizing business processes through the effective management and analysis of data stored in information devices.

The adoption of these innovative technologies not only enhances productivity by optimizing the efficient utilization of limited human resources, but also facilitates skill transfer and enhances the working environment, including workstyles.

## (3) Examples

This subsection outlines instances of addressing labor shortages in the medical care and welfare, accommodations, eating and drinking services, transportation and postal services, and construction industries through the enhancement of the working environment and the adoption of new technologies (Table 3-3-6).

### 1) Medical care and welfare - Sompo Care Inc.

SOMPO Care initiated a demonstration experiment in July 2022 to assess the impact of introducing nursing care robots and information devices on staff workload and the quality of services at multiple nursing care facilities.[4] The results of the verification demonstrated that the implementation of nursing care robots not only reduced the work hours of staff members but also concurrently increased the time available for them to undertake actions aimed at enhancing

Part I

**Part II**

Part III

Part IV

---

4) "DX in nursing care is a dream or an experiment," [in Japanese] Nikkei, November 22, 2022.(https://www.nikkei.com/article/DGXZQOUA1102L0R11C22A1000000/ last viewed June 23, 2023)

| Table 3-3-6 | Examples of Working Environment Improvement and New Technology Introduction |
|---|---|

| Name | Initiative |
|---|---|
| Sompo Care Inc. | Demonstration experiments were conducted to alleviate staff workload through the utilization of nursing care robots, including a "sleep sensor" for remote monitoring of residents' sleep status and an "automatic position changer" designed to prevent bedsores. Furthermore, an "independence support application" was developed to predict patients' conditions by analyzing data such as patient care records in comparison with information accumulated from over 30,000 patients over the preceding years. This initiative represents an effort to transform the observation and prediction of users' conditions, traditionally reliant on the tacit knowledge of skilled staff, by harnessing the insights derived from nursing care data. |
| Jinya Co., Ltd. | A cloud-based system was implemented to centralize the management of information, encompassing customer relations, time and attendance tracking, and business analysis, with the aim of enhancing operational efficiency and fostering information sharing among employees. Additionally, service quality was elevated through the integration of sensors, devices, and IoT technology. The company underwent a shift in work allocation from a strict division of labor to a multitasking approach, minimizing unnecessary waiting times and reducing the duration during which employees were engaged in tasks. Moreover, the adoption of a three-day workweek not only heightened employee satisfaction but also led to a substantial reduction in employee turnover. |
| Sekisui House, Ltd. | The integration and restructuring of disparate systems and databases across departments enabled the efficient utilization of information, resulting in substantial cost reductions and productivity enhancements. Furthermore, the widespread adoption of iPads throughout the company allowed field employees to access the system and conduct work directly through these devices. This approach facilitated direct transitions between the field and home, leading to a significant reduction in overtime hours. To further enhance the working environment at construction sites, the company is actively engaged in the development and implementation of construction robots. |
| Yamato Transport Co., Ltd. | Since 2020, the company has been executing a "data-based management" strategy, enhancing on-site operational efficiency through data analysis and the integration of AI. A notable instance involves the application of machine learning technology to forecast cargo volumes at distribution centers three to four months in advance, allowing for the optimization of employee shifts and vehicle assignments based on these predictions. Additional initiatives comprise the deployment of logistics support robots to streamline sorting and loading operations, resulting in reduced manpower and heightened efficiency. |

the quality of care.[5]

This initiative stems from a pronounced labor shortage in the nursing care industry. In light of the outcomes of this demonstration project, the Ministry of Health, Labour, and Welfare is contemplating the possibility of revising the existing standard, currently set at one staff member per three patients.

SOMPO care has incorporated machines equipped with sensors, aiming to comprehensively understand users' conditions without imposing an additional

---

5) Report on the Project for Measuring the Effectiveness of Efforts to Improve Productivity through the Use of Nursing-care Robots," [in Japanese] Document from the 216th Subcommittee on Nursing-care Benefits, Council on Social Security, April 27, 2023 (https://www.mhlw.go.jp/content/12300000/001091715.pdf last viewed June 23, 2023)

burden on staff. Additionally, the company has developed an application that forecasts a patient's condition several months in advance by analyzing the patient's nursing care data in comparison with information from over 30,000 patients accumulated in the past. This initiative seeks to actualize the observation and prediction of a user's condition, traditionally reliant on the tacit knowledge of skilled staff, through the utilization of nursing care data. The anticipation is that preventing the deterioration of a patient's condition will alleviate the workload on staff and ultimately contribute to the mitigation of staff turnover.[6]

## 2) Accommodation service - Jinya Co., Ltd.

In 2009, Jinya Corporation, a small ryokan (inn) situated in Tsurumaki Onsen, Kanagawa Prefecture, implemented a cloud-based system to efficiently centralize information, spanning from customer management to attendance and business analysis. This initiative aimed to enhance operational efficiency and facilitate the seamless sharing of essential information among employees. Additionally, the integration of IoT technology and equipment, including sensors and cameras, played a pivotal role in elevating service quality. Noteworthy applications included the automatic reading of license plate numbers for arriving cars and the monitoring of user numbers, water temperature, and the availability of towels in the public baths.

Simultaneously, there was a shift in the distribution of work at Jinya, transitioning from a strict division of labor, where each task had a dedicated employee, to a multitasking system. This approach involves one employee performing various tasks, ranging from front desk responsibilities to room cleaning. The adjustment aimed to minimize unnecessary waiting times and reduce the overall time spent by employees. Additionally, a three-day workweek was instituted, incorporating a variable schedule of 10 hours per day starting in 2020. This change led to a notable increase in employee satisfaction and a significant decrease in turnover.[7], [8]

6) "Supporting Unchanged Lifestyles with Digital x Expertise - Transformation into 'Predictive Care'," [in Japanese] SOMPO Holdings News Release, April 18, 2022 (https://www.sompo-hd.com/-/media/hd/files/news/2022/20220418_1.pdf?la=ja-JP last viewed June 23, 2023)
7) "Working with a 'Three-day Weekend' - How Will Working Standards Change? -," [in Japanese] Recruit Works Research Institute, April 3, 2023 (https://www.works-i.com/research/works-report/item/4dayww_2023.pdf last viewed June 23, 2023)
8) Survey on the Management Status of Small and Medium Inns," [in Japanese] Organization for Small & Medium Enterprises and Regional Innovation, March 2017 (https://www.smrj.go.jp/doc/ research_case/h28_ryokan_full.pdf last viewed June 23, 2023)

### 3) Construction - Sekisui House, Ltd.

Commencing in 2010, Sekisui House initiated the "Mansion Information Project" aimed at integrating and restructuring independent systems and databases within each department to achieve company-wide optimization. By centralizing the management of scattered information, the company successfully utilized data and streamlined business processes, resulting in substantial cost reductions and improvements in productivity (Shishikura, 2019). Additionally, from 2013 onwards, the company actively promoted the use of iPads throughout its operations. Field employees leveraged iPads to enter and engage with the system, facilitating a direct transition from the field to home and significantly reducing overtime hours.[9]

In 2018, the company unveiled a robot designed to assist in the installation of plasterboard on ceilings—a physically demanding task. Currently under development for future practical use, the introduction of this robot is anticipated to alleviate the workload of construction workers, potentially reducing it by up to 70%.[10]

### 4) Transportation - Yamato Transport Co., Ltd.

Since 2020, Yamato Transport has actively pursued a "shift to data-based management" strategy, focusing on enhancing on-site operations through data analysis and the integration of AI. A notable application involves the implementation of machine learning technology to establish a system predicting package volume at distribution centers three to four months in advance. This predictive system enables the optimization of employee shifts and vehicle assignments based on the anticipated workload.[11] Furthermore, to enhance safety and efficiency in sorting and loading operations, a logistics support robot was introduced at sorting sites to prevent accidents and reduce manpower. In November 2022, the company conducted a demonstration test of a personal delivery service using unmanned automatic delivery robots in Ishikari City, Hokkaido.

---

9) "17,000 iPads Utilized by All Employees, In-house Apps, 15 Hours Less Overtime per Month," [in Japanese] Nikkei Computer, January 10, 2019.

10) "Robot Technology to be Introduced to Housing Construction Sites to Reduce Workload by up to 70% and Improve Construction Site Environment," [in Japanese] Sekisui House, Ltd. press release, May 16, 2018 (https://www.sekisuihouse.co.jp/library/company/topics/datail/__icsFiles/afieldfile/2018/05/16/20180516_2.pdf last viewed June 23, 2023)

11) "Yamato Transport Achieves Optimal Allocation of Management Resources with MLOps," [in Japanese] ExaWizards Corporation, Case Study, August 3, 2022 (https://exawizards.com/works/20297 last viewed June 23, 2023)

## 3. Summary

While the labor market in the Kansai region is gradually rebounding from the impact of the COVID-19 pandemic, the extent of recovery exhibits variations based on gender and age group. Women, predominantly constituting informal workers in service industries with face-to-face interactions, experienced more pronounced setbacks during the pandemic; however, they have largely recuperated. Conversely, for men, the pandemic's impact was comparatively milder than for women, but the recovery of the employment situation has decelerated, particularly within the prime working age cohort.

The current pressing concern revolves around the escalating labor shortage in the non-manufacturing sector. Industries such as medical care and welfare, services involving face-to-face interactions with clients, and transportation and postal services have witnessed substantial job openings, even predating the COVID-19 pandemic. Simultaneously, the construction industry, which remained relatively unaffected during the pandemic, has been experiencing a consistent and growing demand for labor. Concerns are emerging regarding potential labor supply constraints in certain services, including transportation and postal service, and construction in the future due to persistent labor shortages.

To address these challenges, it is crucial to prioritize the enhancement of the working environment, aiming to elevate the accession rate and attachment within the mentioned industries. An integral component of this improvement involves the introduction of new technologies. Technological innovation serves not only to boost labor productivity, but also to enhance working conditions and workstyles, as evidenced by several successful cases. Anticipated to gain further momentum in the future, this trend holds the potential to foster positive changes across various sectors.

## References

Higuchi, M., Sakamoto, K., and Hagiwara, R. (2016), "Women's Constraints to Marriage, Childbearing, and Employment and Verification of the Effects of Various Measures: A Work-Life Balance Analysis Using a Household Panel Survey" (Japanese title: *Josei no Kekkon Shussan Shugyo no Seiyaku Yoin to Shotaisaku no Kouka Kensho: Kakei Paneru Chosa Niyoru Waku-Raifu-Baransu Bunseki*), [in Japanese] Mita Journal of Commerce 58 (6), pp. 29-57

Kondo, A., and Shigeoka, H. (2017), "The Effectiveness of Demand-side Government Intervention to Promote Elderly Employment: Evidence from Japan," ILR Review 70(4), pp.1008-1036

Part I

**Part II**

Part III

Part IV

Ministry of Land, Infrastructure, Transport and Tourism (2021a), White Paper on Land, Infrastructure, Transport and Tourism 2021 [in Japanese]. (https://www.mlit.go.jp/hakusyo/mlit/r02/hakusho/r03/html/n1221000.html, last viewed June 14, 2023).

Ministry of Land, Infrastructure, Transport and Tourism (2021b) "Current Status and Issues of Workplace Reform in the Construction Industry" (Japanese title: *Kensetsugyo no Hatarakikata Kaikaku no Genjo to Kadai*), [in Japanese] (https://www.kensetsu-kikin.or.jp/news/57a42379796b2a6c1d23286d40ea5b611f163364.pdf, last viewed June 14, 2023).

Nakayama, T. (1987) "The Progress of Microelectronics and Its Impact on the Production Process and Employment" (Japanese title: *Maikuroerekutoron-ikusuka no Shinten to Sono Seisan Katei Koyo eno Inpakuto*), [in Japanese] Hitotsubashi Journal of Economics 11(4), pp. 43-57

New Energy and Industrial Technology Development Organization (2014), NEDO Robot White Paper 2014. [in Japanese] (https://www.nedo.go.jp/content/100567345.pdf, last viewed June 20, 2023).

Nishioka, S. (2022), "Severe Labor Shortages Put Uptick in Japan's Wages: Unemployment Rate Could Break Below 2% as Labor Participation Rate Stagnates" (Japanese title: *Shinkoku na Hitode Busoku de Wagakuni Chingin ni Josyo Atsuryoku -Rodo Sankaritsu no Teitai de Shitugyoritsu 2% Ware mo Shiya-*), [in Japanese] Japan Research Institute Research Focus No. 2022-051. (https://www.jri.co.jp/MediaLibrary/file/report/researchfocus/pdf/13880.pdf, last viewed June 14, 2023).

Shishikura, M. (2019), "Sekisui House's IT Department's Approach to Using Data in the Enterprise" (Japanese title: *Sekisui Hausu no IT Bumon ga Kakaeru Kigyonai Deta Katsuyojutsu*), [in Japanese] UNISYS TECHNOLOGY REVIEW 142, pp. 19-25

Yamada, A. (2017), "Rising Employment Rates and Income Blankets Associated with Raising the Starting Age for Pension Benefits: Analysis Based on the Ministry of Health, Labour and Welfare's Longitudinal Survey of Middle-aged and Older Workers (2014)" (Japanese title: *Nenkin Shikyu Kaishi Nenrei Hikiage ni Tomonau Shugyoritsu Josho to Shotoku no Kuhaku: KoseiRodoSho 'Chukonensha Judan Chosa (2014nen)' ni Motozuku Bunseki*) [in Japanese] Japan Institute for Labour Policy and Training (ed.), Employment of Older People in a Declining Society, pp. 194-216.

Yamaguchi, S., Asai, Y., and Kambayashi, R. (2018) "Effects of Subsidized Child-care on Mothers' Labor Supply under a Rationing Mechanism," Labour Economics, 55, pp. 1-17

# Chapter 4

# INBOUND DEMAND RECOVERY AND TOURISM STRATEGY

## Section 1
### REVIEWING TEN YEARS OF KANSAI'S TOURISM STRATEGY: THE TOURISM AGENCY'S BUDGET AND LARGE HOTEL CONSTRUCTION TRENDS

*NOMURA, Ryosuke; INADA, Yoshihisa; INOUE, Kenji*

Section 1 reviews 10 years of tourism strategies from the viewpoints of the national government and private sectors, and clarifies the challenges of tourism strategies for the future. Specifically, Subsection 1.1 reviews the budget of Japan Tourism Agency for the past 10 years and discusses the characteristics of the national tourism strategy. In Subsection 1.2, we focus on micro-based hotel construction trends in the Kansai region to extract the characteristics of the response to inbound tourism demand, considering the challenges posed by the COVID-19 pandemic and the upcoming Osaka-Kansai Expo. While this white paper has focused mainly on the demand side, this section discusses the supply side and sustainability of the tourism industry. Finally, we present a summary of Section 1.

## 1. Characteristics of the tourism strategy based on a 10-year budget allocation

### (1) Budget trends of the Japan Tourism Agency
First, we will examine the Tourism Agency's budget from FY 2014 to FY 2023[1] (Figure 4-1-1).

The budget increased sharply from JPY 9.8 billion in FY 2014 to JPY 20 billion in FY 2016. Looking back at the inbound tourism demand during this period, "Bakugai" (explosive buying) became a social phenomenon in 2014 and

---

1) The budget amounts are the total of the initial budget, and do not include reconstruction quotas or economic measures.

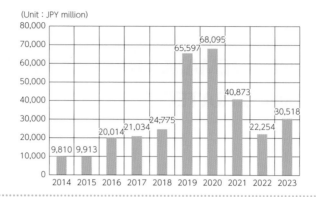

(Unit : JPY million)

**Figure 4-1-1**  Trends in Tourism Agency Budget: FY 2014-23

Source: Compiled from Japan Tourism Agency

2015, during which the number of Chinese tourists visiting Japan skyrocketed.

This trend continued after FY 2017, reaching JPY 65.6 billion in FY 2019 and a record high of JPY 680 billion in FY 2020. However, inbound tourism demand disappeared due to the COVID-19 pandemic, and the budget fell sharply to JPY 40.9 billion in FY 2021 and JPY 22.3 billion in FY 2022. In FY 2023, the budget increased to JPY 30.5 billion in expectation of a recovery in demand.

The trends in budgets thus indicate a response to the trend of foreign visitors to Japan. Next, we will clarify the characteristics of the budget by purpose.

## (2) Characteristics of the budget by purpose

Table 4-1-1 shows the budget allocated for each fiscal year, categorized by purpose. In addition to public relations activities and improvement of the environment for foreign visitors to Japan, the budget also includes items related to SDGs, D&I and DX (Digital Transformation).

Next, Figure 4-1-2 shows the changes in the budget amount by purpose. "Attracting foreign visitors", promotions targeting foreign countries, accounted for more than 80% of the total budget in FY 2014 and FY 2015.

From FY 2016 to FY 2018, the budget for "Improving the environment for foreign visitors" increased, possibly because local regions were improving their receptions of foreign visitors in response to a steady increase in international tourists. From FY 2019 to FY 2020, there was a large increase in the budget for "regional visitor attraction". This suggests that the funds were allocated to the discovery and improvement of tourism resources to increase the number of foreign visitors to each region. In FY 2019, there was an increase in the budget for regional development for tourism and DMO". The increase reflected the reform

| Table 4-1-1 | Tourism Agency Budget Classified by Purpose |
| --- | --- |

| Classification by purpose | Classification Definition |
| --- | --- |
| Attracting foreign visitors | Budget related to PR activities for foreign countries |
| Improving the environment for foreign visitors | Budget for measures to improve the environment for foreign visitors to Japan, such as immigration and tourist information |
| Attracting foreign visitors to the region | Budget for measures to explore and refine local tourism resources |
| Tourism development and DMO | Budget for measures to create tourism regions before the institutionalization of DMOs, and for measures to support and reform DMOs |
| Human Resource Development | Budget for the development of tourism-related human resources, including specialized personnel and interpreters |
| Accommodations and private lodging | Budget for measures to improve the lodging environment, such as improving the lodging facilities and optimizing the private accommodations |
| Exchange population | Budget for measures to increase the exchange population with other regions in Japan |
| Value added and DX | Budget for measures to increase productivity and value added in the tourism sector and support digitalization |
| SDGs | Budget for the creation of a model for promoting sustainable tourism |
| D&I | Budget for universal tourism measures |
| EBPM | Budget related to the collection and analysis of tourism-related data |
| Others | Budget not applicable to the above |
| Budget for reconstruction | Budget for reconstruction and promotion of tourism after the Great East Japan Earthquake (separate appropriation) |
| Economic measures | Budget for measures to support tourism in the COVID-19 pandemic (separate appropriation) |

Source: Compiled from Japan Tourism Agency website

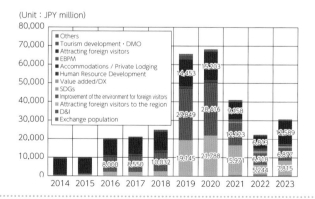

(Unit : JPY million)

| Figure 4-1-2 | Budget of Japan Tourism Agency: FY 2014-2023 |
| --- | --- |

Source: Compiled based on Japan Tourism Agency

of DMO, which plays a role in tourism regional development, in accordance with word-standard DMO formation[2].

From the FY 2021 - to FY 2022, a new category "value added and DX" was established in response to the changes caused by the COVID-19 pandemic. Specifically, anticipating a full-fledged recovery in inbound tourism demand, the budget allocated funds to projects that promote online tourism using DX or create tourism content using digital technology. In FY 2023, a large share of the budget was again allocated to "attracting foreign visitors" in response to the recovery of inbound demand. Utilizing cultural resources to develop tourism contents aiming towards inbound tourism led to a larger budget for "regional tourism promotion" compared to previous fiscal year, indicating that tourism resources were being improved in preparation for the recovery of inbound demand.

The above trends suggest five phases of Japan Tourism Agency's budget: (1) overseas promotion, (2) improving of the reception environment for inbound tourists, (3) creating local contents, (4) responding to COVID-19, and (5) recovery in inbound tourism demand.

## 2. COVID-19 pandemic and hotel construction

Subsection 1.1 reviewed the changes in national tourism strategy over the past decade using budget data of the Japan Tourism Agency. Subsection 1.2 draws attention to the private sector. Specifically, we look at how private sectors respond to COVID-19 by focusing on the supply side of hotel construction in the Kansai region.

### (1) Planned Construction Costs of Lodging Industry in Kansai

First, let's review the construction trends of the lodging industry. Table 4-1-2 shows the planned construction cost of accommodation facilities in each of the prefectures in the Kansai region, based on the "Survey of Construction Starts" by the Ministry of Land, Infrastructure, Transport and Tourism. The estimated cost in Osaka Prefecture increased six-fold from JPY 26.7 billion in 2015 to JPY 154.8 billion in 2017. Similarly, the cost in Kyoto Prefecture increase significantly from JPY 4.9 billion in 2015 to JPY 92.8 billion in 2017. The surge in the construction of accommodation facilities might be due to the aforementioned rapid increase in the number of foreign visitors to Japan triggered by the "bakugai".

In Osaka Prefecture, the planned amount peaked in 2017 and remained

---

2) For more information on the government's DMO policy, refer to the Tourism Chronology.

at the JPY 90 billion level from 2018 to 2019. On the other hand, the planned amount in Kyoto Prefecture peaked in 2018, and reached the same amount as Osaka Prefecture in 2019.

In 2020, the amount decreased in both Osaka and Kyoto prefectures from the previous year due to the COVID-19 pandemic. In 2021, it increased slightly to JPY 75.1 billion in Osaka Prefecture, but continued to decline further to JPY 13 billion in Kyoto Prefecture.

In 2022, the planned costs significantly decrease to JPY 13.3 billion in Osaka Prefecture, but Kyoto Prefecture increased substantially to JPY 46.2 billion from the previous year. As shown, the planned construction cost reveals the response of the private sectors to inbound tourism demand. In the next subsection, we will examine the response to inbound tourism demand after the COVID-19 pandemic, using microdata on the movements of large-scale hotel construction.

**Table 4-1-2**  Planned Construction Costs for Buildings in the Lodging Industry: 2011-2022

[Number of building]

Unit : number of building

| | 2011 | 2012 | 2013 | 2014 | 2015 | 2016 | 2017 | 2018 | 2019 | 2020 | 2021 | 2022 | Total |
|---|---|---|---|---|---|---|---|---|---|---|---|---|---|
| Shiga pref. | 3 | 13 | 4 | 9 | 13 | 8 | 30 | 4 | 4 | 49 | 40 | 80 | 257 |
| Kyoto pref. | 13 | 9 | 33 | 27 | 35 | 150 | 254 | 265 | 195 | 110 | 21 | 44 | 1,156 |
| Osaka pref. | 13 | 18 | 11 | 12 | 29 | 100 | 133 | 85 | 99 | 54 | 27 | 24 | 605 |
| Hyogo pref. | 17 | 28 | 40 | 24 | 34 | 41 | 68 | 43 | 38 | 40 | 62 | 159 | 594 |
| Nara pref. | 10 | 0 | 7 | 5 | 7 | 6 | 22 | 7 | 15 | 7 | 0 | 10 | 96 |
| Wakayama Pref. | 22 | 16 | 33 | 31 | 19 | 22 | 22 | 19 | 13 | 10 | 9 | 30 | 246 |
| Total | 78 | 84 | 128 | 108 | 137 | 327 | 529 | 423 | 364 | 270 | 159 | 347 | 2,954 |

[Planned Construction Cost]

Unit : JPY million

| | 2011 | 2012 | 2013 | 2014 | 2015 | 2016 | 2017 | 2018 | 2019 | 2020 | 2021 | 2022 | Total |
|---|---|---|---|---|---|---|---|---|---|---|---|---|---|
| Shiga pref. | 564 | 1,355 | 57 | 940 | 745 | 3,610 | 14,033 | 157 | 2,337 | 1,402 | 789 | 2,512 | 28,503 |
| Kyoto pref. | 9,963 | 1,731 | 18,666 | 16,680 | 4,915 | 32,204 | 92,837 | 106,212 | 91,247 | 48,974 | 12,953 | 46,168 | 482,550 |
| Osaka pref. | 3,385 | 10,738 | 13,552 | 1,948 | 26,701 | 77,902 | 154,810 | 94,200 | 89,829 | 66,711 | 75,145 | 13,338 | 628,258 |
| Hyogo pref. | 1,131 | 1,559 | 4,473 | 6,955 | 11,652 | 18,895 | 9,591 | 27,771 | 15,564 | 3,141 | 4,845 | 10,579 | 116,156 |
| Nara pref. | 290 | 0 | 1,210 | 1,143 | 3,511 | 259 | 8,212 | 5,080 | 6,290 | 4,515 | 0 | 7,508 | 38,019 |
| Wakayama Pref. | 377 | 460 | 753 | 626 | 516 | 508 | 608 | 479 | 967 | 582 | 2,804 | 2,938 | 11,617 |
| Total | 15,710 | 15,843 | 38,710 | 28,293 | 48,040 | 133,378 | 280,091 | 233,898 | 206,235 | 125,325 | 96,537 | 83,042 | 1,305,102 |

Source: Compiled from Ministry of Land, Infrastructure, Transport and Tourism, "Survey of Construction Starts

## (2) Inbound tourism demand and hotel construction response

As mentioned earlier, the rapid increase of inbound tourism demand since the mid-2010s has stimulated construction investment in hotels and other accommodation facilities. Here we focus on the trend of hotel construction in the Kansai

Part I

Part II

Part III

Part IV

region by utilizing APIR's own survey[3]. Specifically, we summarize and analyze the number of large-scale hotels that opened in the six prefectures of the Kansai region from 2017 to 2023 and their construction costs. Similar analysis is also conducted for properties scheduled to open by 2026.

Figure 4-1-3 shows the number of new hotel openings in each prefecture. Of the 75 large-scale hotels that have opened or are scheduled to open, Osaka Prefecture accounts for about 51% (38 openings) and Kyoto Prefecture accounts for about 36% (27 openings). making up more than 80% of the Kansai region. Figure 4-1-4 shows the construction cost (estimated) of large-scale hotels. The

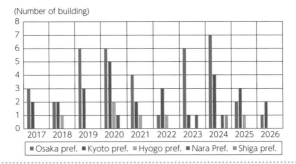

| Figure 4-1-3 | Number of large-scale hotels opened in Kansai: 2017-2026 |

Note: Actual opening until 2022; scheduled openings from 2023 onwards.
Source: Compiled by APIR from various press articles

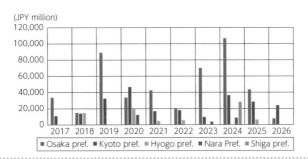

| Figure 4-1-4 | Trends in construction value of large-scale hotels in Kansai: 2017-2026 |

Note: Actual openings until 2022; scheduled openings from 2023 onwards.
Source: Compiled by APIR from various press articles

---

3) Hotels in this study are selected if their estimated construction cost is JPY 4 billion or more and the total floor area is 3,000 tsubo or more. For more details, see Inoue, Nomura and Inada (2023).

total construction cost (JPY 794.6 billion) during this period indicates that Osaka and Kyoto prefectures have by far the largest shares, at 58% and 30%, respectively. In terms of both number and scale, the construction of large-scale hotels is concentrated in Osaka and Kyoto. The geographical distribution in Osaka and Kyoto Prefectures is shown in Reference Figure 4-1-1 below.

## (3) Features of Hotel Construction
Next, let us focus on the brand and grades of lodging expense of large-scale hotel construction.

Figure 4-1-5 shows the number of hotels that opened or are scheduled to open between 2017 and 2026, divided into domestic and overseas hotels. the number of large hotels openings (75 openings) peaked in 2020 with 14 openings. Although the COVID-19 pandemic slowed the pace of new openings from 2021 to 2023, the number of new openings is expected to increase again in 2024, with 13 new openings planned in expectation of a recovery from the pandemic. The number of openings of domestic hotels peaked at 10 in 2020, partly due to the pandemic, and has averaged about 4 annually since 2021. On the other hand, while the number of foreign hotels was 4 in 2000 and decreased from 2021 to 2022, it started to increased again in 2023. The number is expected to increase steadily to 9 in 2024 and 5 in 2025.

Figure 4-1-6 shows the trends of hotel construction by grades of lodging expense[4] (per room per night). Until 2020, the majority of the properties had relatively reasonable rates (B and A). However, as more foreign-brand hotels

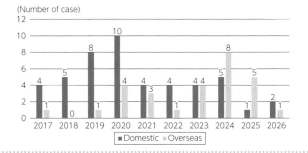

**Figure 4-1-5**   Hotel openings by brands: 2017-2026

Note: Actual openings until 2022; scheduled openings from 2023 onwards
Source: Compiled by APIR from various press articles

---

4) The grades of the unit price per night are as follows: B: from about JPY 10,000, A: from about JPY 30,000, S: from about JPY 50,000, and H: from about JPY 100,000.

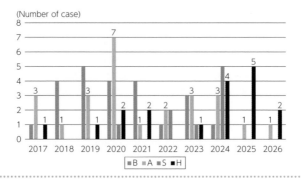

**Figure 4-1-6**    Hotel construction by grades of lodging expense: 2017-2026

Note: Actual openings until 2022; scheduled openings from 2011 onwards.
Source: Compiled by APIR from various press articles

started to open, the number of hotels with high room rates (S, H) has been increasing since 2023.

Thus, as the number of foreign guests increases, the number of openings also increased steadily at peak at 2020, when the COVID-19 started. Some of the opened hotels were shut down and later transferred to other brands before reopening, while others continued to be built and opened after the construction was suspended.[5] However, expecting a recovery from the pandemic, overseas top luxury brand and major hotels in Japan continue to steadily build their hotels. Since it takes a minimum of four years from the acquisition of land to the opening for large hotels, many of the hotels scheduled to open around 2024 are probably planning for the Osaka-Kansai Expo. As such, the construction of major hotels in the Kansai region is focusing on quality rather than quantity, in response to the growing number of wealthy foreign visitors.

## 3. How did the lodging business operators respond to the COVID-19 pandemic?

In June 2019, Prime Minister Shinzo Abe met with Chinese President Xi Jinping at the G20 Osaka Summit and invited him to visit Japan. On January 15, 2020, Chief Cabinet Secretary Suga headed the 36th meeting of the Tourism Strategy Promotion Council and discussed about "Promoting foreigner-friendly accommodation in rural areas". The discussion agreed on: 1) the government and

---

5) For more information on hotel construction trends in the Kansai region, see Tourism Chronology.

financial institutions should cooperate to encourage aggressive capital invest-ment to increase the value added and attractiveness of lodging facilities; 2) the government should promote multilingualization and the separation of lodging and food services.

Many lodging businesses had been optimistic about the bright future of the industry and invested aggressively. However, Japan was hit by the COVID-19 pandemic as cherry blossoms were blooming, and "state of emergency" and "Priority measures to prevent the spread" were repeatedly issued and lifted from April 2020 to until March 2022. How did domestic lodging businesses respond to this unprecedented crisis situation?

Because of the pandemic, hotels were forced out of business, or had their properties sold and rebranded by other firms. Some suspended constructions or delayed their opening. On the other hand, some business owners looked towards the post-COVID and continued to invest steadily in construction and make new developments. The followings are some notable examples.

## (1) Examples of well-established and emerging businesses affected by the setbacks of the COVID-19 pandemic

### Fujita Kanko

Originating from the Fujita zaibatsu established in 1869, Fujita Kanko is a prom-inent lodging business that owns 62 hotels domestic and abroad (as of August 2023), including the Chinzanso, Kowakien, and Washington Hotel. In June 2019, the historic banquet facility Taikoen, which had been used as guesthouse during the G20 Osaka Summit, faced several closures and openings due to the COVID-19 pandemic and a significant decline in demand for weddings and banquets. In June 2021, the establishment ended its operation. By selling the assets, Fujita Kanko managed to improve its deteriorating financial situation.

Meanwhile, a new brand "Hotel Tabinos" with a "MANGA" motif was devel-oped in Hamamatsu-cho, Asakusa, and Kyoto from 2019 to 2021. The once out of business Hotel Kirara Resort Kanku was also reopened as Kanku Izumiotsu Washington Hotel in 2021. Similarly, the Hakone Hotel Kowakien, which was closed down in 2018 due to deterioration, was rebuilt and reopened in July 2023.

### White Bear Family.

White Bear Family went bankrupt in 2020 with the largest debt in the travel and lodging industry (total debt of the three companies exceeded JPY 51 billion). The company as a travel planner and travel agency since 1977, based in Hyogo Prefecture. From 2004, starting in Okinawa and then expanding national wide, it operated 27 hotels, including the Hotel WBF. In January 2020, the company opened its first large-scale project, the 400-room WBF Shin-Osaka Sky Tower, but the hotel operator (WBF Hotel & Resort) went bankrupt in April. The hotel was then sold to APA Group in June and reopened as APA Hotel Shin-Osaka Station Tower (case 1).

In August 2020, Hoshino Resort initiated rehabilitation plan after concluding a share transfer agreement to acquire the White Bear Family and hotel management company (WBF Hotel & Resort), which were in the process of applying for the Civil Rehabilitation Law. About 350 employees transferred to the new Hoshino Resort subsidiary and continued to operate the hotel. Meanwhile, construction of the WBF Grande Kansai Airport (case 2), which was suspended due to the pandemic, was resumed by Hoshino Resort and opened in 2023 as the OMO Kansai Airport (700 rooms). In October 2021, the company completed the civil rehabilitation proceeding, sold its hotel division, and restarted its core business of travel planning and sales agency (Table 4-1-3).

| Table 4-1-3 | Examples of hotels that abandoned continued operations and rebranded |
|---|---|

| Case number | Opening name | Operator (Brand) | Operator at time of con-struction | Date of opening | Properties (<Reference> Press Release/Home Page/ Newspaper Report) |
|---|---|---|---|---|---|
| ① | Hotel WBF Shin-Osaka SKYTOWER ⇒APA Hhotel Shin-Osaka Eki Tower | WBF Hotels & Resorts ⇒APA Hotel (20/6~) | White Bear Family Co., Ltd | 2020/1 | The 32-story building is the highest in the Shin-Osaka area. There is an observation restaurant and a rooftop bar on the rooftop with a spectacular view of central Osaka. Closed due to COVID-19 pandemic; reopening as APA Hotel in June 2020. |
| ② | (計画時) Hotel WBF Grande Kansai Interna-tional Airport OMO Kansai Airport | Hoshino Resorts | White Bear Family Co., Ltd | 2023/3 | Largest hotel development in "Rinku Town" by WBF in 2018. Construction was suspended due to the COVID-19 pandemic. After Hoshino Resort acquired the property, construction resumed and the hotel opened under the "OMO" brand. |
| ③ | Hotel WBF ⇒OMO3 Kyoto Toji | WBF Hotels & Resorts ⇒Hoshino Resorts (21/6~) | White Bear Family Co., Ltd | 2019/10 | Within walking distance of Toji Temple, a World Heritage Site. The hotel will be closed in June 2020 due to the COVID-19 pandemic, and will reopen in April 2009 under the brand "OMO3". |

## (2) New developments by APA Hotel and Hoshino Resort, while facing the setbacks by COVID-19 pandemic

### APA Hotel.

APA Hotel operates 737 hotels domestic and abroad (as of August 2023), including franchised hotels, and 43 of them were repurposed as "hotels for people with minor symptoms of COVID-19" (as of August 2009, according to Airstair). Opened in 2019, the APA Hotel & Resort (Yokohama Bay Tower), boasting the largest number of rooms for one hotel building in Japan with 2311 rooms, was repurposed as "hotels for people with minor symptoms of COVID-19" in response to the requests from the Ministry of Health, Labour and Welfare and Prefecture. Such repurposed properties and deteriorating properties were then renewed and reopened one after another. As a result, the number of hotels had increased by approximately 17% over the past two years, from 583 hotels (95,130 rooms) in January 2020 to 683 hotels (105,290 rooms) in January 2022 (according to figures published in the company's news release).

### Case study of Hoshino Resort.

In Kansai, before the COVID-19, Hoshino Resort only had "Hoshinoya Kyoto" (formerly known as "Arashiyama Onsen Rankyokan"), which was bought and renovated by Hoshino Resort in 2009. In 2021, other than the "Hotel WBF Kyoto Toji (case 3)" in Kyoto City from WBF, it acquired properties that were closed or were completed but could not be opened due to the COVID-19 pandemic, including two from "OMO5" before reopening as "OMO3" hotel. In Osaka City, it opened a new large-scale property, "OMO7 Shin-Imamiya (case 4)" (436 rooms), in 2022. Currently in 2023, after rebranding part of the Hyatt Regency Osaka (currently Grand Prince Hotel Osaka Bay) (64 rooms on 4 floors) to "Resonare Osaka", and acquiring "OMO Kansai Airport" from WBF, the company increased its number of hotels to the total of 7 in Kansai, 4 in Kyoto and 3 in Osaka.

During the unprecedented crisis situation from April 2020 to March 2022, APA Hotels and Hoshino Resort responded flexibly and continued to increase their number of guest rooms. Both brands also have planned to capture the inbound visitors to Japan after the pandemic (Table 4-1-4).

Part I

**Part II**

Part III

Part IV

Table 4-1-4    New large properties built by Hoshino Resort and APA Hotel

| Case number | Opening name | Operator (Brand) | Operator at time of construction | Date of opening | Start of construction | Properties (<Reference> Press Release/Home Page/ Newspaper Report) |
|---|---|---|---|---|---|---|
| ④ | OMO7 Osaka | Hoshino Resorts | Shin-Imami-ya Development Special Purpose Company | 2022/4 | 2019/6 | OMO Ranger will guide you to the Shinsekai area, where you will have a unique encounter.Guests can interact with each other in the common space. |
| ⑤ | APA Hotel & Resort Midosuji Hommachi Eki Tower | APA Hotel | APA apartment | 2019/12 | 2017/6 | APA Hotel has the largest number of guest rooms in western Japan (at the time of opening).The hotel has the latest specifications of the company's new urban hotels, with a large indoor and outdoor bath and an outdoor terrace pool, providing a resort-like atmosphere. |
| ⑥ | APA Hotel &Resort Osaka Umeda Eki Tower | APA Hotel | APA Home | 2023/2 | 2020/8 | A new landmark tower in the Umeda area of Osaka, with an observation restaurant and swimming pool on the top floor, as well as a large public bath and open-air bath facilities, providing a resort-like atmosphere while remaining in the city. |
| ⑦ | APA Hotel &Resort Osaka Namba Eki Tower | APA Hotel | APA Home APA apartment | 2024/10 | 2022/3 | APA Hotel, a high-rise tower with the largest number of guest rooms in western Japan. Aiming to become a new landmark in the Namba area as an "urban resort" where guests can enjoy their stay, including a restaurant and swimming pool on the top floor. |

## 4. Summary

We have reviewed 10 years of tourism strategies in Japan and analyzed trends in hotel construction to determine the characteristics of how lodging business operators were responding to changes in inbound tourism demand due to the COVID-19 pandemic and the forthcoming Osaka-Kansai Expo. The results can be summarized as follows.

The Tourism Agency's budget indicates that before the rapid increase in the number of foreign visitors to Japan, most of the allocation was for overseas PR. However, after 2014, in order to cope with the rapid increase in the number of foreign visitors to Japan, the budget was reallocated to focus on improving the reception environment of tourist destinations in response to jump in the number of inbound tourists. From 2018, as the number of foreign visitors to Japan had been increasing steadily, the budget was focusing on discovering local tourism resources to draw visitors to regions outside of urban areas. However, after 2020, the budget is allocted to Tourism DX, SDGs, and D&I in response to the changes caused by COVID-19 pandemic.

Regarding the hotel construction trend in the Kansai, the number of lodging facilities had been steadily increasing, especially in Osaka and Kyoto prefectures, following the increase in the number of foreign visitors. However, after 2020, hotel construction projects came to a halt due to the COVID-19 pandemic. Expecting the recovery in inbound tourism demand and the Osaka-Kansai Expo, hotels with high rates per night are now being constructed not only in Osaka and Kyoto prefectures, but also in other prefectures.[6]

After the pandemic started in 2020, many large hotels have opened. As a result, several hotels went out of business or were acquired by other companies; while others suspended their construction or delayed their opening. Among them, APA Hotel continued to operate by converting a number of its properties into " hotels for people with minor symptoms of COVID-19". On the other hand, Hoshino Resort acquired properties that were closed or under construction, and put the hotel operations and employees under its management. APA Hotel and Hoshino Resort have increased the number of guest rooms while responding flexibly to the pandemic, and have begun to steadily attract not only domestic guests but also the resumed inbound foreign visitors to Japan.

## References

Inoue, K., Nomura, R., and Inada, Y. (2023), "The COVID-19 pandemic and hotel construction in Kansai: How did lodging businesses respond to the COVID-19 pandemic?", (Japanese title: *Koronaka to Kansai no Hoteru Kensetsu -Koronaka ni Shukuhaku Jigyosha wa Donoyouni Taiou Shitanoka-*), APIR Trend Watch No. 87, August 9, 2023, (https://www.apir.or.jp/research/12454/).

Japan Tourism Agency HP, "Budget and Procurement Information," (https://www.mlit.go.jp/kankocho/siryou/yosan/youbou.html, last viewed July 5, 2023).

Part I

Part II

Part III

Part IV

---

6) For more information on large hotel construction projects, see the Tourism Chronology section of this publication.

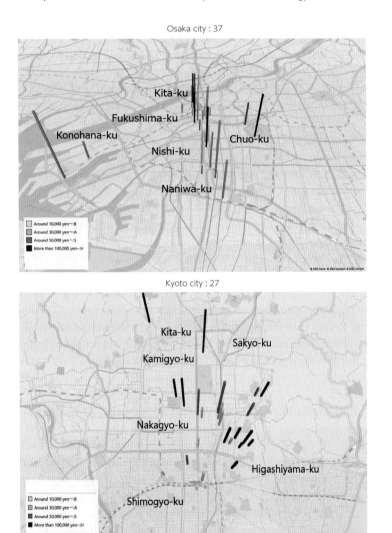

**Reference Figure 4-1-1**  Hotel Construction Map 2017-26: Osaka City and Kyoto City

Note: The height of the bar indicates the construction project cost of the hotel in question in Reference Charts 1.1 and 1.2, and the color indicates the grade of lodging cost.

## Section 2
# CHARACTERISTICS OF RECOVERING INBOUND TOURISM DEMAND

*NOMURA, Ryosuke; INADA, Yoshihisa*

Section 2 reviews the dynamics of tourism in the Kansai region in 2022/23.

Subsection 2.1 focuses mainly on inbound tourism demand, analyzing trends in the number of foreign visitors to Japan and the expense by foreign visitors. Subsection 2.2 focuses on domestic tourism demand in the Kansai region, analyzing domestic travel consumption and the total number of Japanese overnight stays. Finally, Subsection 2.3 addresses future issues of the rapid recovery in tourism industry.

## 1. Rapidly recovery of inbound tourism demand

This subsection discusses the rapid recovery of inbound tourism demand. Specifically, we will examine the recovery in the number of inbound foreign visitors and the expense by these visitors since the COVID-19 pandemic.

### (1) Number of foreign visitors

In response to the global spread of COVID-19, the Japanese government implemented strict border control measures after February 1, 2020[1]. As a result, the previously strong inbound tourism demand disappeared, striking a very serious blow to the tourism industry.[2] The number of inbound foreign visitors to Japan from the "Statistics on Foreign Visitors to Japan" of the Japan National Tourism Organization (JNTO) (Figure 4-2-1) shows that the number of inbound foreign visitors reached only 1,663 in May 2020, a record low since the statistics began, due to the strict border control measures. The number of cases recovered somewhat to 58,673 in December 2020, partly because the infection calmed down in the second half of 2020, and people were allowed to enter Japan only for business and study purposes. In January 2021, however, a new strain of COVID-19 led to another strict border control measure, causing the number to decrease to 7,355 in February 2021. In July, the number of visitors temporarily increased to

---

1) For a detailed description of the border control measures taken by the government, see Asia Pacific Institute of Research (2021), pp. 242.
2) The impact of the loss of inbound tourism demand on the tourism industry is analyzed in Chapter 5, Section 1 of Asia Pacific Institute of Research (2022).

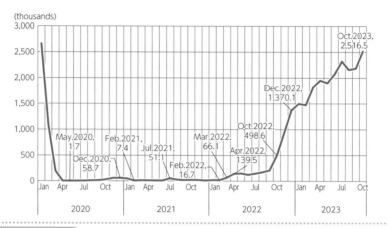

**Figure 4-2-1** Trends in the number of foreign visitors to Japan: January 2020-October 2023

Source: Compiled from Japan National Tourism Organization (JNTO), "Statistics on Foreign Visitors to Japan

51,055 due to the Tokyo Olympics and Paralympics but, again, remained at low level after the games.

Inbound tourism demand showed a recovery trend in 2022 as the government gradually relaxed border control measures in preparation for the recovery of international traffic. In March 2022, the number of visitors sharply increased to 66,121 (compared to 16,719 in February), possibly because the entry limit was raised from 5,000 to 7,000 people per day. In April, the limit was further raised to 10,000, and the number exceeded 100,000 for the first time since the pandemic began, reaching 139,548. As border control measures were lifted in October, the number of visitors greatly increased to 498,646, and to over 1,370,114 in December, exceeding 1 million.

Since the beginning of 2023, the number of foreign visitors to Japan has remained above the one-million mark, and reached 2,516,500 in October, exceeding the two-million mark and recovering to the pre-pandemic level. The pace of recovery, however, varies by country and region and will be discussed in the following subsections.

Figure 4-2-2 compares the number of inbound tourism visitors to Japan by country and region in October 2023 with the pre pandemic level of October 2019. The number of visitors from South Korea and the United States exceeded the pre-pandemic level, while the number of Chinese visitors, who had previously accounted for 30% of all visitors to Japan (average for 2019), was only at 35% of the pre-pandemic level. The slowdown of Chinese economy and the deterioration of Japan-China relations might be the reasons for the slow recovery,

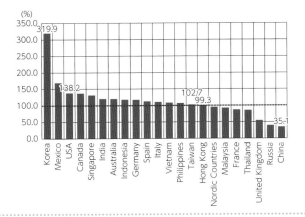

**Figure 4-2-2**  Comparison of recovery from before the COVID-19 pandemic by country/region: October 2023

Source: Compiled from Japan National Tourism Organization (JNTO), "Statistics on Foreign Visitors to Japan

despite all border control measures have been lifted. Thus, while the overall number of foreign visitors to Japan was steadily recovering, the pace of recovery differed by country and region. As will be discussed later, however, the recovery of consumption exceeded that of foreign visitors to Japan.

## (2) Trends in the expenditure by foreign visitors to Japan

Let us look at trends in the amount spent by foreigners visiting Japan (all purposes) on a quarterly basis using the Japan Tourism Agency's "Survey of Trends in Consumption by Foreign Visitors to Japan" (Figure 4-2-3)[3].

Before the COVID-19 pandemic, consumption by foreign visitors in 2019 was generally above JPY 1 trillion (on a quarterly basis) and was approximately JPY 4.8 trillion for the entire year of 2019. However, due to the pandemic, it decreased to JPY 707.1 billion in Q1 2020, and has continued to decreased[4].

As mentioned above, border control measures were gradually relaxed since 2022 and, as a result, consumption by foreign visitors has steadily recovered since the Q1 period. During the Q4 period, border control measures were fully lifted and consumption amounted to JPY 594.9 billion, approximately 50% of the level for the same period in 2019.

---

3) The figures for 2019, Q1 2020, and Q4 2022 are revised figures. Those for Q4 2021 through Q3 2022 are estimated figures. Those for Q1 and Q2 of 2023 are second preliminary figures and those for Q3 2023 are first preliminary figures.
4) As the survey was suspended from Q2 2020 to Q3 2021 due to the spread of COVID-19, data on inbound travel spending during this period is missing.

Part I

Part II

Part III

Part IV

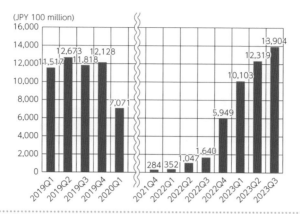

(JPY 100 million)

**Figure 4-2-3**    Trends in Foreign Visitors Expenditure in Japan: from Q12019 to Q32023

Source: Compiled from Japan Tourism Agency, "Survey of Foreign Visitor Consumption Trends in Japan

In the current Q3 of 2023, as inbound tourism demand rapidly recovered, the consumption value increased JPY 1,390.4 billion, up 17.7% from the same period in 2019, surpassing the pre- pandemic level. A steady rise in the per-consumption price might be why number exceeds the pre-pandemic level. Regarding the per-unit expenditure and the average number of nights spent in Japan, according to the Japan Tourism Agency's "Survey of Trends in Foreign Visitor Expenditure in Japan," travel expenditures per capita for all purposes (Table 4-2-1) were JPY 218,110 in the Q3 of 2023, up 29.4% from the same period of 2019, exceeding the pre-COVID-19 pandemic level. By country and region, France was the highest at JPY 357,775 (+40.2%), followed by Spain at JPY 349,718 (+57.8%), Italy at JPY 341,870 (+63.6%), the UK at JPY 328,422 (+84.9%), and Australia at JPY 320,286 (+46.6%). The depreciation of the Japanese yen, increasing in the number of long-stay travelers, mainly from Europe, the U.S., and Australia, might have contributed to the rise in unit prices.

Next, looking at the average number of nights (Table 4-2-1), the overall average was 11.2 nights, an increase of 0.8 nights from the same period in 2019 (10.4 nights). By country and region, China increased to 14.6 nights compared to the same period in 2019 (7.7 nights). This was followed by the United Kingdom (14.6 nights) and Singapore (11.9 nights), both of which increased from the same period in 2019 (UK: 12.7 nights, Singapore: 9.1 nights).

## (3) Kansai economy and inbound tourism demand

Next, let us examine the rapid recovery process of inbound tourism demand in the Kansai region using the number of foreign visitors to Kansai International

Airport (KIX).

Figure 4-2-4 shows the number of international arrivals to KIX, which reached a record low of 181 in May 2020.

In 2021, however, the number of arrivals in February was 1,879 and has remained at a low level since then, due to the tightening of border control measures.

From the beginning of 2022, border control measures were relaxed, and the number of arrivals started to increase. In March 2022, the number reached 10,284, the highest since December 2020. It reached 116, 658 in October, exceeding 100,000, and raised to 331,249 in December 2022, about 50% of the pre-pandemic level.

In 2023, the number of international arrivals continued to recover, reaching 655,571 (+0.6% over the same month in 2019) in October, approaching the

**Table 4-2-1** Comparison of pre-unit expenditure and average number of nights spent by inbound foreign visitors by country/region: Q3-2019 vs. Q3-2023

| Country/Region | 2023Q3 (JPY/person) | 2019Q3 (JPY/person) | Comparison with 2019(%) | Country/Region | 2023Q3 (number of nights) | 2019Q3 (number of nights) | Comparison with 2019 |
|---|---|---|---|---|---|---|---|
| Total | 210,810 | 162,860 | 29.4 | Total | 11.2 | 10.4 | 0.8 |
| Korea | 110,686 | 87,032 | 27.2 | Korea | 4.9 | 7.6 | -2.7 |
| Taiwan | 177,823 | 114,360 | 55.5 | Taiwan | 7.5 | 6.7 | 0.8 |
| Hong Kong | 233,887 | 153,544 | 52.3 | Hong Kong | 7.6 | 6.7 | 0.9 |
| China | 284,934 | 203,576 | 40.0 | China | 14.6 | 7.7 | 6.9 |
| Thailand | 180,543 | 149,850 | 20.5 | Thailand | 16.0 | 20.0 | -4.0 |
| Singapore | 256,496 | 153,238 | 67.4 | Singapore | 11.9 | 9.1 | 2.8 |
| Malaysia | 215,478 | 133,041 | 62.0 | Malaysia | 10.2 | 16.8 | -6.6 |
| Indonesia | 201,116 | 135,682 | 48.2 | Indonesia | 18.5 | 19.7 | -1.2 |
| Philippines | 166,434 | 95,811 | 73.7 | Philippines | 24.6 | 25.6 | -1.0 |
| Vietnam | 188,835 | 181,017 | 4.3 | Vietnam | 30.4 | 36.3 | -5.9 |
| India | 215,085 | 148,328 | 45.0 | India | 22.7 | 21.7 | 1.0 |
| UK | 328,422 | 177,608 | 84.9 | UK | 17.7 | 12.7 | 5.0 |
| Germany | 274,691 | 189,867 | 44.7 | Germany | 14.6 | 12.4 | 2.2 |
| France | 357,775 | 255,267 | 40.2 | France | 20.4 | 24.5 | -4.1 |
| Italy | 341,870 | 208,944 | 63.6 | Italy | 11.8 | 12.7 | -0.9 |
| Spain | 349,718 | 221,568 | 57.8 | Spain | 16.2 | 16.1 | 0.1 |
| Russia | — | 188,173 | — | Russia | — | 24.6 | — |
| US | 291,537 | 198,736 | 46.7 | US | 12.8 | 14.1 | -1.3 |
| Canada | 261,416 | 170,991 | 52.9 | Canada | 13.2 | 12.1 | 1.1 |
| Australia | 320,286 | 218,474 | 46.6 | Australia | 13.4 | 11.9 | 1.5 |
| Others | 314,812 | 224,345 | 40.3 | Others | 23.3 | 18.5 | 4.8 |

Source: Compiled by Japan Tourism Agency from "Survey of Foreign Visitor Expenditure Trends in Japan

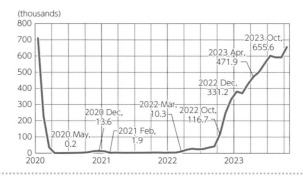

**Figure 4-2-4**　Trends in the number of visitors to KIX: Jan. 2020-Oct. 2023

Source: Compiled from Ministry of Justice, "Immigration Statistics.

pre-COVID-19 pandemic level. Similar to the national trend above, the number of international arrivals to the Kansai region is rapidly recovering, but the pace of recovery differs by country and region.

Table 4-2-2 compares the number of foreign arrivals at KIX in 2019 and 2022 by major country and region. As the table shows, before the pandemic, the number of arrivals from China was the highest, especially in Kansai, with a share of 39.4%. However, looking at 2022, China's share has declined significantly to 3.6%, while Korea's has greatly increased to 38.1%. In addition, the shares of Hongkong and Vietnam are also higher than the pre-pandemic level at 10.1% and 8.9%, respectively.

Figure 4-2-5 show the number of visitors to KIX of the top 5 countries and regions in Q3-2023 and compare them to Q3-2019 level. Korea was the highest at 555,000 (+98.6% compares to Q3-2019), China was at 404,000 (-58.0%), Taiwan was at 295,000 (+5.7%), Hongkong was at 160,000 (+15.9%), and US was at 49,000 (-2.8%).

While inbound tourism demand is rapidly recovering in Japan and Kansai, inbound visitors from China, which accounted for a large portion of the total number before the pandemic, is still lagging behind. Therefore, a full recovery will require more time. In the next subsection, we will shift our analysis to domestic travel demand, which was hit as hard by the pandemic, and examine its recovery process.

| Table 4-2-2 | Comparison of the number of visitors to KIX by country/region: 2019 vs. 2022 |
|---|---|

| Country/Region | The number of international arrivals at KIX | | | |
|---|---|---|---|---|
| | 2019 | Share(%) | 2022 | Share(%) |
| Total | 8,378,039 | 100.0 | 885,470 | 100.0 |
| China | 3,302,710 | 39.4 | 32,291 | 3.6 |
| Korea | 1,510,776 | 18.0 | 337,644 | 38.1 |
| Taiwan | 1,098,555 | 13.1 | 85,002 | 9.6 |
| Hong Kong | 604,787 | 7.2 | 89,693 | 10.1 |
| US | 220,341 | 2.6 | 21,201 | 2.4 |
| Thailand | 310,615 | 3.7 | 34,026 | 3.8 |
| Australia | 94,752 | 1.1 | 10,875 | 1.2 |
| Philippines | 198,265 | 2.4 | 30,411 | 3.4 |
| Malaysia | 150,760 | 1.8 | 16,595 | 1.9 |
| Vietnam | 148,247 | 1.8 | 79,204 | 8.9 |
| Singapore | 114,459 | 1.4 | 34,161 | 3.9 |
| UK | 59,632 | 0.7 | 6,765 | 0.8 |
| Indonesia | 85,643 | 1.0 | 21,164 | 2.4 |
| Canada | 55,437 | 0.7 | 5,497 | 0.6 |
| France | 61,340 | 0.7 | 9,219 | 1.0 |
| Germany | 35,255 | 0.4 | 3,648 | 0.4 |
| India | 21,599 | 0.3 | 4,020 | 0.5 |
| Italy | 24,571 | 0.3 | 2,723 | 0.3 |
| Spain | 28,072 | 0.3 | 2,130 | 0.2 |
| Russia | 9,496 | 0.1 | 1,027 | 0.1 |
| Mexico | 4,574 | 0.1 | 303 | 0.0 |

Source: Compiled from Ministry of Justice, "Immigration Statistics.

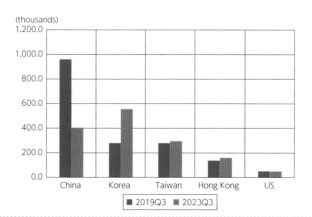

| Figure 4-2-5 | Comparison of the number of visitors to KIX by country and region: Q3 2019 vs. Q3 2023 |
|---|---|

Source: Compiled from Ministry of Justice, "Immigration Statistics.

## 2. Recovery of domestic travel demand

In this subsection, we focus on domestic travel demand in the Kansai region[5] and examine its recovery process from the COVID-19 pandemic.

### (1) Trends in the Total Number of Japanese Overnight Stays

We use the "Overnight Travel Statistics Survey" conducted by the Japan Tourism Agency to examine the recovery process of the total number of Japanese overnight stays in Kansai. As shown in Figure 4-2-6, the number of overnight stays declined sharply by 82.5% in May 2020 compared to the same month in 2019. As the "Go to Travel" program started in July, the decline was reduced to -8.1% in November compared to November 2019. However, the decline increased again in January 2021 to -51.1% due to another wave of COVID-19 infection and the suspension of the "Go to Travel" program. The pace of recovery was slow but steady, declining at -20.5% and -7.2% in October and November, respectively, comparing to the same month in 2019. In December, the number of Japanese overnight stays steadily recovered and exceeded the pre-pandemic level by +5.2%.

Due to the government's measures to prevent infection in 2022, however, the number of Japanese overnight visitors decreased by -14.1% in January, and -35.1% in February. Then, it started to recover from March to September, and turned positive in October with +10.8%. The increasing trend continued and

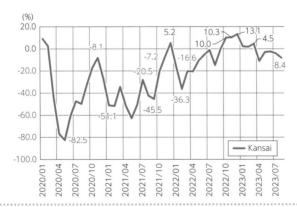

Figure 4-2-6    Total Number of Japanese Overnight Stays in 2019 % Change from the Same Month in 2019: Kansai: Jan 2020 - Aug 2023

Source: Compiled from the Japan Tourism Agency, "Overnight Travel Statistics Survey"

5) Greater Kansai here is based on Fukui, Mie, Shiga, Kyoto, Osaka, Hyogo, Nara, Wakayama, Tottori and Tokushima prefectures.

reached 11.2% in November and 12.7% in December.

The number of Japanese overnight stays had been on a recovery trend from January to March since the beginning of 2023, but has shown a downward trend since April, and in August, it has been below the pre-COVID-19 pandemic level for five months in a row, at 8.4%.

## (2) Domestic Travel Consumption

Figure 4-2-7 shows the quarterly trend of domestic travel consumption in the Kansai region. Domestic travel consumption declined sharply to JPY 202.8 billion in the Q2 of 2020 due to the declaration of a state of emergency[6]. In Q3 and Q4, the consumption recovered as the government launched the "Go to Travel" program.

In 2021, however, domestic travel consumption for Q1 totaled JPY 315.6 billion since the infection situation got worse and the "Go to Travel" program got suspended, and the pace of recovery slowed thereafter. In Q4, the consumption rose sharply to JPY 751.4 billion as the pandemic slowed down, and local governments stimulated travel demand with their own policies[7].

In 2022, , domestic travel expenditure in Q1 was JPY 475.9 billion due to the worsening infection situation and the government's priority measures to prevent

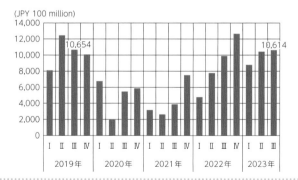

| Figure 4-2-7 | Trends in domestic travel expenditure: Kansai: Q1 2019-Q3 2023 |

Note: The data from 2019 to 2022 are revised figures. 23 years are preliminary figures.
Source: Compiled from Japan Tourism Agency, "Travel and Tourism Consumption Trends Survey"

6) The period of emergency declarations and priority measures to prevent the pandemic spread are as follows. Emergency declaration (1st: April 7 to May 25, 2020; 2nd: January 7 to March 21, 2021; 3rd: April 25 to June 20, 2021; 4th: July 12 to September 30, 2021). Priority measures to prevent the pandemic spread (April 5 to September 30, 2021; and January 9 to March 21, 2022).

7) See Chapter 5 Section 1 of Asia Pacific Institute of Research (2022) and COVID-19 Chronology for the Kansai prefectures' own measures to stimulate travel demand.

pandemic spread. In Q2, the consumption recovered, reaching JPY 1,263.6 billion and exceeding the pre-pandemic level, due in part to the "National Travel Support Program" that was initiated on October 11, 2023.

In Q1 of 2023, although the consumption totaled to JPY 834.9 billion, exceeding the pre-pandemic level for two consecutive quarters, it dropped in Q3 to somewhat lower than the pre-pandemic level at JPY 1,061.4 billion (-0.4% from the same period in 2019).

As described above, since the latter half of 2022, domestic travel expenditure and the number of Japanese overnight stays in the Kansai region have been steadily recovering to pre-pandemic levels, partly because of the subsided pandemic and because of government measures to stimulate demand. In the future, it is important to maintain a sustained growth of both inbound tourism demand and domestic travel demand. In the following subsection, we will identity some future issues in the tourism industry.

## 3. Future issues

As we have seen, both inbound tourism demand and domestic travel demand are recovering from the COVID-19 pandemic.

Looking at the recovery of inbound tourism demand, it is particularly interesting to note that both the unit consumption price and the average number of nights spent have increased. This point has also been addressed in the Japan Tourism Agency's Tourism Nation Promotion Plan. In anticipation of the recovery in inbound tourism demand, the Japan Tourism Agency revised its new Tourism Nation Promotion Plan in March 2023[8]. Table 4-2-3 compares the targets for inbound tourism in the previous plan with those in the revised plan.

**Table 4-2-3**    Contents of the Newly Revised Tourism Nation Promotion Plan

|  | Foreign visitors | Expenditure by foreign visitors | Unit price for foreign visitor | Number of overnight stays per foreign visitor in local areas |
|---|---|---|---|---|
| 3rd Revision | 40 million people | JPY 8 trillion | — | — |
| Target values | Until 2020 | Until 2020 | — | — |
| 4th Revision | 2019 level exceeded | JPY 5 trillion | JPY 200,000 | 2 nights |
| Target values | Until 2025 | at an early date | Until 2025 | Until 2025 |

Source: Compiled from Japan Tourism Agency, "Tourism Nation Promotion Plan

---

8) The specific measures that the Japan Tourism Agency will take in 2023 are detailed in the Japan Tourism Agency (2023).

The fourth revision of the plan aims to increase the number of inbound visitors to Japan to exceed the 2019 level by 2025, and to achieve JPY 5 trillion in consumption as soon as possible. A new target of JPY 200,000 by 2025 has also been set for the per-unit expenditure. As mentioned above, per-unit expenditurewas approximately JPY 210,000 in Q3 2023 and, thus, the JPY 5 trillion target is achievable, but it is important to maintain and improve the per-unit expenditure.

The recovery of Chinese visitors to Japan is also important for the Kansai economy, which was severely damaged by the pandemic. Before the pandemic, Chinese visitors to Japan accounted for 39.4% of all arrivals at KIX, but by 2022, they accounted for 3.6%. In addition, there is still a high degree of uncertainty about the future due to deteriorating Japan-China relations and the slowdown of the Chinese economy.

After the pandemic, issues regarding future tourism strategies became clear. These are: (1) improving and sustaining the per-unit spending of foreign visitor, (2) promotion of regional tourism, and (3) improving the profitability and labor supply constraints in the tourism industry.

Regarding (1), as mentioned above, the per-unit expenditureof foreign visitors to Japan is steadily increasing, maintaining it will be important in the future.

Regarding (2), from the perspective of the "tourism regionalization" that APIR has been emphasizing, it is necessary to eliminate the overtourism phenomenon concentrated in Osaka and Kyoto prefectures in the Kansai region, and to attract visitors to other prefectures. In this case, the tourism strategy of each municipality and the role of DMOs will become even more important.

Regarding (3), the recovery and productivity improvement of female non-regular employees, who have been supporting the tourism industry, is a challenge. In Kansai particularly, the number of female non-regular employees has been hit hard by the pandemic[9] and has yet to recover to its pre- pandemic level.

Although the face-to-face service industry is recovering from the pandemic, the pace of recovery of female workers in the Kansai region varies by industry. Figure 4-2-8 shows that the index of female workers in the face-to-face service industry in the Kansai region in Q3 of 2023 (2019 average = 100) declined by 2.2 points in the "wholesale and retail industry", 8.6 points in the "accommodation and food services industry", and 3.0 points in the "lifestyle-related services and

---

9) The impact of the COVID-19 pandemic on female part-time workers in the Kansai region is analyzed in detail in Chapter 3, Section 5 of Asia Pacific Institute of Research (2021). The current state of labor supply constraints in the Kansai region is discussed in detail in Chapter 3, Section 3 of this report.

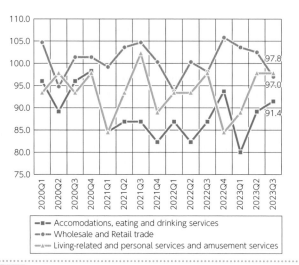

Trends in the index of female workers in face-to-face service industries: Kansai: from Q1-2020to Q3-2023

Note: Index for each industry with 2019 average number of workers as 100
Source: Compiled from Ministry of Internal Affairs and Communications, 2Labour Force Survey"

entertainment", all are below the pre-pandemic level, indicating a slow recovery. Thus, the future issue for the Kansai region is how to resolve the labor supply constraint.

## References

Asia Pacific Institute of Research (2021), Kansai and the Asia Pacific Economic Outlook 2021.

Asia Pacific Institute of Research (2022), Kansai and the Asia Pacific Economic Outlook 2022.

Japan Tourism Agency (2023), White Paper on Tourism in Japan, 2023.

# Chapter 5

# GREATER EXPO DEVELOPMENT AND DX

## Section 1
## GREATER EXPO AND THE ECONOMIC IMPACT OF PROMOTING TOURISM TO A WIDER EXTENT

*IRIE, Hiroaki; SHIMOYAMA, Akira; SHIMODA, Mitsuru;*
*NOMURA, Ryosuke; INADA, Yoshihisa; TAKABAYASHI, Kikuo*

## Introduction

This section lists examples of initiatives already underway in the Kansai region aimed at creating "profitable industries" and "profitable regions," and presents an overview of these initiatives, and their economic impact. The section also focuses on the Osaka-Kansai Expo, which will be held in 2025. However, for the future economic growth in Kansai, it is necessary to ensure that the economic effects of the Osaka-Kansai Expo are not temporary and localized, but are sustained and spread over a wide geographical area. In consideration of this, this section discusses the key concepts of 1) a Greater Expo and 2) the promotion of region-wide sightseeing tours.

The first part of this article (Subsection 1.1) discusses the Greater Expo, which was also the subject of last year's Economic Outlook. In particular, this year we present an updated version of the economic effects of the Greater Expo, we outline, Yao City's "Open Factory" initiative the Hanazono Expo held in Higashi-Osaka City in 2022 as examples of Expo expansions in various regions in Kansai.

The second part of this article (Subsection 1.2) focuses on the promotion of region-wide sightseeing tours for foreign visitors in Kansai. In view of the upcoming Expo, various efforts have been made to promote tourism throughout the Kansai region. We outline several such initiatives, and we discuss their economic impact on travel demand and higher value added by inbound tourism in Kansai. We pay special attention to the tour programs created as part of "The

Exciting Kansai" initiative by the Kansai Tourism Bureau.

# 1. A "Greater Expo": Economic Impact and Examples

Subsection 1.1 presents an updated version of the economic impact of the Greater Expo, which was featured in last year's white paper.

The "Greater Expo" refers to efforts to expand the concept of the Expo theme, time axis, and spatial axis, and to develop a variety of economic activities with the entire Kansai region as a virtual pavilion. The extension of the time axis includes long-term activities before and after the Expo. Spatial expansion could include the development of activities that are highly compatible with Expo, not only in the Yumeshima site where the Expo will be held, but also in the greater Kansai region (and even the entire country). Examples of Greater Expo activities include special events, such as special visits to temples and shrines, music festivals, lighting, illumination, food festivals, and other events that reflect the Expo's concept of a "People's Living Lab" and the SDGs. The use of MaaS(Mobility as a Service)is also being considered to facilitate transportation between regions. In addition to encouraging Expo visitors to tour the Kansai region, it is hoped that the Expo will not be a one-time event, but will become a permanent event.

Below, Subsection 3.1 (1) presents an updated version of the economic effects of the Greater Expo. Next, Subsection 3.1 (2) introduces the Open Factory in Yao City and the Hanazono Expo held in Higashi-Osaka City in November 2022 as examples of Greater Expo in practice.

## (1) The Economic Impact of a "Greater Expo": An Update in our Estimations

Here, we re-estimate the economic impact of the Osaka-Kansai Expo and Greater Expo using the 2015 Interregional Input-Output Table for the Kansai Region (final version), which was developed by the APIR[1]. In the Greater Expo scenario, we assume an increase in repeat visitors due to the momentum created by participation in the Expo and additional participation in events held at locations other than the Yumeshima site. In the re-estimation, assumptions, such as trends of one-day trips were reexamined based on the recent developments. In addition, the daily expenditures by domestic and overseas visitors were updated based on the latest data. In addition to the case in which final demand is generated mainly by the pavilion at the Yumeshima site (hereinafter referred to as the

---

1) See Inada, Irie, Shimoyama, and Nomura (2023) for details of the analysis method and results in Subsection 3.1 (1).

"baseline scenario"), we estimate the economic impact for the case in which the number of participants and related events increases in the entire Kansai region (i.e. the "Greater Expo scenario").

## (1) Assumptions about final demand

Final demand generated by the Expo can be roughly divided into operating expenses incurred by the organizers and exhibitors, and consumption expenditures by visitors.

The project operation cost is JPY 727.5 billion, based on data released by the Association for International Expositions and the City of Osaka, which reflects the progress of Osaka-Kansai Expo related projects. The breakdown is JPY 337.4 billion for venue construction, JPY 238.6 billion for operations, JPY 30.6 billion for related infrastructure development and JPY 15.6 billion municipal expenses for hosting the Expo. These amounts are unchanged from the previous year's estimates and are the same for both the baseline scenario and the Greater Expo scenario.

The consumption expenditure by visitors is calculated by multiplying the per capita consumption unit price by the estimated number of visitors.

In the baseline scenario case, per capita spending per day for transportation, lodging, food and beverages, shopping, and entertainment services is calculated for one-day visitors, domestic overnight visitors, and international visitors based on the Japan Tourism Agency's "Survey of Travel and Tourism Consumption Trends" and "Survey of Foreign Visitors to Japan". The number of visitors in the baseline scenario is assumed to be approximately 28.2 million, based on the "Basic Plan" of the Japan Association for International Expositions. Of the total 18.2 million visitors,15.6 million are expected to come from the six prefectures in Kansai, 9.1 million from domestic areas outside Kansai, and 3.5 million from overseas. It is assumed that visitors from the two and four prefectures in Kansai will visit the Expo on a one-day trip, while those from other parts of Japan will stay overnight in the Kansai region. Visitors from overseas are assumed to stay in Kansai for three nights (four days).

The Greater Expo scenario assumes an increase in repeat visitors due to the momentum created by participation in the Expo and additional participation in events held at locations other than the Yumeshima site. In this case, two patterns are considered: one in which the number of overnight stays increases (hereinafter referred to as Greater Expo Case 1), and the other in which the number of day-trippers increases by an additional 20% relative to Greater Expo Case 1 (hereinafter referred to as Greater Expo Case 2).

In both Greater Expo Cases 1 and 2, the number of nights for domestic guests is assumed to increase from one to two, and the number of nights for overseas guests is assumed to increase from three to five. Within the two-night increase for overseas guests, one night is assumed to be spent in Osaka and the other night is assumed to be spent either in Osaka or in another place in the same proportion as domestic guests.

Greater Expo Case 2 assumes a 20% increase in transportation, food and entertainment expenses by day-trippers on top of the increase in Greater Expo Case 1. This is based on the assumption that the efforts of each municipality in the Kansai region will lead to the pavilionization of the entire Kansai region, and that domestic day-trippers will increase by another 20% and visit areas outside of Osaka. The above assumptions about consumption expenditures by visitors are shown in Table 5-1-1. The total consumption expenditure would be JPY

**Table 5-1-1**    Consumption Expenditures by Visitors

Conventional Expo                                                    Unit: JPY 100 million

| | Domestic day visitors | Domestic over-night visitors | Overseas |
|---|---|---|---|
| Transportation expenses | 1,241 | 803 | 224 |
| Lodging expenses | 0 | 1,054 | 681 |
| Food and drinks expenses | 665 | 495 | 459 |
| Shopping expenses | 941 | 421 | 505 |
| Entertainment services expenses | 964 | 370 | 117 |
| Total | 3,784 | 3,784 | 1,986 |

Greater Expo Case1

| | Domestic day visitors | Domestic over-night visitors | Overseas |
|---|---|---|---|
| Transportation expenses | 1,241 | 1,204 | 335 |
| Lodging expenses | 0 | 2,108 | 1,136 |
| Food and drinks expenses | 665 | 743 | 688 |
| Shopping expenses | 941 | 421 | 505 |
| Entertainment services expenses | 964 | 555 | 175 |
| Total | 3,784 | 5,031 | 2,839 |

Greater Expo Case2

| | Domestic day visitors | Domestic over-night visitors | Overseas |
|---|---|---|---|
| Transportation expenses | 1,457 | 1,204 | 335 |
| Lodging expenses | 0 | 2,108 | 1,136 |
| Food and drinks expenses | 798 | 743 | 688 |
| Shopping expenses | 1,129 | 421 | 505 |
| Entertainment services expenses | 1,157 | 555 | 175 |
| Total | 4,541 | 5,031 | 2,839 |

Source: Prepared by the author

891.3 billion in the Conventional Expo (baseline scenario), JPY 1,165.4 billion in Greater Expo Case 1 (+29.0% over the baseline), and JPY 1,241.1 billion in Greater Expo Case 2 (+35.4% over the baseline).

## (2) Estimation Results and Discussion

Based on the final demand assumptions shown in (1), we calculate the induced production for the baseline scenario and the Greater Expo scenario based on the 2015 Interregional Input-Output Table for the Kansai Region (tentative version). Table 5-1-2 shows the induced production in each region, the difference between the cases, and the share of induced production by region.

Induced production in the Kansai region as a whole would be JPY 2,745.7 billion in the baseline scenario, and JPY 3,238.4 billion in Greater Expo Case 1, an increase of JPY 492.7 billion. The Greater Expo Case 2 shows an increase of JPY 621.0 billion to JPY 3,366.7 billion. The difference between Greater Expo Case 2 and Greater Expo Case 1 is at least JPY 128.3 billion.

Looking at the differences between Greater Expo Case 2 and the baseline scenario by region (Greater Expo 2 -Conventional in Table 5-1-2), the largest increase was JPY 188.2 billion in Kyoto Prefecture, followed by JPY 104.4 billion in other regions, JPY 99.7 billion in Hyogo prefecture, and JPY 50.6 billion in

**Table 5-1-2**    Induced production by region

| | Conventional Expo | Greater Expo case1 | Greater Expo case2 | Greater Expo1-Conventional | Greater Expo2-Conventional | Greater Expo1-Expo2 | Conventional Expo share | Greater Expo case1 share | Greater Expo case2 share |
|---|---|---|---|---|---|---|---|---|---|
| Unit | JPY 100 million | JPY 100 million | JPY 100 million | JPY 100 million | JPY 100 million | JPY 100 million | % | % | % |
| Fukui | 78 | 278 | 359 | 199 | 280 | 81 | 0.3 | 0.9 | 1.1 |
| Mie | 359 | 719 | 865 | 360 | 506 | 146 | 1.3 | 2.2 | 2.6 |
| Shiga | 201 | 452 | 535 | 251 | 334 | 83 | 0.7 | 1.4 | 1.6 |
| Kyoto | 242 | 1,963 | 2,124 | 1,721 | 1,882 | 161 | 0.9 | 6.1 | 6.3 |
| Osaka | 20,621 | 20,874 | 21,069 | 254 | 448 | 194 | **75.1** | 64.5 | 62.6 |
| Hyogo | 722 | 1,515 | 1,719 | 793 | 997 | 204 | 2.6 | 4.7 | 5.1 |
| Nara | 76 | 165 | 246 | 88 | 170 | 81 | 0.3 | 0.5 | 0.7 |
| Wakayama | 192 | 385 | 436 | 193 | 244 | 51 | 0.7 | 1.2 | 1.3 |
| Tottori | 32 | 156 | 193 | 125 | 161 | 37 | 0.1 | 0.5 | 0.6 |
| Tokushima | 89 | 210 | 232 | 121 | 142 | 22 | 0.3 | 0.6 | 0.7 |
| Other regions | 4,846 | 5,668 | 5,889 | 822 | 1,044 | 221 | 17.6 | 17.5 | 17.5 |
| Total | 27,457 | 32,384 | 33,667 | 4,927 | **6,210** | **1,283** | 100.0 | 100.0 | 100.0 |

Source: Prepared by the author

Mie Prefecture.

The share of economic impact by region shows that the share of Osaka Prefecture decreases from 74.5% in the baseline scenario to 62.4% in Greater Expo Case 2. It can be said that the increase in the number of extra nights and day-trippers further increases the economic impact on prefectures other than Osaka in the Kansai region. A comparison of the baseline scenario and the Greater Expo scenario shows that the increase in overnight stays and day-trippers associated with the development of the Greater Expo will have a relatively higher economic impact on areas outside of Osaka Prefecture. By developing a Greater Expo with contents that are attractive to tourists, day-trip and stay-over consumption can be expected to increase in areas outside of the Expo site. In other words, the economic effects of the Expo can be expected to ripple out over a wider area and into other prefectures in the Kansai region, thereby turning the entire Kansai region into a pavilion. There have already been a number of events that aim at the development of a Greater Expo and the pavilionization of the Kansai region. The following subsection introduces some examples of such efforts.

## (2) Examples of a Greater Expo: Open Factories in Yao City and Higashi-Osaka City

As described in Subsection 3.1 (1), the development of a Greater Expo envisions additional participation in events held at locations other than the Yumeshima site as well as the creation of pavilions throughout the Kansai region that will have an economic effect on the Greater Kansai region. This subsection introduces Yao City's "Open Factory" initiative called "*Miseruba-Yao*" and its efforts toward the Osaka-Kansai Expo, as well as the Hanazono Expo held in Higashiosaka City in 2022 as examples of the Greater Expo in practice.

## (1) What is an "Open Factory"?

According to the Kinki Bureau of Economy, Trade and Industry, Yao City's "Open Factory" is an initiative in which manufacturing companies open their production sites to the outside world and allow visitors to experience the manufacturing process. In addition, in recent years, many companies, mainly in regions with a certain level of industrial concentration, have begun to organize events together rather than independently. Such events attract many visitors from within and outside the region by showing the attractiveness of the region in an integrated manner. In the Kansai region, in particular, such open factory events are expected to serve as a means of communicating the attractiveness of Kansai in anticipation of the 2025 Osaka-Kansai Expo.

According to the Kansai Bureau of Economy, Trade and Industry (METI-Kansai), as of March 2023, 41 regionally integrated open factories have been held nationwide. Of these, 14 have been held in two in Kansai (including Fukui Prefecture), or about one-third of all open factory events. Figure 5-1-1 shows the number of open factories in the Kansai region, mainly in Osaka and Kyoto prefectures. In Osaka Prefecture, in particular, there are areas where the manufacturing industry is flourishing, such as Higashi-Osaka City and Yao City, and each municipality is taking advantage of its regional strengths.

## (2) "*Miseruba-Yao*" and "Osaka Health Care Pavilion" in Yao City

"*Miseruba-Yao*", inaugurated in Yao City in 2018, is a typical example of the open factory described in (1) (see Figure 5-1-2). It is a consortium (joint venture) of local small and medium-sized companies, major companies, universities,

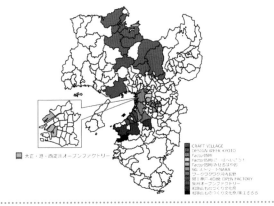

**Figure 5-1-1**    Open Factories in Kansai

Source: Compiled by METI Kinki from "OPEN FACTORY REPORT 1.0

**Figure 5-1-2**    View of "*Miserubayao*"

Source: Courtesy of Yao City

financial institutions, and the government, aiming at promoting co-creation among companies to bring about new innovations. Specifically, the consortium contributes to the local community through "manufacturing workshops," communicates the attractiveness of manufacturing and the appeal of manufacturing companies, and conducts collaborative projects, product development, and events among the companies. In the five years since its establishment, more than 50 new collaborative projects and products have been created. As of the end of January 2023, there were 130 participating companies. The total number of visitors as of the end of January 2023 was about 84,000, and the goal is to attract 100,000 visitors during the period of Osaka-Kansai Expo.

Yao City will be the only municipality to have a booth at the Osaka-Kansai Expo in the "Osaka Health Care Pavilion," where Osaka Prefecture and Osaka City will exhibit their products. In addition, the city is actively promoting Yao City to attract visitors from the Expo site in cooperation with the *Miseruba-Yao* mentioned above.

## (3) Hanazono Expo in Higashi-Osaka City

A similar initiative to Yao City's "Open Factory" was the Hanazono Expo held by Higashi-Osaka City in 2022. The city held the "Hanazono Expo: Let's experience 'the future society full of shining lives'[2]" at Hanazono Central Park on November 5 and 6, 2022 (see Figure 5-1-3). The purpose of this event was to allow visitors to experience new lifestyles and values in a post-pandemic society,

**Figure 5-1-3**    Hanazono Expo poster and scenes from the day

Source: Provided by Higashi-Osaka City

---

2) An adapted translation of the official the logo of the Osaka-Kansai Expo,

as well as digitalization through cutting-edge technology, and to publicize the significance and the potential of the Expo. Hanazono Central Park was used as the Expo site, and nearly 200 booths of companies and other organizations were lined up to display actual "flying cars," performances by Expo producers, a corner where visitors could try using VR goggles, and a drone piloting experience. The official Expo character *Myaku-myaku* was also on display.

According to the city of Higashi-Osaka, the event attracted 70,000 visitors compared to the originally planned 20,000, resulting in a production inducement effect of JPY 420 million for Osaka Prefecture as a whole and JPY 160 million for Higashi-Osaka City. It can be said that the event succeeded in fostering momentum toward the Osaka-Kansai Expo, and in generating economic effects. Aiming to promote local small and medium-sized businesses, the city is planning to hold the same event in 2023 and 2024, before the Osaka-Kansai Expo.

## 2. Economic effects of promoting sightseeing tours

In Chapter 5, it was pointed out that a major challenge for tourism in Japan is to eliminate the phenomenon of overtourism in urban areas and to attract visitors to other regions. With the Osaka-Kansai Expo scheduled to be held in 2025, several promotions and specific tour programs are under consideration to promote wide-area tourism in the Kansai region.

Subsection 3.2 (1) introduces efforts to promote sightseeing tours in the Kansai region. Subsection 3.2 (2) presents a model case of a high value-added tour as exemplified by the Kansai Tourism Bureau, as well as the results of our analysis of its impact on the regional economy using the Kansai Interregional Input-Output Table.

### (1) Efforts to promote sightseeing tours, wide-area expansion, and high value-added tourism in Kansai

Below, we introduce two initiatives by various institutions working toward the development and promotion of tourism in Kansai.

### (1) Action Plan for the 2025 Osaka-Kansai Expo (an initiative by the International Exposition Promotion Headquarters)

The "Action Plan for the 2025 Osaka-Kansai Expo" (Version 3, released in December 2022), published by the Expo Promotion Headquarters, outlines the policies and measures to be implemented by each ministry and agency in the lead-up to the 2025 Osaka-Kansai Expo. The first version was released in December 2021 and it has been revised every six months since then. The key themes for tourism are "Promotion of inbound travel to Japan using the opportunities provided by the Osaka-Kansai Expo" (Versions 1 and 2) and "Promotion of the Osaka-Kansai Expo as an opportunity to attract visitors to the entire country" (Version 3). The basic idea of the project is that the Cabinet Secretariat and the Japan Tourism Agency will take the lead and work with exposition associations and DMOs (Destination Marketing/Management Organizations) to refine tourism resources, enrich contents, and promote digital technologies, which will lead to the rebranding of the region. The project also envisions the construction of high-quality, attractive sightseeing routes, the creation of model courses including wide-area tours, and the enrichment of sightseeing content.

## (2) Kansai Tourism Action Plan for Osaka-Kansai Expo (a joint initiative by the Kinki Regional Development Bureau, Kinki District Transport Bureau, Kansai Tourism Bureau)

Next, the "Kansai Tourism Action Plan for Osaka-Kansai Expo" (Ver. 2, revised in August 2023) by the Kinki Regional Development Bureau, the Kinki District Transport Bureau, and the Kansai Tourism Bureau, based on the "Action Plan for the 2025 Osaka-Kansai Expo" above, provides more specific details of efforts specifically for the tourism industry. For example, the plan lists the creation of new tourism contents based on changes in travel demand (improvement of attractiveness), the creation of sustainable tourism regions (regional initiatives), and the strengthening of the tourism industry (introduction of digital technologies, etc.) as initiatives to promote the recovery of tourism in the Kansai region. In order to make Kansai an internationally competitive tourist region, the Bureau aims to create a tourist region that is "good to live in and good to visit" by linking regions from the four perspectives of "theme and story," "human resources," "information," and "transportation" to coordinate regional tourist resources as an "area. For inter-regional travel, the Bureau plans to use MaaS(Mobility as a Service)to promote seamless inter-regional travel by public transportation.

In preparation for the Osaka-Kansai Expo, it is stated that "the entire Kansai region will be transformed into a pavilion to encourage Expo visitors to tour the Kansai region" (Figure 5-1-4). The Bureau also states that efforts will be made to create content that takes advantage of regional characteristics and to promote high value-added tourism, which is the plan of action that we suggested in last year's white paper.

## (3) "The Exciting Kansai" (an initiative by the Kansai Tourism Bureau)

The Kansai Tourism Bureau has created "The Exciting Kansai," an initiative aiming at promoting sightseeing route for foreign visitors in the Greater Kansai

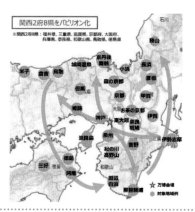

**Figure 5-1-4**    A representation of the pavilionization of the entire Kansai region

Source: "Kansai Tourism Action Plan for Osaka-Kansai Expo" by Kinki Regional Development Bureau, Kinki District Transport Bureau, and Kansai Tourism Bureau.

**Table 5-1-3**    Tourist Routes in "The Exciting Kansai"

| Area Name | target prefectures |
|---|---|
| KII PENINSULA | WakayamaPref., Nara Pref., Mie Pref. |
| HARIMA | Hyogo Pref. |
| WEST LAKE BIWA & FUKUI | Shiga Pref., Fukui Pref. |
| FUKUI, EAST LAKE BIWA & MIE | Fukui Pref., Shiga Pref.,  Mie Pref. |
| KOBE, AWAJI ISLAND & TOKUSHIMA | Hyogo Pref., Tokushima Pref. |
| SAN'IN COAST | Tottori Pref., Hyogo Pref., Kyoto Pref., Fukui Pref |
| ISE &NARA | Nara Pref., Mie Pref. |
| TANABA | Kyoto Pref., Hyogo Pref |

Source: Compiled by KANSAI Tourism Bureau from "The Exciting Kansai" website and materials.

region. The initiative has developed eight sightseeing routes in the Kansai region.  The idea is that Kyoto, Osaka, Kobe, and Nara are core areas, from where visitors can go on tours around in the Greater Kansai region (see Table 5-1-3 for the routes). The website of "The Exciting Kansai" provides examples of model courses and experience programs for each of the eight routes based on the key concepts of touring, wide-area tourism, and high value added.

In the next paragraph, we introduce a model self-guided tour course in the

San'in Kaigan area, one of "The Exciting Kansai" tourist routes[3]. The results of an analysis of the impact on the regional economy using the Kansai Interregional Input-Output Table are also presented.

## (2) Economic effects of the promotion of region-wide sightseeing tours by Kansai Tourism Bureau

We selected the San'in Kaigan area as an example, because it straddles multiple prefectures, and is therefeore a concrete example of a wide-area, round-trip tour that includes overnight stays.

Table 5-1-4 shows an overview of the San'in Kaigan area tour. Using a rental car, visitors will tour the area centering on Toyooka City in Hyogo Prefecture and the Tango region along the sea in the northern part of Kyoto Prefecture. On the first day, visitors will rent a car at Kansai International Airport, explore Izushi Town in Hyogo Prefecture, visit the Toyooka Bag Factory in Toyooka City, and stay at a luxurious hotel in Kinosaki (a famous hot spring resort). On the third day, visitors will experience activities such as a sightseeing boat ride in the area near Amanohashidate before returning to Kansai International Airport. The tour is characterized by the fact that it incorporates a wide variety of tourist resources (food, local specialties, and souvenirs from each region), and by the fact that it is a value-added plan that increases tourist satisfaction through accommodation in luxurious facilities and a higher value added than conventional individual tours.

Using the Kansai Interregional Input-Output Table (tentative table), we measure the economic impact on the regional economy of increased tourism demand and higher value added by international visitors to Japan (referred to as the "high value-added scenario"), based on the assumption of the excursion tours shown in Table 5-1-4. As a comparison, we also measure the economic effects of conventional tours to Hyogo and Kyoto prefectures (hereinafter referred to as the "baseline scenario").

Table 5-1-5 compares the per capita cost (unit cost) in the baseline scenario and the high value-added case. In the baseline scenario, the per capita costs in Hyogo and Kyoto prefectures are taken from the Japan Tourism Agency's "Survey on Trends in Foreign Visitor Consumption in Japan." In the high value-added scenario, each unit cost was assumed based on the program shown in Table 5-1-4.

---

3) Self-guided tours are a form of travel that is spreading mainly among wealthy Europeans and Americans, in which travelers arrange their itinerary, transportation, and accommodations in advance, and enjoy sightseeing and staying at their own pace with a dedicated map and guidebook in hand.

**Table 5-1-4**    Outline of San'in Kaigan Area Tour (part of "The Exciting Kansai")

| |
|---|
| Tour Name: Kinosaki ~ Tango Peninsula ~ Amanohashidate 3 days / 2 nights |
| Fee: JPY 128,000 per person |
| Route: Kansai International Airport → Kinosaki Hot Spring → Amanohashidate → Kansai International Airport |
| Day1: Kansai airport to Kinosaki Onsen<br>Arrival at Kansai Airport and depart after renting a car. Depart for Izushi Town by self-drive.<br>[Recommended Model Course]<br>　Izushi soba lunch and walking around Izushi castle town.<br>　Izushi Castle Town Highlights: Shinkoro Clock Tower, Eirakukan, Takumi Crafts<br>[Recommended Options]<br>(Izushi Area)<br>　Soba making experience and lunch (reservation required / time required about 1 hour)<br>(Toyooka Area)<br>　Shopping at Toyooka KABAN Artisan Avenue<br>　Genbudo Cave Park & Genbudo Cave Museum<br>Accommodation: Nishimuraya Hotel Shougetsutei or similar *dinner & breakfast is included |
| Day2: Breakfast at the ryokan and Check-out. Depart for self-drive tour. Kinosaki Onsen to Amanohashidate<br>[Recommended Model Course]<br>　Kinosaki Onsen Ropeway to Matsudaisan Onsenji temple and observation deck<br>　Lunch at Wakuden MORI Arts and Crafts Restaurant<br>Chirimen (crepe) road / Former Bito Family House<br>[Recommended options]<br>(Kinosaki Area)<br>　Kinosaki straw work experience (reservation required / time required about 1 hour)<br>(Kyotagngo Area)<br>　Authentic crepe kimono dressing & walking experience (reservation required / time required about 4 hours)<br>　Crepe coaster making and hand-weaving experience (reservation required / time required about 1 hour)<br>Accommodation: Amanohashidate Rikyu Hoshi no Oto or similar |
| Day3: Breakfast at the hotel and Check-out. Self driver tour Tango peninsula. Amanohashidate to Kansai Airport<br>[Recommended Model Course]<br>　Walking around the Ine Funaya (boat house) area (please enjoy recommended options)<br>　Sea food lunch at "Funaya Restaurant" or "Wadatsumi"<br>　Amanohashidate (Motoise Konos Shrine / Kasamatsu Park)<br>[Recommended options in Ine]<br>(Ine)<br>　Ine experience with Funaya guide (reservation required / group tour about 1 hour)<br>　Ine e-bike / electric assist bicycle rental (reservation required)<br>　Sightseeing around Ine Funaya by sea taxi (reservation required / time required about 30 minutes)<br>　Ine Bay Sightseeing Boat (time required: about 30 minutes) |

Source: Compiled by KANSAI Tourism Bureau from "THE EXCITING KANSAI" website.

　　The first difference between the baseline scenario and the high value-added case is the cost of lodging. The baseline scenario includes relatively inexpensive hotels, but the high value-added case assumes that the tourists will stay at luxurious facilities, resulting in a higher cost per person. Second, in the high value-added case, the purchase of Toyooka bags in Hyogo Prefecture and traditional crafts in Kyoto Prefecture are assumed based on the tour itinerary, and these purchases are reflected in the shopping costs. Therefore, the unit price of the shopping cost is larger than that of the baseline scenario. Third, in the high value-added case, it is assumed that the travel expenses include car rentals and expressway charges in Osaka Prefecture.

Based on the unit costs in Table 5-1-5, the economic impact was calculated by multiplying 41,000 (person-nights), which is the total number of foreign overnight stays in Toyooka City in 2019, and assigning it to each industry in each region using the Kansai Interregional Input-Output Table (tentative version). The induced production, value added, and employment income for both cases are shown in Figure 5-1-5. The induced production amount is JPY 5.0 billion in the baseline scenario case and JPY 13.4 billion in the high value-added scenario. Meanwhile, the induced value added is JPY 2.7 billion in the baseline scenario and JPY 7.0 billion in the high value-added scenario. Finally, the induced employment income is JPY 1.3 billion in the baseline scenario and JPY 3.4 billion in the

| Table 5-1-5 | Comparison of Per Capita Expenditures in the baseline versus the high value-added scenario |||||

| | Base Case | | high value added case | | |
| (Unit: JPY/person) | Hyogo | Kyoto | Hyogo | Kyoto | Osaka |
|---|---|---|---|---|---|
| Lodging expenses | 7,600 | 10,531 | 45,000 | 60,000 | 0 |
| Food and drinks expenses | 8,412 | 8,598 | 1,200 | 6,030 | 0 |
| Transportation expenses | 545 | 778 | 935 | 1,953 | 8,599 |
| Entertainment services expenses | 1,630 | 1,319 | 1,200 | 3,200 | 0 |
| Shopping expenses | 7,445 | 7,593 | 20,000 | 10,000 | 0 |
| Other | 4,261 | 4,840 | 1,000 | 3,500 | 0 |

Source: Compiled by the author based on the Japan Tourism Agency's "Survey of Foreign Visitor Spending Trends" and the Kansai Tourism Bureau' "The Exciting Kansai" program, etc.

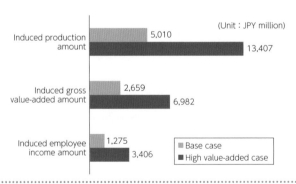

| Figure 5-1-5 | Comparison of the economic impact of the baseline versus the high value-added scenario |

Source: Prepared by the author

high value-added scenario. In both cases, the economic effect in the high value-added scenario is about 2.5 times larger than that of the baseline scenario.

Table 5-1-6 shows the economic impact by region in terms of induced production. In both the baseline scenario and the high value-added scenario, Kyoto Prefecture accounts for about 40% of the total induced production effect, while Hyogo Prefecture accounts for about 35%. In both cases, Kyoto Prefecture receives the largest share of the induced production effect because the cost of lodging is higher in Kyoto Prefecture. In the high value-added scenario, Kyoto Prefecture's share increases while the share of the rest of the Kansai region decreases by 1.1 %pt. These results suggest that the economic ripple effects of tours that effectively utilize regional tourism resources remain within the region.

Table 5-1-7 shows the production inducement effect by region and industry. In the baseline scenario, the service industry has the largest effect, followed by the manufacturing and commerce industries. In the high value-added case, the service sector also has the largest effect, but its share of the total is slightly lower than in the baseline scenario case. Instead, the shares of the manufacturing and transportation/communication sectors increase. In the high value-added case, the induced production effect in the manufacturing sector in Hyogo Prefecture is about five times larger than in the baseline scenario, while the manufacturing sector in Kyoto Prefecture also increases by about 2.5 times.

Finally, we outline the impact of the promotion of region-wide sightseeing tours on value added in the regional economy. In Table 5-1-8 we compare the gross value added in Kyoto and Hyogo prefectures, as well as the ratio of the effect to the gross regional product (nominal GRP) of the Tango region in

**Table 5-1-6**    Production Inducement Effects by Region

| | Base case | | High value-added case | | Difference between the two cases (JPY million) |
|---|---|---|---|---|---|
| | Induced production amount (JPY million) | Share by Region | Induced production amount (JPY million) | Share by Region | |
| Kyoto Pref. | 2,011 | 40.1% | 5,523 | 41.2% | 3,512 |
| Hyogo Pref. | 1,734 | 34.6% | 4,595 | 34.3% | 2,861 |
| Osaka Pref. | 273 | 5.5% | 768 | 5.7% | 495 |
| Other Kansai | 152 | 3.0% | 414 | 3.1% | 262 |
| Other regions | 841 | 16.8% | 2,108 | 15.7% | 1,267 |
| Total | 5,010 | 100.0% | 13,407 | 100.0% | 8,397 |

Note: Other Kansai includes Fukui, Mie, Shiga, Nara, Wakayama, Tottori and Tokushima prefectures. The "Other Kansai" includes Fukui, Mie, Shiga, Nara, Wakayama, Tottori, and Tokushima prefectures.
Source: Prepared by the author

| Table 5-1-7 | Production Inducement Effects by Region and Industry |

Base case                                                                    (Unit: JPY million)

| Industry | Kyoto Pref. | Hyogo Pref. | Osaka Pref. | Other Kansai | Other regions | Total | Share (%) |
|---|---|---|---|---|---|---|---|
| Agriculture, forestry and fisheries | 11 | 13 | 1 | 9 | 61 | 94 | 1.9% |
| Manufacturing | 187 | 137 | 66 | 86 | 252 | 729 | 14.6% |
| Commerce | 203 | 194 | 63 | 16 | 127 | 603 | 12.0% |
| Transportation and communications | 142 | 121 | 52 | 15 | 149 | 479 | 9.6% |
| Service and others | 1,228 | 1,077 | 61 | 13 | 177 | 2,555 | 51.0% |
| Others | 240 | 192 | 30 | 12 | 74 | 549 | 11.0% |
| Total | 2,011 | 1,734 | 273 | 152 | 841 | 5,010 | 100.0% |

High value-added case                                                          (Unit: JPY million)

| Industry | Kyoto Pref. | Hyogo Pref. | Osaka Pref. | Other Kansai | Other regions | Total | Share (%) |
|---|---|---|---|---|---|---|---|
| Agriculture, forestry and fisheries | 15 | 21 | 1 | 19 | 128 | 184 | 1.4% |
| Manufacturing | 462 | 635 | 176 | 233 | 589 | 2,095 | 15.6% |
| Commerce | 365 | 532 | 159 | 40 | 312 | 1,407 | 10.5% |
| Transportation and communications | 431 | 368 | 173 | 48 | 421 | 1,442 | 10.8% |
| Service and others | 3,507 | 2,499 | 169 | 37 | 460 | 6,671 | 49.8% |
| Others | 744 | 540 | 90 | 36 | 197 | 1,607 | 12.0% |
| Total | 5,523 | 4,595 | 768 | 414 | 2,108 | 13,407 | 100.0% |

difference                                                                   (Unit: JPY million)

| Industry | Kyoto Pref. | Hyogo Pref. | Osaka Pref. | Other Kansai | Other regions | Total |
|---|---|---|---|---|---|---|
| Agriculture, forestry and fisheries | 4 | 8 | 1 | 10 | 67 | 90 |
| Manufacturing | 275 | 498 | 110 | 147 | 337 | 1,366 |
| Commerce | 162 | 338 | 95 | 24 | 185 | 804 |
| Transportation and communications | 289 | 248 | 121 | 33 | 272 | 963 |
| Service and others | 2,279 | 1,422 | 108 | 24 | 283 | 4,116 |
| Others | 503 | 348 | 60 | 24 | 123 | 1,058 |
| Total | 3,512 | 2,861 | 495 | 262 | 1,267 | 8,397 |

Note: Regional classification is the same as in Table 5-1-6.
Source: Prepared by the author

| Table 5-1-8 | Impact on the local economy (in terms of gross value added) |

(Unit:JPY million)

| | | | |
|---|---|---|---|
| Tango Area Nominal GRP | 300,612 | Toyooka City Nominal GRP | 302,512 |
| Kyoto Prefectural Effect | 1,471 | Hyogo Prefectural Effect | 1,783 |
| Ratio (%) | 0.49% | Ratio (%) | 0.59% |

Note: Nominal GRPs are based on the latest available data for 2019. The Tango region includes Miyazu City, Kyotango City, Ine Town, and Yosano Town.
Source: Prepared by the author based on "Statistical Report of Toyooka City for FY 2022" by Toyooka City and "Kyoto Prefecture's Municipal Accounts for FY 2022" by Kyoto Prefecture.

Kyoto Prefecture and Toyooka City in Hyogo Prefecture. The ratio of the effect in Kyoto Prefecture to the economy of the Tango region is 0.49%, and the ratio of the effect in Hyogo Prefecture to the economy of Toyooka City is 0.59%. The results show that changing the tour itinerary to a high value-added course generates an additional economic ripple effect in the region.

## Conclusion: Kansai's Economy Should Aim for High Value-Added Opportunities related to Expo 2025

In Section 1 we discussed the possibility for a Greater Expo and introduced examples of how to brand and add value to regions and industries in the Kansai region, or more simply put, how to create profitable industries and profitable regions.

Subsection 1.1 presented an updated version of our estimates of the economic impact of the Osaka-Kansai Expo and a potential Greater Expo, and introduced the concept of "open factories" which can be integrated into a Greater Expo, with specific examples from Yao City and Higashi-Osaka City. Subsection 1.2 outlined efforts to promote sightseeing tours in the Kansai region, introducing examples of high value-added tours in the San'in Kaigan area by the Kansai Tourist Organization, and measuring the economic impact of such tours. Our analysis indicates that the promotion of sightseeing tours and high value-added tours has an economic impact not only in the region concerned, but also more broadly throughout the Kansai region.

The Osaka-Kansai Expo is scheduled to be held in 2025, and it is necessary to work toward expanding the economic effects of the Expo throughout the entire Kansai region in a sustainable. Rather than limiting the economic effects of the Expo to specific regions or specific times, it is necessary to proactively prepare mechanisms to ensure that the effects are sustained and spread over a wider area. Even after the Expo, it is important to design events and tour programs that fully utilize the characteristics and attractions of each region and succeed in attracting tourists. We hope to see more initiatives in the Kansai region similar the ones described in Section 1 of this article, as we believe that such initiatives will lead to the rebranding of the region and generate high added value.

## References

Cabinet Secretariat (2022), "2025 Osaka-Kansai Expo Action Plan Ver. 3," (https://www.cas.go.jp/jp/seisaku/expo_suisin_honbu/pdf/Action_Plan_Ver.3.pdf).

Inada, Y., Nomura, R., APIR IO project team (2024), "Economic Ripple Effects of Osaka-Kansai EXPO: Estimates based on the latest data and the economic impact of the Greater EXPO" (Japanese title: *Osaka-Kansai Banpaku no Keizai Hakyu Koka -Saishin Deta wo Fumaeta Shisan to Kakucho Banpaku no Keizai Koka-*), APIR Trend Watch No.92, January 24, 2024, (https://www.apir.or.jp/research/13926/).

Kansai Bureau of Economy, Trade and Industry (2023), "OPEN FACTORY REPORT 1.0," (https://www.kansai.meti.go.jp/1-9chushoresearch/openfactory/R4fybooklet.html).

Kinki District Transport Bureau, Kinki Regional Development Bureau, and KANSAI Tourism Bureau (2023), "Kansai Tourism Action Plan for Osaka-Kansai Expo: Connecting the Region from Four Perspectives," (https://www.kkr.mlit.go.jp/news/top/press/2023/lpe01g0000002ilo-att/20230801-1actionplan.pdf).

KANSAI Tourism Bureau (2021) "THE EXCITING KANSAI", (https://www.the-kansai-guide.com/en/exciting/).

# Section 2
## LEVERAGING DX IN KANSAI AND OSAKA

*SHIMOJO, Shinji; ASHIKAGA, Tomoyoshi*

## 1. Two types of economic effects of DX

With the adoption of the "Osaka Super City Concept" as a super city-type national strategic special zone by the Cabinet Office in April 2022, the "Osaka Prefecture Super City Concept" has begun to move toward the social implementation of a data collaboration infrastructure (ORDEN) known as an urban operating system (OS). A super city is an effort to promote sustainable urban development at a higher level than before by utilizing DX, and an urban OS is a digital platform for a super city that efficiently manages the entire city by utilizing sensors, networks, big data, artificial intelligence (AI), etc. (Figure 5-2-1). The Osaka Prefecture Super City Concept has two green fields, Yumeshima (Yumeshima Construction, Osaka-Kansai Expo) and Umekita Phase 2, where rapid demonstration and social implementation of cutting-edge services is being promoted by taking advantage of the nature of green fields, where urban development is conducted from the ground up.

This section analyzes the effects of applying DX in a super city based on the definition in the Cabinet Office's "Smart City Guidebook": "Smart cities solve various problems faced by cities and regions, and continue to create new value." The "solution of various problems" refers to the streamlining of existing businesses through data visualization and analysis and is an aspect of "quantitative

**Figure 5-2-1**    Difference between Smart Cities and Super Cities

Source: IoT News, "What is the 'Super City' Concept of Urban DX?" Source: IoT News, "What is the 'Super City' Concept?"

improvement effects." "Creating value" refers to new value and new business created from data and is an aspect of "qualitative business transformation."

In the following, we will introduce two aspects of service cases using DX: "quantitative improvement effects" and "qualitative business transformation."[1]

## 2. Quantitative improvement effects

Here, we introduce two cases in which data analysis and visualization were incorporated into existing businesses to improve process efficiency. The first is the case of Mitsubishi UFJ Trust and Banking Corporation, which used the information banking service "Dprime" to integrate user communication into a company's product development process, and developed a final product based on the results of collecting and analyzing personal data and questionnaire data. The second is a case study of "Yumeshima Construction," a project to use DX to facilitate the construction of the Expo site and related infrastructure for the 2025 Osaka-Kansai Expo, including countermeasures against traffic congestion of construction vehicles and smooth movement of workers.

### (1) Product development based on analysis of users' personal data

In July 2022, Mitsubishi UFJ Trust and Banking Corporation launched the "Beer Development Project with Your Data and Waste Ingredients" based on the concept of "Let's Make Beer Together to Raise Food Loss Issues." Users experience the process of creating products using their own data, and companies develop products from the user's perspective while sharing the social significance of the product and gaining the empathy of the user. This is a service that can only be provided by an information bank that connects individuals and companies with data.

In this project, participants were recruited through the "Dprime" application, and a pilot version was developed by the company through in-depth analysis of personal data and questionnaire data for 1,400 participants. Since feedback to participants must be simple to gain their sympathy and be seen by them, the results of the analysis for participants were presented in an easy-to-understand graphical format with four cut-off points, according to the data on beer tastes and preferences. For example, for those who do not like beer, we created a slightly sweet and fruity one that does not show bitterness from the viewpoint of user comprehensibility. For other analyses, we decided on a case-by-case

---

1) The case studies are taken from the Asia Pacific Institute of Research's "Urban DX in Kansai and Osaka" study group report (FY2022).

basis how to communicate with the participants and published the results on our website and in videos to make it easier for them to understand how to use the data. The beer development process was conducted by actually making four kinds of beer, having 600 people drink a set of the four kinds, and collecting questionnaires afterward.

The "food loss countermeasure" in the development of this beer was the use of grapefruits that were to be discarded by farmers and cacao husks (cacao peels discarded during chocolate processing). The grapefruit was produced in cooperation with a company called "Midori-no-Sato Ryokun" in Miyazaki Prefecture, and the cacao husk was produced in cooperation with "Dandelion Chocolate." By communicating the concerns and thoughts of these partner companies on food loss issues through videos and websites, the project has gained the sympathy of users not only for the brewing of beer, but also for efforts to address social issues.

In the questionnaire results before the tasting, few people answered that they would "actively choose products that solve social issues," with 24% saying that they would "actively want to choose," but in the questionnaire results after the tasting, those who changed their attitude to "actively want to choose" increased by 26% to 50%, indicating the "achievement of empathy," which was the significance of the project.

The use of "Dprime" in this product development project not only enabled the construction of customer contact points by disclosing the development process, but also enabled the sequential reflection of massive data obtained from users in product development, as well as the acquisition of empathy from users.

## (2) Yumeshima Construction

A large number of construction vehicles are expected to come to Yumeshima during the large-scale construction of the Osaka-Kansai Expo. In addition to construction vehicles, container trucks and general vehicles are also expected to travel on Yumeshima, potentially causing large-scale traffic congestion. There are two major routes to Yumeshima, one from Maishima in the north and the other from Sakishima in the south. Even if these two routes flow smoothly, there is a gate to the construction site on the route, and delays near this gate will lead to congestion. Even if the gate can be passed, there is a limit to the number of parking spaces available due to the limited area of the Expo construction site, and these factors must be considered (Figure 5-2-2).

However, while the number of construction vehicles must be planned so as not to cause traffic congestion, the plan should not be adjusted on a monthly basis. In addition, the Osaka-Kansai Expo project involves coordination among

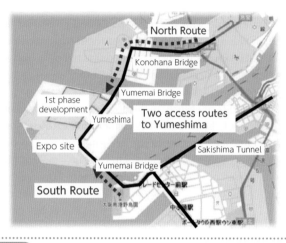

**Figure 5-2-2**    Access route to Yumeshima

Source: Osaka Super City Council, "Osaka Super City Overall Plan," p.24; figure processed by APIR.

multiple construction companies, resulting in an enormous amount of coordination man-hours. In order to reduce the coordination man-hours, we use "DX at construction sites" that utilizes mathematical optimization.

In the past, for example, data for each construction area was managed individually by the company managing the construction area, but Yumeshima Construction's "Data Standardization and Visualization System" centralizes the vehicle management data held by each construction company and displays it on a dashboard for a one-stop view of the data.

Specifically, in order to estimate the adjusted number of construction vehicles in the operation plan, the total number of vehicles in the operation plan for each north-south route is calculated. The number of general vehicles is also estimated based on historical traffic volume data, and the sum of the number of vehicles on each route is calculated. This sum is then used to determine the number of vehicles that exceed the upper traffic limit for each route using traffic engineering. In addition, the conditions required for the planning include the vehicle adjustment conditions from each general contractor and weather information data necessary for making decisions when adjusting the vehicles. For example, ready-mixed concrete trucks cannot work if they are brought in on a rainy day, so if it is known that it will rain tomorrow, it is necessary to shift these trucks to the day before or the day after, or to a time when it will not rain.

The Yumeshima Construction dashboard displays a revised operation plan for construction vehicles based on mathematical optimization with the objective function of minimizing the number of adjustment man-hours and the time spent traveling before and after adjustment. Although this is a hypothetical simulation, it is estimated that the system will reduce the number of man-hours required to adjust construction vehicles by about 420 hours per month, assuming that there are about 300 vehicles per day and that each vehicle takes 2 minutes to adjust (Figure 5-2-3).

## 3. Qualitative business transformation

Here, we present the Pasona Metaverse from Pasona Inc., a company that is working to create new industries, jobs and career opportunities in rural areas using virtual spaces (metaverse).

In September 2020, Pasona relocated part of its head office functions to Awaji Island. The relocation of a portion of Pasona's head office functions is not only from a BCP perspective, but also from the perspective of the decline of rural areas and agriculture, the falling birthrate and aging population, children on waiting lists, the separation of employees from nursing care, and the physical

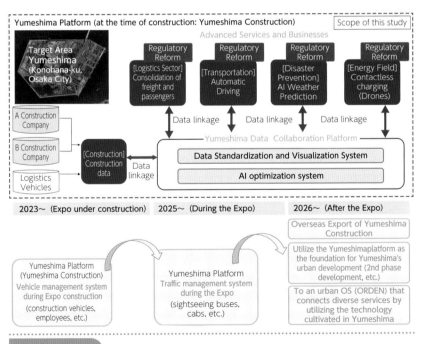

**Figure 5-2-3    Yumeshima Construction's System Configuration**

Source: Super City Smart City Forum 2022 Lecture "Kankeiren's Approach to Yumeshima City Planning Starting with 'Yumeshima Construction,'" p.21.

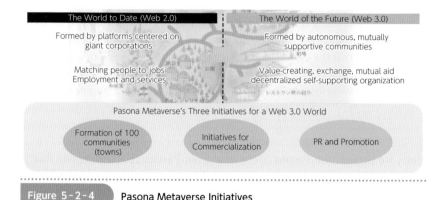

| The World to Date (Web 2.0) | The World of the Future (Web 3.0) |
|---|---|
| Formed by platforms centered on giant corporations | Formed by autonomous, mutually supportive communities |
| Matching people to jobs Employment and services | Value-creating, exchange, mutual aid decentralized self-supporting organization |

Pasona Metaverse's Three Initiatives for a Web 3.0 World

Formation of 100 communities (towns)

Initiatives for Commercialization

PR and Promotion

**Figure 5-2-4**    Pasona Metaverse Initiatives

Source: "FY2022 SDGs Public-Private Partnerships for Local Development: Excellent Examples of Efforts," p.14, International Forum on SDGs for Local Development 2023

and mental environment, as well as the value of the option to end Tokyo's concentration. Awaji Island is about the same size as the 23 wards of Tokyo or Singapore, with a population of 120,000.

Pasona aims to create new industries, employment and career opportunities by multiplying Awaji Island activities with the Metaverse. In order to create work opportunities and business operations in the metaverse, Pasona has created a new community industry with "100 communities (towns)" and presented the working environment, facilities and values on Awaji Island (Figure 5-2-4).

The community allows users to participate in real content on Awaji Island, and when there is a "shortage of people or poor response from facilities," a mechanism is in place to send customers to each other. When using a car, one would conventionally go to Awaji Island and then car-share, or rent a car in Shin-Kobe or Sannomiya, but in Pasona's metaverse, one owns their own car in the metaverse space before going to Awaji Island, and when one arrives, they can get into their own car in the virtual space in real time.

Pasona has launched the Avatar Human Resource Creation Project and created the Awaji Avatar Center on Awaji Island. The center provides opportunities for staff who want to serve customers to work in sales and reception. For example, there is a theme park called "Nijigen-no-mori" on Awaji Island, which has a large digital signage display at the entrance that shows video clips. When you say "Hello" in front of this display, a staff member at the Avatar Center answers your question. The avatars do not have faces, and voice conversion is also possible, so that a person of a different age or gender can serve customers as if she were a woman in her 20s without any discomfort. The avatar concierge can be connected to the chatbot on the Web. For example, if the system is installed in a store that is closed at night, it can respond via the Web from Awaji Island because the number of customers is not known even if the store is open at night. The system can also be used for event reception, to find new customers, and to utilize specialized human resources. In the field of digital marketing, placing avatar consultants on the Internet has the effect of increasing conversion rates and inquiries. Currently, the Avatar Center on Awaji Island handles this service, but in the future, we are considering offering this service at home. This method allows a wide range of skilled personnel to be utilized throughout the country, such as by making it possible to respond from a different location if one location becomes congested.

## 4. How a super city (urban DX) should be

In order for the development plan of the "Osaka Super City Concept" to ensure the sustainable development of the city in the future, it is necessary to provide services that solve the problems of consumers and visitors and improve their quality of life (QoL), and to maintain their level of satisfaction.

The fact that a city continuously enhances and evolves the attractiveness of its services to its residents and users has something in common with the subscription-based business model: Tzuo (2018) describes subscription from the perspective of the service provider as "focusing on the needs of specific customer desires and creating services that bring continuous value to them. If this subscription approach is applied to cities, "a state of high QoL" can be realized by analyzing the inconveniences (who is troubled and why) latent in the city and providing services to satisfy those inconveniences.

There are two ways to increase the value of a service to a customer in subscription: up-selling and cross-selling. Up-selling is proposal of a new service that brings new value to the current situation. Cross-selling is creating new value by linking with other services.

In order to sustainably improve the quality of services, optimizing services for individual users (personalization) using user response and evaluation data will strengthen the residents' intention to continue living in the community. In addition, new services must be created through up-selling and cross-selling to increase the value to customers. The three case studies presented in this report have in common that they have both real and virtual user contact points and continue to generate high QoL through data-driven service provision, which provides suggestions on how to gain community engagement.

It will become increasingly important for Osaka Prefecture and Super Cities to continue to increase and retain residents by enhancing their services, in an environment where cities around the world are competing for population.

## References

Asia Pacific Institute of Research, "Comprehensive digital transformation in Kansai and Osaka," Report of the Research Project (FY 2022)
https://www.apir.or.jp/research/11175/

International Forum on SDGs for Regional Revitalization 2023 "Introduction of Excellent cases of Public-Private Partnerships for SDGs in FY 2022"
https://future-city.go.jp/sdgs-event/assets/pdf/2023/20230207_1700_awaji_jp.pdf

Osaka Super City Council, "Osaka Super City Overall Plan."
https://www.pref.osaka.lg.jp/attach/22971/00428630/01_zentaikeikaku.pdf

Super City Smart City Forum 2022, "Kansai Economic Federation's Approach to Yumeshima City Planning Starting with 'Yumeshima Construction'" (in Japanese).
https://www.chisou.go.jp/tiiki/kokusentoc/supercity/supercityforum2022/Forum2022_3-10.pdf

# Part III

## EXPO 2025 Chronology

# Table of Contents

## About the Editing of the EXPO 2025 Chronology

- The EXPO 2025 Chronology was written by the Chronology Group of the Asia Pacific Institute of Research (APIR).
- The last check date of the following data is November 30, 2023 (exceptions noted).
- EXPO 2025 OSAKA, KANSAI, JAPAN is referred to as "Osaka-Kansai Expo" and The Japan Association for the International Exposition, 2025 is referred to as "Expo Association" due to space limitation.
- EXPO 2025 OSAKA, KANSAI, JAPAN is referred to as "Expo" only in "1. Chronology" due to space limitation.
- Kansai is defined as Shiga, Kyoto, Osaka, Hyogo, Nara, and Wakayama prefectures, unless otherwise noted.

# 1. Chronology

○July 18, 2022: The Expo Association announced the nickname of the official character 1,000 days before the Expo.
○October 25, 2022: The first international meeting was held between the Expo Association and representatives of the participating countries and regions, and the construction of pavilions for each country began in earnest.
○December 20, 2022: The Headquarters for the World Expo, Cabinet Secretariat revised the Action Plan for the Expo, incorporating the requests of Osaka Prefecture, Osaka City, and other related organizations.
○April 13, 2023: A groundbreaking ceremony was held in Yumeshima, the planned venue, two years before the opening of the Expo.
○November 30, 2023: Advance ticket sales began 500 days before the Expo.

**Table 1**    Movements related to Expo: April 2022 - November 2023

| Year | Month | | Expo-Related Movements |
|---|---|---|---|
| 2022 | 4 | 8 | Participation Pledges Reach 100 Countries/Regions. |
| | | 18 | Expo Association announces basic plans for eight core pavilions. |
| | | 27 | Expo Association releases "Expo 2025 Green Vision". |
| | 5 | 13 | Tokushima Prefecture opens the Tokushima Virtual Pavilion. |
| | 6 | 3 | The Osaka-Kansai Expo establishes the "Basic Policy for Visitor Transportation". |
| | | 10 | Expo Association releases license plates commemorating the Expo. |
| | | 17 | Osaka Prefecture and City released the exterior image of Osaka Pavilion. |
| | 7 | 1 | Osaka Prefecture and City hold "Conference on Status of International Medical Treatment in Yumeshima". |
| | | 13 | Osaka Prefectural and City governments name the Osaka Pavilion "Osaka Health Care Pavilion: Nest for Reborn". |
| | | 18 | Expo Association announces the nickname of the official character 1000 days before the Expo event. |
| | 8 | 8 | Expo association selects 23 young architects to design rest areas and restrooms at Expo site. |
| | | 24 | Osaka Prefecture announces that has selected eight decarbonization technology projects to present their results during the Expo. |
| | 9 | 15 | The Kansai region's 7 prefectures and 41 chambers of commerce and industry have formed a working group to help build momentum for the Expo. |
| | | 18 | The Kansai 3 Airports Advisory Committee increases the limit of the number of departures and arrivals at Kansai International Airport, Osaka International Airport, and Kobe Airport to 500,000 per year. |

| Year | Month | Day | Event |
|---|---|---|---|
| 2022 | 10 | 25 | Expo Association holds first international meeting with representatives of participating countries and regions. |
| | | 26 | Expo Association begins coordinating pavilion construction with 30 participating countries. |
| | | 27 | Osaka Chamber of Commerce and Industry and Osaka Bureau of Industry approve 26 businesses to participate in the Osaka Pavilion. |
| | | 27 | 44 organizations affiliated with Kansai Science City establish the Keihanna Expo Event Preparation Committee. |
| | | 28 | Expo Association signs pavilion exhibition contract with Austria. |
| | 11 | 5 | "HANAZONO EXPO" event held in Higashi-Osaka City of Osaka Prefecture, to build momentum for Expo. |
| | | 8 | Seven major railroad companies in the Kansai region establish the "Kansai MaaS Council" and will start providing "MaaS" applications in the summer of 2023. |
| | 12 | 1 | Osaka Metro, NTT Communications, and six other companies begin demonstration tests of "Level 4" self-driving bus in Maishima. |
| | | 5 | Expo Association selects companies to sign official character licensing agreements. |
| | | 20 | The government's Expo Promotion Headquarters announces the "Osaka-Kansai Expo Action Plan Ver. 3". |
| | | 23 | Cabinet approves FY 2023 budget proposal, which allocates JPY 2.4 billion for the construction of the Japanese Government Pavilion and other projects at the Expo. |
| | | 27 | Expo Association begins accepting applications for "Advanced Air Mobility (AAM)" operators to connect the Expo site with the center of Osaka City and other areas. |
| 2023 | 1 | 18 | Expo Association introduce "Theme Weeks" at the Expo, where each theme is held for approximately one week. |
| | | 18 | Expo Association announces the introduction of Artificial Intelligence (AI) multilingual translation system at the Expo venues. |
| | 2 | 1 | Switzerland announces the outline of its pavilion "LA SUISSE ENCHANTÉE" at the Expo. |
| | | 14 | Osaka City announces FY 2023 budget plan of 13.4 billion JPY to support the Expo infrastructure and demonstration experiments. |
| | | 21 | Expo Association announces the selection of five companies, including ANA Holdings and Japan Airlines, to operate "AAM". |
| | 3 | 3 | Osaka Prefecture and City announce the selection of three candidate sites for the takeoff and landing sites of the "AMM". |
| | | 14 | Expo Association announces its plan to hold about 8,000 events of various sizes during the Expo. |
| | | 24 | The Japanese government announces that 153 countries and regions (excluding Japan) and 8 international organizations have pledged their participation. |
| | 4 | 6 | Expo Association announces its policy to make all payment cashless at the Expo. |
| | | 12 | Expo Association launches merchandise featuring official Expo character "Myaku-Myaku". |
| | | 13 | The Imperial Household Agency announces the appointment of His Imperial Highness Prince Akishino as honorary president of the Expo. |
| | | 13 | Groundbreaking ceremony is held for the pavilion and other major facilities on Yumeshima, the planned venue of the Expo. |
| | | 25 | Expo Association signs pavilion exhibition contract with the US. |
| | 5 | 17 | Expo Association announces the appointment of Hiroshi Osaki, former chairman of Yoshimoto Kogyo Holdings, as co-chairman of the Event Review Committee. |
| | | 29 | Osaka-Kansai Expo Kyoto Promotion Committee, co-chaired by the Governor of Kyoto Prefecture, the Mayor of Kyoto, and others, holds its first meeting. |
| | | 31 | Osaka Metro announces the introduction of 65 EV buses for commuting by venue construction workers. |
| | 6 | 5 | The Netherlands announces the outlines of its pavilion "Common Ground". |
| | | 6 | Expo Association holds International Planning Meeting (IPM) on the Expo in Osaka City. |

| 2023 | 6 | 7 | Mayoral Alliance for EXPO 2025 announces "Expo Bento Lunchboxes" featuring ingredients from 34 cities and towns throughout Japan. |
|---|---|---|---|
| | | 12 | Expo Association draws up an action plan to build momentum for the Expo both at home and abroad. |
| | | 12 | Austria announces pavilion outline "Composing the Future". |
| | | 30 | Expo Association decides to set the base price of admission tickets at JPY 7,500 for adults (18 years and older). |
| | 7 | 13 | The Expo Association approaches participating countries and regions with the idea of having the Japanese side construct the pavilion on their behalf (Type X). |
| | | 18 | Osaka Prefecture announces that "Osaka Week" will be held as part of the Expo's "Theme Weeks". |
| | | 19 | Expo Association holds briefing for businesses on the status of preparations for water transportation during Expo. |
| | 8 | 2 | Expo Association announces the outline of the pavilion where 11 businesses will jointly exhibit "Cities of the Future". |
| | | 7 | The Mint held a ceremony to commemorate the Expo by striking the first 1,000 JPY silver coins. |
| | | 25 | NPO Zeri-Japan announces outline of pavilion "Reviving the Ocean". |
| | | 30 | Osaka Prefecture announces that children between the ages of 4 and high school age living in Osaka Prefecture will be invited to the Expo free of charge. |
| | 9 | 6 | The first official Expo store opens at Abeno Harukas Kintetsu Main Store. |
| | | 11 | Groundbreaking ceremony held for the "Japan Pavilion" on Yumeshima, the planned site of the Expo. |
| | | 20 | Musician Sachiko Nakajima outlines the theme pavilion "Playground of Life: Jellyfish Pavilion". |
| | 10 | 6 | Groundbreaking ceremony held for "Kansai Pavilion," a pavilion led by the Union of Kansai Governments, on Yumeshima, the planned venue of the Expo. |
| | | 19 | Expo Association announces new information content to help build momentum for the Expo on its official YouTube channel. |
| | | 23 | Expo Association announces concrete plans for a complete cashless payment nicknamed "Myaku-pe!". |
| | | 26 | The Federation of Electric Power Companies holds a groundbreaking ceremony for the pavilion "Electric Power Pavilion – Eggs of Possibilities" in Yumeshima, the planned venue of the Expo. |
| | | 30 | Canada announces the outline of the pavilion, with the theme "Regeneration". |
| | 11 | 3 | "HANAZONO EXPO", an event to build momentum for the Expo, is held in Higashi Osaka City, Osaka Prefecture. |
| | | 10 | NTT held a groundbreaking ceremony for the pavilion "NTT Pavilion natural(Tentative)" in Yumeshima, the planned venue of the Expo. |
| | | 14 | Nine new countries have announced their participation in the Expo, bringing the total to 160 countries and regions. |
| | | 30 | 500 days until the Expo opens. Expo Association begins selling advance tickets. |

Source: Prepared by APIR based on various press materials.

Part I

Part II

Part III

Part IV

## 2. Countries, Regions and International Organizations

○Figure 1 shows the latest status of countries and regions that have announced their participation in Osaka-Kansai Expo. As of November 14, 2023, the number of countries and regions that have officially announced their participation has reached 160, surpassing the goal of 150 countries and regions. On the other hand, the number of participating international organizations is 9, which is still short of the target (25) (Tables 2 and 3).

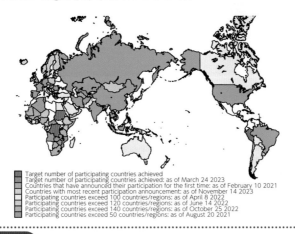

Target number of participating countries achieved
Target number of participating countries achieved: as of March 24 2023
Countries that have announced their participation for the first time: as of February 10 2021
Countries with most recent participation announcement: as of November 14 2023
Participating countries exceed 100 countries/regions: as of April 8 2022
Participating countries exceed 120 countries/regions: as of June 14 2022
Participating countries exceed 140 countries/regions: as of October 25 2022
Participating countries exceed 50 countries/regions: as of August 20 2021

**Figure 1**    Map of countries/regions that have announced their participation

Source: Prepared by APIR based on Expo Association press release.

**Table 2**    Changes in International Organizations Declaring Participation

| Total | Date | Institution |
|---|---|---|
| 1 | 2021/2/10 | International Fusion Energy Organization (ITER) |
| 2 | 2/10 | International Solar Alliance (ISA) |
| 3 | 4/7 | International Red Cross and Red Crescent Movement |
| 4 | 5/28 | African Union Commission (AUC) |
| 5 | 7/2 | European Union (EU) |
| 6 | 2022/1/7 | Association of Southeast Asian Nations (ASEAN) Secretariat |
| 7 | 4/8 | Pacific Islands Forum (PIF) Secretariat |
| 8 | 7/5 | United Nations (UN) |
| 9 | 2023/11/14 | International Science and Technology Center (ISTC) |

Source: Prepared by APIR based on Expo Association press release.

| Table 3 | | Countries/regions that have announced their participation |
|---|---|---|

| Total | Date | Country |
|---|---|---|
| 7 | 2021/2/10 | Republic of Yemen, Republic of Greece, Republic of Djibouti, Turkmenistan, People's Republic of Bangladesh, Kingdom of Bhutan, Republic of Mali |
| 14 | 3/12 | Islamic Republic of Afghanistan, Republic of Uzbekistan, Republic of Senegal, Kingdom of Bahrain, Federative Republic of Brazil, Burkina Faso, Kingdom of Lesotho |
| 18 | 4/7 | Republic of Qatar, Republic of Guinea-Bissau, Republic of Zimbabwe, Nepal |
| 19 | 4/13 | Kingdom of Thailand |
| 25 | 4/21 | Democratic People's Republic of Algeria, Republic of India, Federal Republic of Germany, French Republic, Jordan, Russian Federation |
| 29 | 5/14 | Republic of Angola, Republic of Zambia, Swiss Confederation, Lao People's Democratic Republic |
| 34 | 5/28 | Islamic Republic of Iran, Republic of Ghana, Republic of Guinea, People's Republic of China, Grand Duchy of Luxembourg |
| 43 | 6/15 | United Kingdom (United Kingdom of Great Britain and Northern Ireland), Kingdom of Cambodia, Republic of Cuba, State of Kuwait, Union of Comoros, Central African Republic, United Mexican States, Republic of Mozambique, Romania |
| 46 | 7/2 | United Arab Emirates, Republic of Kazakhstan, Kingdom of Spain |
| 48 | 7/16 | United States of America, Republic of Korea |
| 49 | 7/27 | Portuguese Republic |
| 54 | 8/20 | Republic of Indonesia, Arab Republic of Egypt, Kyrgyz Republic, Republic of Suriname, Socialist Republic of Viet Nam |
| 57 | 9/28 | Argentine Republic, Dominican Republic, Republic of Burundi |
| 58 | 10/15 | Kingdom of Saudi Arabia |
| 63 | 11/17 | Italian Republic, Republic of Uganda, Republic of Tajikistan, Brunei Darussalam, Republic of South Sudan |
| 64 | 11/24 | Republic of Paraguay |
| 67 | 12/14 | Republic of Austria, Sultanate of Oman, Kingdom of Tonga |
| 72 | 2022/1/7 | Republic of Azerbaijan, Republic of Estonia, Commonwealth of Australia, Republic of Serbia, Republic of Turkey |
| 78 | 1/28 | Republic of Armenia, Canada, Saint Lucia, Independent State of Papua New Guinea, Republic of Honduras, Republic of Rwanda |
| 86 | 3/4 | Republic of The Gambia, Democratic Socialist Republic of Sri Lanka, Republic of Equatorial Guinea, Saint Vincent and the Grenadines, Islamic Republic of Pakistan, Kingdom of Belgium, Republic of Madagascar, Republic of Latvia |
| 87 | 3/11 | Republic of Slovenia |
| 100 | 4/8 | Antigua and Barbuda, Republic of El Salvador, Republic of Guyana, Republic of Cote d'Ivoire, Democratic Republic of Sao Tome and Principe, Saint Kitts and Nevis, Tuvalu, Republic of Togo, Republic of Vanuatu, Palestine, Republic of Benin, Plurinational State of Bolivia, Republic of the Marshall Islands |
| 105 | 4/19 | Ireland, Eastern Republic of Uruguay, Republic of Guatemala, Republic of Kosovo, Malaysia |
| 106 | 5/10 | Mongolia |
| 115 | 5/31 | Republic of North Macedonia, Republic of Kenya, Independent State of Samoa, Republic of Singapore, Solomon Islands, Republic of Niger, Republic of Haiti, Republic of Bulgaria, Federated States of Micronesia |

| 119 | 6/7 | Federal Democratic Republic of Ethiopia, Kingdom of the Netherlands, Niue, Republic of Poland |
| 120 | 6/14 | Republic of the Philippines |
| 126 | 7/5 | United Republic of Tanzania, Czech Republic, Republic of Trinidad and Tobago, Republic of Palau, Belize, Montenegro |
| 130 | 7/29 | Hungary, Republic of Fiji, Republic of Mauritius, Islamic Republic of Mauritania |
| 137 | 9/9 | Kingdom of Eswatini, Republic of Gabon, Federal Republic of Somalia, Federal Republic of Nigeria, Republic of Nauru, Democratic Republic of East Timor, Republic of Botswana |
| 142 | 10/25 | Slovak Republic, Republic of Tunisia, Republic of Panama, Republic of Malta, Republic of South Africa |
| 153 | 2023/3/24 | State of Israel, Democratic Republic of Congo, Republic of Sudan, Republic of Seychelles, Vatican City State, Republic of Peru, Republic of Malawi, Principality of Monaco, Republic of Moldova, Republic of Lithuania, Republic of Liberia |
| 160 | 11/14 | Kingdom of Denmark, Republic of Finland, Kingdom of Norway, Iceland, Kingdom of Sweden, Republic of Croatia, Republic of Chile, Jamaica, Republic of Cameroon (Declined) United Mexican States, Republic of Estonia |

Source: Prepared by APIR based on Expo Association press release.

## 3. Comparison of Admission Fees for Past International Expositions

○Table 4 compares the admission fees of major international expositions held in Japan and the EXPO 2025 Osaka, Kansai, Japan. Admission for adults was JPY 800 for the first Expo held in Japan (Japan World Exposition Osaka 1970) and JPY 4,600 for the 2005 World Exposition, Aichi, Japan, while the admission fee for the EXPO 2025 Osaka, Kansai, Japan is set at JPY 7,500.

○Table 5 lists the admission fees for the EXPO 2025 Osaka, Kansai, Japan. The introduction of the "Summer Pass," which was not available at the 2005 World Exposition, Aichi, Japan, is a unique feature of this exposition in order to diversify the number of visitors.

**Table 4**    Comparison of Admission Fees for Past International Expositions

| | | Adult | Junior | Child | Season pass | [Reference Example] Starting salary for college graduates |
|---|---|---|---|---|---|---|
| 1970 | Japan World Exposition Osaka 1970 | 800JPY | 600JPY (15 to 22 years old) | 400JPY | – | 39,900JPY |
| 2005 | The 2005 World Exposition, Aichi, Japan | 4,600JPY | 2,500JPY (12 to 17 years old) | 1,500JPY | 17,500JPY | 196,700JPY |
| 2025 | EXPO 2025 Osaka, Kansai, Japan | 7,500JPY | 4,200JPY (12 to 17 years old) | 1,800JPY | 30,000JPY | 235,100JPY (2023) |

Note: Children under 3 years old are free of charge, basic price (one-day ticket) is compared.
Source: Prepared by APIR based on various press materials.

| Table 5 | List of Admission Fees for Osaka-Kansai Expo |

| Group | Name | | Outline | Adult 18 years old over | Junior 12 to 17 years old | Child 4 to 11 years old |
|---|---|---|---|---|---|---|
| Tickets sold before the exposition | Opening ticket | | One entry allowed from 13/April to 26/April | 4,000JPY | 2,200JPY | 1,000JPY |
| | First-half period ticket | | One entry allowed from 13/April to 18/July | 5,000JPY | 3,000JPY | 1,200JPY |
| | One-day ticket | Super early bird (From the start of sale until October 6, 2024) | One entry allowed at any time during the exhibition period | 6,000JPY | 3,500JPY | 1,500JPY |
| | | Early bird (From October 7, 2024 until the opening of the Expo) | One entry allowed at any time during the exhibition period | 6,700JPY | 3,700JPY | 1,700JPY |
| Tickets sold during the exposition | One-day ticket | | One entry allowed at any time during the exhibition period | 7,500JPY | 4,200JPY | 1,800JPY |
| | Weekday ticket | | One entry allowed after 11:00 a.m. on weekdays, excluding weekends and holidays | 6,000JPY | 3,500JPY | 1,500JPY |
| | Night ticket | | One entry allowed after 5:00 p.m. | 3,700JPY | 2,000JPY | 1,000JPY |
| Tickets sold before/during the exposition | Special ticket | | One entry allowed for the guest with a disability certificate or the accompanying guest | 3,700JPY | 2,000JPY | 1,000JPY |
| | Multiple entry pass | Summer pass | Multiple entries allowed from 19/July to 31/August after 11:00 a.m. | 12,000JPY | 7,000JPY | 3,000JPY |
| | | Season pass | Multiple entries allowed from 13/April to 3/October after 11:00 a.m. | 30,000JPY | 17,000JPY | 7,000JPY |
| | Group ticket | | One simultaneous entry for a group of 15 or more | 6,300JPY | 3,500JPY | 1,500JPY |
| Group | | | | High School students | Kindergarteners, elementary and junior high school students | |
| | School group ticket (First half) | | One simultaneous entry for a school group from 13/April to 18/July | - | 2,000JPY | 1,000JPY |
| | School group ticket (Second half) | | One simultaneous entry for a school group from 19/July to 13/October | - | 2,400JPY | 1,000JPY |

Source: Excerpt from Expo Association press release, "Ticket Types and Prices for Admission to the 2025 Japan International Expo" (June 30, 2023).

Part I

Part II

Part III

Part IV

## 4. Efforts by Local Governments to Host the Expo

○Based on the idea of "Greater EXPO", the Osaka-Kansai Expo is being promoted in the entire Kasai region to attract "visitors to Yumeshima" to the region, using the whole Kansai region as a virtual pavilion. Table 6 is a list of major initiatives being undertaken by the prefectures in the Kansai region.

| Table 6 | | Initiatives in Kansai Prefectures |

| Municipality | Name | Details of Initiatives |
| --- | --- | --- |
| Osaka Pref. | Portal site "Eyan! Osaka Shopping Street" | A portal site that disseminates information on the attractiveness of Osaka's shopping arcades and stores. The goal is to use the Expo as an opportunity to improve the attractiveness of the shopping district and increase the number of visitors. |
| Osaka Pref. /City | Virtual Osaka | Creating and disseminating the attractiveness of Osaka by proposing urban experiences through an urban-linked metaverse. |
| Hyogo Pref. | Hyogo Field Pavilion | An initiative to invite many people to see, learn, and experience the "SDGs acitivities onsite" in the region, with the local people taking the initiative in disseminating the information. |
| Kyoto Pref. | Osaka-Kansai Expo Kyoto Promotion Committee | The Osaka-Kansai Expo is an opportunity to promote the strengths of Kyoto's industries, as well as the culture and tourism resources of the prefecture, both domestically and internationally, and to promote exchanges that will lead to the steady development of Kyoto. |
| Shiga Pref. | Osaka-Kansai Expo Shiga Prefecture Basic Plan | This report summarizes Shiga Prefecture's participation in the Osaka-Kansai Expo and its significance, plans for a booth in the "Kansai Pavilion," and efforts to promote visits to Shiga Prefecture using the Expo. |
| Nara Pref. | Osaka-Kansai Expo 2025 x SDGs Symposium | A symposium was held under the auspices of Nara Prefecture and the Nara Chamber of Commerce and Industry to deepen understanding of the SDGs. |
| Wakayama Pref. | Let's Liven up Expo2025 in Wakayama | The Expo 2025 Wakayama Promotion Council (a joint industry-government-academia organization) will take the lead in promoting momentum within the prefecture, and in order to maximize the ripple effect of the Expo, will promote the attraction of visitors and disseminate information to businesses and other organizations. |
| Tokushima Pref. | Tokushima Marugoto Pavilion | The Expo site will be used as a gateway, and the entire Tokushima Prefecture will be used as a "Marugoto" pavilion, with the charms of the entire prefecture communicated to the world through video and images. |
| | Tokushima Virtual Pavilion | The entire charms of Tokushima, including culture, food, and cutting-edge technology, will be presented to the world. Visitors can dance with avatars of the Awa Odori dance in the "Metaverse. |

Source: Prepared by APIR based on information on each prefecture's website.

# 5. Infrastructure Map

○On May 26, 2023, the Expo Association released the second edition of its Action Plan for Visitor Transportation (first edition in October 2022). The three main routes are (1) Osaka Metro Chuo Line, (2) JR Sakurajima Line (shuttle bus from Sakurajima Station), and (3) Yodogawa Left Bank Line (shuttle bus from Shin-Osaka Station and Osaka Station). In addition, shuttle bus transportation from major railroad stations and parking lots outside the venue and marine transportation from Osaka City and Hyogo Prefecture are also planned. Figure 2 is an excerpt of the main transportation routes.

○Since the event will be held on an artificial island with limited access routes, a balanced transportation system is being developed to ensure the safe and smooth transportation of visitors without concentrating on specific means of transportation or routes.

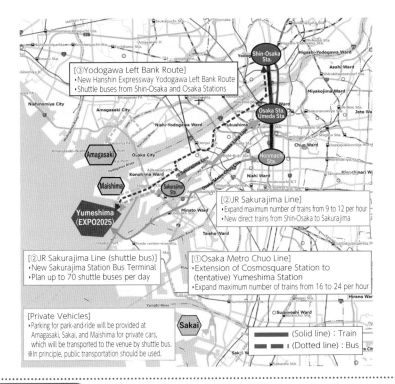

| Figure 2 | Map of main transportation routes to Expo site (Yumeshima) |

Source: Prepared by APIR based on the Osaka-Kansai Expo Specific Policies for Visitor Transport (Action Plan) Ver. 2

# 6. Expo-related budget: Osaka-Kansai Expo

○Tables 7-8 show the total projected costs of the Expo as of December 2023 for the national government and Osaka Prefecture and City, as well as the budget appropriations. The total cost, including future costs, is expected to be JPY 162 billion for the national government and JPY 137.77 billion for Osaka Prefecture and City.

| **Table 7** | Government Expenditures Related to Osaka-Kansai Expo |

(Unit: JPY 100 billion)

| | Total national cost expectations, including future | Status of appropriations to the national budget to date | | |
| --- | --- | --- | --- | --- |
| | | ~Initial Budget for FY 2023 | FY2023 Revised Budget | Total |
| (1) Exposition site construction costs by the Exposition Association. (government expense share) (Ministry of Economy, Trade and Industry) | **Up to JPY 78.3 billion** (The national government, Osaka Prefecture and City, and the business community will each contribute a third of the maximum JPY 235 billion.) | 121 | 510 | 631 |
| (2) Expenses for the construction of the Japan Pavilion. (Ministry of Economy, Trade and Industry) | **Up to JPY 36.0 billion** | 92 | 171 | 263 |
| (3) Supporting developing countries to exhibit. (Ministry of Economy, Trade and Industry·Ministry of Foreign Affairs) | **Approx. JPY 24.0 billion** (Total amount of Japanese financial support for developing countries pledged to the Bureau International des Expositions (BIE) as the host country.)[1] | 9 | 92 | 101 |
| (4) Expenses for ensuring safety in the exhibition site. (Ministry of Economy, Trade and Industry)" | **Approx. JPY 19.9 billion** | 0 | 4 | 4 |
| (5) Expenses required for Creating the Expo 2025 momentum, etc. | **Approx. JPY 3.8 billion + Future expenses** | 5 | 3 | 38 |

Note 1: The total amount of Japanese support for developing countries promised to the BIE is approximately JPY 24 billion, which includes approximately JPY 5 billion of the construction cost of the venue by the Exposition Association (1/3 of the national expense). In addition to the expenses for supporting developing countries, approximately JPY 1.1 billion is forecast for expenses for supporting the UN's participation in the exhibition.

Note 2: Figures have been rounded to the nearest million yen, so some fractions may not add up to the totals.

Source: Secretariat of the Headquarters for the World Expo, Cabinet Secretariat website.

| Table 8 | Osaka Prefecture and City Expenses for Osaka-Kansai Expo |
|---|---|

(Unit: JPY 100 billion)

| | Forecast of total cost for Osaka Prefecture and City including future years*1 | Status of appropriation to the budgets of Osaka Prefecture and the City of Osaka to date | | |
|---|---|---|---|---|
| | | ~Initial budget request for FY2024*2 | | Total |
| | | Osaka Pref. | Osaka City | |
| (1) Construction cost of venue by Osaka Prefecture and City<br>(Osaka World Expo Promotion Bureau) | **Up to approx. JPY 78.3 billion**<br>(The national government, Osaka Prefecture and City, and the business community will each contribute 1/3 of the up to JPY 235 billion) | 305.9 | 305.9 | 611.8 |
| (2) General account burden for reclamation work in Yumeshima area<br>(Osaka World Expo Promotion Bureau) | **Approx. JPY 2.14 billion**<br>(Reclamation work that was hastily constructed to improve the Expo site) | 10.7 | 10.7 | 21.4 |
| (3) Osaka Metro Chuo Line transportation capacity expansion, etc.<br>(Osaka World Expo Promotion Bureau) | **Approx. JPY 4.70 billion**<br>(including general traffic outreach TDM) | 17.6 | 17.6 | 35.2 |
| (4) Construction of Osaka Healthcare Pavilion, etc.<br>(Osaka World Expo Promotion Bureau) | **Approx. JPY 11.86 billion**<br>(Including regenerative medicine dissemination project. There is a separate sponsorship from a private company.) | 54.1 | 54.1 | 108.2 |
| (5) Promotion of participation<br>(Osaka World Expo Promotion Bureau) | **Approx. JPY 4.04 billion**<br>(Preparation for receiving volunteers, preparation of activity bases, local government events, etc.) | 6.2 | 6.2 | 12.4 |
| (6) Creating the Expo 2025 momentum, etc.<br>(Osaka World Expo Promotion Bureau) | **Approx. JPY 3.92 billion**<br>(large scale events, city dressing in major areas, information dissemination, etc.) | 10.5 | 11.9 | 22.4 |
| (7) Expenses incurred in attracting<br>(Osaka World Expo Promotion Bureau) | **Approx. JPY 420 million**<br>(Separately paid for by the business community.) | 2.3 | 1.8 | 4.2 |
| (8) Expenses other than (1) through (7)<br>(Other departments) | **Approx. JPY 5.89 billion + Approx. JPY 26.50 billion + Future expenses**<br>(Previous amount) + (Initial budget request for FY 2024 (including debt obligations, etc.)) | 61.2 | 181.1 | 242.3 |
| (1)-(8) Total | **Up to approx. JPY 111.27 billion + approx. JPY 26.50 billion**<br>(Previous amount) + (Initial budget request for FY 2024 (including debt obligations, etc.))<br>**=Up to approx. JPY 137.77 billion + Future expenses** | 468.5 | 589.3 | 1,057.8 |

Note 1: Figures (1) through (7) include future expenses currently projected.
Note 2: Figures are rounded to the nearest whole number, so some fractions do not add up to the total.
Source: Osaka Prefecture and Osaka City websites.

○Table 9 shows the budgets for Expo projects in each of the prefectures in the Kansai region. Hyogo has the largest budget of JPY 920 million, followed by Wakayama with JPY 254.42 million and Mie with JPY 98.12 million.

| Table 9 | Budget Overview of Kansai Prefectures |
| --- | --- |

(Unit: JPY million)

| FY | prefecture | Project | Budget |
| --- | --- | --- | --- |
| 2023 | Mie | Strengthening Promotion of the Kansai Region on the Occasion of the Osaka-Kansai Expo | 9,812 |
| | Shiga | Expo 2025 Osaka-Kansai Expo exhibition | 1,500 |
| | Kyoto | Expo 2025 Osaka-Kansai Expo Kyoto Attractiveness Promotion Project | 2,600 |
| | Hyogo | Development of Hyogo Field Pavilion | 25,000 |
| | | Exhibitions in the Hyogo Building (tentative name) and Hyogo Prefectural Museum of Art | 6,000 |
| | | Promoting Hyogo's attractiveness through Hyogo Theme Weeks | 23,000 |
| | | Implementation of projects to create momentum | 37,000 |
| | | Establishment of a promotion system | 1,000 |
| | Wakayama | Promotion of Osaka-Kansai Expo | 25,441.80 |
| | Tottori | Measures to attract visitors from Japan and abroad to the Osaka-Kansai Expo | 4,548 |
| | Tokushima | Osaka-Kansai Expo Tokushima Pavilion development project | 2,500 |
| | | Osaka-Kansai Expo Promotion Project | 5,498 |

Source: Prepared by APIR based on each prefecture's website

# Tourism Chronology

# Table of Contents

## About the Editing of the Tourism Chronology

- This Tourism Chronology was written by the Chronology Group of the Asia Pacific Institute of Research (APIR).
- The last check date of the following data is November 30, 2023 (exceptions noted).
- Kansai is defined as Shiga, Kyoto, Osaka, Hyogo, Nara, Wakayama, Fukui, Mie, Tottori and Tokushima prefectures, unless otherwise noted.
- DMO is an abbreviation for Destination Management/Marketing Organization.

# 1. Chronology ①: 2014-2019

○In June 2014, the Japanese government set a target of 20 million foreign visitors to Japan at the Council on the Promotion of Japan as a Tourism-Oriented Country. In December, the Cabinet approved the "Comprehensive Strategy for Vitalization of Towns, people, and Jobs", and in February 2016, the first batch of Japanese DMO candidate corporations were registered. In 2017, the Private Lodging Business Act was enacted to accommodate the rapidly increasing number of foreign visitors to Japan, which exceeded 30 million in 2018.

○After Osaka City decided in February 2015 to attract IR, the local government passed the IR Promotion Act in December of the following year. In July 2018, the IR Development Act was enacted to set forth the specific licensing and approval system related to IRs.

○JR West Japan, Kintetsu, Nankai, Keihan, Hankyu, and Eizan Railway companies operated new types of trains (luxury sightseeing, express, sleeper, and cable cars) to promote travel diversification.

○Luxury brands of overseas hotel chains, such as Hilton and Marriott opened new hotels, and domestic companies such as Hotel Okura and Mitsui Fudosan also opened luxury hotels targeting wealthy customers.

○Before the COVID-19 pandemic in 2019, amidst the discussions about overtourism, a joint declaration for sustainable growth was adopted at the G20 Tourism Ministers' Meeting (Kutchan, Hokkaido) in October . In November, Kyoto City announced its basic policy for "sustainable cities".

**Table 1**   National and private events related to tourism: 2014-2019

| Year | | National and Local Governments | | Private sector |
|---|---|---|---|---|
| 2014 | 6/17 | Council on the Promotion of Japan as a Tourism-Oriented Country formulates action plan for 20 million foreign visitors to Japan. | 3/8 | Kintetsu to fully open Abeno Harukas. Project cost: JPY130 billion |
| | 10/1 | Expansion of duty-free coverage to cosmetics, medicines, food, etc. | 7/15 | USJ opens new Harry Potter area. 2 million more visitors expected. |
| | 12/27 | Cabinet approves "Comprehensive Strategy for Vitalization of Town, People, and Work". | 9/2 | KIX celebrates the 20th anniversary of its opening. New Kansai International Airport aims to sell its management rights. |
| 2015 | 2/9 | Osaka City decides to attract IR to Yumeshima. | 1/16 | Prefectural police increase the number of Minami sightseeing bus stops along Sakaisuji from 2 to 5. |
| | 6/12 | Minister of Land, Infrastructure, Transport and Tourism approves plans for seven "wide-area tourism" routes. | 8/1 | Passenger volume at KIX reaches a record high of 2.29 million for a single month In August. |
| | 10/27 | Osaka Prefectural Assembly passes nation's first ordinance on private lodging. | 9/1 | Passenger volume at KIX reaches a record high of 11.98 million in the April-September period. |
| | 12/15 | Registration of Japanese DMO candidate corporations started | 11/19 | Mitsui Fudosan opens the largest 220,000m² Expo City. |

| | | | | |
|---|---|---|---|---|
| **2016** | 2/26 | 24 organizations registered in the first batch of Japanese DMO candidate corporations. | 3/7 | USJ visitors topped 12.7 million in FY 2015, setting a new record. |
| | 4/1 | Osaka Prefecture enacts ordinance on private lodging. | 3/17 | Hoshino Resort "Hoshinoya Kyoto" opened after renovation, adding the view of Arashiyama Katsuragawa River |
| | 6/29 | Establishment of "Umi-no-Kyoto" DMO. | 4/5 | Himeji Castle, for the first ime, ranks 1st with 2.86 million visitors in FY 2015. |
| | 10/1 | Osaka City enacts ordinance on private lodging. | 4/26 | Kumamoto earthquake affects visitors to Japan; cancellations increase at hotels in Kansai. |
| | 12/15 | The House of Representatives agrees and passes an amendment to the IR Promotion Act by the House of Councillors. | 10/15 | Resdential hotel for the wealthy "Four Seasons Kyoto" opened in Higashiyama-ku, Kyoto. |
| **2017** | 3/30 | Visa relaxation for visitors to Japan from five priority countries, including China and India. | 6/9 | Hilton opens luxury hotel "Conrad Osaka" in Nakanoshima. |
| | 6/9 | Private Lodging Business Act (Minpaku Law) is enacted. | 6/17 | JR West Japan begins operation of "Mizukaze" luxury sleeper train, targeting the wealthy |
| | 11/28 | 41 organizations registered as the first batch of Japanese version of DMO. | 12/19 | USJ records 2 million international visitors in 2017, doubling in 3 years. |
| **2018** | 1/17 | Osaka Tourism Bureau announces the number of international visitors to Osaka Prefecture in 2017 exceeds 10 million. | 4/1 | Privatization of Kobe Airport. Kansai Airport begins integrated operation of 3 airports. |
| | 7/20 | IR Development Act passed and enacted by the House of Councillors. | 5/15 | Two new Sunflower Ferry vessels begin service between Kagoshima and Osaka. |
| | 12/17 | The Japan Tourism Agency holds a ceremony to commemorate the 30 millionth visitor to Japan in 2018. | 9/4 | Kansai International Airport closed until 9/20 due to damage from Typhoon No. 21 - a hard hit on export and tourism. |
| **2019** | 10/25 ~26 | G20 Tourism Ministers meet and make a joint declaration for sustainable growth of the tourism industry. | 3/1 | Nankai operates a new "Koyasan Cable Car" between Koyasan and Gokurakubashi. |
| | 11/20 | Kyoto City announces basic guidelines for realizing a "sustainable tourism city". | 3/26 | KIX's international scheduled flights exceeded 3,000 per week for the first time, Asian routes increase. |
| | 12/12 ~13 | "United Nations Conference on Tourism and Culture in Kyoto 2019" to be held in Kyoto City. | 9/20 | Daimaru Shinsaibashi main building to be rebuilt with 40,000m$^2$ and an investment of JPY 37 billion. |
| | 12/20 | Cabinet approves the second phase of the "Comprehensive Strategy for Vitalization of Town, People, and Workplace". | 11/27 | Hankyu Hanshin opens "Hotel RESPIRE" in Umeda with 1030 rooms. |

Source: Prepared by APIR based on press releases from various sources

# Chronology ②: 2020-2023

○Domestic tourism was reviewed during the pandemic, and measures to stimulate demand, such as "Go To Travel" in July 2020 and "National Travel Assistance" from October 2022 to January 2023, were set forth.

○After the government made a cabinet decision on the basic policy regarding IR in December 2020, Osaka Prefecture/City announced the outline in September 2021.The government approved the development plan for "Osaka IR" in April 2023.

○The government received a new proposal for the Osaka Prefecture/City Super City Initiative in October 21, and made a Cabinet decision to adopt the plan in April 2022.

○In anticipation of a recovery in inbound tourism demand after the pandemic, Osaka Prefecture/City set a new goal of ranking MICE among the top 10 in the world in January 2023. A partnership agreement between the Kansai Tourism Bureau and Mastercard was announced in February of the same year. The Japan Tourism Agency's "Tourism Restart Project" was announced in March of the same year.

○Ferry Sunflower, a car ferry operator between Kyushu and Kansai, and four other companies have launched 10 newly built vessels on five routes. The new ships feature larger hulls and all private rooms, changing the traveling style for those who enjoy traveling by boat.

○Urban tower hotels with relatively low prices and more rooms were constructed to meet the needs of a diverse range of travelers. Many properties that were closed or failed to open due to the pandemic were acquired by, for example, APA Hotel and Hoshino Resort before rebranded.

**Table 2**    National and private events related to tourism: 2020-2023

| Year | | National and Local Governments | | Private sector |
|------|------|-------------------------------|------|----------------|
| 2020 | 4/8 | Municipalities in the vicinity of Osaka and Hyogo Prefectures request voluntary restraint on travel between prefectures. | 2/4 | Carnival cancels "Diamond Princess" port call to Kobe Port. |
| | 7/22 | Launching of "GoTo Travel" | 5/13 | Arrivals and departures at KIX over the long holiday : 2,150 people, a 99.8% sharp drop YoY |
| | 12/18 | Cabinet approves IR basic policy. | 7/22 | Marriott opens first class "JW Marriott Hotel" in Nara City |
| | 12/28 | The government temporarily suspends GoTo Travel. | 11/3 | Mitsui Fudosan opens first class "Hotel Mitsui" Near Nijo Castle in Kyoto |

| | | | | |
|---|---|---|---|---|
| | 4/1 | "Regional Tourism Business Support" for travel within prefecture begins. | 3/16 | "Fauchon Hotel Kyoto" opens in Kyoto by Fauchon of France |
| | 9/16 | MGM-ORIX alliance selected as candidate for Osaka IR project. | 3/18 | USJ opens a new Nintendo area with "Mario" theme. |
| | 9/28 | Osaka Prefectural Government and City of Osaka Announce IR Outline | 3/30 | APA Group opens Shin-Osaka Station Tower, acquires buildings under construction with 400 rooms. |
| 2021 | 10/15 | Osaka Prefecture and City submit new proposal for "Super City" Initiative | 4/9 | Kyoto International Conference Center acquires international hygiene certification, the first MICE facility in Japan. |
| | 12/2 | Osaka Prefecture resumes lodging discount campaign for Osaka residents. | 4/26 | Hankyu Hanshin Fudosan opens hotel "remm plus Kobe Sannomiya" directly above the station. |
| | 12/9 | Shiga Prefecture extends lodging discount campaign to residents of Fukui Prefecture | 9/1 | Hilton opens first class "LXR Hotels" in Rakuhoku, Kyoto |
| | 4/1 | Prefectural discount expands to all prefectures within regional blocs | 1/10 | Hotel Okura opens "Okazaki Bettei" in Higashiyama, Kyoto |
| | 4/12 | Cabinet approves the designation of Osaka City as the "Super City" concept. | 4/22 | Hoshino Resort opens "OMO7" hotel in front of Shin-Imamiya Station |
| 2022 | 9/29 | Comprehensive cooperation agreement with Osaka Convention & Tourism Bureau and Airbnb agree on a comprehensive cooperation about tourism promotion. | 6/25 | JR Tokai resumes "Let's go to Kyoto" commercials for the first time in two and a half years. |
| | 10/11 | "Nationwide Travel Assistance" covering nation-wide begins. | 11/1 | Sekisui House and Marriott open "Michi no Eki" hotel in Toyooka City. |
| | 1/10 | Nationwide Travel Assistance resumes | 1/2 | Hoshino Resort opens "OMO Kansai Airport", a transferred property |
| | 3/31 | Japanese government approves "Tourism Nation Promotion Basic Plan" for FY2023-FY2025 at Cabinet meeting. | 1/20 | RIHGA Royal Osaka is sold and bought by a Canadian investment company. |
| | 7/28 | Kyoto Prefecture revises prefectural comprehensive tourism strategy | 2/1 | APA G opens the urban resort Osaka Umeda Station Tower with 1,704 rooms. |
| 2023 | 9/22 | Japan Tourism Agency approves IR implementation agreement up by Osaka Prefectural and Osaka city | 8/29 | "Shisui Luxury Collection Hotel Nara" opens. |
| | 11/16 | Japan National Tourism Organization announces that the number of international visitors in October exceeded that before the COVID-19 pandemic. | 10/4 | Koyasan Shukubo Association reopens the Central Information Center. |
| | 11/22 | Osaka Convention & Tourism Bureau and Catalonia (Spain) enter a reciprocal tourism prmotion agreement. | 10/26 | Tourism Expo Japan held at INTEX Osaka for the first time in four years. |

Source: Prepared by APIR based on press releases from various sources

## 2. Tourism Goals of Government and Administration

○Prior to the COVID-19 pandemic, taken into account the rapid increase in inbound tourism demand, the target number of inbound tourism visitors at the
end of 2020 was 40 million (calculated in 2017, Table 3).

○In 2023, the by the end of 2025 was revised downward to "exceed the pre-
COVID-19 pandemic level (31.88 million visitors)".

○Facing the pandemic, domestic tourism was reevaluated and a target of 320
million overnight stays by domestic travelers in rural areas was set for 2023.

○The outbound target (number of Japanese traveling overseas) has remained
virtually unchanged at 20 million since it was set in 2007.

| Table 3 | Government's Goals for Realization of "Tourism Nation" |
|---|---|

| Year of formu-lated | Contents and Targets |
|---|---|
| 2007 | [Number of foreign visitors to Japan]<br>· 10 million by 2010 |
| | [Number of international conferences held]<br>· Increase by 50% or more by 2011 (252 or more conferences) |
| | [Number of overnight stays per capita by Japanese domestic tourist travelers]<br>· 4 nights per year by FY 2010 |
| | [Number of Japanese traveling abroad]<br>· 20 million by 2010 |
| | [Domestic travel expenditure]<br>· JPY 30 trillion by FY 2010 |
| 2012 | [Number of foreign visitors to Japan]<br>· 18 million by 2016 |
| | [Number of international conferences held]<br>· Increase by 50% or more by 2016 (1,111 or more conferences) |
| | [Number of overnight stays per capita by Japanese domestic tourism]<br>· 2.5 nights per year by 2016. |
| | [Number of Japanese traveling abroad]<br>· 20 million by 2016. |
| | [Domestic tourism expenditure]<br>· JPY 30 trillion by FY 2016 |
| | [Satisfaction level of international visitors to Japan]<br>· 45% to answer ""Very satisfied" and 60% to answer "Definitely want to revisit" in the "International Visitor Survey" by 2016. |
| | [Traveler satisfaction in tourist areas]<br>· By 2016, 25% to answer "Very satistified" when asked about overall satisfaction, and 25% to answer "Strongly agree" when asked whether to visit Japan again. |

| | |
|---|---|
| 2017 | [Number of foreign visitors to Japan]<br>· 40 million by 2020 |
| | [Number of international conferences held]<br>· 30% or more conferences held by major Asian countries* by 2020<br>*Japan, China, Korea, Australia, and Singapore |
| | [Number of Japanese traveling abroad]<br>· 20 million by 2020. |
| | [Domestic tourism expenditure]<br>· JPY 21 trillion by 2020 |
| | [Tourism expenditure by international visitors]<br>· JPY 8 trillion by FY 2020. |
| | [Number of repeat international visitors]<br>· 24 million by 2020 |
| | [Total number of overnight guests by international visitors in local areas*]<br>· 70 million person-nights by 2020<br>*Areas outside the three major metropolitan areas (Saitama, Chiba, Tokyo, Kanagawa, Aichi, Kyoto, Osaka, and Hyogo Prefectures) |
| 2023 | [Number of international visitors to Japan]<br>· Exceed the 2019 level (31.88 million) by 2025. |
| | [Number of international conferences held]<br>· 30% or more conferences held by major Asian countries* by 2025.<br>*Top 5 countries in terms of the number of international conferences held in the Asia-Pacific region (as of 2019: Japan, China, South Korea, Australia, and Taiwan) |
| | [Number of Japanese traveling abroad]<br>· Exceed the 2019 level (20.08 million) by 2025. |
| | [Domestic travel expenditure]<br>· JPY 20 trillion at an early date and JPY 22 trillion by 2025. |
| | [Tourism expenditure by international visitors]<br>· JPY 5 trillion at an early date. |
| | [Tourism expenditure per trip by international visitors]<br>· 200,000 JPY by 2025. |
| | [Number of overnight stays by international visitors in local areas*]<br>· 2 nights by 2025<br>*Areas outside the three major metropolitan areas (Saitama, Chiba, Tokyo, Kanagawa, Aichi, Kyoto, Osaka, and Hyogo Prefectures) |
| | [Total number of overnight guests by Japanese in rural areas*]<br>· Will be 3.2 million person-nights by 2025<br>*Areas outside the three major metropolitan areas (Saitama, Chiba, Tokyo, Kanagawa, Aichi, Kyoto, Osaka, and Hyogo Prefectures) |

Source: Prepared by APIR based on each year's Basic Plan for the Promotion of Tourism

○The goals set by each of the six prefectures in the Kansai region indicates that tourists are clustered in Kyoto, Osaka, and Hyogo prefectures, which further raise the importance of the currently discussed issue of "Creating a mechanism to attract tourists to the rural regions" at the broader Kansai level (Table 4).

**Table 4**   Tourism Strategy Goals for Kansai Six Prefectures

| Prefecture | Outcome Indicators | Target Value | Period |
|---|---|---|---|
| Shiga | Total number of visitors | 54.1 million people | By FY 2024 |
| | Total number of overnight guests | 41 million people | |
| | Number of visitors who experienced Biwaichi | 110,000 people | |
| | Tourism expenditure per trip (day trip) | JPY 4,600 | |
| | Tourism expenditure per trip (overnight stay) | JPY 21,000 | |
| | Tourism expenditure (Total) | JPY 213.9 billion | |
| | Tourist satisfaction | 87.4% | |
| | Repeat visitor rate | 68.8% | |
| | Willingness of prefectural residents to recommend tourism in Shiga Prefecture | 100.0% | |
| | Business operators engaging in Shiga Rhythm | 100.0% | |
| Kyoto | Rate of tourists interacting with locals during their trip to Kyoto | Increase by 1 point annually | By 2026 |
| | Visitors satisfaction | 90.0% | |
| | Repeat visitor (visiting 4 times or more) rate | 50.0% | |
| | Number of international conferences held in the prefecture | 50 conferences | |
| | Rate of residents thinking that tourism resources in their area are utilized | 63.0% | |
| | Off-season to peak season ratio (tourists in off-season months/tourists in peak months) | 67.5% | |
| | Tourism expenditure per trip within the prefecture | JPY 5,500 | |
| | Number of times information on training and seminars for developing, securing, and retaining human resources provided | 100 cases | |
| Osaka | Total number of overnight stays by Japanese | 30 million person-nights | By 2023 |
| | Number of international visitors to Osaka | 11.525 million people | Two years after the lifting of entry restrictions |

Part I

Part II

Part III

Part IV

| | | | |
|---|---|---|---|
| Hyogo | Tourism expenditure | JPY 1,450 billion | By FY 2027 |
| | Average number of nights | 1.5 nights | |
| | Total number of overnight stays (domestic) | 15 million people | |
| | Total number of overnight stays (international visitors) | 3 million people | |
| | Rate of lodging by international visitors | 17.0% | |
| | Tourism expenditure per trip (domestic, overnight) | JPY 64,000 | |
| | Tourism expenditure per trip (domestic, day trip) | JPY 19,000 | |
| | Tourism expenditure per trip (international visitors) | JPY 60,000 | |
| | Repeat visitor rate | 70.0% | |
| | Visitor satisfaction | 80.0% | |
| | Resident satisfaction | 75.0% | |
| Nara | Tourism expenditure | JPY 210 billion | By FY 2025 |
| | Tourism expenditure per trip (overnight) | JPY 28,000 | |
| | Tourism expenditure per trip (day trip) | JPY 5,000 | |
| | Total number of overnight stays | 3.5 million people | |
| | Number of visitors | 51 million people | |
| | Number of international visitors | 4.5 million people | |
| | Number of hotel and inn guest rooms | 12,000 rooms | |
| Wakayama | Number of guests (day trip) | 33 million people | By FY 2026 |
| | Number of guests (overnight) | 7.13 million people | |
| | Number of international guests | 1.4 million people | |
| | Number of cruise ship calls | 30 ships | |

Source: Prepared by APIR based on the "First Action Plan of Cigarism Tourism Promotion Vision" for Shiga Prefecture, "Kyoto Prefecture Tourism Strategy (March 2020)" for Kyoto Prefecture, "Osaka Urban Attractiveness Creation Strategy 2025 (March 2024)" for Osaka Prefecture, "Nara Prefecture Tourism Strategy
(July 2021)" for Nara Prefecture, "Hyogo Prefecture New Tourism Strategy (March 2023)" for Hyogo
Prefecture, and "Wakayama Prefecture Tourism Promotion Vision Phase 1 Action Plan (March 2020)"
for Wakayama Prefecture. For Wakayama Prefecture, based on the "Wakayama Prefecture Comprehensive Strategy for Urban, Human and Cultural Development (March 2020)".

# 3. DMO Measures

○In FY 2017, DMO Net were strengthened, and since FY 2018, contents such as human resource matching and human resource development programs have been enhanced. From FY 2021, seminar and symposiums have been held with the help of DMO Net.

○"Strategies development using big data" has been promoted since FY 2017. In FY 2020, model project of a specific system design and development was implemented. In FY 2021, collection of concrete data on the lodging, GPS information, and SNS of tourists was promoted. In FY 2022, support for the application of DMP (Data Management Platform) and CRM (Customer Relationship Management) in strategy development was presented.

○From FY 2020, DMO support will focus on "DMOs with high motivation and potential". In FY 2021, "DMO registration requirements are tightened". In FY 2023, a policy of strategic support was established for "'pioneering DMO' that are candidates for 'globally-recognized DMO'".

**Table 5**    DMO measures indicated by the government

| FY | Targets |
|---|---|
| 2017 | ·Enhance "DMO Net" functions<br>·DMO Net contents: Human resource matching<br>·Promote strategy development using big data<br>·Establise a human resource development program for tourism destination management.<br>·Financial support for establishing organizations, autonomizing operations, entrepreneurship, and improving productivity<br>·Support for establishing and managing Japanese version of DMO by DBJ<br>·Promote and utilize the "Tourism Forecasting Platform"<br>·Submit the "Investment in the Regional Future Promotion Bill (Cabinet Submission No. 30)" to the Diet. |
| 2018 | ·DMO Net Contents: Business process optimization support, human resource matching, and human resource development programs (basic and applied)<br>·Promote strategy development using big data<br>·Facilitate human resource matching of those who have finished the human resource development program<br>·Financial support for organizational establishment, autonomous operations, entrepreneurship, and productivity improvement<br>·Support for establishing and managing Japanese version of DMO by DBJ<br>·Support for the region-wide DMO managing the seven prefectures in the Setouchi area through investment of Cool Japan Organization<br>·Support for the enhancement of tourism contents, improvement of reception environment, and promotion of tourism in region-wide cooperation<br>·Consulting support and promotion know-how by JNTO |
| 2019 | ·DMO Net Contents: Business process optimization support, promoting human resource exchange and collaboration, cooperation among DMOs. Human resource development programs (basic and applied)<br>·Promote strategy development using big data<br>·Facilitate human resource matching of those who have finished the human resource development program<br>·Financial support from organizational establishment to initiatves aimed at autonomizing operations<br>·Support for the region-wide DMO managing the seven prefectures in the Setouchi area through investment of Cool Japan Organization<br>·Support for promoting travelling and staying through region-wide cooperation<br>·Discuss a system of selection criteria and selection process for "globally-recognized DMO"<br>·Accelerate the formation of "globally-recognized DMO" by providing consulting support and promotional know-how |

| | |
|---|---|
| 2020 | ·DMO Net contents: marketing (basic and applied), human resource development programs (basic and applied), and other e-learning materials<br>·Promote strategy development using big data<br>·Implemente a model project to design and develop a system for collecting and analyzing tourist data for strategy development<br>·Support for the region-wide DMO managing the seven prefectures in the Setouchi area through investment of Cool Japan Organization<br>·Enchance stay-related content through region-wide collaboration, and provide support for infrastructure development for region-wide excursion tourism<br>·Raise the level of DMOs based on guidelines<br>·Focused support for DMOs with high motivation and potential<br>·Support for matching with human resources possessing professional expertise and foreigner's perspectives, as well as for the cost of hiring<br>·Comprehensive support through collaboration among related ministries and agencies |
| 2021 | ·DMO Net Contents: Information on various trainings, seminars, and symposiums<br>·Rebuild and implement model projects for data collection platform and CRM application<br>·Promote collection and analysis of DMO's big data such as tourist accommodation, characteristics, GPS data, SNS, etc.<br>·Support for the region-wide DMO managing the seven prefectures in the Setouchi area through investment of Cool Japan Organization<br>·Supporting infrastructure investment in projects that leverage tourism resources to improve the local economy<br>·Raise the level of DMOs in accordance with stricter registration requirements<br>·Focused support for DMOs with high motivation and potential<br>·Matching with human resources possessing professional expertise and foreigner's perspectives. Support for hiring cost<br>·Conduct nationwide training programs and symposiums, and provide support for participation<br>·Conduct meetings to exchange opinions among DMOs in each area to promote the sharing of roles and cooperation<br>·Support for initiatives to promote region-wide excursion tours |
| 2022 | ·DMO Net Contents: Information on various training programs, seminars, symposiums, etc. Support for training courses for human resource development<br>·Expand horizontally the mechanism for collecting and analyzing tourist data, strategy development based on data, and implementing the according initiatives<br>·Support for analysis and strategy development using DMP and CRM<br>·Support for the hiring and training of digital tourism human resources<br>·Support the efforts to improve the distribution environment by disseminating information through websites and SNS and listing travel products on OTAs<br>·Registration and renewal of DMO registration based on guidelines<br>·Provide various information to DMOs, strengthening their systems, and provide support to facilitate destination development<br>·Focused support for pioneering DMOs with high motivation and potential<br>·Based on guidelines, promote the establishment of CFO for DMOs to manage finances and ensure stable funding. Disseminate guidebooks, horizontal deployment of best practices, and provide information through training and seminars regarding independent financial resources<br>·Matching with human resources possessing professional expertise and foreigner's perspectives. Support for hiring cost<br>·Support for the region-wide DMO managing the seven prefectures in the Setouchi area through investment of Cool Japan Organization<br>·Supporting infrastructure investment in projects that leverage tourism resources to improve the local economy |
| 2023 | ·Select "pioneering DMOs" that are candidates for "globally-recognized DMO" to provide strategic support<br>·Support DMOs in securing financial resources based on guidelines<br>·Horizontal expansion of best practices, and sharing initiatives that address challenges<br>·Promote the division of roles and cooperation based on the guidelines of the registration system. Support for integrated regional initiatives<br>·Aim to create a virtuous cycle in which media outlets share tourism contents of developed regions. The regions then use the received market responses to improve the next tourism resources.<br>·Cooperate with region-wide DMO to share information, and provide the latest mark trends obtained from overseas network<br>·Provide consultation. Introduce and share the latest market trends and domestic inbound initiatives to regions through online seminars and the "Regional Inbound Promotion Website"<br>·Utilize the "DMO Net" to provide information on various training programs, seminars, symposiums, etc.<br>·Support for participating in training sessions regarding recruitment and development of talents to secure human resource<br>·Matching with human resources possessing professional expertise and foreigner's perspectives. Support for hiring cost<br>·Dispatch experts to regions that are promoting region-wide excursion tourism to help attract domestic and foreign tourists<br>·Publish and horizontally deploy information on challenges regarding reception infrastructure development, as well as related initiatives and results on the websites of regional Transport Bureaus |

Source: Prepared by APIR based on each year's Tourism White Paper

○Table 6 shows the registered and candidate DMOs operating in the Kansai region. Each prefectures has DMOs that managed the whole region, except for Tottori Prefecture and Tokushima Prefecture, while Kansai Tourism Headquarter manages the entire Kansai region.

○As of June 2023, there are 51 registered DMOs in Kansai, of which 1 is a region-wide partnership DMO, 23 are regional partnership DMOs, and 27 are regional DMOs. In addition, there are 10 DMOs candidate, of which 3 are regional partnership DMOs and 7 are regional DMOs.

## 4. Trends in Large Hotel Construction

○From 2017 to 2026, there are 30 properties (large hotels) valued more than JPY 10 billion. As of 2023, 17 have been opened, of which 10 are domestic brands. 11 out of 17, or about 60%, of the hotels have relatively reasonable unit price per night (Table 6-1, Table 6-2).

| Table 6-1 | List of construction projects (estimated) costing more than 10 JPY billion, in order of year of opening (2017-2023) |
|---|---|

Grade (per night per person): "B" around 10,000 JPY~ , "A" around 30,000 JPY~ , "S" around 50,000 JPY~ , "H" around 100,000 JPY~

| Date of opening | Brand-Name | Brand | Grade | Pref. | Operator | Property Introduction (<Reference> Press Release/Home Page) |
|---|---|---|---|---|---|---|
| Jun-17 | CONRAD OSAKA | US | H | Osaka | Hilton Worldwide | The second Conrad, Hilton's most luxurious brand, hotel in Japan. Magnificent panoramic views from the upper floors of Festival Tower West (33rd to 40th floors). Located in Nakanoshima. Directly connected to Higobashi Subway Station. |
| Mar-18 | Hotel Monterey Himeji | JP | B | Hyogo | MARUITO Co., Ltd. | Conveniently located 15 minutes from the World Heritage and National Treasure "Himeji Castle". Hotel Monterey Himeji offers chic and elegant guest rooms that blend Art Deco designs with accented Japanese elements, making for a pleasant and relaxing stay for both business and leisure travelers. Directly connected to "Himeji Station" of JR Shinkansen and conventional lines. |
| Jan-19 | THE THOUSAND KYOTO | JP | A | Kyoto | Keihan Hotels & Resorts | New flagship hotel built adjacent to Keihan H&R's Century H Kyoto. The three rings in our corporate log firmly link people, society, and the future as we provide hotel stays foreseeing the coming one thousand years.. 2 minutes north of JR Kyoto Station. |
| Oct-19 | Park Hyatt Kyoto | US | H | Kyoto | Hyatt Hotels and Resorts | Renovation of the ryotei "Sanso Kyoyamato" with elements of a world-class luxury hotel. Preservation and restoration of the Higashiyama Niningsaka district and its historical architecture and gardens. Fusion of tradition and new culture. 14 minutes from Gion-Shijo Station on Keihan Line. |
| Nov-19 | LIBER HOTEL AT UNIVERSAL STUDIOS JAPAN | JP | A | Osaka | MUSASHINO | Developed by Musashino, a major delicatessen company, under the theme of "offering a stylish hotel stay like never before," the first to open in the Kansai region. The 8th (and largest) official hotel of USJ. 1 minute from JR West Japan Sakurajima Station. |

Part I

Part II

Part III

Part IV

| | | | | | | |
|---|---|---|---|---|---|---|
| Nov-19 | Hotel Hankyu RESPIRE OSAKA | JP | B | Osaka | Hankyu Hanshin Hotels Co., Ltd | The first branch of the new hotel brand "Respire" based on the concept of "Healing Rest" and "Vitality Inspire". Located on the upper floor of Yodobashi Umeda Tower, it offers a space free from the hustle and bustle of the city. 5 minutes west of Osaka Umeda Station on the Hankyu Line. |
| Dec-19 | HOTEL ROYAL CLASSIC OSAKA | JP | A | Osaka | Bellco HOTEL ROYAL CLASSIC OSAKA | Wedding and Funeral Service "BELCO" inherited the design of the former "New Kabuki-za". The magnificent appearance has been restored in the lower part of the building. The hotel offers various services such as bridal, sightseeing, and business. Directly above "Namba" subway station. |
| Jun-20 | ACE HOTEL KYOTO | US | S | Kyoto | Ace Hotel | Ace Hotel, the new trend of hotels in the world, opens its first branch in Asia in the redevelopment complex of "Shinpukan", which inherited the building of the former Kyoto Central Telephone Station and has long been loved as a local exchange center. 1 minute from Karasuma-Oike Subway Station. |
| Jun-20 | Takarazuka Hotel | JP | A | Hyogo | Hankyu Hanshin Hotels Co., Ltd | The official hotel of Takarazuka Grand Theatre, established in 1926, has been relocated and reconstructed under the concepts of "Dream Continues Here" and "CLASSIC ELEGANT". A gallery is set up in the hotel. 4 minutes from Takarazuka Grand Theater and Hankyu/JR Takarazuka Station. |
| Jul-20 | JW Marriott Hotel Nara | US | A | Nara | Marriott International | Marriott Int'l's top-of-the-line "JW Marriott" brand. The core facility of the "Omiya-dori Interaction Hub Project", which includes convention facilities, NHK, etc. Located at the west end of Nara Park. 9 minutes from Shin-Omiya Station on the Kintetsu Line. |
| Nov-20 | HOTEL THE MITSUI KYOTO | JP | H | Kyoto | Mitsui Fudosan Hotel Management Co., Ltd. | Located to the east of Nijo Castle, Mitsui Fudosan's flagship hotel will be revived along with the remains of the Mitsui Soryo family's residence, which has been in use for over 250 years. We aim to be the best hotel brand in Japan. 3 minutes from JR Nijojo-mae Station. |
| Mar-21 | W Osaka | US | H | Osaka | Marriott International | Marriott Int'l's luxury "W" brand. Facing Midosuji Avenue, the hotel transmits "Whatever/Whenever" and "Osaka merchants' playful spirit" as a new culture to the world. 4 minutes from Shinsaibashi Subway Station. |
| Sep-21 | ROKU Kyoto LXR Hotels & Resorts | US | H | Kyoto | Hilton | Hilton's luxury brand "LXR" first entry in Asia Pacific. Located in Takagamine, northern part of Kyoto City. Under the concept of "Dive into Kyoto," the hotel offers "the charm of Kyoto known only to those in the know" as a staycation resort. 30 minutes from JR Kyoto by car. |
| Apr-22 | OMO7 Osaka by Hoshino Resorts | JP | A | Osaka | Hoshino Resort | Pass through the garden area in front of JR Shin-Imamiya Station, which is easily accessible from Kansai Airport, to the hotel. The OMO Rangers will guide you to an extraordinary encounter in the "Shinsekai" area. Guests can interact with each other in the common space. |
| Feb-23 | APA Hotel & Resort Osaka Umeda Eki Tower | JP | B | Osaka | APA Hotel | A new landmark tower in the Umeda area of Osaka, with an observatory restaurant on the top floor, an observatory pool, a large public bath and open-air bath facilities, etc., providing a resort-like atmosphere while remaining in the city. 3 minutes from Higashi Umeda Subway Station. |

Country Code: "**JP**" Japan, "**US**" USA, "**GB**" Great Britain, "**SG**" Singapore, "**TH**" Thailand, "**HK**" Hong Kong, "**CA**" Canada
Source: Prepared by APIR based on press releases from various sources.

○After 2024, foreign brands will account for 8 of the 13 properties, 4 of which are non-U.S. luxury hotel groups. 10 out of 13, or about 80%, of the hotels have relatively high unit price per night. (Table 6-2).

| Table 6-2 | List of construction projects (estimated) costing more than 10 JPY billion, in order of year of opening (2023-2026) |
|---|---|

Grade (per night per person): "B" around 10,000 JPY~ , "A" around 30,000 JPY~ , "S" around 50,000 JPY~ , "H" around 100,000 JPY~

| Date of opening | Brand-Name | Brand | Grade | Pref. | Operator | "Property Introduction (<Reference> Press Release/Home Page)" |
|---|---|---|---|---|---|---|
| Mar-23 | OMO Kansai Airport by Hoshino Resorts | JP | B | Osaka | Hoshino Resort | The largest hotel development in "Rinku Town" by WBF. After Hoshino Resort acquired the property, it resumed construction and opened under the "OMO" brand. One minute from JR and Nankai "Rinku Town" station. |
| Jul-23 | CENTARA GRAND HOTEL OSAKA | TH | A | Osaka | CENTARA HOTELS RESORTS | Centara Hotels' first foray into Japan. With the concept of "fusion of Thai and Japanese beauty and culture," the hotel offers an authentic Thai spa, cuisine, and other services. Bunk beds and connecting rooms are available for families. 6 minutes from Nankai "Namba" station. |
| Apr-24 | Candeo Hotels Osaka Dozimahama | JP | A | Osaka | Candeo Hotels | The largest and most prestigious 4-star flagship of Candeon H. Located on the upper floors of a high-rise tower complex. The top floor has an open-air bath with a view of Midosuji Boulevard from the guest rooms. 4 minutes from Yodoyabashi Station on the subway and Keihan lines. |
| Apr-24 | Doubletree by Hilton Osaka Castle | US | S | Osaka | Hilton | Hilton's up-scale hotel, Doubletree. Upper floors of the former Nikkei Shimbun Osaka headquarters development complex. Seasonal views of Osaka Castle and Sakuranomiya Park. 5 minutes from Tenmabashi Station on the water bus, Keihan and subway. |
| May-24 | Four Seasons Hotel Osaka Douzima | CA | H | Osaka | Hotel Properties Limited | "Four Seasons Hotel" opens for the first time in Osaka City. The concept is "Travel and Art". Luxury hotel located on the upper floors of a high-rise residential complex tower. 4 minutes from Nishi-Umeda Subway Station and 5 minutes from JR Kitashinchi Station. |
| Jun-24 | Canopy by Hilton Osaka Umeda | US | S | Osaka | Hilton | Hilton's new "Canopy" brand is like a Neighborhood where you can relax and recharge. Simple service, comfortable space. Located on the upper floor of the North District complex. 7 minutes north of JR "Osaka Station". |
| Jul-24 | THE OSAKA STATION HOTEL, Autograph Collection | JP | S | Osaka | WEST JAPAN RAILWAY HOTEL DEVELOPMENT, LTD. | The concept is "The Osaka Time". Built on the first Osaka Station land, the hotel is named "Osaka Station Hotel," a new brand by JR West Japan Hotels. Marriott Int'l's "Autograph Collection" is the fourth hotel in Japan. |
| Oct-24 | Sanctuary Court Biwako | JP | H | Shiga | Resorttrust, Inc. | Located on the west side of Lake Biwa. The concept is "Venetian Modern. A membership-only resort resembling a water palace where the vast water basin and the lake are combined. All rooms are suites with a lake view. 10 minutes drive from JR Takashima Station. |

| Oct-24 | APA Hotel & Resort Osaka Nanba Eki Tower | JP | B | Osaka | APA Hotel | APA Hotel is the skyscraper tower with the largest number of guest rooms in western Japan. Aiming to become a new landmark in the Namba area as an "urban resort" where guests can enjoy their stay with restaurants and swimming pool on the top floor. 3 minutes from JR Namba Station. |
|---|---|---|---|---|---|---|
| Dec-24 | Hilton Kyoto | US | S | Kyoto | Hilton | The concept is "Kyo SYNAPSE," meaning to connect guests with the various attractions of Kyoto. The exterior of the building is based on the theme of "Kyoto's deep and profound style" and the interior is based on the theme of "ORIMONO (textile)". 6 minutes from Sanjo Station on Keihan Line. |
| Dec-24 | Hotel Hankyu GRAN RESPIRE OSAKA | JP | A | Osaka | Hankyu Hanshin Hotels Co., Ltd | Hankyu Hanshin Hotels' "Respire" is an upscale hotel with "GRAN" meaning "wonderful," adding a cozy atmosphere of nature and peacefulness in the city and a mature quality to the hotel. East wing of the South Wing. 3 minutes north of JR Osaka Station. |
| Mar-25 | Hotel Patina Osaka | SG | H | Osaka | Capella Hotels and Resorts | Capella Hotel Group's hotel brand "Patina" opens its second hotel worldwide. A new generation lifestyle hotel that applies its unique sensibility and design to a location steeped in the history of Osaka Castle and Naniwanomiya Palace. 5 minutes from Tanimachi 4 Subway Station. |
| Apr-25 | Waldorf Astoria Osaka | US | H | Osaka | Hilton | Hilton's premier luxury hotel brand, Waldorf Astoria, promises personalized service and a pursuit and commitment to food. Located on the upper floor of the West Wing of the South City complex. 4 minutes from JR Osaka Station. |
| Jul-25 | Capella Kyoto | SG | H | Kyoto | Capella Hotels and Resorts | "Capella" first appearance in Japan. Offering the world's finest hospitality. Located on Yamato-oji Dori in the flower district of Miyagawa-cho. Creating "new coexistence value" through the integrated development of a hotel, an opera house, and local facilities. 4 minutes from Keihan Shijo Station. |
| Nov-26 | ROSEWOOD KYOTO | HK | H | Kyoto | Rosewood Hotel Group | Provide authentic experiences in cooperation with Shokokuji Temple, which is located adjacent to the south side of the building. By incorporating traditional industrial products into the accommodation space, the hotel aims to be a high-quality accommodation facility that contributes to the transmission of local history and culture and to the revitalization of the area. 7 minutes from Kuramaguchi Subway Station. |

Country Code: "**JP**" Japan, "**US**" USA, "**GB**" Great Britain, "**SG**" Singapore, "**TH**" Thailand, "**HK**" Hong Kong, "**CA**" Canada
Note: The properties in red in the table are those that will open in 2024 or later.
Source: Prepared by APIR based on press releases from various sources.

# STATISTICAL ANNEX

The definitions of the geographical regions used in the annex are as follows unless otherwise noted.

| Region | Prefecture |
|---|---|
| Kansai | Type A: Shiga, Kyoto, Osaka, Hyogo, Nara, Wakayama |
| | Type B: Shiga, Kyoto, Osaka, Hyogo, Nara, Wakayama, Fukui |
| | Type C: Shiga, Kyoto, Osaka, Hyogo, Nara, Wakayama, Fukui, Mie, Tottori, Tokushima |
| Kanto | Ibaraki, Tochigi, Gunma, Saitama, Chiba, Tokyo, Kanagawa, Yamanashi |
| Chubu | Nagano, Gifu, Shizuoka, Aichi, Mie |
| Japan | All prefectures including the Kansai, Kanto and Chubu regions |

## Figure 1    Total population by region

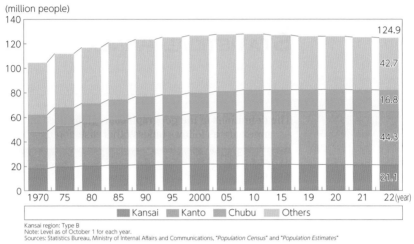

(million people)

Kansai region: Type B
Note: Level as of October 1 for each year.
Sources: Statistics Bureau, Ministry of Internal Affairs and Communications, "*Population Census*" and "*Population Estimates*"

## Figure 2    Kansai population by age group

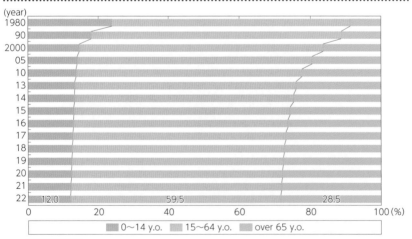

Kansai region: Type B
Note: Does not include persons with unspecified ages.
Sources: Statistics Bureau, Ministry of Internal Affairs and Communications, "*Population Census*", "*Population Estimates*" and "*Internal Migration in Japan Derived from the Basic Resident Registration (for 2010-22data)*"

## Figure 3    Population aging rates

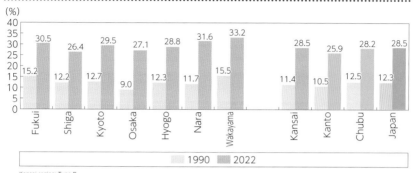

Kansai region: Type B
Note: Population aging rate (%) = Population aged 65 and above/total population x 100. Level as of October 1 for 1990 and as of January 1 for 2022.
Sources: Health and Welfare Bureau for the Elderly, Ministry of Health, Labour and Welfare, "Table of Figures for Health and Welfare Services
Map for the Elderly (1990)" Statistics Bureau, Ministry of Internal Affairs and Communications, "Population Estimates" and "Internal
Migration in Japan Derived from the Basic Resident Registers (for 2022data)"

## Figure 4    Gross regional product(GRP) trends

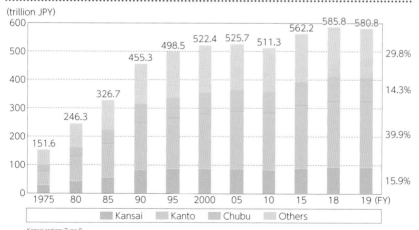

Kansai region: Type B
Note: The 1975-90 period is based on the 1968 SNA, the 1990-2005 period on the 1993 SNA, and the 2006-19 period on the 2008 SNA.
Source: Cabinet Office, "Annual Report of Regional Accounts Statistics"

## Figure 5    Trends in the GRP shares of economic sectors

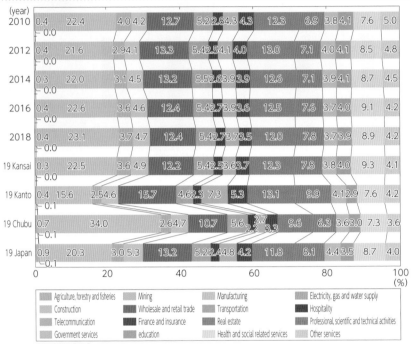

Kansai region: Type B
Note: The values used for the calculation of the shares do not include imputed interest. However, we used the GDP figures by industry to
        calculate the total GDP.
Source: Cabinet Office, *"Annual Report on Prefectural Accounts"*

## Figure 6    GRP per capita

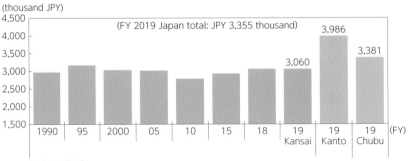

Kansai region: Type B
Source: Cabinet Office, *"Annual Report on Prefectural Accounts"*

## Figure 7    Kansai's GRP and sovereign states' nominal GDP (2020)

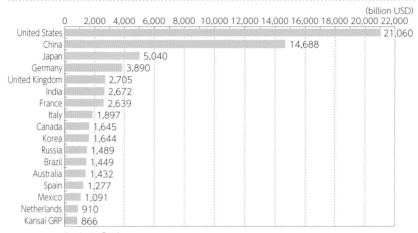

(billion USD)

| | |
|---|---|
| United States | 21,060 |
| China | 14,688 |
| Japan | 5,040 |
| Germany | 3,890 |
| United Kingdom | 2,705 |
| India | 2,672 |
| France | 2,639 |
| Italy | 1,897 |
| Canada | 1,645 |
| Korea | 1,644 |
| Russia | 1,489 |
| Brazil | 1,449 |
| Australia | 1,432 |
| Spain | 1,277 |
| Mexico | 1,091 |
| Netherlands | 910 |
| Kansai GRP | 866 |

Kansai region: Type A
Note: Nominal GDP in 2020. The figure for Kansai is based on its nominal GRP for FY 2019 (April 2019-March 2020) The 2020
exchange rate was JPY 106.82 to the US dollar.
Sources: UN, "*National Accounts Main Aggregates Database*", Cabinet Office, "*Annual Report of Regional Accounts Statistics*"

## Figure 8    Value of manufactured goods shipments

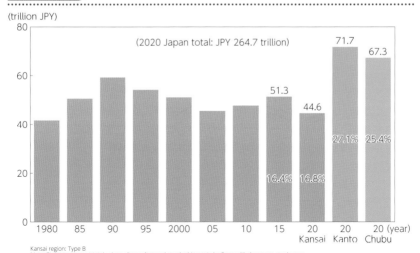

(trillion JPY)

(2020 Japan total: JPY 264.7 trillion)

- 2015: 51.3
- 2020 Kansai: 44.6 (16.4%)
- 2020 Kansai: (16.8%)
- 2020 Kanto: 71.7 (27.1%)
- 2020 Chubu: 67.3 (25.4%)

Years: 1980, 85, 90, 95, 2000, 05, 10, 15, 20 Kansai, 20 Kanto, 20 Chubu (year)

Kansai region: Type B
Note: Figures represent total values of manufactured goods shipments by firms with 4 or more employees.
Source: Ministry of Economy, Trade and Industry, "Statistics Table on Census of Manufactures" The Ministry of Internal Affairs and Communications
and Ministry of Economy, Trade and Industry, "*Economic Census for Business Activity (for 2015 and 2020 data)*"

## Figure 9　Capital investment in Kansai

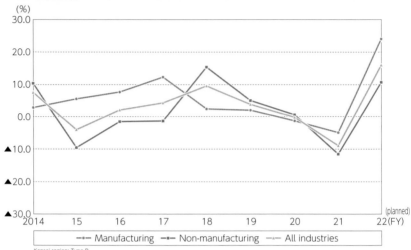

Kansai region: Type B
Note: YoY. Figures for FY 2022 are the planned values as of December 2022.
　　　Includes investments in land, but does not include investments in software.
Source: Bank of Japan, Tankan (Short-Term Economic Survey of Enterprises in Japan)

## Figure 10　Capital investment in Japan

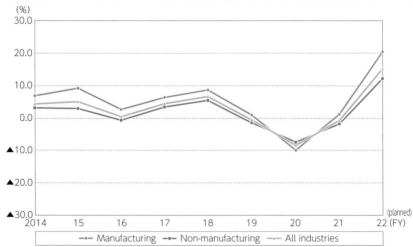

Note: YoY. Figures for FY 2022 are the planned values as of December 2022.
　　　Includes investments in land, but does not include investments in software.
Source: Bank of Japan, Tankan (Short-Term Economic Survey of Enterprises in Japan)

## Figure 11    Index of industrial production (IIP)

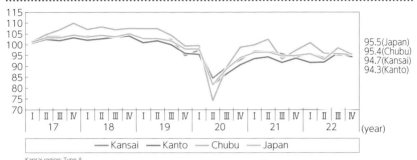

95.5(Japan)
95.4(Chubu)
94.7(Kansai)
94.3(Kanto)

—— Kansai    —— Kanto    —— Chubu    —— Japan

Kansai region: Type A
Note: 2015 = 100. Seasonally adjusted. The Kansai, Kanto, and Chubu regions are under the jurisdiction of the Kansai, Kanto, and Chubu Bureaus of Economy, Trade and Industry, respectively.
Source: Ministry of Economy, Trade and Industry, "Production, Shipments and Inventories"

## Figure 12    Employment by industry (2022)

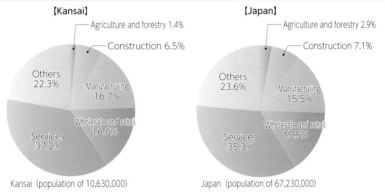

【Kansai】

Agriculture and forestry 1.4%
Construction 6.5%
Others 22.3%
Manufacturing 16.7%
Wholesale and retail 16.0%
Services 37.2%

Kansai (population of 10,630,000)

【Japan】

Agriculture and forestry 2.9%
Construction 7.1%
Others 23.6%
Manufacturing 15.5%
Wholesale and retail 15.5%
Services 35.3%

Japan (population of 67,230,000)

Kansai region: Type A
Note: "Services" represents the total employment in the following industries: Hotels and Restaurants, Entertainment, Health and Social Work, Education, Mixed services, and Other services(services that cannot be categorized).
Source: Statistics Bureau, Ministry of Internal Affairs and Communications, "Annual Report on the Labor Force Survey"

## Figure 13    Exports by product category (2022)

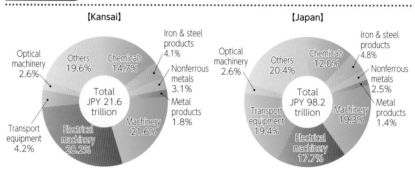

Kansai region: Type A
Source: Ministry of Finance, "*Trade Statistics for2022*", Osaka Customs, "*Trade Statistics of the Kinki Region for 2022*"

## Figure 14    Imports by product category (2022)

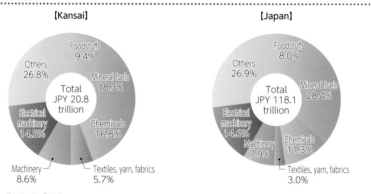

Kansai region: Type A
Source: Ministry of Finance, "*Trade Statistics for2022*", Osaka Customs, "*Trade Statistics of the Kinki Region for 2022*"

## Figure 15  Destination of exports from Kansai

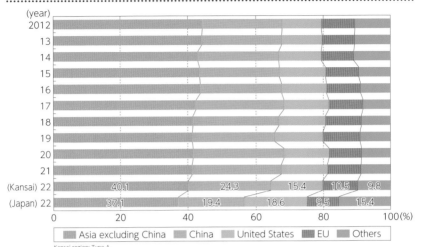

(Kansai) 22: Asia excluding China 40.1 | China 24.3 | United States 15.4 | EU 10.5 | Others 9.8
(Japan) 22: Asia excluding China 37.1 | China 19.4 | United States 18.6 | EU 9.5 | Others 15.4

Legend: Asia excluding China | China | United States | EU | Others

Kansai region: Type A
Note: The figure for 2022 are definite.
Source: Ministry of Finance, "*Trade Statistics for2022*", Osaka Customs, "*Trade Statistics of the Kinki Region for 2022*"

## Figure 16  Origin of imports into Kansai

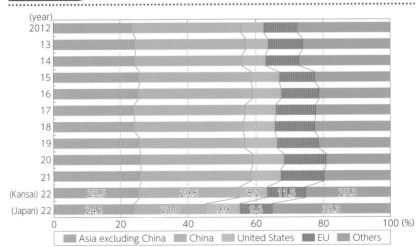

(Kansai) 22: Asia excluding China 25.5 | China 29.5 | United States 8.2 | EU 11.5 | Others 25.3
(Japan) 22: Asia excluding China 24.1 | China 21.0 | United States 9.9 | EU 9.6 | Others 35.3

Legend: Asia excluding China | China | United States | EU | Others

Kansai region: Type A
Note: The figure for 2022 are definite.
Source: Ministry of Finance, "*Trade Statistics for2022*", Osaka Customs, "*Trade Statistics of the Kinki Region for 2022*"

Part I

Part II

Part III

Part IV

## Figure 17  Number of universities, junior colleges and enrolled students

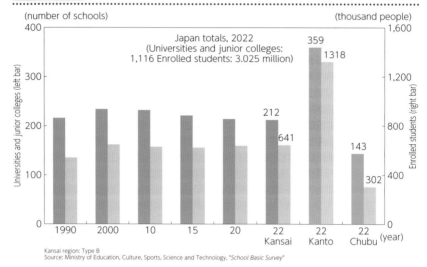

(number of schools)                                    (thousand people)

Japan totals, 2022
(Universities and junior colleges:
1,116 Enrolled students: 3.025 million)

Kansai region: Type B
Source: Ministry of Education, Culture, Sports, Science and Technology, "School Basic Survey"

## Figure 18  Number of national treasures and important cultural properties (2023)

| | National treasures | Important cultural properties | National treasures, domestic share (%) | Important cultural properties, domestic share (%) |
|---|---|---|---|---|
| Fukui | 6 | 114 | 0.5 | 0.9 |
| Shiga | 56 | 829 | 4.9 | 6.2 |
| Kyoto | 237 | 2,201 | 20.9 | 16.5 |
| Osaka | 62 | 682 | 5.5 | 5.1 |
| Hyogo | 21 | 473 | 1.9 | 3.5 |
| Nara | 206 | 1,331 | 18.2 | 9.9 |
| Wakayama | 36 | 396 | 3.2 | 3.0 |
| Kansai | 624 | 6,026 | 55.1 | 45.0 |
| Kanto | 340 | 3,755 | 30.0 | 28.1 |
| Chubu | 44 | 1,105 | 3.9 | 8.3 |
| Japan | 1,132 | 13,377 | 100.0 | 100.0 |

Kansai region: Type B
Note: Values are as of April 1, 2023
Source: Agency for Cultural Affairs, "List of National Treasures and Important Cultural Properties Designated by Prefecture."

## Figure 19    International overnight visitors

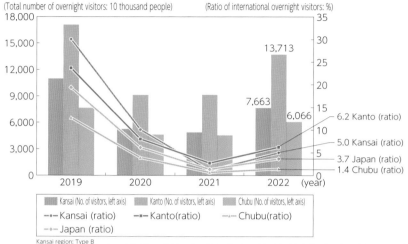

(Total number of overnight visitors: 10 thousand people)    (Ratio of international overnight visitors: %)

- 13,713
- 7,663
- 6,066
- 6.2 Kanto (ratio)
- 5.0 Kansai (ratio)
- 3.7 Japan (ratio)
- 1.4 Chubu (ratio)

■ Kansai (No. of visitors, left axis)  ■ Kanto (No. of visitors, left axis)  ■ Chubu (No. of visitors, left axis)
--●-- Kansai (ratio)   --■-- Kanto(ratio)   --▲-- Chubu(ratio)
--◆-- Japan (ratio)

Kansai region: Type B
Note: Ratio of international overnight visitors = Total number of international overnight visitors/ (Total number of overnight visitors) x 100
Sources: Ministry of Land, Infrastructure, Transport and Tourism, "*Overnight Travel Statistics Survey*".

## Figure 20    Visit rates of international visitors by prefecture

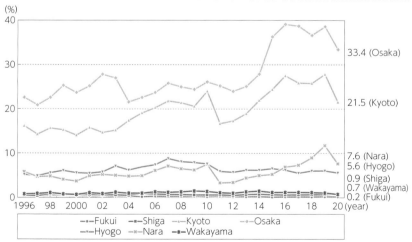

(%)

- 33.4 (Osaka)
- 21.5 (Kyoto)
- 7.6 (Nara)
- 5.6 (Hyogo)
- 0.9 (Shiga)
- 0.7 (Wakayama)
- 0.2 (Fukui)

--●--Fukui   --■--Shiga   --▲--Kyoto   --◆--Osaka
--▼--Hyogo   --✕--Nara   --■--Wakayama

Note: Visit rate = the number of respondents who visited the prefecture during their stay/the total number of respondents (N) × 100
The figures of 2020 are average for Jan-Mar as the survey was cancelled after the onset of the COVID 19 pandemic in April
The survey was cancelled in 2021-2022 due to the impact of the COVID-19 pandemic.
Sources: Japan National Tourism Organization (JNTO), "*Destination Survey of Overseas Visitors to Japan*". From 2011, Japan Tourism Agency "*Consumption Trend Survey for Foreigners Visiting Japan*"

## Figure 21    Average expenditure per visitor by nationality (2022)

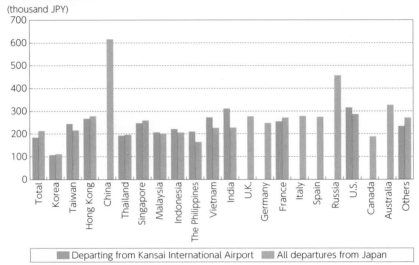

(thousand JPY)

Departing from Kansai International Airport    All departures from Japan

Note 1) Travel spending per person departing from Japan.
     The figures of 2022 are average for Oct-Dec as the Jan-Mar, Apr-Jun, and Jul-Sep surveys were scaled back due to the COVID-19 pandemic.
Note 2) No data country shows no respondents.
Source: Japan Tourism Agency, "*Accommodation Survey*"

**About Us**
Organization Name: Asia Pacific Institute of Research (APIR)
Date of Establishment: December 1, 2011
Research Director: MIYAHARA, Hideo
Address: 7th Floor., Knowledge Capital Tower C, GRAND FRONT OSAKA
3-1 Ofuka-cho, Kita-ku, Osaka 530-0011 Japan

Kansai and the Asia Pacific
Economic Outlook 2023-24

2024 年 4 月 25 日　初版発行

| 編　著 | ASIA PACIFIC INSTITUTE OF RESEARCH （一般財団法人アジア太平洋研究所） | ©2024 |

発行所　**日経印刷株式会社**
〒102-0072　東京都千代田区飯田橋 2-15-5
電　話（03）6758-1011
https://www.nik-prt.co.jp/

発売所　**全国官報販売協同組合**
〒100-0013　東京都千代田区霞が関 1-4-1
電　話（03）5512-7400
https://www.gov-book.or.jp/

組版・印刷・製本／日経印刷株式会社

ISBN 978-4-86579-409-0　C0033